Assessing Allegations

of

CHILD SEXUAL ABUSE

Kathryn Kuehnle, PhD

Professional Resource Press
Sarasota, Florida

Published by Professional Resource Press
(An imprint of Professional Resource Exchange, Inc.)
Post Office Box 15560
Sarasota, FL 34277-1560

The copy editor for this book was David Anson; the managing editor was Debra Fink; the production coordinator was Laurie Girsch; typesetting, charts, and graphs formatted by Robert Lefebvre; and Carol Tornatore created the cover.

Library of Congress Cataloging-in-Publication Data

Kuehnle, Kathryn.
    Assessing allegations of child sexual abuse / Kathryn Kuehnle.
       p.   cm.
    Includes bibliographical references (p.   ) and index.
    ISBN 1-56887-009-4 (alk. paper)
    1. Child sexual abuse. 2. Sexually abused children--Mental health. 3. Sexually abused children--Interviews. I. Title.
    RC560.C46K84 1996
    616.85'836--dc20
                                 95-31514
                                     CIP

Dedication

This book is dedicated to the three most important men in my life - John, Peter, and Kit.

Acknowledgement

This book would not have been completed without the support and assistance from school psychologist, Lorene Heuvelman, who spent endless hours in the University of South Florida library, finding research and helping me review hundreds of research studies. She also read and reread the drafts of this book almost as many times as I did. Her dedication was further evidenced by her return to the library 4 days after she gave birth to her daughter, Rachel. I also am deeply grateful to my typists, Deborah Dupree and Eve Perry. Furthermore, I am indebted to Debra Fink, Managing Editor, who spent endless hours editing the manuscript and organizing the book into a final product.

I also wish to express my gratitude to those individuals for whom I hold such high regard, who gave their time to review all or part of this book. Dr. Barbara Boat's review of the book at its first draft helped me organize the book with subheadings, making the voluminous material more understandable. Dr. Sylvia Carra's review of a later draft assisted me in the chronological reorganization of several chapters. I would also like to thank Dr. Stephen Ceci for taking the time to review my book. Dr. Karen Saywitz and Dr. Stephen Ceci assisted with the section on children's suggestibility. Discussions with Dr. Saywitz regarding her work on the interaction between developmental factors and interviewing factors also have been immensely helpful.

Ms. Nancy Berson and Dr. Mark Everson's review of the chapter on anatomical dolls assisted me in interpreting the research to the reader in a clear manner. Additionally, conversations with Dr. Everson on the state of the art of the anatomical dolls were thought provoking. Furthermore, I am very grateful to Dr. Everson for allowing me to observe his multidisciplinary team and am grateful to Ms. Berson for allowing me to observe her interview techniques. I also wish to thank Dr. William Friedrich for his review of the chapter on assessment instruments and Dr. Richard Gelles for his review of the chapter on incidence and prevalence research. Dr. Glenn Wolfner's review of this book and comments on actuarial versus clinical methods were of great assistance. Thank you to my readers, Dr. Robert Woody, Dr. Robert Green, and Dr. Debra Carter.

I am especially grateful to Dr. Randy Otto, who read the final draft of this book in its entirety and provided me extensive feedback. I also wish to thank my mentor, Dr. Irving Weiner, from whom I have learned so much about evaluating children. Finally I am deeply grateful to my publisher, Dr. Larry Ritt, who suggested that I write this book and who patiently waited.

Table of Contents

Assessing Allegations

of

CHILD
SEXUAL
ABUSE

Introduction

Research examining child sexual abuse has yet to provide accurate numbers on child victims or definitive markers that differentiate true cases of child sexual abuse from those cases that are not true. In the majority of child sexual abuse cases, the victim and the perpetrator are the only eyewitnesses. Typically, there is an absence of medical evidence, and admission by the perpetrator is unusual. Thus, in most cases, the child's statements become the critical factor for determining whether sexual abuse has occurred (Myers, 1992).

Reliance on young children's statements for factual information is complicated by the fact that young children are only able to provide limited information to nondirective questions and may be susceptible to interviewer influence, including pre- and post-event suggestions. While school-age children appear to be reliable reporters of events they have experienced when the interviews are well done (Saywitz, 1995a), preschool children appear to be less reliable and, under certain conditions, may be highly susceptible to suggestions presented by the adult interviewer (Ceci & Bruck, 1993).

Further complicating the determination of whether sexual abuse has occurred is the fact that sexual abuse is not an external event that triggers an internal process which then sets off a range of predictable symptoms and characteristics (Friedrich, 1990). Because children, as a group, are heterogeneous, the event of sexual abuse interacts with a matrix of factors, including the child's personality, the child's and family's interpretation of the event, the family and socioeconomic environment, and the abuse characteristics. Children's immediate and long-term responses to sexual abuse can range from neutral to very negative (Friedrich, Urquiza, & Beilke, 1986; Mannarino & Cohen, 1987).

The personality characteristics which impact children's coping resources and resilience are still not thoroughly understood. How children's personalities help them cope with an event, such as sexual exploitation, continues to be investigated. Child victims are found to process their experience of sexual abuse in a number of different ways (Friedrich, 1990). A large number of adults who were sexually abused as children do not interpret their experience(s) as traumatic (Kilpatrick, 1992). Conversely, profound trauma is the experience for many other childhood victims (Browne & Finkelhor, 1986).

While Browne and Finkelhor (1986), in their review of the research, were unable to identify a definite relationship between specific characteristics of sexual

1

abuse and behavioral outcomes for the child, some characteristics of sexual abuse appear to have a greater impact than others. Sexual abuse perpetrated by a father figure, a poor mother-child relationship, and sexual exploitation that involves intercourse and violence has been found to cause the greatest psychological harm to the child (Browne & Finkelhor, 1986). Sexual behavior problems exhibited by young sexually abused children have been found to be related to the number of perpetrators who abuse them and the frequency of the sexual abuse (Friedrich et al., 1986).

Because children's responses to sexual abuse are not consistent and predictable, evaluating allegations of child sexual abuse is a complicated process. Professionals continue to search for reliable techniques and tools to assist them in their evaluations. To date, there is no single assessment tool that can serve as a "litmus test" for determining whether sexual abuse has occurred.

This book presents empirical information on what is known and unknown about evaluating child sexual abuse allegations with preschool and latency-aged children. The purpose of this book is to summarize how children respond to sexual abuse and how children respond during sexual abuse evaluations. This book hopes to assist professionals in the use of valid techniques that will enable the evaluator to provide the courts with accurate information. The information presented throughout this book draws heavily from the work of Karen Saywitz, Gail Goodman, Stephen Ceci, Mark Everson, Barbara Boat, and Kathleen Faller.

This book does not cover a review of medical evidence in child sexual abuse cases. Determining the veracity of an allegation of child sexual abuse based on medical findings can be a complicated process and is beyond the scope of this book. Typically, when sexual abuse is suspected, the physical examination of the child does not uncover physical evidence of sexual abuse (A. P. Giardino et al., 1992). Because many children are not seen until weeks or months after their involvement in sexual activity, superficial physical trauma typically has healed, leaving no evidence of the abuse (Finkel, 1989). Physical findings have been found to be more common when the sexual abuse has involved physical violence and when the perpetrator was an adolescent family member or extrafamilial perpetrator (Finkel, 1988). The reader is referred to A. P. Giardino et al. (1992) for a thorough review of the medical evaluation of sexual abuse.

Chapter 1 of this book delineates the numerous sources of "incidence" and "prevalence" statistics on child sexual abuse. The reader will be made aware of the sources of commonly cited child abuse statistics and the methodological problems that confound these statistics. Chapter 2 addresses the role of the mental health professional in evaluations of child sexual abuse allegations. Some of the most legitimate criticisms of evaluations conducted by mental health professionals have focused on these professionals simultaneously engaging in multiple professional roles. Within this chapter, delineation of therapist and evaluator roles is emphasized.

Chapter 3 reviews normative behavior throughout childhood, while Chapter 4 reviews the development of children's memory and children's suspectibility to memory alterations. Conducting forensic child sexual abuse evaluations without a solid understanding of children's cognitive, social, and emotional abilities will handicap the evaluator and impair the evaluator's ability to interpret the interview data. The younger and the more developmentally delayed or disturbed the children, the more specialized the evaluators must be in their academic training in child development. For example, the evaluation of children ages 6 and younger presents special problems due to limitations of cognitive and linguistic development. Younger children also are thought to be more vulnerable than older children and adults to pre- and post-event suggestions by authority figures.

Chapters 5 through 7 review evaluation models, specific interview techniques, and the empirically derived criteria used to assess the veracity of a child's statements of sexual abuse. Individuals who specialize in the assessment of child sexual abuse allegations have yet to unanimously endorse any evaluation protocol that functions as a standard of practice in the field.

Because verbal questioning of a child may present problems when evaluating very young children or mentally handicapped children who possess limited verbal communication skills, concrete interviewing props have been utilized as an interview aid by many professionals. Chapter 8 reviews both normative and comparative studies on the most common of these props - the anatomical dolls.

Since the evaluation of child sexual abuse requires multiple pieces of information, Chapter 9 reviews standardized observation systems, behavior rating scales, and projective assessment tools for evaluating child sexual abuse. When evaluating an allegation of child sexual abuse, sound clinical assessment skills maximize the accuracy of the information acquired. Misinterpretation of data can lead to faulty conclusions.

Chapter 10 presents a case study of an allegation of child sexual abuse. The case study is utilized to demonstrate the assessment process delineated in the first nine chapters of this book.

It is the premise of this book that both true and false allegations of sexual abuse exist. While there exist thousands of child victims of sexual abuse, false allegations of sexual abuse do occur. Although older elementary school-aged children and adolescents may be capable of independently initiating a false allegation, it is highly unlikely that toddlers, preschool-aged children, or younger elementary school-aged children independently create false allegations. Rather, younger children's false allegations are most likely the products of leading questioning and/or prompting by adults.

The result of a poorly conducted evaluation may leave a true victim of sexual abuse unprotected from further abuse or, conversely, destroy a relationship between a child and a wrongfully accused parent or caretaker. The far reaching impact of the sexual abuse evaluation is further articulated by Berliner (1988):

Determining whether a child has been sexually abused is a matter of great importance. If the judgement is wrong, a child's physical and mental health may be permanently jeopardized, additional children needlessly abused and their families and communities traumatized. Just as important, an individual's reputation, access to and custody of children, and even liberty, may be lost over a false accusation. Children's recovery from the effects of abuse, the protection of the community, and the protection of innocent persons depends on accurate decision-making. (p. 48)

When the sexual abuse of a young child is alleged, the following possibilities must be considered:

- The child is a victim of sexual abuse, and the allegation is credible and accurate.
- The child is a victim of sexual abuse, but due to age or cognitive deficits, does not have the verbal skills to provide a credible description of his or her abuse.
- The child is a victim of sexual abuse, but due to fear, will not disclose his or her abuse.
- The child is a victim of sexual abuse, but due to misguided loyalty, will not disclose his or her abuse.
- The child is not a victim of sexual abuse and is credible but has misperceived an innocent interaction.
- The child is not a victim of sexual abuse but has been *unintentionally* contaminated by a concerned or hypervigilant caretaker or authority figure.
- The child is not a victim of sexual abuse but has been *intentionally* manipulated by a caretaker or authority figure into believing that he or she has been abused.
- The child is not a victim of sexual abuse but knowingly falsely accuses someone of sexual abuse because of pressure by caretakers or authority figures who believe the child has been abused.
- The child is not a victim of sexual abuse but knowingly falsely accuses someone of sexual abuse for reasons of personal aggrandizement or revenge.*

Over the past several decades, research has been inspired by the divergent views of experts involved in the area of child sexual abuse. Debates have ensued over children's memory, suggestibility, and truthfulness, as well as the method and structure of the evaluation process. These different positions have forced us to support our beliefs with data. We must not lose sight of the benefit of this diversity as the intense emotions evoked by the topic of children's sexual abuse swirl around us.

---

*Although preadolescent and adolescent children may be capable of knowingly falsely accusing someone of sexual abuse for secondary gains (i.e., escape from the family, revenge, removal of an adult from the family, etc.), preschool and young school-age children are probably not cognitively sophisticated enough to initiate a false sexual abuse allegation.

CHAPTER 1

Elusive Numbers: Determining the Incidence and Prevalence of Child Sexual Abuse

This chapter presents information on the extent of child sexual abuse. Both incidence and prevalence studies on child sexual abuse are reviewed. Research on children's disclosures of sexual abuse is examined in order to address the issue of whether incidence figures represent over- or underestimates. Research on adults' memory for childhood sexual abuse related to the issue of prevalence figures also is examined.

*   *   *

Two forms of study for determining the extent of child abuse and neglect are categorized as "incidence studies" and "prevalence studies." Incidence studies are the research attempts to estimate the number of new cases of child abuse and neglect occurring in a given time period. Prevalence studies are the research attempts to estimate the proportion of a population that has been abused and neglected during the course of their childhood.

INCIDENCE RATES*

Because national data on reported cases of child abuse and neglect only reflect the number of cases that are reported to agencies, some experts believe the national figures underestimate actual cases. These experts purport that many cases are never reported to state agencies. Conversely, others believe that because the national figures include large numbers of unsubstantiated cases reported to state agencies, the national figures reflect overestimates of child abuse and neglect cases.

Some observers argue that the proliferation of child abuse and neglect reports over the past two decades is the result of professionals mislabeling minor problems as child abuse. To date, empirical evidence does not exist to support this argument.

---

*See Appendices A through F, pages 299-310, for a detailed review of incidence figures.

Conversely, in support of an underreporting hypothesis, according to the National Incidence Study (Sedlak, 1991), professionals only made reports to state authorities on about half of the abused and neglected children they encountered. These professionals failed to report approximately 40% of the sexual abuse cases, 30% of the fatal or serious physical abuse cases (defined as life threatening or requiring treatment to prevent long-term impairment), and approximately 50% of the moderate physical abuse cases (defined by bruises, depression, emotional distress, or other symptoms lasting over 48 hours). They also failed to report approximately 70% of the fatal or serious physical neglect cases and approximately 75% of the moderate physical neglect cases (Sedlak, 1991).

While the accuracy of child physical abuse and child neglect incidence figures is debated, child sexual abuse incidence figures have become the most hotly debated statistics. The child sexual abuse figures have generated intense disagreement because of the difficulty in identification of sexually abused children. Child sexual abuse typically leaves little corroborative evidence, and behavioral symptoms associated with sexual abuse can also be linked to other causes.

ACCURATE OR INACCURATE STATISTICS BASED ON CHILDREN'S DISCLOSURES OF SEXUAL ABUSE

Accurate figures representing physically abused, sexually abused, and neglected children continue to elude us. Despite its importance to the identification of sexually abused children, there has been little research devoted to sexually abused children's initiations of disclosure and these children's resistance to disclosure. Recently, a number of researchers have examined sexually abused children's disclosures in order to analyze whether national child sexual abuse incidence figures may represent overestimates or underestimates of child sexual abuse cases (see Table 1.1, pp. 8-11).

In a study by Keary and Fitzpatrick (1994), 251 children were divided at the time of referral into two groups: (a) children who had disclosed sexually abusive experiences prior to the investigative interview, and (b) children who had not made any disclosures. Results showed a positive correlation between having previously told someone about sexual abuse and disclosure of sexual abuse during the investigative interview. Results also showed an age effect: children under the age of 5 were least likely to disclose abuse during the investigative interview, irrespective of whether they had previously told someone about the abuse. Disclosure of sexual abuse during the investigative interview was further positively correlated with the abuse being confirmed by additional data. Based on these results, the researchers question use of formal sexual abuse investigations with children who have not previously told someone about the sexual abuse. They speculate that in their subject sample, the threshold for suspicion of sexual abuse may have been too low, and as a result, many children who were not abused were undergoing unnecessary assessments.

Conversely, other research suggests the issue of lack of disclosure is more complex than lack of sexual experiences. In the study by Lawson and Chaffin (1992), 28 children, ages 4 years to premenarcheal, were identified solely by a physical complaint that was later diagnosed as a venereal disease. Many of the sexually abused children, even when asked directly, did not disclose their sexual abuse. Only 43% of the children who were diagnosed with venereal disease made a verbal disclosure of sexual abuse during the initial interview. A caretaker's belief or disbelief of the occurrence of sexual abuse was significantly associated with the child's disclosure of the abuse. While 63% of children with supportive caretakers disclosed their abuse, only 17% of the children with unsupportive caretakers disclosed their abuse. Because almost half of the children showed no behavioral symptoms of sexual abuse, Lawson and Chaffin postulate, "Without the STD, the abuse of many of these children would likely not have been even remotely suspected by professionals. . . ." (p. 540).

Other researchers have also investigated children's disclosures and the probability of the occurrence of false-negatives when interviewing children. Sauzier's (1989) investigation of 156 children, ranging in age from infancy to 18 years old, identified children as sexually abused if the clinicians evaluating the victim and family concurred that it was very likely that the child had experienced sexual contact. Fifty-five percent of the children identified as sexually abused initiated the disclosure. Six percent of the children disclosed abuse after suspicions were raised. The children who initiated disclosure were most likely to first tell a parent or parent surrogate. Reviewing the time lapse before disclosure, 24% told within a week of being abused, 21% disclosed within a year, 17% after more than a year, and 39% never disclosed.

As discussed by Sauzier (1989), disclosure appeared to be related to abuse specific characteristics, including type of abuse, strategy used by the perpetrator to gain the child's compliance, relationship of the offender, and duration of the abuse. Children who experienced (a) sexual abuse that was attempted but not completed, or (b) sexual abuse that involved nonpenetrating fondling were more likely to initiate the report than children subjected to intercourse or penetration. Most children subjected to intercourse with aggression never told. When the strategy used by the perpetrator to gain the child's compliance relied on manipulation, children were less likely to disclose immediately. Additionally, only 23% of the children who were verbally threatened told immediately. Approximately one-half of the children abused by a natural parent did not disclose their abuse and were identified through accidental disclosure. Children abused by an extrafamilial perpetrator were more likely to disclose immediately. Short duration of abuse was related to late disclosure or lack of disclosure. Age or gender of the child, race, and family composition (one or two parents) were not related to disclosure. Previous mental health treatment also had no effect on whether the child disclosed.

Research by Sorenson and Snow (1991) provides further support for the hypothesis that national figures represent an underestimate rather than overestimate of sexual abuse reports. In this research, 116 children, ranging in age from 3 to 17

TABLE 1.1
Research on Children's Disclosure of Sexual Abuse

	Elliott and Briere (1994)	Keary and Fitzpatrick (1994)	Lawson and Chaffin (1992)	Sauzier (1989)	Sorenson and Snow (1991)

Subjects of Abuse	• 399 children between 8 and 15 years of age (79 subjects in the *unclear* group were not used in the data analysis)
	  - 251 females
	  - 69 males
	  - 30 had a developmental or physical handicap
		• 251 children suspected of having been sexually abused
		• Ages:
		  29% - 0 to 5 years
		  38% - 6 to 10 years
		  28% - 11 to 15 years
		  5% - 16 years and older
			• 28 children identified as sexually abused
			• Ages:
			  4 years to premenarcheal
				• 156 children attending the Family Crisis Program for Sexually Abused Children
				• Ages: Infancy to 18 years
				  7% - 4 years and younger
				  22% - 4 to 6 years
				  49% - 7 to 13 years
				  22% - 14 to 18 years
					• 116 children identified as sexually abused
					• Ages:
					  23% - 3 to 5 years
					  40% - 6 to 9 years
					  13% - 10 to 12 years
					  27% - 13 to 17 years

Confirmation of Abuse	• Disclosure of abuse that was considered credible
	• External evidence regardless of disclosure credibility
		• 129 children confirmed to have been sexually abused
		• 122 unconfirmed cases
		• Confirmation of cases based on "all available information and were framed in terms of the balance of probabilities"
			• 100% - Sexually transmitted disease (STD)
			• 68% - gonorrhea alone or in combination with another STD
			• Additional behavioral or physical findings (apart from the STD and its associated symptoms) that might have suggested sexual abuse were noted
				• Clinicians at the Family Crisis Program for Sexually Abused Children evaluated the victim and the family and concurred that it was very likely the child had experienced sexual contact
				• The cases were confirmed when there was
				  - confession by the perpetrator, medical evidence, a witness to the abuse, or perpetrator had known multiple victims
				  - other evidence used to confirm abuse included everyone involved in the family believed the abuse occurred, or there was consensus among evaluators that abuse occurred (if any one evaluator disagreed, it was considered unconfirmed)
					80% - offender confession
					14% - criminal conviction
					6% - medical evidence

Procedure				

• Based on evaluation by a multi-disciplinary team, which included the administration of the Trauma Symptoms Checklist for Children (TSC-C), children placed in one of six groups:
 	
Disclosing-Credible
- 149 children who made a credible disclosure with or without external evidence
 	
Disclosing-Partial
- 60 children made incomplete but credible disclosures
 	
Nondisclosing-Evidence
- 19 children who did not make a disclosure, but for whom there was strong external evidence indicative of sexual abuse
 	
Nondisclosing-Recanter
- 20 children who had previously given a disclosure, later rancanted but there was external evidence indicative of sexual abuse
 	
Nonabused
- 72 children with either no external evidence indicative of sexual abuse, who made a credible denial, or made a noncredible disclosure that was later recanted
 	
Unclear
- 79 children for whom no determination regarding sexual abuse could be made
	• Assessment involved a multi-disiplinary team of professionals. Parental interviews, child interviews, and physical examinations were administered
	• Guidelines of Royal College of Psychiatrists were followed for child interviews so as to not be suggestive or leading
	• Two mental health professionals carried out the assessment
	• Children placed into two groups:
	
	Prior Disclosure Group
	- 123 children disclosed abuse to their families or community network prior to assessment. These children were referred due to similar behaviors as the "Other Group" below
	
	Other Group
	- 128 children referred for assessment due to such problems as emotional, behavior, sexual, or physical signs of abuse
		• Following diagnosis of STD
		  - parents interviewed
		  - child interviewed by social worker trained in disclosure techniques
		• Physical exams completed by pediatric residents, and a specialized sexual abuse examination form was completed
		• Support by caretaker was qualitatively evaluated as either "supportive" or "nonsupportive"
		• Disclosure of sexual abuse defined as "some indication that sexual contact of some sort had occurred"
			• Retrospective analysis of disclosure process data that was provided by the child's and family's therapists
			• Child and family administered clinical interviews, received crisis intervention, and completed the Louisville Behavior Checklist and the Piers Harris Self-Esteem Scale
			• Additional measures from "other child sexual abuse programs" and interview measures designed for this study were also administered
			• Follow-up information 18 months later was obtained from 115 of the original 156 cases. The same battery of measures was administered
				• Disclosure process analyzed retrospectively from case records in 116 confirmed cases of child sexual abuse
				• Disclosure process contained four progressive variables:
				
				Denial
				- Child's initial statement to any individual that she had not been sexually abused
				
				Disclosure
				Contained two phases:
				- *Tentative* - child's partial, vague acknowledgement of sexual abuse activity
				- *Active* - personal admission of child having experienced a specific sexually abusive activity
				
				Recant
				- Child's retraction of previous allegation formally made and maintained for a period of time
				
				Reaffirm
				- Child's reassertion of the validity of a previous statement that was recanted

TABLE 1.1 (Continued)
Research on Children's Disclosure of Sexual Abuse

	Elliott and Briere (1994)	Keary and Fitzpatrick (1994)	Lawson and Chaffin (1992)	Sauzier (1989)	Sorenson and Snow (1991)
Findings	• Among the four sexually abused groups, there were higher rates of developmentally delayed children and children with mothers who did not believe their child had been abused • Among the 248 abused or probably abused children, medical evidence was available on 138 children, of which 60 had less than completely credible disclosures • Differences among the subjects was noted by the characteristics of those subjects classified as the Unclear group. These subjects were more likely to be male, more frequently engaged in sexual acting-out behaviors, referred by mandated reporters, and more likely to recant an allegation of sexual abuse • Mother's disbelief of abuse was predicted most powerfully when she was residing with alleged perpetrator • The six groups varied based on symptomatology as assessed by the TSC-C • Children who disclosed abuse were found to be the most symptomatic while those who did not disclose their abuse, yet were abused, reported the lowest levels of symptomatology. Nonabused children reported an intermediate level of symptomatology which is consistent with the nonabused population • Handicapped children and children with histories of neglect were more likely to make less than credible disclosures	• 86 % of the "Prior Disclosure Group" disclosed again during assessment • 18% of the "Other Group" disclosed abuse during assessment interviews • Within the "Prior Disclosure Group," only 59% of children below the age of 5 disclosed the abuse again during assessment, while over 90% of the children over 6 disclosed again • Sexual abuse confirmed in 85% of the "Prior Disclosure Group" • Sexual abuse more likely to be confirmed in cases where children disclosed abuse during assessment • Prior disclosure was not related to age but was related to gender with girls more likely to make prior disclosure than boys	• Only 43% disclosed sexual abuse during the initial interview • 63% of children with supportive caretaker disclosed sexual abuse during initial interview • 17% of children with unsupportive caretaker (denied possibility of sexual abuse) disclosed sexual abuse during initial interview	• 55% of children initiated the abuse report • 24% disclosed immediately (within 1 week) • 21% disclosed within 1 year • 17% disclosed after more than 1 year • 39% never disclosed • Percentage of victims who told immediately by sexual abuse act performed: - 33% of those who were fondled - 23% of those who were engaged in intercourse - 17% of those who were subjected to nonpenile penetration • Percentage of victims who never disclosed by sexual abuse act performed: - 22% of those who were fondled - 54% of those who were engaged in intercourse - 32% of those who were subjected to nonpenile penetration • No significant differences in demographics of sexual abuse experiences differentiated the families at follow-up	• Disclosures were more commonly accidental versus purposeful • Preschool children more likely than adolescents to disclose accidentally • 72% initially denied sexual abuse - only 7% of these children moved immediately to active disclosure - 78% of these children moved to a middle step of a tentative disclosure - 96% of these children eventually actively disclosed the abuse • 22% recanted • 4% never disclosed

	Study 1	Study 2	Study 3	Study 4	Study 5
Weaknesses	• Data cannot be generalized to younger children • Interviews conducted by variety of staff possibly making interview techniques inconsistent • Evaluation techniques not clearly defined • Ethnic composition in groups differed significantly	• Difficult to determine if assessment measures used were standardized • Many different pairs of mental health professionals completing assessments • Confirmation of abuse poorly defined • Weak definition of "disclosure of abuse," which was defined as verbal information that the individual had experienced sexual abuse	• Small sample size • Age range too broad - developmental differences would confound results • Due to the epidemiology of STDs in the study, the selection process resulted in a sample that was nonrepresentative of the general population • Pediatric residents completed physical exams as a part of training possibly resulting in more false-positives and false-negatives • Weak definition of sexual abuse	• Sample may not be representative of population • Age range too broad for sample • Number of subjects should have been expanded to include enough subjects in each age cell for meaningful statistical analysis • Large variability of sample sizes makes comparisons between categories difficult • Retrospective analysis • Differing interpretations among clinicians evaluating the subjects could introduce bias	• Sample may not be representative of the population • Retrospective analysis • Number of subjects should have been expanded to include enough subjects in each age cell for meaningful statistical analysis
Strengths	• Multidisciplinary team approach to evaluation • Conceptually sound and organized study • Categorization of children into groups indicated the need for thorough evaluations which include more than one interview	• Used team approach in assessment • Child interviews videotaped • Many interviews were observed • Children interviewed two or three times over 3 to 4 week period • Demonstrates that very young children are not consistent in their disclosure of abuse, but children above 6 can be more consistent in the type of information they disclose	• Restricting subject sample to STD diagnosis reduces chance of false-positives • Adds to body of knowledge about abuse by examining the caretaker's belief related to the impact on the disclosure process	• Adds to body of knowledge about abuse by examining process and effects of disclosure • Overall good sample size • Subjects limited to those who had disclosed abuse within past 6 months • Consistency of information at follow-up	• Adds to the body of knowledge about abuse by defining disclosure as a multistep process and then defining the steps of that process • Good overall sample size • Inclusion criteria clear and concise • Examined each age subcategory separately as well as collectively

years old, were confirmed as sexually abused by (a) confession or guilty plea by the offender (80%), (b) a conviction in criminal court for one or more of the alleged offenses (14%), and/or (c) medical evidence highly consistent with sexual abuse (6%). The majority (72%) of the subjects denied sexual abuse when they were initially questioned. Almost a fourth (22%) of the children recanted, and 4% never disclosed. Preschool children were more likely to disclose accidentally, while adolescent disclosures were more likely to be purposeful. School-age children were as likely to accidentally disclose as they were to purposefully disclose. While anger was seen as an impetus for purposeful disclosure, this was found exclusively in the adolescent age group (24%). Of the 22% of the children who recanted their allegations, 92% reaffirmed their abuse allegations over time. Sorenson and Snow (1991) concluded that disclosure of child sexual abuse is best described as a process, not an event.

In a more recent study of children's disclosures, Elliott and Briere (1994) classified three hundred and ninety-nine 8- to 15-year-old children into six groups:

1. *Disclosing-Credible:* subjects who reported sexual abuse and whose report of abuse was considered credible.
2. *Disclosing-Partial:* children whose statements were considered partially credible.
3. *Nondisclosing-Evidence:* individuals who at no time had made a disclosure of sexual abuse but for whom . . . there was external evidence.
4. *Nondisclosing-Recanter:* individuals who had previously given a disclosure of sexual abuse, later recanted their statements, and for whom there was external evidence of abuse.
5. *Nonabused:* if there was no external evidence indicative of sexual abuse and if they either: (a) made a credible denial of sexual abuse, or (b) made a noncredible disclosure of abuse that was later recanted.
6. *Unclear:* No determination regarding sexual abuse could be made. There was no external evidence of abuse in any of these cases and all subjects in this group gave a noncredible disclosure or denial of abuse. (p. 265)

Among the sexually abused groups, two important findings were revealed. First, comparisons of those children who disclosed their abuse with those children who did not disclose, yet had been abused, found differences in maternal support. More supportive mothers were found with those children who had disclosed their abuse. These findings are consistent with the research findings of Lawson and Chaffin (1992), which also showed that nondisclosing children are more likely to have nonbelieving mothers. Elliott and Briere (1994) postulate that maternal disbelief is more likely to be a precursor to nondisclosure rather than disbelief occurring from the child's lack of disclosure. The researchers base this hypothesis on their data, which showed the mother's disbelief existed in the presence of confirmatory external evidence in more than 50% of the cases in their study.

A second important finding was that there was a higher rate of developmentally delayed children and neglected children in the Disclosing-Partial group. Children with cognitive handicaps and children from neglectful environments were more likely to be judged as having made less than completely credible statements. These children's assignment to the confirmed sexually abused group was more likely to be made on external evidence rather than on their statements.

Elliott and Briere (1994) also found notable ethnic and racial differences. Hispanic children were less likely to make complete, credible disclosures that would place them in the confirmed sexually abused group. These researchers speculated that because English was learned as a second language for many of the Hispanic subjects in their study, this finding most likely reflected a language barrier. Findings also indicated that Black children were more likely to have never disclosed their abuse and to be identified by external evidence. Caucasian children were found to be more likely to recant their disclosure. Children assigned to the Unclear category were more frequently males, more likely to have been referred by a mandated reporter than a family member, more likely to have exhibited sexually acting-out behaviors, and more likely to have recanted the abuse at some point.

While these studies offer preliminary information that some sexually abused children may deny sexual abuse or may not be credible reporters, other research suggests that very young children contaminated by repetitive, highly leading interviews may provide consistent credible statements about events that never occurred (Bruck, Ceci, Francouer, & Barr, 1995; Ceci, Crotteau, et al., 1994; Ceci, Loftus, et al., 1994). Together, the research indicates that, at least within the child sexual abuse incidence statistics, there exist both false-negative and false-positive cases.

PREVALENCE RATES
OF SEXUAL ABUSE

Because of the significant problems with estimating actual numbers of sexually abused children from incidence studies, prevalence studies were developed from the premise that a more valid measure would be obtained from retrospective victim or offender self-reports. As discussed by Finkelhor (1986), while the early prevalence studies utilized community volunteers as subjects, studies in the 1970s utilized college students. The research utilizing community volunteers and college students as subjects showed inconsistent findings, leaving questions about the true prevalence of child sexual abuse unanswered.

Beginning in the early 1980s, in an attempt to acquire a more representative population sample, prevalence studies began to focus on probability samples of the general population. However, these prevalence studies also showed great disparity in findings, with the reported rates of subjects sexually abused as children ranging from 3% to 31% for males and 6% to 62% for females (see Finkelhor [1986] for more complete descriptions of these prevalence studies).

Similar to problems with the incidence studies, the comparison of prevalence studies has been confounded by the variability in definitions of sexual abuse, as well as diversity of the subject samples. Methodological factors, including recruitment of subjects, how subjects were interviewed, wording of the questions, and who interviewed the subjects have created further comparison problems (Finkelhor, 1986).

The largest and most methodologically sound prevalence study was conducted by Finkelhor et al. (1990); this study was the first national survey of child sexual abuse. Finkelhor's survey utilized The Los Angeles Times Poll, an experienced research organization, to interview a sample of 1,145 men and 1,481 women over the phone. The sampling frame was all residential telephones in the United States, including Alaska and Hawaii.

In this study, sexual abuse was broadly defined as someone touching, grabbing, kissing, or rubbing against the individual in a manner the respondent would consider sexual abuse. Also included in the definition were nude photos being taken of the respondent, someone exposing himself or herself or performing a sex act in the presence of the respondent, and someone trying or succeeding with intercourse, sodomy, or oral sex. Finkelhor et al. (1990) based their use of broad screening questions on an analysis of prevalence studies which found that respondents, when provided a variety of event cues and multiple opportunities to disclose, disclosed more experiences than when they were given a single screening question. A problem with this study is that these screening questions allowed for a partially undefined interpretation of sexual abuse (S. D. Peters, Wyatt, & Finkelhor, 1986).

Finkelhor et al. (1990) found a history of child sexual abuse was disclosed by 27% of the women and 16% of the men surveyed (see Table 1.2, p. 15). Over one-third of the males and females who identified themselves as sexually abused had not previously disclosed their abuse. Approximately one-fourth of the female victims were abused by a family member. However, only a small percentage of these perpetrators were biological fathers or stepfathers. While the majority of the perpetrators were known to the girls, this finding was not the case for boys. Boys were more likely than girls to have been sexually abused by a stranger, and their abuse was more likely to have involved intercourse. The majority of the sexual abuse for both boys and girls did not involve force. However, these results may only include the most severe type of force since the screening question gave respondents examples, such as "did this person strike you, use a weapon, or threaten to harm you in any way or to restrain you by physical strength" (Finkelhor et al., 1990, p. 23).

PREVALENCE RATES – OVERESTIMATES OR UNDERESTIMATES?

Similar to the debate on whether national incidence figures represent overestimates or underestimates of child sexual abuse cases, prevalence figures also are similarly debated. Recently, a number of studies have examined adult memory for child sexual abuse experiences in order to analyze whether retrospective research may represent overestimates or underestimates of cases (see Table 1.3, pp. 16-18).

TABLE 1.2
Characteristics of the Sexual Abuse Experience of Subjects from 1985 Los Angeles Times Poll*

	MALE	FEMALE
Prevalence	16%	27%
Mean Age at Time of Abuse	9.9 (22% younger than age 8)	9.6 (23% younger than age 8)
Perpetrator Relation • Stranger • Biological Parent • Stepparent • Grandparent • Uncle/Aunt • Cousin • Sibling (Refer to Finkelhor et al., 1990 for a complete listing of perpetrators)	40% 0% 0% 0% 5% 5% 1%	21% 3% 3% 2% 14% 5% 2%
Gender of Perpetrator • Male • Female	83% 17%	98% 1%
Actual or Attempted Intercourse	62%	49%
Force Used	15%	19%
Never Disclosed Before Telephone Interview	42%	33%
Study Weaknesses	• Subjects limited to those who had telephones, who answered their phone, and who agreed to participate (24% of those approached refused to participate) • Reporting bias - no way to confirm statements made, either denial or confirmation • Questions used in study allowed for broad interpretation of sexual abuse by subjects	
Study Strengths	• Large sample size • Representative sample	

* Adapted from "Sexual Abuse in a National Survey of Adult Men and Women: Prevalence, Characteristics, and Risk Factors," by D. Finkelhor, G. Hotaling, I. A. Lewis, and C. Smith, 1990, *Child Abuse & Neglect, 14*, pp. 19-28.

Briere and Conte (1993) studied amnesia for childhood sexual abuse in women and men who reported being victims of child sexual abuse. In response to an extensive questionnaire, 59% of the subjects reported amnesia for sexual abuse at some point before the age of 18. Factors related to amnesia included initiation of sexual abuse at an earlier age, longer duration of abuse, sexual abuse by multiple perpetrators, greater likelihood of physical injury, fear of death if they disclosed, and abuse perpetrated by a nonfamily member.

Herman and Schatzow (1987) also found high rates of amnesia for childhood sexual abuse with their adult subjects. Sixty-four percent of their subjects had

TABLE 1.3
Research on Adults' Memory for Childhood Sexual Abuse

	Briere and Conte (1993)	Herman and Schatzow (1987)	Loftus, Polonsky, and Fullilove (1994)	Williams (1994)

Subjects	• 438 women, 30 men
	• Subjects recruited by their therapists
	• Self-reported history of psychologically or physically forced sexual contact at age 16 or younger
		• 53 women treated by the researchers in time-limited group therapy
		• Age range 15 to 53
		• Self-reported histories of sexual abuse
			• 57 of 105 women in a substance abuse treatment program (all free of drug use; 85% for at least 1 week)
			  - 46% between ages 20 to 30
			  - 54% between ages 31 to 53
			• Previous addictions
			  - 30% alcohol, 74% crack, 46% cocaine, 20% heroin
			  - 67% were mandated into treatment by courts
				• 136 women
				• Histories of childhood sexual abuse documented in hospital records

Procedure	• Subjects, currently in therapy, completed an extensive questionnaire regarding their childhood environment, various aspects of the victimization, and their current psychological functioning.
	• Memory was assessed by the question, "During the period of time before the first forced sexual experience happened and your 18th birthday, was there ever a time when you could not remember the forced sexual experience?"
		• Patient records examined retrospectively.
		• Subjects self-reports, during group therapy, of childhood sexual abuse were rated by the therapists/authors as full recall, mild to moderate memory deficits, or severe memory deficits.
		• Ratings of degree of violence and of amnesia were made independently by the two authors.
			• Interviewed one-on-one with mental health professional trained in the use of the survey instrument.
			• Sexual abuse was introduced as "behaviors ranging from exposing his or her genitals to you, to someone having intercourse with you. These experiences may have involved a relative, a friend of the family, or a stranger."
			• 11 "yes-no-don't know" questions followed which inquired about specific sexual experience the individual may have endured.
			• Participants indicating one or more episodes of sexual abuse in the past were asked to describe the memory about the *worst* event. The following instructions to assess "persistence of memory" were given:
			  1. *Some people have always remembered abuse throughout their lives, even if they never talked about it.*
			  2. *Some people have remembered parts of the abuse their whole lives, while not remembering all of it.*
			  3. *Some people forget the abuse for a period of time, and only later have the memory return.* (p. 75)
				• From April 1973 through June 1975, 206 reported female victims of sexual abuse (age 10 months to 12 years) were examined in a city hospital emergency room and interviewed as a part of a larger National Institute of Mental Health funded study. Details of the sexual assault were recorded contemporaneous to the report of abuse and documented in both hospital medical records and research interviews.
				• In 1990 and 1991, 136 (66%) of these females were located and interviewed to assess their memory for the sexual abuse event. The subjects were interviewed for approximately 3 hours in a one-to-one structure; they were not informed of their victimization history. The subjects were asked a series of detailed questions in order to elicit information about childhood sexual experiences. The interviewers were not blind to the purpose of the study but did not know any of the specific details of any subject's abuse.

Findings

• Delayed Memory	• 59% amnestic for sexual abuse during a period before age 18	• 64% reported incomplete or absent memories of abuse at some time period during the past • 36% reported no memory deficits	• 12% reported incomplete memory for the sexual abuse • 19% amnestic for the sexual abuse during a period but later recalled • 69% reported always maintaining a complete memory	• 38% amnestic of the documented child sexual abuse or chose not to report the abuse during a research interview 17 years later • 68% of those subjects who did not recall or report the documented sexual abuse disclosed other sexual abuse involving different perpetrators and circumstances
• Differences in Amnestic Versus Nonamnestic Groups	• Molested at earlier age - 5.8 years versus 7.3 years • Abused over a longer period of time - 11.5 years versus 9.3 years • Victimization by more individuals - greater likelihood of having been physically injured as a result of the abuse • Greater fear that they would die if they ever reported the abuse • Took longer to disclose abuse • More frequently abused outside of the family • More symptomatic as adults	• 9 out of 12 subjects who suffered overtly violent abuse reported that they had been amnestic for the abuse for a prolonged period of time • Subjects who reported no memory deficits had abuse begin or continue well into adolescence • Subjects with marked memory deficits had abuse begin in preschool years and end before adolescence	• Always remembered group greater than Partial memory group on components of memory (e.g., clarity, visual pictures, order of events) and intensity of feelings at time of the abuse • Partial memory group remembered stronger intensity of feelings at the time of the abuse compared to the Forgot group • No significant difference for groups on violence of sexual abuse: - 68% violence in Always remembered group - 58% violence in Partial and Forgot groups • No significant difference for groups on familial relationship of perpetrator (incestuous vs. nonincestuous): - 56% incest in Always remembered group - 47% incest in Partial and Forgot groups	• Those who recalled abuse were, on average, 2 years older at the commencement of the abuse than those who did not recall their abuse • Those who did not recall abuse were more likely to have: - been abused by family members - had a closer relationship to the perpetrator - been subjected to more force

TABLE 1.3 (Continued)
Research on Adults' Memory for Childhood Sexual Abuse

	Briere and Conte (1993)	Herman and Schatzow (1987)	Loftus, Polonsky, and Fullilove (1994)	Williams (1994)
Study Weaknesses	• Subjects not representative of the general population • Retrospective study • Broad definition of sexual abuse • Recall bias	• Subjects not representative of the general population • Some subjects identified as sexually abused based on their "strong suspicion" even if they could not clearly remember sexual abuse • Broad age range may confound results • Broad definition of sexual abuse included sexual propositions • Retrospective study • Recall bias	• Subjects not representative of the general population • Retrospective study • Broad definition of sexual abuse included exposure of genitals to the subjects • "Forgot" abuse not clearly defined leaving subjects to determine definition (questions do not clearly indicate repression/amnesia vs. willful forgetfulness) • Recall bias	• Interviewers not blind • Age of abuse may confound finding of amnesia versus infants' inability to store an event in long-term memory
Study Strengths	• Overall good sample size • Adds to the body of knowledge about sexual abuse by examining memory for abuse with violence of abuse and age when abuse initiated	• Adds to the body of knowledge about sexual abuse by examining memory for abuse with violence of abuse and age when abuse commenced	• Sexually abusive behaviors were specifically defined for the subjects • The clarity of memories was specifically defined through questions and consistently assessed through a rating scale	• Large sample size • Although retrospective, childhood documented data not subject to recall bias

incomplete or absent memories of abuse at some time in their past. These data also indicated that characteristics, including age at commencement and termination of abuse, as well as violence accompanying the abuse, were related to memory deficits. Nine of 12 subjects who suffered overtly violent abuse reported a prolonged period of amnesia for the abuse. Subjects with prolonged amnesia also experienced initiation of sexual abuse in preschool with termination of abuse before adolescence. Thus, memory impairments in both the Briere and Conte (1993) and Herman and Schatzow (1987) studies were associated with more violent sexual abuse experiences and occurrence of abuse at a younger age. A problem with these studies is that the subjects were in therapy or had received therapy prior to their participation in the research. Therefore, it cannot be determined what influence therapy may have had on enhancing the memory or contaminating the memory of the subjects.

Loftus, Polonsky, and Fullilove (1994) examined recovering female drug abusers for memories of childhood sexual abuse. The majority (69%) of the subjects in this study claimed that they always remembered the sexual abuse. Only 12% of the women claimed to remember parts but not all of the abuse, while 19% reported they forgot the sexual abuse for a time and then later recalled the memory. Forgetting the sexual abuse for a period of time was associated with deteriorated memory. These women's memories were less clear and contained less of a visual picture. The women who had forgotten their abuse for a period of time also showed deteriorated memory for the intensity of the feelings at the time of the sexual abuse. Results further indicated that whether the women remembered their sexual abuse throughout their entire life or forgot the sexual abuse and then regained the memory, the duration of memory was unrelated to whether the abuse was violent. However, in this research, violent sexual abuse was defined as any completed act of vaginal, oral, or anal sex. Duration of memory was also unrelated to whether the abuse was incestuous.

Williams (1994), examining adult memories of childhood sexual abuse, found over one-third of the women who, as children, were brought to a hospital because of sexual abuse were amnestic for the abuse or chose not to report the abuse when interviewed 17 years later. It must be noted that this study was not able to differentiate whether the women who were amnestic for the sexual abuse repressed the memory of abuse, never stored the abuse event in long-term memory due to age limitations, forgot the abuse, or simply refused to disclose their abuse.

In response to the concern that some of the women in the study may not have been true victims of abuse, Williams (1994) reexamined the data using a more conservative estimate of the rate of forgetting. Inclusion of data for reanalysis was restricted to those girls (a) who had medical evidence of genital trauma and (b) whose accounts also received the highest credibility rating by interviewer rating in the 1970s. In the 23 cases that met Williams' more conservative standard, over half (52%) of these women, when interviewed in the 1990s, did not recall or did not report their sexual abuse. Factors other than cognitive development are thought to have played a role in the adults' lack of recall of the abuse. Not only did the women who were abused at age 3 and younger have a high rate of no recall (55%), but also, women who were abused at ages 4 to 6 years old were just as likely (62%) to have been amnestic for the abuse. Williams (1994) concluded

> The high rate of no recall for these older children (4 to 6 years of age) may be due to other factors such as the degree of psychological trauma they suffered, their ability to understand the seriousness and meaning of the abuse, or the resources that were available to them for dealing with the abuse. (p. 1171)

The results of the studies by Briere and Conte (1993), Herman and Schatzow (1987), Loftus et al. (1994), and Williams (1994) suggest that child sexual abuse figures based on retrospective research may be underestimates due to victims' inability and/or unwillingness to report their sexual abuse. Conversely, a number of researchers and clinicians argue that prevalence rates may be overestimates due to the reports by adults of false memories of childhood sexual abuse.

Some memory experts argue that "decades delayed discoveries" based on repressed memories are not accurate memories. Researchers, such as Loftus (1993), base their argument on the following:

- Memory is not like a videotape that permanently stores everything a person does and sees. Rather, some experiences are never stored and others are permanently lost or changed over time.
- Memory can be changed, and/or a complete memory for something that never happened can be implanted in memory.
- Even relatively traumatic memories can be implanted in adults who, upon accepting the basic premise, will generate additional "factual" and subjective details of the fictitious event.
- A review of 60 years of research provides no empirical support for the authenticity of repressed memories that return.

As discussed by Saywitz and Goodman (in press), one of the most controversial claims of repressed memory comes in the form of allegations of ritualistic child sexual abuse. Often, such reports involve repressed memories that emerge in therapy and include events, such as (a) having been sexually abused by groups of Satanists, (b) being impregnated and forced to have abortions so that the Satanists could use the fetuses in rituals, and (c) being forced to murder other children (Saywitz & Goodman, in press). Saywitz and Goodman report that although some acts of sexual abuse may be carried out in the name of Satan, there is no evidence for a large Satanic conspiracy of child abusers. They further suggest that it is more likely that for some cases involving allegations of ritualistic sexual abuse, some form of sexual abuse may have occurred, even if the Satanic components are false.

Although the term "False Memory Syndrome" has been coined in the debate surrounding the phenomena of adults' recovery of repressed memories of childhood sexual abuse, research has yet to substantiate the existence of a "false memory syndrome." Further research is needed to adequately address the issue of false memories.

CONCLUSION

Numerous methodological problems interfere with empirical attempts to determine the extent of child sexual abuse through incidence and prevalence studies. Issues with children's disclosures, repressed memories, and false memories cause professionals to question the accuracy of incidence and prevalence research.

Although researchers agree that the study of a phenomenon when it occurs is more desirable than the study of a phenomenon in retrospect, researchers who study child sexual abuse at the time of the abuse encounter many difficulties (Kilpatrick, 1992). The issues of informed consent and mandatory reporting of abuse all impact upon data collection (Kilpatrick, 1987).

While retrospective research has offered another avenue for studying the problem of child sexual abuse, significant problems also exist with retrospective study, including that the event was never stored in memory or that the memory deteriorated over time (Loftus, 1993). Furthermore, there usually is no way to verify the retrospective data collected (Kilpatrick, 1987).

Over a period of several decades, nationally derived figures on child abuse and neglect reports have shown a significant increase in reported child sexual abuse cases, as well as other abuse and neglect cases. Authorities from various states have identified economic stress, substance abuse, and reporting changes as major factors underlying the escalating reports. However, the identification of these factors is based on speculation rather than empirical data. Because there does not exist a reliable baseline to compare current factors with past conditions, the contribution of economic and social conditions to an increase in child abuse and neglect reports cannot be substantiated.

Researchers have studied children's disclosures of sexual abuse in order to further determine the accuracy of incidence figures. These findings suggest that when children disclose sexual abuse, disclosure tends to be a process rather than a single event, with children disclosing further pieces of information over time. Many sexually abused children are reluctant to disclose their sexual abuse. One factor related to children's resistance to disclose their sexual abuse is the lack of maternal support.

Research also indicates that developmentally delayed children and those children who have learned English as their second language are more likely to be judged by evaluators as providing less-credible disclosures. Conversely, some preschool-age children have been found to provide consistent and credible statements about events that never occurred when interviewed repeatedly by evaluators using highly leading questions.

While the research literature suggests that the lack of symptoms coupled with verbal denial by the child cannot be relied upon to distinguish nonsexually abused from sexually abused children, neither can symptoms of stress coupled with a verbal affirmation of sexual abuse be solely relied upon to differentiate these two groups.

GUIDELINES
Considerations and Cautions

- Children, at times, do not disclose their sexual abuse during an initial interview.
- Children's disclosure of sexual abuse may be associated with the caretaker's belief or disbelief of the occurrence of the sexual abuse. Children with supportive caretakers may be more likely to disclose their abuse than children with unsupportive caretakers.
- Children may be less likely to disclose their sexual abuse if the perpetrator is a natural parent versus an extrafamilial perpetrator.
- The disclosure of sexual abuse is best considered a process rather than a single event.
- Commencement of sexual abuse when the child is very young may lead to memory impairment for the event.
- Research correlating memory impairments in adults with more violent child sexual abuse experiences is inconclusive.
- The national incidence figures collected from state child protection agencies are not inclusive figures and are not accurate estimates of child sexual abuse victims.
- Statements that 1 in 4 children are sexually abused before they reach the age of 18 is an estimate based on one prevalence study. Prevalence studies have found estimates of childhood sexual abuse ranging from 3% to 31% for males and 6% to 62% for females.
- Incidence substantiation rates (i.e., 42% - American Humane Association Study [American Association for Protecting Children, 1988] or 52% - the National Incidence Study [Sedlak, 1991]) are based on a mathematic average of the states reporting substantiation rates.
- Substantiation rates derived from national incidence figures cannot be generalized to child sexual abuse cases. To date, substantiation rates have not been calculated on the individual abuse categories (i.e., physical, sexual, and emotional) from national data.
- Children who have learned English as their second language, if interviewed in English, may not provide a highly credible disclosure.
- Children who have cognitive handicaps may not appear as credible as children without handicaps.
- There is no evidence of the existence of a large Satanic conspiracy of child abusers.

CHAPTER 2

Multiple Roles of the Mental Health Professional in Child Sexual Abuse Cases

This chapter defines and describes the roles of the therapist, forensic evaluator, and expert witness. Definitions of professional roles and conflict of interest issues are addressed. Mental health professionals' testimony in cases of child sexual abuse are also reviewed.

* * *

A SHIFT IN FOCUS - FROM CHILD TO INTERVIEWER

Beginning in the mid-1980s, a shift within the professional community began to take place regarding the assessment and interview process in allegations of child sexual abuse. A 1984 landmark case in Jordan, Minnesota, in which 25 children were removed from their families and placed in foster homes for over 1 year, may have precipitated this movement. While attempting to gather information for the prosecution of the Jordan parents for their alleged involvement in a sex ring, the state attorney's office was accused of repeated interviewing that undermined the credibility of the children alleged to have been sexually abused. The Attorney General was eventually brought in to investigate the techniques of weekly interviewing that had been conducted over a period of months by the state attorney's office.

Minnesota Attorney General Hubert Humphrey, III, concluded that the repetitive pattern of questioning the children, conducted by the state attorney, often occurred in circumstances which threatened the integrity of the children's statements (Humphrey, 1985). In many cases, the children had been removed from their homes and isolated from all family contact for prolonged periods even though many of the children denied having been sexually abused. In some cases, the children did not admit that their parents had abused them until several months after separation, marked by continuous questioning about abuse. In the most extreme cases, these children were also told that reunification with their families would be facilitated by admissions that their parents were perpetrators of their sexual abuse.

Records indicated that one child was interviewed between 30 and 50 times; other children were interviewed up to 20 times by law enforcement authorities. Ultimately, the majority of charges against the children's families were dropped. Attorney General Humphrey concluded that it was impossible to determine whether the sexual abuse actually occurred. He further wrote

> The best way to protect children is to conduct investigations in a responsible manner, in a way that will lead to discovery of what really happened and lead to convictions, if justified by the evidence. It is in this regard that the Scott County cases foundered. (Humphrey, 1985, p. 3)

Following this controversial Minnesota case and several other well-publicized cases of child sexual abuse allegations, the legal community began to move away from a sole focus on the credibility of the child's statements to a focus on the interviewer's techniques and interpretations. In response to this shift, the mental health community began to focus its attention on the study of interview techniques and, specifically, the effect of interviewer and interview techniques on children's reports and memory for events.

The majority of professionals agree that experienced, specially trained professionals are needed to conduct the interviews with children alleged to have been sexually abused. However, it has been argued by some professionals that there is a paucity of well-trained professionals to evaluate suspicions and allegations of child sexual abuse. A policy statement from the American Academy of Child and Adolescent Psychiatry (1990) addressed this problem:

> The explosion of cases involving allegations of child sexual abuse exceeds the resources available to deal with the problem. Many clinicians lack specific training in this area, and the legal profession is often confronted with an array of self-identified experts who have emerged to fill the void. Unfortunately, these evaluators often use inadequate diagnostic techniques or fail to evaluate the child within the context of the family. If conclusions are drawn on the basis of inadequate or insufficient information, children may be harmed, parent-child relationships seriously damaged, and these cases contaminated to the point that courts and other professionals have great difficulty sorting out what did or did not occur. (p. 1)

GUIDELINES FOR PROFESSIONALS CONDUCTING SEXUAL ABUSE EVALUATIONS

Regarding the evaluation of child sexual abuse allegations, a definitive standard of practice does not exist for professionals either at the state or national level within professional mental health organizations or within government. Currently, the American Professional Society on the Abuse of Children (APSAC, 1990) has developed the most comprehensive guidelines for evaluating suspected sexual abuse in young children. APSAC qualifies these guidelines by stating that the guidelines are not intended to be used as a standard of practice to which professionals are expected to adhere in all cases. Regarding professional roles, the APSAC guidelines recommend "Psychosocial evaluators should first establish their role in the evaluation process. . . . The difference between the evaluation phase and the clinical phase must be clearly articulated if the same professional is to be involved" (p. 1). The APSAC guidelines address, among other areas, the qualifications of the evaluator:

- The evaluator should possess an advanced mental health degree in a recognized discipline (e.g., MD or Masters or PhD in psychology, social work, counseling, or psychiatric nursing).
- The evaluator should have experience evaluating and treating children and families. A minimum of two years of professional experience with children is expected, three to five years is preferred. The evaluator should also possess at least two years of professional experience with sexually abused children. If the evaluator does not possess such experience, supervision is essential.
- It is essential that the evaluator have specialized training in child development and child sexual abuse. This should be documented in terms of formal course work, supervision, or attendance at conferences, seminars, and workshops.
- The evaluator should be familiar with the current professional literature on sexual abuse and be knowledgeable on the dynamics and the emotional and behavioral consequences of abuse experiences.
- The evaluator should have experience in conducting forensic evaluations and providing court testimony. If the evaluator does not possess such experience, supervision is essential.
- The evaluator should approach the evaluation with an open mind to all possible responses from the child and all possible explanations for the concern about possible sexual abuse. (p. 2)

As indicated by these guidelines, evaluators who do not have a firm background in child development, including cognitive, social, and emotional development, may overlook important information or misinterpret data. For example, without a solid understanding of normative behaviors and behavior problems exhibited at different developmental stages, it would be difficult to conclude which behaviors exhibited by sexually abused children are aberrant.

IMPACT OF POORLY CONDUCTED EVALUATIONS

The impact of a poorly conducted evaluation can be profound. While there is great diversity of opinion in the field regarding what is good practice, there is consensus that the negligent use of concepts and techniques or irresponsible use of data can produce great harm. Whether a sexually abused child is left unprotected with an abusive parent or whether a parent is falsely accused of abuse and the parent-child relationship is permanently destroyed, either cost is too high. In the following example, the therapist drew a conclusion from inadequate data.

> Tiffany, age 12, is a shy child who has never had a boyfriend. She has never been a behavior problem either at home or at school. She is described by others as a very compliant child. After being told that she would be left alone with her mother's live-in boyfriend for the evening, Tiffany ran away to a friend's house. When brought home by her mother, Tiffany disclosed that her mother's boyfriend was engaging her in sexual activities. She stated that the abuse had been ongoing since this man moved into their home a year ago. The mother confronted her boyfriend who denied the allegation. The mother then took Tiffany and her boyfriend to a therapist. At her session with the therapist, Tiffany disclosed to the therapist that she was being sexually abused by her mother's boyfriend. The therapist's case notes indicate that she believed Tiffany's statements to be truthful until she talked to the boyfriend who then convinced her that Tiffany was a chronic liar. Tiffany was sent home with the boyfriend and her mother. The therapist concluded abuse had not occurred and a child abuse report was not made by the therapist. Tiffany's sexual abuse continued, until Tiffany disclosed her sexual abuse to her best friend 3 months after her initial disclosure. Tiffany's best friend called the police. Tiffany was evaluated by a state caseworker and a therapist who had extensive training in the assessment of child sexual abuse allegations. This therapist also was knowledgeable about the current research on false allegations and child sexual abuse disclosures. Tiffany's statements were found to be consistent and plausible. Medical evidence suggesting sexual contact was present.

The next example describes a professional who "assumes" a child has been sexually abused and then engages in an ongoing investigation under the guise of "therapy." This therapist, too, had minimal training on the topic of child sexual abuse. Although the therapist had attended several workshops on child sexual abuse, he had received no formal training regarding assessment of sexual abuse allegations. This therapist also had not kept abreast of the empirical research or literature on this topic. In this case, the therapist did not separate the evaluation phase from the therapy phase.

> Kathy, age three and a half, was brought to the therapist by her mother. Kathy's parents recently had separated, and the mother feared Kathy was being sexually abused by the father. The mother informed the therapist that Kathy's toileting, eating, and sleeping patterns had changed. Kathy, reportedly, had begun to wet her pants, did not want to eat, and had begun to have nightmares. The mother further reported Kathy did not want to go on visits with her father. During Kathy's first session with the therapist, according to the therapist, the child appeared "unusually interested in the penis on the anatomically correct doll." The child did not make any statements to the therapist about her father touching her vagina. The therapist did not conduct a formal evaluation, nor did he attempt to get a history from the father. The therapist concluded after the first visit that, based on his work with adult victims and what they had told him about their experiences as children, he felt strongly that Kathy was a victim of sexual abuse. The therapist then continued to schedule sessions with the child.

However, it was unclear whether the therapist provided therapy or continued assessment. From the therapist's case notes, it appeared that the therapist continued to
interview the child about her father and the alleged sexual abuse. The therapist at the
fourth session was informed by the child that "the monster touched her," and "her
father was the monster." An abuse report was then called into the state child abuse
registry. By the time Kathy was evaluated by the state caseworker, she was very
confused.

These two examples illustrate the need for specially trained professionals to
conduct a thorough sexual abuse evaluation following suspicions or any disclosure
of child sexual abuse. If a mental health professional is not qualified to conduct
this type of formal evaluation, it is his or her ethical responsibility to refer the child
to a qualified professional prior to drawing any conclusion or conducting any therapy.

In the first example, this 12-year-old child may have spent the remainder of
her childhood in a sexually abusive relationship with her mother's boyfriend because of a conclusion formulated on inadequate information. The therapist did not
bother to obtain further information about Tiffany, other than information on her
"character" which was provided by the accused. In the second example, there are
alternative hypotheses other than sexual abuse that may explain Kathy's behavior,
symptoms, and resistance to go with her father. For example, Kathy may have
developed symptomatic behavior because of her parents' conflictual separation and
impending divorce. The therapist working with Kathy formulated his conclusion
based on inadequate information and possibly contaminated the child's memory
through the process of ongoing evaluation sessions that were labeled as "therapy."
Regarding this second case, the question must be raised about the implementation
of therapy prior to the completion of an evaluation.

THERAPY OR EVALUATION?

Professionals may, at times, lose their boundaries and blend roles of evaluator
and therapist. After suspicions of child sexual abuse surface, when the child does
not make statements to substantiate the sexual abuse, the child may be placed in
"therapy" for ongoing observation. The therapy conducted with these children
may actually be an extended evaluation process rather than therapy. By placing
children in "therapy" for ongoing observation, the premise is that given a therapeutic environment, the child may then disclose the "secret" of sexual abuse. Unfortu-
nately, therapy under these circumstances may not offer a neutral therapy environment. As such, suspected victims may be read stories about children who are victims of sexual abuse. They also may be repeatedly exposed to anatomical dolls
after exposure to these stories and so on. To date, we do not have empirically
derived answers to the effect of this type of "therapy" on children's psyches or
their disclosure of sexual abuse. While this type of a setting could be fertile ground
for the child to disclose sexual abuse, it may be difficult within this context to
separate the true from the false allegation of sexual abuse. It also does not offer the

child a truly therapeutic setting. Children should not be provided therapy for sexual abuse if there is any question whether the child is or is not a victim of sexual abuse. This does not mean that the child should not be provided therapy with other treatment goals.

IMPLEMENTING THERAPY WHEN
CHILD SEXUAL ABUSE IS ALLEGED

In order to provide children appropriate treatment, treatment goals must be identified. In order to create treatment goals, a therapist conducts an evaluation, draws conclusions, makes a diagnosis, and develops objectives prior to the commencement of therapy. For example, if a 7-year-old child presents with symptoms of overactivity, inattention, impulsivity, negativity, and oppositional behaviors, a number of diagnoses are possible, one of which is Attention-Deficit/Hyperactivity Disorder (ADHD). The development of treatment goals, such as treatment modality and medication intervention, would not be appropriate without an empirically based evaluation. A diagnosis of ADHD, based on observation of the child in play therapy and collection of collateral information from a single source - the parent - would be highly inadequate and inappropriate. Conversely, negating a diagnosis of ADHD, based on the absence of hyperactive, inattentive behaviors demonstrated by the child in play therapy, would also be inappropriate.

Yet, in some cases where sexual abuse is alleged, these same inadequate evaluation methods are utilized. For example, a child suspected of being a victim of sexual abuse is placed in play therapy for observation. The only collection of collateral information is from the accusing parent. A thorough evaluation is not performed, and the therapist renders a finding of sexual abuse based on the limited information from the accusing parent and observation of the child's doll play. Conversely, a child suspected of being a victim of sexual abuse denies sexual abuse during a one-time interview by a therapist who does not collect any collateral information. Negating a finding of sexual abuse, based on these inadequate data, would also be inappropriate.

An example follows of a 5-and-a-half-year-old child referred to a mental health professional for sexual abuse therapy following an allegation that her father had sexually abused her. In this case, the professional determined the child might have inappropriately been identified as a sexual abuse victim. As a result, the professional determined that she could not provide therapy to the child prior to further evaluation.

Sasha, age 5½, was interviewed by a state investigator and policeman at her school following an allegation by Sasha's friend, Crystal, that Sasha's father had sexually abused both her and Sasha. When Sasha was interviewed by these two male investigators, she initially denied that her father had sexually abused her. When Sasha was informed that Crystal had reported Sasha's father touched the privates of both she and Sasha, Sasha stated to the investigators that "Crystal is a liar." According to the investigators, after this line of questioning "did not work," they told Sasha that they were going to meet with her daddy, and they wanted to know what Sasha wanted them to tell her daddy about him hurting her. Sasha then, reportedly, told the professionals that she wanted them to tell her daddy to "stop hurting her." Following this line of questioning, Sasha reportedly gave information that her father touched her private with his hand. The father was arrested, and the mother was notified of Crystal's and Sasha's allegations. The mother was told by the investigators that she should seek sexual abuse therapy for Sasha. She was also told that Sasha should not be lied to but should be told her father was in jail for sexually abusing her. Based on this information, the mental health professional contacted by Sasha's mother informed the mother that she would need to further evaluate Sasha due to what appeared to be a questionable initial evaluation by the state investigator and policeman. Throughout the evaluation by the mental health professional, Sasha was found to be a very confused child who had few details regarding how her father had sexually abused her.

Comment: The mental health professional concluded it was impossible to substantiate whether Sasha was or was not a victim of sexual abuse. Sasha was found to be very depressed over the loss of her father. Sasha was referred to another mental health professional for therapy with goals of addressing the disruption and losses in Sasha's life. It was strongly advised not to provide Sasha sexual abuse therapy at that time.

CLINICAL VERSUS FORENSIC ROLES

Some of the most intense legitimate criticisms of the interviews and evaluations conducted by mental health professionals have centered around multiple professional roles and conflict of interest issues. In cases of child sexual abuse, mental health professionals may be asked to assume forensic and therapeutic roles. These roles are separate and distinct and potentially involve a conflict of interest if simultaneously conducted during the investigative phase. Table 2.1 (p. 32) presents Everson's (Everson & Faller, 1994) delineation of roles for the clinician and forensic evaluator.

Mental health professionals involved in cases of child sexual abuse have not always clearly defined their role. In such cases, the question of neutrality versus advocacy has been appropriately raised. As discussed by Kendell-Tackett (1991), when the evaluator acts as an advocate rather than as a scientist, the evaluator may be prone to overvalue evidence that will substantiate the abuse and ignore evidence that weakens a conclusion of abuse.

When maintaining a clinical role, the mental health professional may act as a therapist or a clinical evaluator. When maintaining a forensic role, the mental health professional may act as a forensic evaluator and/or educator. Although both the clinical and forensic roles may involve evaluation, the goals of the clinical and forensic evaluators differ. Mental health professionals' clinical and forensic roles are defined in the following sections.

TABLE 2.1 Delineation of Roles: Clinical Versus Forensic Evaluator		
FACTORS	**CLINICAL**	**FORENSIC**
Ultimate Client	Child and Child's Parents	Judicial System
Goal	Understanding the Child's Psychological State	Obtaining Uncontaminated Data
Role of Professional	Advocate	Fact Finder
Stance	Pro-Child	Neutrality
Assumptions	Trustworthiness of the Child	Existence of Multiple Hypotheses
Techniques	Therapeutic	Legally Defensible

CLINICAL ROLES

Psychotherapist. The psychotherapist acts as an advocate whose goal is to alleviate suffering and to help the client develop more adequate coping mechanisms for dealing with stress. While information validating the sexual abuse of the child may be obtained as trust is established, the use of treatment primarily to validate allegations is counterproductive and undermines the therapeutic potential (Wehrspann, Steinhauer, & Klajner-Diamond, 1987).

Evaluator. The clinical evaluator focuses specifically on the assessment of the child's developmental status, including social, emotional, and cognitive functions. The goal of the clinical evaluation is not to evaluate an allegation of sexual abuse.

FORENSIC ROLES

Forensic Evaluator. The forensic evaluator acts as an impartial scientist who collects data from a number of sources. The evaluation process is designed to answer a question or a set of questions of relevance to the legal system. The forensic evaluator's focus is on a single question. The forensic evaluation of child sexual abuse differs from the clinical evaluation in that more effort is invested in obtaining corroborating information from other sources, such as medical evaluations, school reports, prior interviews, and collateral interviews with relevant persons (American Academy of Child and Adolescent Psychiatry, 1990).

Expert Witness. Similar to the role of the forensic evaluator, the expert witness acts as an impartial scientist who provides an objective professional opinion based upon appropriate evaluation methods. The role of an expert witness is to assist the court in making a just and fair decision in a particular case. Given the limited empirical data presently available, the expert witness must identify the data from which conclusions are drawn and the limitations of the data (Minnesota Psychological Association, 1986).

MULTIPLE ROLES AND CONFLICT OF INTEREST

Because of the potential conflict of interest between the roles of therapist and forensic evaluator, several professional associations have advised their members not to engage in dual roles of forensic evaluator and therapist; the members are advised not to conduct therapy if they have conducted the forensic evaluation. The guidelines from the American Academy of Child and Adolescent Psychiatry (1990) advise "the evaluator and the child's or adolescent's therapist should be two different individuals. This clarifies roles and preserves confidentiality in treatment" (p. 2).

Regarding clarification of roles, The Specialty Guidelines for Forensic Psychologists (Committee on Ethical Guidelines for Forensic Psychologists, 1991) and The American Psychological Association's Ethical Principles (American Psychological Association, 1992) also address this issue. The American Psychological Association's Ethical Principle 7.03 - Clarification of Roles - reads, "In most circumstances, psychologists avoid performing multiple and potentially conflicting roles in forensic matters" (p. 1610). The American Psychological Association (1994) Guidelines for Child Custody Evaluations in Divorce Proceedings also address the issue of multiple role conflicts with the following statements:

> Psychologists generally avoid conducting a child custody evaluation in a case in which the psychologist served in a therapeutic role for the child or his or her immediate family or has had other involvement that may compromise the psychologist's objectivity. . . . In addition, during the course of a child custody evaluation, a psychologist does not accept any of the involved participants in the evaluation as therapy clients. Therapeutic contact with the child or involved participants following a child custody evaluation is undertaken with caution. (p. 678)

While these American Psychological Association (1994) custody guidelines do not specifically address child sexual abuse evaluations, they may be relevant to all forensic evaluations of children.

EVALUATORS' BOUNDARIES

In order to minimize role confusion and boundary diffusion, it is advisable for the professional to clearly delineate his or her role as the forensic evaluator to the child's parents. The forensic evaluator must also make clear to the parents and child that, unlike therapy, what the parents, child, and collateral sources disclose to the evaluator is not confidential for the forensic report. In order to further clarify one's role, it is advisable, in cases involving allegations of sexual abuse, that the forensic evaluator request that he or she be court appointed. This court appointment may serve a dual purpose. First, through appointment by the court, the evaluator is defined as a neutral party or "friend of the court." Additionally, in cases where parents are separated or divorced and there is conflict, this court appointment may deter both parents from seeking their own independent evaluations of the child, thus reducing the child's involvement with multiple professionals and the repeated questioning of the child.

It is the forensic evaluator's ethical responsibility to conduct an objective evaluation through the collection of multiple pieces of information. As discussed by White and Quinn (1988), within the forensic evaluator role, objectivity is sought through both "external" and "internal" independence. External independence involves the evaluator's ability to remain objective and to avoid alliances with any particular individual involved in the evaluation. Internal independence involves the evaluator's ability to avoid personal biases that will influence the collection or interpretation of information presented by any party. During the evaluation process, advocacy for the child is inappropriate and may contaminate the child's cognitions and confound the evaluation data (White, 1994).

When the forensic evaluator is involved in cases of alleged child sexual abuse, the evaluator may feel drawn into a dual role, demonstrated by the following example:

> Ms. Kercher, a licensed social worker, was the court appointed evaluator in a case involving an allegation of sexual abuse by 9-year-old Sonya against her stepfather. During questioning, Sonya tearfully disclosed "and he told me if I told, he'd find a way to get even." Ms. Kercher followed Sonya's disclosure by stating, "Oh, that must have been so terrible for you." She then stated, "I'm so glad you told. We're going to do everything we can to see that he gets punished." Ms. Kercher then continued to question Sonya for details of the sexual abuse.

> *Comment: The supportive statements made by Ms. Kercher are therapeutic and should not be made by a forensic evaluator. These therapeutic statements have the potential of shaping a child's responses and/or can be used by an astute attorney to discredit a child's statements and the evaluator's conclusions.*

THERAPISTS' BOUNDARIES

Prior to conducting therapy with a child, the therapist, like the forensic evaluator, should delineate the parameters of his or her role to the child's parent(s). The therapist should discuss with the parent(s) that the therapist's role is to provide therapy. Clear delineation of roles may help the therapist avoid being manipulated into legal proceedings by a parent with a hidden agenda or with inappropriate expectations.

When the therapist is involved in cases involving allegations of child sexual abuse, the therapist may find himself or herself pulled into a dual role, demonstrated by the following example:

> Dr. Jones, a licensed psychologist, began providing therapy for 7-year-old Randy, whose parents had recently finished a bitter divorce. Following the court's decision to award joint custody to the parents, the mother was ordered to make Randy available for the father's visitations. The mother reported that Randy did not want to visit his father. Under a court order filed by the father's lawyer, Randy was provided therapy. Several months after therapy commenced, Dr. Jones was contacted by a state social service caseworker and alerted that a report of sexual abuse was made, naming Randy as the victim and Randy's father as the perpetrator. The caseworker asked Dr. Jones to conduct an evaluation of Randy in order to determine the veracity of the sexual abuse allegation. Dr. Jones declined the sexual abuse evaluator role, citing a dual role conflict, and referred the caseworker to another professional who could conduct the evaluation.

> *Comment: In this case, Dr. Jones refused to become engaged in a forensic evaluator role that would have compromised his therapeutic role. A formal sexual abuse evaluation should not have been conducted by Randy's therapist but, instead, by an independent mental health professional.*

In a second scenario:

> Dr. Smith, a licensed psychologist, began providing therapy for 7-year-old Jorge, whose parents had recently finished a bitter divorce. Following the court awarding joint custody to the parents, the mother was ordered to make Jorge available for the father's visitations. The mother reported that Jorge did not want to visit his father. Under a court order filed by the father's lawyer, Jorge was provided therapy. Several months after therapy commenced Jorge was evaluated by another mental health professional regarding an allegation of sexual abuse reported to the state social services. Jorge was named as the victim and his father was identified as the perpetrator. Following the forensic evaluation, Dr. Smith was subpoenaed to testify in family court. In court, Dr. Smith testified to Jorge's emotional stability over the course of treatment but refused to give an opinion on the question of whether Jorge was or was not the victim of sexual abuse perpetrated by his father.

> *Comment: In this case, Jorge had not made any statements to Dr. Smith about sexual abuse. Dr. Smith refused to give an opinion about the veracity of the sexual abuse allegation. As the child's therapist, Dr. Smith appropriately commented on the course of Jorge's treatment and offered no opinion about the forensic question. The forensic role of making legal decisions regarding sexual abuse would have placed him in a dual role.*

THE COURT ARENA

Professionals acting in either the role of therapist or forensic evaluator also may be required to assume a second role, that of the witness in court. The Specialty Guidelines for Forensic Psychologists (Committee on Ethical Guidelines for Forensic Psychologists, 1991) speak to the issue of multiple roles and warn the professional to recognize the potential for conflict of interest. The American Psychological Association (1994) Guidelines for Child Custody Evaluations in Divorce Proceedings also address the issue of the expert witness and the potential for conflict of interest. Although these guidelines do not specifically address child sexual abuse evaluations, the recommendations are still applicable. The Custody Evaluation Guidelines state

> A psychologist asked to testify regarding a therapy client who is involved in a child custody case is aware of the limitations and possible biases inherent in such a role and the possible impact on the ongoing therapeutic relationship. Although the court may require the psychologist to testify as a fact witness regarding factual information he or she became aware of in a professional relationship with a client, that psychologist should generally decline the role of a expert witness. (p. 678)

THE THERAPIST'S ROLE IN COURT

There are basically two types of witnesses that testify in court proceedings: the "lay" witness and the "expert" witness. As a lay witness, the mental health professional withholds any expert opinion. In legal terminology the "opinion rule" requires that all witnesses other than expert witnesses testify only as to the facts known or observed by them. Witnesses who are not expert witnesses may only make statements which are based upon the known or observed facts to which they testify. The following could be testimony from the professional who is acting in the role of a lay witness:

> "During the three individual therapy sessions I have conducted with Suzie, she has made several spontaneous statements about her grandfather, such as, 'I am Pop Pop's girlfriend,' 'Pop Pop thinks my pussy smells good.' " (No opinions are given by the witness regarding the meaning of these statements.)

Conversely, "expert" witnesses are allowed to give an opinion (i.e., clinical opinion) based on the facts to which they testify. Therapists must use caution when acting in the role of the expert witness because they may have difficulty maintaining neutrality; therefore, the data upon which their opinion is based may be biased.

When subpoenaed, the therapist should not automatically assume that he or she should immediately submit the case records to the attorney. First, the therapist should contact the child's parents. If the parents give the therapist written permission to release records or to honor the subpoena, the therapist should comply with the directions of the subpoena. However, if the parents direct the therapist not to divulge information about their child through records or court testimony, the therapist should request an Order of Protection. An Order of Protection can be submitted to the court by the therapist's attorney or by the parents' attorney.

Furthermore, a therapist may conclude that releasing the case records of a child may be detrimental to a child. In this circumstance, if the child's parent(s) demand(s) that the therapist release the child's records to the court, the therapist again may request an Order of Protection. The judge will then be left to rule on whether case records must be released by the therapist or whether the therapist will be required to testify during the court proceedings.

An example of one possible response to a request by a parent's attorney for testimony on visitation or custody recommendations when acting in the role of the child's therapist is found on page 38.

THE FORENSIC EVALUATOR'S
ROLE IN COURT

Unlike the role of the therapist, the role of the forensic evaluator in child sexual abuse cases typically involves the court arena, whether this be family, juvenile, or criminal court. Evaluators, unlike therapists, typically are chosen to evaluate allegations of child sexual abuse in order to assist the court in the determination of whether sexual abuse did or did not occur. As discussed by Myers (in press), expert testimony is used when the judge or jury requires assistance to understand technical, clinical, or scientific issues. Myers writes that expert testimony in child sexual abuse litigation falls into two categories: (a) testimony offered as substantive proof that a child was sexually abused, and (b) testimony offered for the more limited purpose of rehabilitating a child's impeached credibility.

EXPERT TESTIMONY:
SUBSTANTIVE

Testimony offered as substantive evidence utilizes the expert by having him or her give a clinical opinion or educate the court on a specific issue. As presented by Myers (in press), this type of testimony is directed at the main issue that is to be decided by the court. Within this role, the expert is allowed to rely upon any data that would normally be relied upon in clinical practice to formulate decisions. These data could include the child's developmental history, reports from collateral sources (i.e., teachers, doctors, etc.), and published literature (Myers, in press). Myers uses

ATTORNEY'S REQUEST

Dear Dr. Kuehnle:

I represent Walter Killian in his dissolution of marriage action. As you know, he presently has temporary primary care of his two children. Walter is very concerned about his children being alone with their mother without adult supervision. He believes that her personality disorder and past suicide attempts are a present danger to his children. He further worries that the children are at risk for sexual abuse when with their mother. Since he feels this way, he has insisted on supervised visitation, which has created a few problems. Now his wife is asking that temporary primary care of these children be changed to her. Case law does not favor temporary primary care being changed because, of course, the courts presume it is not in the best interests of the children to be continually changed from one primary caretaker to another.

However, this is exactly the situation that Walter is facing, and I would like to know if you will come to court on August 15, 1994 at 2:30 p.m. (the case begins at 1:30 p.m.) to testify: (a) It would not be in the best interests of these children to have their primary residence changed and then in a few months have it changed again (one change, if any, would be more than enough); (b) these children have changed for the better since they have been coming to you (since they have been primarily in their father's care); (c) about any concerns you may have about them being with their mother without any other supervision (if you don't have that concern, I would like to know); and (d) if you can say what is in the long-range best interest of the children with respect to primary residential care and visitation.

THERAPIST'S RESPONSE

Dear Mr. Morris:

I am in receipt of your letter of July 25, 1994. In response to your request that I testify in Court on August 15, 1994 on behalf of Katey and Kyle Killian, I previously have made my position very clear. My role is as the children's therapist, and I will not become involved in the divorce/custody/visitation litigation. I made this very clear prior to my involvement as the therapist of the Killian children.

Both Katey and Kyle are very open with me in therapy and, I believe, they share with me many of their feelings. It is very important that they have someone, such as myself, with whom to talk who they know does not take sides with - or judge - either parent. Thus, I will continue to keep my neutrality and the confidentiality in what the children tell me by not becoming involved in the court process.

While I understand your desire to use me in the legal proceedings, in my opinion, this would interfere in my role as the children's therapist. Furthermore, since I have not conducted a custody evaluation, it would be highly inappropriate for me to make any recommendations about the adequacy of either parent. I would advise the court to appoint an evaluator to make visitation and custody recommendations regarding this family.

the acronym HELP as a useful organizer for the principles that should underlie expert testimony:

H onesty
E venhandedness
L imits of expertise
P reparation

The following could be testimony offered as substantive evidence from an expert:

Case Facts - Mrs. Smith stated that on October 3rd, she observed 3-year-old Rosey take her 3-year-old cousin's penis and lick it. When Mrs. Smith asked Rosey what she was doing, she said she does that to her grandfather so that he can feel good. Rosey was not further questioned by her mother but immediately taken to her pediatrician. The pediatrician did not question the child but, instead, called state investigators. Rosey was only questioned on one occasion by state authorities. This interview took place and was videotaped at the Child Interview Center. She was then evaluated by mental health professional Lauren Carter.

Expert Testimony - Lauren Carter, acting in the role of an expert witness, testified, "Three-year-old Rosey reported to this evaluator that she put her cousin's penis in her mouth. Rosey's initiation of fellatio on her 3-year-old cousin is developmentally aberrant behavior. This type of sexual behavior, which imitates adult sexual activity, typically is not one that would developmentally unfold on its own. Research by Boat and Everson (1994) found that none of the 209 nonsexually abused 2- and 3-year-old children in their study demonstrated this behavior when given anatomical dolls in free play." Ms. Carter further testified "While some sexual behaviors that mimic adult sexual acts have been found to be demonstrated by sexually abused children more frequently than nonsexually abused children, a finding of sexual abuse cannot be made based on these behaviors in isolation. However, during an evaluation session, Rosey made verbal statements regarding sexual abuse. When asked open-ended questions, Rosey stated that she licked her 'Poppy's wiggle waggle.' Rosey was only interviewed one time prior to my interview. This videotaped interview was conducted by a state investigator and was found to be nonleading." Ms. Carter closed her testimony by saying that "Rosey's statements, coupled with her sexual behavior with her cousin, would be consistent with characteristics of children who have a known history of child sexual abuse."

Wakefield and Underwager (1988) write that the expert can only provide information to the justice system based on probability rather than certainty (e.g., The child's behaviors and statements are consistent with the behaviors and statements of children who have been sexually abused). According to Wakefield and Underwager, it is the role of a mental health expert to provide nomothetic (i.e., group) data to assist the court in making idiographic (i.e., individual) decisions about each individual case of alleged child sexual abuse.

Mental health professionals base their opinions on "reasonable clinical certainty," which is defined as the degree of certainty required to make a diagnostic decision. Conversely, the courts rely upon different criteria to make legal decisions and use terms such as Beyond a Reasonable Doubt, Clear and Convincing Evidence, and Preponderance of Evidence. When mental health professionals are asked by attorneys to testify to levels of legal certainty, they should refuse since this is not within their role.

Currently there exist differing opinions regarding whether the expert can offer opinions to the court about ultimate legal issues (i.e., "This child was sexually abused by her father"). Professionals debate whether an expert opinion that a child was abused is an opinion of ultimate fact (permissible), or an opinion on the ultimate issue (impermissible) (Myers, 1992). Melton and Limber (1989) argue that a mental health professional offering an opinion to the court that sexual abuse occurred is providing a legal conclusion, and, therefore, this opinion should not be allowed. Conversely, Myers argues that mental health professionals use clinical judgments to reach conclusions about sexual abuse, and in doing so, reach factual, not legal, conclusions.

EXPERT TESTIMONY: REHABILITATIVE

Because it is not unusual for children to change their reports of sexual abuse (Sorenson & Snow, 1991), rehabilitative testimony is utilized to educate lay persons about the causal factors that underlie changes in children's statements (Myers, in press). In these cases, the expert witness does not examine, and does not testify about, the alleged child victim. Rather, the expert witness educates the court about children in general so that the court may better understand inconsistencies in the children's statements. The following could be testimony offered as rehabilitative evidence by an expert:

> *Case Facts* - Heather, age 10, disclosed a history of sexual abuse several years after the abuse had commenced. She initially disclosed the abuse to her best friend and then recanted when questioned by authorities.

> *Expert Testimony* - Mental health professional Robert Otto, acting in the role of the expert witness, testified, "I have considered the following facts of Heather's case: (a) ten-year-old Heather's initial statement to her best friend that she was sexually abused by her father, (b) her later recantation of sexual abuse when questioned by authorities, and (c) later redisclosure to her counselor at school. This pattern of recantation has been found in cases of validated child sexual abuse and, thus, does not necessarily provide evidence that Heather fabricated the sexual abuse. Supporting the conclusion that Heather's delayed disclosure and recantation do not substantiate fabrication are preliminary research findings which suggest many children do not disclose

their sexual abuse during initial interviews with authorities. Research by Lawson and Chaffin (1992) found that 57% of the children in their study did not disclose their abuse during an initial interview. The children in the Lawson and Chaffin study were identified as sexually abused based on the presence of a sexually transmitted disease. Furthermore, in the study by Sorenson and Snow (1991), 22% of the children who disclosed sexual abuse, shortly after disclosing to authorities, recanted their disclosure. While some of these children may have falsely reported abuse, current research does not support a finding that initial denials or later recantations are a 'litmus test' for fabricated allegations. Research conducted by Elliott and Briere (1994) found that children's denial of sexual abuse was sometimes related to their mothers' lack of support for disclosure. Heather's mother has not been supportive of her daughter's disclosure and has chosen to keep her husband in the home while placing Heather in a state shelter home pending further investigation."

HOW ACCURATE ARE EVALUATORS OF CHILD SEXUAL ABUSE ALLEGATIONS?

Dawes, Faust, and Meehl (1989) address the issue of data accumulated from clinical observations and interpretation versus actuarial methods. Dawes and his colleagues argue that when evaluating allegations of child sexual abuse, the clinician must utilize actuarial methods that rely on empirically derived data over clinical methods that rely on subjective observations. In the clinical method, the therapist typically relies on past clinical experience to draw conclusions. In the actuarial (or statistical) method, human judgment is eliminated, and conclusions rest solely on empirically established relations between data and the behavior of interest (see Dawes et al., 1989, for a more complete delineation of clinical versus actuarial judgments). Dawes and his colleagues write:

> The possession of unique observational capacities clearly implies that human input or interaction is often needed to achieve maximal predictive accuracy (or to uncover potentially useful variables) but tempts us to draw an additional, dubious inference. A unique capacity to observe is not the same as a unique capacity to predict on the basis of integration of observations. (p. 1671)

In support of the argument by Dawes et al. (1989), preliminary research indicates that when professionals rely solely on their subjective observations of children's narratives to assess the accuracy of preschool-age children's statements, their conclusions are not more accurate than chance. In research conducted by Ceci, Loftus, et al. (1994) videotapes of children's narratives of their experience of 5 fictitious and 5 real events were presented to 109 professionals in psychology, law enforcement, social work, and psychiatry. The children's narratives were obtained from a study by these same researchers in which children, over a 12-week period, were repeatedly told that they had experienced the fictitious events. The mental health professionals and law enforcement officers in this study were not told how many of the narratives were true and how many were false. The results indicated that the professionals were no more accurate than chance at detecting which events described by the children were fictitious or real. Ceci, Loftus, et al. (1994) speculated that many of the children had come to believe what they were narrating to the interviewer and, as a result, they appeared very believable to the professionals who observed them.

In another study, Leichtman and Ceci (1995) showed videotapes of children's fictitious narratives to experts who provided therapy to children suspected of being sexually abused, conducted research on children's testimonial capacity, or conducted law enforcement interviews with children. The children's narratives were obtained from a study by these same researchers in which children were repeatedly presented pre-event negative stereotyping information and post-event erroneous suggestions. The mental health professionals, researchers, and law enforcement officers were told that all of the children in the videotapes had observed the visit of a man named Sam Stone to their daycare setting. These professionals then were asked to watch the tapes carefully and decide which of the statements that were alleged by the children actually transpired during Sam Stone's visit and which did not, to rank the children in terms of overall accuracy, and to rate the accuracy of specific statements the children had made. The majority of these professionals were highly inaccurate despite being confident in their mistaken opinions. The overall credibility ratings that were made on the individual children were also highly inaccurate; the children that were the least accurate were rated the most credible.

In a study by Horner, Guyer, and Kalter (1993), the beliefs about sexual abuse held by the evaluator of a sexual abuse allegation were found to be correlated with the evaluator's final clinical conclusion on whether the abuse did or did not occur. Using an actual case of alleged child sexual abuse, Horner and his colleagues examined a total of 129 mental health specialists in child psychiatry, clinical psychology, clinical social work, and allied disciplines. These professionals evaluated the likelihood that a 3-year-old child had been sexually molested by her father, when she was age 2, as alleged by the mother. The clinician subjects were asked to provide two estimates on the likelihood of a true positive finding based on presentation of specific materials. The first estimated probability was based on the clinicians' participation in an extensive and detailed case conference given by the actual evaluating clinician. During this case conference, the subjects were given opportunities to view videotaped interactions of the child with each parent. Clinicians were also given detailed histories and descriptions of the child by each parent, as well as each parent's interpretation of the child's behavior that caused the mother to allege abuse. The clinicians were given further information derived from protective services, police investigators, and previous evaluators. The second estimated probability was based on an extensive discussion of the case by the clinicians, during which opportunities to argue specific interpretations of the findings were structured.

In reference to the estimated likelihood that the child had been molested, results showed that the professionals' conclusions were diverse. Specifically, the clinical case conference format that was used seemed to provide the clinicians with no apparent means for eliminating or reducing differences in their clinical opinions. The authors concluded that regardless of the specificity of the details presented, clinicians deliberating alone or in consultation with other clinicians do not agree on the significance and implication of particular clinical observations and findings. Horner et al. (1993) argue that mental health experts "may provide avenues toward facts that courts do not inherently possess; but as a class of interpreters of facts, they appear no more equipped or specially qualified than any other class of witness whose opinions might be sought" (p. 289). These researchers argued that their findings question the benefit to the courts of utilizing mental health experts when these experts are asked to interpret data to determine whether sexual abuse did or did not occur.

Based on their single study using a preschool-age child, Horner et al. (1993) appear to overgeneralize their research findings with their statement that mental health experts are not better qualified than lay people to interpret facts presented in child sexual abuse cases. The results may have been significantly different if the subject had been a school-age child and/or the sexual abuse allegation had not been embedded in a divorce situation.

In contrast to Horner et al. (1993), proponents for the use of mental health professionals as expert witnesses in the courtroom argue that the testimony of any expert is beneficial because it provides essential educational information about child sexual abuse to the judge and jury (Myers et al., 1994). In examining the question regarding whether mental health professionals do possess knowledge that may assist the court, Morison and Greene (1992) compared professionals' knowledge and jurors' knowledge about child sexual abuse variables. A 40-item Child Sexual Abuse Questionnaire was developed for the study from a review of the current literature of child sexual abuse. Topics included definitions of child sexual abuse; prevalence; demographics; victim, offender, and offense characteristics; and typical symptoms of and reactions to abuse.

Of the 40 items on the Child Sexual Abuse Questionnaire, the majority of experts showed high consensus on child sexual abuse dynamics. Experts were more knowledgeable than jurors about issues associated with the reliability of victim reports, typical victim responses, characteristics of the offender, offense characteristics, extent of the consequences, or typical medical and legal responses to child sexual abuse. The authors concluded that the data from their research satisfies the legal admissibility requirement that testimony supplied by an expert witness be beyond the common knowledge of the lay person. Morison and Greene (1992) argue, "Witnesses with expertise in child sexual abuse can formulate opinions based on reliable data and supply valuable information to assist jurors in their decisions" (p. 609).

In drawing final conclusions on these opposing positions of Horner et al. (1993) and Morison and Greene (1992), a number of confounding variables must be considered when attempting to determine evaluator accuracy and the use of experts in the courtroom. Child variables, evaluator variables, and context variables will influence degrees of evaluator accuracy and, thus, impact the usefulness of expert testimony in the legal arena.

With regard to child variables, the younger the alleged victim, the more difficult the assessment. Young children do not provide eloquently narrated descriptions of their sexual abuse experiences; therefore, other sources of information must be utilized. Because the children in the studies conducted by Horner et al. (1993), Ceci, Loftus, et al. (1994), and Leichtman and Ceci (1995) were preschool age, generalizations cannot be made about the competency of mental health professionals to interpret data derived from cases of school-age children or adolescents. What the data from these three studies does suggest is that determining whether a preschool child is or is not the victim of sexual abuse can be a very difficult task. Furthermore, the data suggest that professionals are not good judges of the veracity of young children's verbal statements when they rely solely on their skills as clinical observers.

The knowledge and training of the evaluator also confounds conclusions regarding evaluator accuracy and information that may be provided to the judge and jury. While there may be consensus by experts on the dynamics of sexual abuse, as shown in the Morison and Greene (1992) study, this consensus does not ensure that these dynamics will be applied by professionals in a consistent manner in drawing conclusions about young children's sexual victimization. As reported in the Horner et al. (1993) research, consensus of experts on interpretation and conclusions may be a very complex issue.

In summary, this research suggests that mental health professionals who have kept abreast of the current scientific literature on child sexual abuse may be helpful in the legal arena by providing essential empirical information to the legal fact finder. However, the role of the mental health professional as interpreter of data when a preschool child is an alleged victim of sexual abuse remains fraught with problems.

CONCLUSION

The discussion in this chapter on role delineation is not presented to suggest abandoning advocacy for children. Rather, the discussion hopes to reinforce advocacy used within the appropriate role so that it will assist and not harm children and families. In some cases, reports have been unprofessionally biased in the direction of supporting a conclusion of sexual abuse or conversely in the direction of supporting a conclusion of a false report. In some cases, professionals have placed themselves in the role of judge and jury and have decided on the guilt or innocence of the accused, sometimes without ever having observed or evaluated the person they have so judged.

Advocacy for children must be used with empirically derived knowledge. In 1960, Henry Kempe advocated for a law to protect children who were identified as physically abused. Kempe was able to first diagnose child physical abuse based on empirically derived data from x-rays of children's broken bones (Kempe & Helfer, 1968). We must continue, in the tradition of Henry Kempe, to strive to make our decisions based on empirically derived data and not on our "gut feelings." While sexual abuse can create significant psychological trauma, we must also consider the trauma that is created for a child over the loss of an innocent parent who is falsely jailed for sexual abuse. We may never know the psychological damage caused to a nonsexually abused child who falsely believes that he or she is a victim of sexual abuse perpetrated by a loved one.

In summary, it is essential for the mental health professional to clearly understand and define his or her role as an impartial scientist when accepting the role of a forensic evaluator in cases involving suspicions or allegations of child sexual abuse. As a forensic evaluator, the professional acts as a scientist who organizes, interprets, and integrates data drawn from a number of sources in order to understand behavior. Forensic evaluators review all relevant hypotheses and data and tend to speak of "probabilities" rather than provide definitive answers. The forensic evaluator does not attempt to use himself or herself as an instrument to change the child's subjective reality; rather, the evaluator attempts to present himself or herself as an instrument of neutrality. If the professional attempts to combine the roles of evaluating the child for sexual abuse with providing therapy to the child for the alleged sexual abuse, the likelihood of error during the process of evaluation is increased.

In the role of the therapist, the professional is interested in the subjective reality of the child. The goal of therapy, unlike the evaluation, is to change the child's subjective reality in a manner that will allow the child to adequately function within his or her world. These changes in the child are brought about through the interactions that take place between the child and therapist.

The dilemma, at the present time, for those professionals who seek to become effective forensic evaluators is the lack of available quality training in the area of child sexual abuse. National conferences on child sexual abuse have recently offered more comprehensive training, and several national organizations now offer intensive training programs in order to fill this void.

Since child sexual abuse is a crime, the professional who assumes the role of forensic evaluator will most likely find himself or herself within the legal arena as a conveyor of information to the trier of fact. Conclusions must be drawn by mental health professionals with caution and conveyed to the court in an unbiased, empirically based manner.

```
┌─────────────────────────────────────────────────────────────────┐
│                         GUIDELINES                                │
│                  Considerations and Cautions                      │
└─────────────────────────────────────────────────────────────────┘
```

- The mental health professional conducting sexual abuse evaluations should have formal graduate level course work in child development, assessment of children, and assessment of child sexual abuse.
- The professional conducting sexual abuse evaluations should have knowledge of the current literature on child sexual abuse, including the research on interview techniques and assessment tools, human memory, contamination of memory, and false allegations of child sexual abuse.
- The mental health professional's role of therapist or forensic evaluator must be identified. Therapist and forensic evaluator roles should not be engaged in by the same professional. The professional should perform only the tasks of the specific role identified.
- While the therapist may act as an advocate, advocacy for children must be used with empirically derived data in order to make sound decisions.
- Individual or group therapy should not be implemented prior to conducting a formal evaluation of an allegation of sexual abuse.
- Children should not be placed in therapy in order to continue an extended evaluation of sexual abuse.
- When therapy is interfered with because the goal is disclosure of the sexual abuse rather than therapeutic intervention, therapy becomes blurred with investigation.
- The professional engaging in the forensic evaluator role must function as an impartial examiner. Forensic evaluators are impartial objective fact finders who do not adopt an advocacy role.
- The mental health professional must be cautious in drawing conclusions based on his or her observations because a capacity to observe is not the same as a capacity to predict.
- Professionals are not able to reliably discriminate sexually abused from nonsexually abused preschool-age children when they rely solely on the subjective evaluation of children's statements.
- Controversy exists regarding whether it is within the mental health professional's role to provide an opinion on the ultimate legal issue (i.e., "She was sexually abused by her father").

CHAPTER 3

Developmental Issues

*This chapter explores developmental stages and children's vulner-
ability to sexual exploitation. Children's sexual development, as well
as the occurrence of "normal" behavior problems within the general
population, are addressed. Children's understanding of their sexual
exploitation is reviewed. The impact of family and environmental
factors and acts of sexual abuse on children's development are also
discussed.*

*   *   *

One of the most important changes in developmental psychology during this
century has been the recognition of the uniqueness of childhood and of the differences among developmental levels with respect to a developing array of physical
and psychological functions (Ginsberg & Opper, 1969). Empirical investigations
have shown that in many ways, children act and think differently than adults. Thus,
when an allegation of child sexual abuse is evaluated, the alleged victim's statements and behavioral symptoms must be viewed in a developmental context.
Children's social knowledge, pre- and post-event emotions, moods, fears, and behavior problems must all be understood prior to drawing conclusions about children's
verbal statements, behavior, and symptomatology in cases of alleged sexual abuse.

In regard to understanding the impact of sexual exploitation on the child's
development, there has been a move away from the medical model that conceptual-
izes the stressor of sexual abuse (disease agent) to activate a negative behavioral
response (illness state) that persists into adulthood (Meiselman, 1978). Friedrich
(1990) proposes that in order to understand how children cope with their sexual
abuse, we need to adjust our perspective on stress and coping to a more complex
systemic model. Using a systemic model to understand the impact of sexual abuse,
Friedrich suggests that the following factors need to be considered:

- The individual characteristics and resources of the child
- The appraisal of the event by the child
- The family characteristics and resources which impact the child
- The social and physical contexts within which the child resides
- The characteristics of the sexual abuse acts perpetrated on the child

INDIVIDUAL CHARACTERISTICS
AND RESOURCES

COGNITIVE DEVELOPMENT

In order to understand children's ability to process the complex meaning of sexual exploitation, practitioners need to understand the complexities in cognitive development.

Theory of Cognitive Development. Through the observation of children's thoughts, the developmentalist Piaget first began to study the process of how intellectual functioning, or the mind, is transformed during the course of development. Based on his observations, Piaget (1970) concluded that the child's thoughts represent the child's attempt to construct an understanding of self, others, and the world. Piaget proposed the cognitive system to undergo a series of major reorganizations, each reflecting an improved equilibrium between organism and environment. These increasingly better organized mental structures are referred to as stages and were proposed by Piaget to appear in an unchanging order.

According to Piaget, each stage, or mental structure, is unique and is regarded as a system of logical operations that organize specific intellectual behaviors. The stages are labeled sensorimotor, preoperational, concrete operations, and formal operations (Piaget, 1970). As discussed by Kuhn (1988), research has shown the process of cognitive reorganization is not invariant. Rather, the cognitive system includes "asynchrony in emergence," "heterogeneous skills" (rather than a single skill contributing to performance), and "susceptibility of performance to environmental influences."

Stages of Cognitive Development and Vulnerability to Sexual Exploitation. Although there are limitations to Piaget's theory that all developmental change occurs from a small number of reorganizations of the cognitive system as a whole, it offers a useful framework for understanding children's vulnerability to sexual exploitation. It also offers a framework for addressing how the cognitive limitations of young children influence their interpretation of sexual exploitation. Table 3.1 (p. 51) presents Piaget's four stages of cognitive development and how the stages relate to the sexually abused child.

Presently, cognitive development is thought to encompass a gradual coordination of the internal individual mind and the external physical and social reality; neither internal nor external forces predominate over the other (Kuhn, 1988). Kuhn discusses that as the child develops, new information is encoded and represented in different ways, and new forms of metacognition (the individual's thinking about his or her own thoughts) are also interacting with the individual's developing cognitions.

TABLE 3.1
The Relationship Between Piaget's Stages of Cognitive Development*
and the Child's Interpretations of Sexual Abuse

DEVELOPMENTAL STAGE	GENERAL AGE RANGE	CHARACTERISTICS OF PIAGET'S STAGES	CHILD'S INTERPRETATIONS OF SEXUAL ABUSE
Sensorimotor	Birth to approximately 18 months	• Preverbal • Child begins to construct basic concepts of objects • Development of the concept of object permanence (approximately 8 or 9 months) • Play primarily involves imitation and copying the actions of others without understanding the purpose of the actions • Self-concept is limited to a physical awareness that one has a body	• Child, if engaged in sex play that was not painful, would not understand it was wrong • Child unlikely to verbally disclose sexual exploitation because does not understand the meaning of it • Sexually abused child would not identify himself/herself as "bad" or "dirty" • Child does not understand "intention" - so would not identify the perpetrator as "bad" if told the sexual behavior was "good"
Preoperational	18 months to approximately 7 to 8 years	• Beginning of organized language and symbolic thought • Child begins to perceive language as a tool to get needs met • Much of child's language is egocentric - he or she talks to self and does not listen to other children • Child does not use logical thinking. As a result, cannot reason by implication • Child's reasoning is transductive reasoning: reasoning from a particular idea to a particular idea without logically connecting them	• Child does not understand "intention" - so would not identify the perpetrator as "bad" • Child can be easily manipulated through curiosity or fear. Child will believe the perpetrator has supernatural powers if given this information by the perpetrator (i.e., if told by the perpetrator he or she at all times will know what the child tells others, child will accept this information as valid) • A child who tells a preposterous story of sexual abuse, whether the story be fabricated out of repeated questioning or an embellishment of an actual abuse experience, will have little awareness of the illogical nature of the story
Concrete Operations	7 to 8 years to 11 to 12 years	• Thinking is concrete rather than abstract • Child can now perform and make basic groupings of classes and relations • Child can now see how consequences follow from actions - reasoning ability enables the child to acquire and follow directions	• Child understands sexual behavior is wrong, child may believe he/she is bad because he/she is engaged in "bad" behavior • A child who is sexually abused can be manipulated into worrying about the consequences to the perpetrator without having insight into consequences for himself or herself
Formal Operations	11 to 12 years to 14 to 15 years	• Formal (abstract) thought marked by the appearance of hypothetical deductive reasoning • Child can now arrange various ideas in various ways	• Child who is sexually abused may now begin to understand the concept of exploitation and think about the consequences to himself or herself of the sexual abuse • Child who is not sexually abused may be capable of independently initiating a false allegation for reasons of attention, of revenge, or to escape an emotionally/physically abusive family

*The Stages of Cognitive Development were adapted from *Carmichael's Manual of Child Psychology* (Vol. 1, 3rd ed., pp. 703-730), by P. Mussen (Ed.), 1970, chapter entitled "Piaget's Theory" by J. Piaget, New York: John Wiley & Sons, Copyright © 1970 by John Wiley & Sons, Inc. Reprinted by permission of John Wiley & Sons, Inc. Also from *Piaget's Theory of Intellectual Development*, by H. Ginsburg and S. Opper, 1969, Englewood Cliffs, NJ: Prentice-Hall. The child's interpretations of sexual abuse were formulated by the author.

The mechanisms of how developmental change occurs is still not fully understood. Despite the limitations in our knowledge, there is clinical evidence to suggest that young children's egocentric and concrete thinking render them especially vulnerable to sexual exploitation, as well as limit the likelihood of their initiating a disclosure.

MORAL DEVELOPMENT

Theory of Moral Development. Morals are a subset of the values that underlie the socially acceptable behavior in which individuals engage. As such, they are the beliefs held by children and adults that help them to determine what is right or wrong behavior. The internalized system of moral values is usually referred to as one's "conscience."

A major focus of cognitive developmental research has been the building of a series of stages that depict the growth of an individual's moral concepts. Piaget and Kohlberg are two important theorists whose work has dominated moral-cognitive stage theories. In his theory of moral development, Piaget proposed that individuals move through two stages of moral development during the life cycle (Piaget, 1932/1965).

Kohlberg, building on Piaget's theory, developed a more comprehensive framework involving a six-stage model (Kohlberg, 1976). Each stage involves a type of conceptual framework for moral reasoning. Kohlberg viewed all individuals, regardless of culture, to move in a consistent progression through stages of moral development, varying only in the rate at which they moved through the stages and how far they moved through the stages. Kohlberg did not view all individuals as capable of reaching the highest stages of moral development.

As discussed by Hoffman (1988), while research supports claims that a highly cognitive system of increasingly complex types of moral reasoning show an age-related progression, research does not validate an age progression through stages in moral reasoning that are "homogeneous" and unfold developmentally in a "universal invariant order."

Stages of Moral Development and Vulnerability to Sexual Exploitation. Similar to Piaget's cognitive development theory, Kohlberg's theory of moral reasoning has limitations yet offers a useful framework for understanding children's vulnerability to sexual exploitation. Table 3.2 (pp. 54-55) presents Kohlberg's stages of moral development and how the stages relate to the sexually abused child.

The child's level of cognitive and moral development is relevant to the child's ability to assess sexual exploitation in terms of right or wrong and good or bad. Due to the cognitive limitations and inability to understand the sexual behaviors in which they are engaged, young child victims of sexual abuse may not exhibit any behavioral symptoms of stress. Evidence of this is found in Lawson and Chaffin's

(1992) study in which 28 children were identified as sexually abused through the medical finding of a sexually transmitted disease.

In the Lawson and Chaffin (1992) study, the children's initial presenting problem was a physical complaint with no prior suspicion of sexual abuse. Over one-half of these children showed no behavioral symptoms.

The following case is an example of how a child might be asymptomatic:

> Clarissa was observed to have a very positive relationship with her Uncle Fred. Her 32-year-old uncle was a regular babysitter and Clarissa's favorite babysitter. Clarissa's sexual abuse eventually was terminated when Clarissa was age 5 and her uncle moved away. Clarissa remembers the wonderful time she had with Uncle Fred, and how he would let her eat cupcakes for her dinner. He would also allow her to stay up past her bedtime. These special privileges were "secrets" the two of them kept from Clarissa's parents. Clarissa rubbing her uncle's penis while they ate popcorn and watched cartoons was also a "secret."

SEXUAL DEVELOPMENT

Because sexually abused children may exhibit aberrant sexual behaviors, it is important to understand what features discriminate normal from abnormal sexual behavior. While there has been little empirical study of the developmental changes in children's sexual behavior, the existing research suggests that both sexually abused and nonsexually abused children are sexually active in a number of different ways throughout their development.

As discussed by Kelley and Byrne (1992) in their excellent review of sexual development

- Male fetuses have been observed to have erections in the uterus
- Female fetuses are believed to have clitoral erections but probably do not have vaginal lubrication because this response is dependent on hormonal secretions
- Infants of both sexes can become sexually excited and reach orgasm, though males do not ejaculate semen until puberty
- Early sexual climaxes are typically the result of masturbation, which begins at approximately 8 months of age
- Babies are observed to massage their genitals with their hands and rub their bodies against objects, furniture, or toys
- Some babies are found to use masturbation to soothe and comfort themselves in the same way that they use sucking to pacify themselves
- Genital play is most likely to occur among babies who live at home as opposed to those who live in institutions, suggesting that close physical contact with parent figures may have a natural sexually stimulating effect on infants

TABLE 3.2
The Relationship Between Kohlberg's Stages of Moral Development*
and the Child's Interpretations of Sexual Abuse

DEVELOPMENTAL STAGE	CHARACTERISTICS OF KOHLBERG'S STAGES	CHILD'S INTERPRETATIONS OF SEXUAL ABUSE
Preconventional Morality (ages 4 to 10) Rules and social expectations are something external to the self Emphasis is on external control - Motivation to conform to external rules is related to avoidance of punishment or acquiring rewards	*Stage 1 (4 yrs to 8 yrs):* • Individual's definition of right or wrong is based on obedience to rules and authority • Individual's motivation to conform to external rules is based on avoidance of punishment or on obtaining rewards • Confusion of authority's perspective with one's own *Stage 2 (8 yrs to 10 yrs):* • Individual conforms to the rules out of self-interest and assessment of what others can do for him or her • Individual's motivation to conform to external rules is based on the desire to collect rewards for conformity	• In the beginning of this stage, the sexually abused child may readily conform to the instructions of adults without understanding that the sexual behavior is wrong • Child can be tricked into believing their sexual involvement is special, fun, or normal • Child most likely will not intentionally verbally disclose the abuse because of obedience to authority • Child is vulnerable to do what others tell him or her to do, including following directions to lie that sexual abuse did not happen or to lie that sexual abuse did happen • Sexually abused child may understand wrongfulness of sexual exploitation but conforms to the instructions of adults to please adults or to avoid punishment • If relationship with perpetrator is child's strongest relationship, child most likely will not disclose. If child's relationship with nonoffending parent is supportive, likelihood of disclosure is greater • Child continues to be vulnerable to do what others tell him or her, including lying about the absence or presence of their involvement in sexual abuse
Conventional Morality or Role Conformity (ages 10 to 13) Rules and expectations of others, especially authority figures, have been internalized by the self Emphasis is on being considered good by those persons whose opinions are important - Children have internalized the standards of others to some extent	*Stage 3 (10 yrs to 12 yrs):* • Control of behavior is externally derived - the standards are set by rules and expectations held by individuals who are identified as authority • The individual's motivation is to gain approval and to please others • Reactions of authority serve as cues to the rightness or wrongness of an act • Motivation becomes internal as the child anticipates the praise or censure of significant others *Stage 4 (12 yrs to 13 yrs):* • Individual's motivation to conform to external rules is based on maintaining social order and showing respect for authority • Individual is able to take the perspective of others	• Sexually abused child understands the wrongfulness of the sexual exploitation and may disclose the abuse • If supportive relationships exist within the home or outside of the home, apart from the perpetrator, and these relationships become more significant than relationship with the perpetrator, child may disclose (to a friend, teacher, etc.) • Child who is not having emotional needs met by caregivers could make a false allegation of abuse in order to gain nurturance from others • Sexually abused child understands the wrongfulness of the sexual exploitation and understands the consequences to the perpetrator if sexual abuse is disclosed

| Postconventional Morality or Principled Morality

(earliest development age 13, some people never develop)

Rules and expectations of others are differentiated from self, and values are defined in terms of independently chosen principles

This level is the attainment of true morality - the individual understands the possibility of conflict between two socially accepted standards and tries to decide between them | **_Stage 5 (early adolescence and up):_**
• Individual's motivation to conform to external rules is based on defining right and wrong in terms of laws. These laws and rules are seen as necessary for institutional functioning
• Considers moral and legal points of view; recognizes that they sometimes conflict

Stage 6 (middle to late adolescence and up):
• A belief in the validity of universal moral principles and a sense of personal commitment to them
• Individual does what he or she thinks is right, regardless of the legal restrictions or opinions of others | • Sexually abused child understands the wrongfulness of the sexual exploitation and may disclose so perpetrator will not hurt others

• Sexually abused child assesses the sexual exploitation and does what he or she thinks is right |

*The Stages of Moral Development adapted from *Moral Development and Behavior: Theory, Research and Social Issues* (pp. 31-53), by T. Lickona (Ed.), chapter entitled "Moral Stage and Moralization: The Cognitive Developmental Approach" by L. Kohlberg, 1976, New York: Holt, Rinehart & Winston. Reprinted with permission. The child's interpretations of sexual abuse were formulated by the author.

Toddlers continue to masturbate and also begin to explore sexually. Toddler and preschool-age children engage in sex play with other children of both sexes. Such sexual play may begin as early as age 2 or 3 but more typically occurs between ages 4 and 7 (Kelley & Byrne, 1992). Gunderson, Melas, and Skar (1981) found that of 60 preschool teachers surveyed, 85% reported that children in their classes masturbated at least occasionally. Sixty-five percent of these teachers also reported that they observed their preschool students engaged in sexual games such as doctor-nurse and mother-father.

With the preschool-age and primary school-age child, the most common type of sexual behavior, other than masturbation, is exposure. With adolescents, the most common type of sexual behavior after masturbation is heterosexual contact with a peer (Sgroi, 1988). Throughout the childhood and adolescent years, same-sex sexual interactions are common (Kinsey, Pomeroy, & Martin, 1948; Kinsey et al., 1953). According to Kelley and Byrne (1992), engaging in same gender sexual activity (e.g., exposure, fondling, and masturbation) during childhood and adolescence tends to be for the purpose of accomplishing the developmental tasks of relationship building and developing intimacy with peers.

According to Sgroi (1988), what is not developmentally normal behavior is the initiation of sexual activities by adolescents with children who are significantly younger than themselves. Nor is it developmentally normal for young children to initiate sexual play or activities with individuals who are significantly older than them. Coercion and/or force to gain compliance of others in sexual activities is also considered aberrant behavior for any age group.

Sexual play between young children is found to have little impact, either positive or negative, on sexual functioning during adulthood, unless force or domination is involved (Leitenberg, Greenwald, & Tarran, 1989). By the age of 10, most children have explored some aspects of sexuality. Because of these experiences, Kelley and Byrne (1992) state that it no longer makes sense to describe puberty as a time of "sexual awakening" but instead to simply define it as a developmental stage, during which physical maturation results in the ability to reproduce. However, this statement ignores the cognitive changes that take place during the course of maturation. While throughout their development children may engage each other in sexual activities, their cognitive processing of these sexual relations change. For example, as adolescents begin to incorporate adult sexual acts into their sexual activities, they also begin to incorporate sexual fantasies into their sexual behavior repertoire to a greater degree than do young children.

Sgroi (1988), using a developmental continuum, has classified children's sexual behavior into three categories: (a) Touching Oneself, (b) Looking at Others, and (c) Touching Others. Table 3.3 (pp. 57-58) presents developmental material adapted from Sgroi's review of sexual growth in children.

Related to children's sexual exploitation and the possible development of aberrant sexual behaviors, both research and clinical observation verify that some

TABLE 3.3
Development of Sexual Behavior in Children*

AGE	NORMAL BEHAVIORS	INHIBITIONS	ABERRANT BEHAVIORS
0 to 3			
Touching Oneself	• Openly masturbates multiple times a day	• Clothing interferes with genital stimulation	• Excessive masturbation that interferes in play behavior and daily activities
Looking at Others	• Walks in on others unannounced		
Touching Others	• If observes adult sexual activity, will be interested at a level similar to watching someone have a bowel movement	• Negative reaction by adults inhibits child grabbing at others' bodies	• Tries to rub and smell adults' genitals • Attempts to penetrate others' vaginal or anal openings with own genitals • Attempts to be penetrated by another's genitals
4 to 6			
Touching Oneself	• Masturbates in private	• Negative reaction by the parent teaches child that genital stimulation is bad	• Excessive masturbation that interferes in play behavior and daily activities
Looking at Others	• Likely to create opportunities to compare their bodies with others' • May hide and observe while person bathing, using toilet, or undressing	• Negative reaction by adults teaches children nudity is socially unacceptable	
Touching Others	• If circumstances permit, children will take advantage of showing each other their bodies and touching each other • Touching is not masturbatory or directed toward sexual gratification but rather exploratory in nature	• Negative reaction by adults inhibits touching others	• Tries to rub and smell adults' genitals • Attempts to penetrate vaginal or anal openings with genitals • Attempts to be penetrated by another's genitals • Forces sexual involvement of peers or younger children with themselves
7 to 10			
Touching Oneself	• Masturbates in private (less likely to get caught)	• Negative reaction of adults	• Excessive masturbation that interferes in play behavior and daily activities
Looking at Others	• May engage in games that involve sexual exposure (i.e., playing doctor) • May engage in competition (i.e., who can "pee" the farthest) • May engage in dares or initiation into groups that have a sexual component (atmosphere is always game-like)	• Negative reaction by adults	• Excessive attempts to observe others' nudity which violates other's privacy
Touching Others	• Touching bodies occurs within context of game or play activity • Behavior would involve stroking genitals rather than sexual penetration unless encouraged or pressured by older person to do so • Force or coercion would be absent • Engagement in behaviors influenced by peer pressure and not out of fear	• Internalized values that behavior is wrong	• Excessive sex play which interferes in other social activities • Initiates sexual activities with adults • Forces sexual involvement of peers or younger children with themselves

*Adapted with the permission of Lexington Books, an imprint of The Free Press, a Division of Simon & Schuster, Inc., from *Vulerable Populations,* Volume 1 (pp. 2-8), by Suzanne M. Sgroi, MD. Copyright © 1988 by Lexington Books.

TABLE 3.3 *(Continued)*			
AGE	**NORMAL BEHAVIORS**	**INHIBITIONS**	**ABERRANT BEHAVIORS**
Preadolescent 11 to 12 through Adolescent 13 to 18			
Touching Oneself	• Masturbates in private or with peers • Achieves greater control over physiological responses to self-stimulation	• Negative reaction of others • Internalized values	• Excessive masturbation that interferes in social activities with peers
Looking at Others	• Intense interest in viewing others' bodies - especially the opposite sex • Deliberate peeking at peers of opposite sex • Viewing pornographic materials	• Negative reaction of others • Internalized values	• Excessive attempts to observe others' nudity which violates other's privacy • Excessive viewing of pornographic materials that interferes in social activities with peers
Touching Others	• Most adolescents engage in some type of interactive sexual behavior with others, including some or all of the following: - open-mouth kissing - fondling - penetration	• Values that identify premarital sex as wrong • Fear of pregnancy • Fear of disease	• Hyposexual-phobic of sexual behaviors, including kissing • Hypersexual-indiscriminate sexual behavior with multiple partners • Initiates sexual activities with young children • Forces sexual involvement of peers or younger children with themselves

child victims of sexual abuse exhibit developmentally aberrant sexual behaviors (Friedrich et al., 1986, 1992).

Friedrich and his collegues found that children who demonstrated unusually high levels of sexualized behaviors were found to have experienced more severe sexual abuse, force or threat of death, and a greater number of abusers. These researchers also found an association between sexual abuse and greater levels of family distress and fewer educational and financial resources in the family.

NORMAL PROBLEM BEHAVIORS

Because sexually abused children may exhibit a number of behavior problems, it is important to understand which behavior problems are developmentally "normal" (for a comprehensive review of early longitudinal, cross sectional, and follow-up prevalence studies, refer to Anthony, 1970). In one of the largest longitudinal studies to date, data on the frequencies of specific problem behaviors that normal children exhibit during childhood were collected by MacFarlane, Allen, and Honzik (1954). The subjects were selected serially from a birth certificate registry in Berkeley, California. Two hundred fifty-two children were divided into control (126) and clinic (126) groups. Subjects were studied from 21 months of age until age 14. The data discussed in this chapter will only focus on the behavior frequencies of the control group, or what MacFarlane and his colleagues referred to as the "normal" children.

The normative data collected by MacFarlane et al. (1954) showed that disturbing dreams were present in over one-fourth of the "normal" children throughout early and late childhood and, thus, appeared to be a common problem for children. Restless sleep, enuresis, and soiling problems were found to be present in a high percentage of the young children but were found to decrease as children matured. Eating problems were found in over one-fourth of the preschool children. While food finickiness remained constant from the toddler years throughout the preschool years, the problem of insufficient appetite increased for both boys and girls during the preschool years.

Although masturbation was reported to be a low-frequency behavior, it was found to be present throughout the toddler and preschool years with both boys and girls. The problem of overactivity was found to increase during the preschool years and was present in over one-third of the 3- and 4-year-old boys and girls.

High percentages of preschool children were found to exhibit oversensitiveness, specific fears, and temper tantrums. These behavior problems were found to be more commonly exhibited among preschool boys and girls than any of the other problem behaviors identified in the MacFarlane et al. (1954) study. Oversensitiveness, fears, and tantrums were present in one-half to one-fourth of the children throughout early and late childhood. Mood swings and somberness were found to increase during the ages of 3 and 4. Irritability increased over the preschool years, while negativism remained fairly constant with over one-fourth of the preschoolers exhibiting this behavior. Irritability and negativism then decreased during the school-age years.

While the MacFarlane et al. (1954) study presented a longitudinal view of normal behavior problems across the childhood years, generalizability of results is limited because of the weaknesses in the study. Whether children born in Berkeley, California between 1928 and 1929 are representative of children and their behavior in the 1990s can be questioned. Additionally, attrition was large; by age 14, the subject sample had dwindled to 41 subjects. Furthermore, attrition of subjects was greatest among lower social economic status (SES) families. Because of these problems, these data may not represent developmental problems exhibited by children in today's society.

In a contemporary study on the behavioral problems and competencies demonstrated by normal children and those referred for professional help, normative data were collected by Achenbach (1991b). Thirteen hundred subjects, ages 4 to 16, were divided into 50 cases of each gender at each age; the Child Behavior Checklist was utilized as the measurement instrument.

Table 3.4 (pp. 60-61) presents Achenbach's (1991b) data on behavior problems found in the general population. The 39 items from the 121-item Child Be-

TABLE 3.4
Child Behavior Checklist Data for
Nonreferred and Clinic Children*

ITEM	Girls Age 4 to 6		Girls Age 7 to 12		Boys Age 4 to 6		Boys Age 7 to 12	
	(Data listed in percentages)							
	Normative (N = 197)	Clinical (N = 197)	Normative (N = 515)	Clinical (N = 515)	Normative (N = 179)	Clinical (N = 179)	Normative (N = 481)	Clinical (N = 481)
Argues a lot	49.3	82.1	74.0	85.3	53.1	81.3	77.1	88.1
Behaves like opposite sex	6.1	17.2	10.3	13.7	2.8	9.1	3.9	7.7
Bowel movements outside toilet	3.6	13.9	1.4	4.0	3.4	14.2	2.5	6.7
Can't concentrate, can't pay attention for long	31.5	74.9	37.6	71.3	42.7	77.0	49.2	83.7
Clings to adults or too dependent	45.7	66.4	27.4	53.4	40.2	57.5	22.2	44.7
Confused or seems to be in a fog	3.0	35.0	9.8	38.8	2.8	32.6	11.0	40.3
Cries a lot	27.4	63.8	21.9	48.9	26.8	49.7	14.1	38.6
Daydreams or gets lost in his or her thoughts	16.7	38.0	36.9	52.6	16.7	38.8	42.2	54.1
Deliberately harms self or attempts suicide	2.0	6.7	.2	8.1	1.2	8.4	.8	8.0
Disobedient at home	46.5	84.1	48.6	76.2	54.2	85.0	52.0	83.1
Doesn't get along with other children	15.3	57.5	18.5	58.4	22.3	57.3	17.9	65.0
Fears certain animals, situations, or places, other than school	38.6	50.8	37.6	39.5	33.5	44.1	29.1	34.1
Feels worthless or inferior	8.2	30.4	17.8	60.1	6.1	35.7	17.6	62.5
Nervous, highstrung, or tense	8.2	59.3	23.7	63.8	15.7	55.1	30.2	66.0
Nightmares	34.5	54.8	22.8	37.2	32.4	41.3	20.4	36.1
Too fearful or anxious	10.7	47.5	16.9	48.2	14.5	37.7	14.6	47.9
Feels too guilty	1.5	16.3	7.8	33.1	3.4	23.5	9.1	28.7
Overeating	10.7	18.3	21.8	27.5	5.0	12.9	19.7	21.8
Plays with own sex parts in public	1.0	8.8	.6	2.3	3.4	15.6	1.7	5.2
Plays with own sex parts too much	1.5	16.3	.6	3.6	1.7	16.9	1.7	7.6
Secretive, keeps things to self	15.8	41.7	28.5	54.8	7.8	37.9	30.5	55.6
Self-conscious or easily embarrassed	43.7	50.8	60.6	67.0	36.9	45.0	57.2	60.6
Sexual problems	—	8.3	.4	6.8	0.6	6.4	—	4.5
Sleeps more than most kids during day and/or night	7.1	13.2	11.0	12.1	2.8	10.2	7.3	11.0
Stares blankly	5.1	27.3	6.0	24.3	5.6	22.0	6.4	23.0
Sudden changes in mood or feelings	23.8	63.4	34.6	64.1	28.6	52.5	27.6	58.8
Talks about killing self	1.0	5.6	2.9	14.8	2.3	9.5	3.5	18.1
Temper tantrums or hot temper	43.7	75.0	31.1	56.0	47.5	68.0	40.7	69.3
Thinks about sex too much	1.5	7.3	3.9	11.3	1.2	6.8	3.5	10.2
Trouble sleeping	7.6	29.0	6.8	23.7	7.3	28.7	5.8	25.7
Unhappy, sad, or depressed	8.1	47.5	15.8	65.0	8.4	39.3	15.2	57.0
Wets self during the day	4.0	24.5	1.0	6.3	5.0	17.8	.6	5.1
Wets the bed	17.9	35.7	6.4	14.4	19.5	35.4	7.5	14.2
Wishes to be of opposite sex	.5	4.1	.6	5.9	.6	6.1	1.0	2.5
Worries	15.2	42.7	37.3	59.7	15.6	40.8	30.8	54.1

*Percentages calculated from "Child Behavior Checklist Normative Data," *Manual for the Child Behavior Checklist/4-18 and 1991 Profile,* by T. M. Achenbach, 1991b, Burlington, VT: University of Vermont, Department of Psychiatry.

ITEM	Girls Age 4 to 6		Girls Age 7 to 12		Boys Age 4 to 6		Boys Age 7 to 12	
	(Data listed in percentages)							
	Normative (N = 197)	Clinical (N = 197)	Normative (N = 515)	Clinical (N = 515)	Normative (N = 179)	Clinical (N = 179)	Normative (N = 481)	Clinical (N = 481)
Aches or pains	6.1	19.1	18.7	27.5	5.1	16.3	11.4	20.2
Headaches	7.1	20.4	22.5	34.4	5.0	15.6	17.3	28.3
Nausea, feels sick	4.6	14.8	11.9	19.7	2.2	7.2	7.5	13.4
Stomachaches or cramps	9.6	26.6	23.8	33.0	8.4	23.0	12.6	24.8

havior Checklist were selected for this table because these particular items encompass behaviors sometimes exhibited by sexually abused children and/or traumatized children diagnosed with Post-Traumatic Stress Disorder.

Consistent with the study conducted by MacFarlane et al. (1954), Achenbach's data indicate that high percentages of young children within the general population exhibit problem behaviors during their development. High percentages of preschool-age and elementary school-age children were found by Achenbach (1991b) to exhibit problems such as disobedience, temper tantrums, sudden changes in mood, nightmares, poor concentration, and fearfulness. Thus, it appears that some problem behaviors may be a normal part of children's development.

Based on the normative data presented in the MacFarlane et al. (1954) and Achenbach (1991b) studies, child sexual abuse cannot be diagnosed solely on the presence of behavioral symptoms. As Myers (1992) notes, the fact that a child has nightmares and displays regressive behavior says little about sexual abuse.

THE EMOTIONAL STATE OF FEAR

Because fear is often cited as an emotion exhibited by many sexually abused children, children's fears must be understood within a developmental context. The topic of children's fears is especially relevant to evaluating child sexual abuse. Children who are not victims of sexual abuse may exhibit a number of different fears, while children who are victims of sexual abuse may or may not exhibit fears.

A child's personal interpretation of the sexual encounters in which he or she was involved may have a great deal to do with whether the child specifically experiences fear of the perpetrator or fear related to the sexual activity. With this in mind, the definition of emotions by Lewis and Michalson (1983) is most relevant. They define emotions as "a complex set of behaviors that occur around an equally complex set of situations or stimulus events." They further postulate, "Although some cognitive events may elicit emotional states, no emotional experience is without some cognitive processing" (p. 26). Hence, the way a child thinks about the sexual exploitation is an important consideration.

Development of Fears. The types of fears that children experience are related to their age. Some fears are specific to developmental level. The basis for these developmental differences includes the various experiences that children encounter as they grow, as well as children's abilities to use language and to evaluate stimuli with respect to their significance. As discussed by Sarafino (1986), in his comprehensive book on childhood fears, while the fears of infants and toddlers typically are related to tangible and immediate events, preschoolers' fears are less tangible. For example, children between the ages of 2 and 6 become increasingly fearful of imaginary creatures, such as monsters and ghosts. They also begin to fear the dark and fear being alone.

Research shows that there are gender and age differences in children's fears (Sarafino, 1986). Girls report a greater number of, and more intense, fears than boys (Graziano, DeGiovanni, & Garcia, 1979). Sarafino reported that the basis of these differences is related to the greater cultural acceptance for girls to express their fears, as well as greater cultural prompting for girls to be more fearful. Girls are provided more restrictions and have more frequent warnings about dangers.

While not all emotions (including fears) are learned, some fears and emotions appear to be. Children are not born with most of their fears. Many of children's fears are conditioned responses. For example, human smells, sounds, or movements may be negatively conditioned through the child's involvement in sexual abuse. The perpetrator may become a negatively conditioned stimuli to which the child may react with fear, especially if the abuse involves violence or physical pain. When compared to children who had not experienced sexual abuse, Wells and his colleagues found that children with confirmed histories of sexual abuse were significantly more likely to be fearful of being left with a particular person and to be fearful of males (Wells et al., 1995).

In assessing fear responses in children alleged to have been sexually abused, developmental phenomena must be considered. An important premise is that child sexual abuse is not the only cause for a child to respond to an adult with fear. A child may react fearfully when asked to interact with unfamiliar people. A very young child also may react with fear to a known family member if the individual has changed his or her appearance. For example

> Ten-month-old Brittany's parents had separated, and Brittany was to have her first visit with her father after not seeing him for several weeks. Brittany's father arrived for the visit with his mustache shaved off and was using a new after shave lotion. Brittany cried when her father attempted to pick her up and take her with him. The mother inaccurately concluded that the father had previously harmed Brittany.
>
> *Comment: Brittany had formed a cognitive schema of her father. Thus, a radical change, such as the change in the father's appearance, could produce an emotional response of fear.*

Infants and toddlers are more likely to be fearful of strangers if they have had very little social contact with people outside of their immediate family, if they encounter the stranger in an unfamiliar place (e.g., a store), or if their parent is not present when the stranger appears (Sarafino, 1986). For example:

> Fifteen-month-old Elizabeth had minimal contact with her babysitter's husband. She would react to his greetings by freezing when he would bend down to say hello. She frowned and did not allow him to come near her. Elizabeth's parents observed Elizabeth to exhibit masturbatory behavior at home. The parents were fearful the babysitter's husband had sexually abused Elizabeth.

> *Comment: The phenomenon displayed by Elizabeth is referred to as stranger anxiety. Children who exhibit stranger anxiety show fear of new people, but positive, affiliative behaviors with familiar people. This phenomenon usually occurs after the first 8 months of life and is considered by some to be a maturationally determined, biologically derived response (Schaffer & Emerson, 1964). Stranger anxiety also has been viewed as the result of children's developing cognitive ability, which enables them to compare various novel events, such as strangers, with an internal representation of their caregiver (Schaffer, 1974).*

Another fear that is common in children 6 months and older is called separation anxiety. The following is an example of a child exhibiting distress when separated from the primary caregiver:

> Jeremy's father was a traveling salesperson who was minimally involved in the parenting of his son. When the parents separated, Jeremy was 18 months old. The father was granted every other weekend visitation. Initially, when the father began taking Jeremy away from the home in which he resided with his mother, Jeremy exhibited significant distress. He would cry and attempt to crawl out of his father's car seat. Jeremy was tearful and oppositional with his mother after weekend visits with his father. During visits with his father, Jeremy did not have contact with his mother for 48 hours. After returning home, Jeremy would refuse to eat, and his toileting would regress. Jeremy's mother incorrectly identified her son's distress as caused by sexual abuse.

> *Comment: Separation anxiety is a phenomenon that may be exhibited by young children when they are separated from their primary caregiver(s). Separation from a parental figure due to visitation schedules must be considered when children are exhibiting distress.*

Children between the ages of 6 months and 4 years are at highest risk to be psychologically affected by parental loss. However, children are found to be variable in their responses to change. For example, the research on attachment (Ainsworth, 1973; Sroufe, 1983) indicates that children who have healthy attachments with their primary caretaker may be more resilient and less upset by changes in their environment.

Another issue underlying children's expression of fear is the demonstration of fear by a parent. It is possible that a parent's modeling and pairing anxiety and distress with the visit of the other parent may condition the child to be anxious and distressed. For example

Four-year-old Sabrina's mother would become very anxious the day that Sabrina's father was scheduled to take Sabrina for a visit. The mother would repeatedly warn the child not to allow her father to take her off by herself away from his girlfriend. When the father would arrive, the verbal exchange between Sabrina's parents was stormy, with the mother typically becoming tearful. Sabrina's mother became more and more anxious over the father's visits. Sabrina also began to exhibit increasingly distressed behavior prior to her father's arrival for the visits. However, when with her father, away from her mother's home, Sabrina was observed to be a happy, playful child. The mother inaccurately interpreted Sabrina's behavior, prior to the visits with her father, as a sign that Sabrina was being sexually abused.

Conversely, the following example demonstrates how an abusive, threatening stepfather became a conditioned elicitor of fear:

Tanya, age 10, had resided in a foster home for approximately 6 months when her biological mother remarried. The mother had been allowed to take Tanya on visits away from the foster home and continued to do so after her marriage. Following several visits with her mother and new stepfather, Tanya would return to the foster home glazy-eyed and immediately hide herself under clothes in her closet. She would not speak to other members in the family for several days after visits. Immediately preceding visits, she would exhibit physiological responses, such as shaking, perspiring, and shortness of breath.

Comment: Tanya eventually confided in an older foster sister that her mother and stepfather were using her and several other children in child pornography. She further disclosed that her stepfather had warned her that if she told anyone about the pornography, he would throw her out of a boat into the middle of the town lake. Tanya had never been taught to swim. The thought of or presence of her stepfather elicited extreme fear in Tanya.

CHILDREN'S APPRAISAL OF EVENTS

In some situations, young children may be better insulated against stressful situations than adults because they do not comprehend the meaning of the event. Preschool-age children's perception of authority figures and their obedient stance toward adult authority protects them from feelings of guilt. Because young children also lack understanding of other people's motives and intentions, they may be further protected from the stresses that come from understanding the meaning of others' actions. Maccoby (1983) proposes that older children may suffer more negative consequences because they are aware of the meaning of an experience and more likely to feel responsible for its occurrence. Maccoby writes:

We cannot be upset by events whose power to harm us we do not understand; we cannot be humiliated by failure to handle problems whose solutions are someone else's responsibility; we cannot be distressed by anticipating other's contemptuous or critical reactions to our weaknesses if we are not aware of others' probable reactions and if our egos are not yet invested in appearing strong and competent. (p. 219)

Cross-cultural data are thought to provide support for the hypothesis that there is a connection between psychological effects and children's interpretation of their sexual abuse. For example, among the Sambia in New Guinea, all young male members of the tribe are required to indulge in exclusively homosexual activities from approximately age 7 years until they are married (Stoller & Herdt, 1985). During the first stage of initiation, young boys are told that the secret of Sambia maleness lies in the amount of semen that is drunk during childhood. The boys then are instructed to suck post-pubertal boys' penises. Until they reach puberty the young boys must ingest as much semen as possible because the Sambia do not believe males naturally produce semen. Semen alone is believed to produce maleness and manliness. The second phase of initiation occurs at puberty when the fellators become the fellatees. From this point on the adolescent must not fellate other males because he would be stealing semen needed by younger boys.

These Sambia males do not show signs of psychological trauma or culturally aberrant sexual behaviors as a result of their early ongoing sexual experiences, which in our culture would be identified as sexually abusive for the young fellators (Stoller & Herdt, 1985). In the Sambia culture, this fellating behavior is not interpreted as sexual nor are other abuse-related factors present. (This author would like to emphasize that this example cannot in any manner be used to justify a child's sexual exploitation by an adolescent or adult.)

FAMILY CHARACTERISTICS
AND RESOURCES

AVAILABILITY OF
NURTURANCE IN THE FAMILY

Family support has been found to be a strong mitigating factor to the harmful effects of sexual abuse (Wyatt & Mickey, 1988). In a study conducted by Friedrich (1988), family conflict and lack of parental support of the child were more strongly correlated with psychological problems in the sexually abused child than the sexual abuse characteristics. In a study of adult women who had been sexually abused as children, S. D. Peters (1988) found that lack of maternal warmth was a stronger predictor of psychological difficulty than frequency of abuse, duration of the abuse, and age at the last incident. Based on her research on adult survivors of child sexual abuse and their early attachments, Alexander and Anderson (1994) reported that family characteristics have as much to do with the psychological outcome of sexual abuse as the specific abuse variables.

Both clinical observations and research evidence indicate that the effects of sexual abuse are difficult to differentiate from the consequences of emotional abuse and physical abuse (Briere & Runtz, 1990) and the dysfunctional family experience (Alexander & Lupfer, 1987). Therefore, attempts to predict or identify the effects of sexual abuse must include a consideration of the family context that mediates the experience of sexual abuse (Alexander, 1992).

ATTACHMENT

Related to the importance of family context is the significant importance of the mother-infant relationship to children's cognitive, social, and emotional development (Ainsworth, 1973; Bowlby, 1969; Erickson & Egeland, 1987; Quinton & Rutter, 1984; Sroufe, 1983). Most infants, by the time that they are a year old, have developed a strong closeness to their parents and react adversely when separated from them. This phenomenon is known as attachment.

Theory of Attachment. Attachment is defined as the relationship that develops between a young child and his or her primary attachment figure. Those behaviors through which such a connection first becomes formed and later serve to mediate the relationship are referred to as attachment behaviors. Attachment (as a relationship) develops over time and is not completely established until after the infant has attained the concept of object permanence (typically during the last part of the first year). The process of attachment occurs throughout the human life cycle and, as the child develops, also occurs with individuals outside of the family.

As discussed by Husain and Cantwell (1991), the type and intensity of care provided by the caretaker to the infant appears to be the major determinant in the development of attachment behavior. Caretakers who play with their children and give them a great deal of attention show a stronger attachment with their children than caretakers who only interact with their child during routine care (Schaffer, 1971). Husain and Cantwell postulate that a very attentive father would be more strongly attached with the infant than a relatively unstimulating mother, even if the mother interacted with the infant on a more frequent basis. Thus, the quality of the relationship between child and adult appears to be more critical than the quantity of time spent with the child.

As described in the writings of Bowlby (1969), an important aspect of attachment theory is the concept of an internal working model that forms the basis of the individual's personality. Attachment research (Ainsworth, 1973; Bowlby, 1969) indicates that through the relationship with the primary caretaker, the child develops an internal working model for relationships and an internal representation of self-value. According to Alexander (1992), the child is believed to

- Develop expectations about his or her own role in relationships (e.g., worthy and capable versus unworthy and incapable)
- Develop expectations about others' roles in relationships (e.g., trustworthy and caring versus untrustworthy, uncaring, or hurtful)

- Learn coping strategies and strategies for modulating emotions that will be used throughout life

As a result, the child's internal working model is both affected by and comes to affect the types of interpersonal experiences and the interpretation of those experiences that are encoded into the self-concept (Alexander, 1992).

The Relationship of Attachment to Abuse and Neglect. Through the empirical examination of parent-child relationships, it was concluded that children's attachment to their primary caretaker was not always a secure attachment (Ainsworth & Bell, 1970). The primary caretaker's behavior with the child has been shown to be causally linked to the security of the child's attachment (Egeland & Farber, 1984; Erickson, Sroufe, & Egeland, 1985; Sroufe, 1983).

Contemporary research indicates that poor attachment in infancy and early childhood can interfere in the child's normal social, emotional, and intellectual growth (Egeland & Sroufe, 1981; Egeland, Sroufe, & Erickson, 1983; Erickson & Egeland, 1987; Erickson et al., 1985). Table 3.5 (pp. 68-69) presents developmental differences reported by Erickson and Egeland during the first 6 years of children's lives in groups of maltreated and nonmaltreated children from the same high risk sample of subjects.

When evaluating a child alleged to have been sexually abused, the child's behaviors and symptomatology must be considered within the context of his or her attachment to the primary caregiver. As such, a child's anger at, avoidance of, or ambivalent clinginess with a primary caregiver may reflect sexual abuse, another form of maltreatment, or some other stressor. The following example illustrates this point:

> Sylvia's mother suffered from a chronic illness that caused the mother to spend a great deal of time in bed. During these periods of bedrest, she did not want contact with her family. Sylvia's father, as a result, did the majority of the caretaking. Sylvia's father was overindulgent with his daughter and set few limits. When Sylvia's mother was available to her daughter, the mother was pervasively intrusive. As Sylvia's behavior became more unmanageable, her mother began to suspect that Sylvia was the victim of sexual abuse perpetrated by Sylvia's father.
>
> **Comment:** *A thorough assessment of the family and of Sylvia did not support a finding of sexual abuse. The family was provided multiple modalities of therapy, including individual therapy for Sylvia, as well as marital and parenting therapy for the parents.*

Erickson and Egeland (1987) concluded from their research findings that although patterns of behavior problems vary with the specific pattern of maltreatment experienced by the child, there are more similarities than differences among the groups of maltreated children:

TABLE 3.5
Summary of Behavior of Children Who Were Maltreated During the First 2 Years of Life (or Later Identified as Sexually Abused)*

AGE	ASSESSMENT INSTRUMENT	PHYSICALLY ABUSED	VERBALLY ABUSED	SEXUALLY ABUSED	NEGLECTED	EMOTIONALLY NEGLECTED (PSYCHOLOGICALLY UNAVAILABLE CAREGIVER)
18 months	Attachment Classification	• Anxiously attached - significant difference between maltreated and nonmaltreated groups		• No sexually abused children identified	• Anxiously attached significant difference between neglected and nonmaltreated groups	• Almost all children in this group anxiously attached
24 months	Bayley Scales of Infant Development	• Lower scores than nonmaltreated group	• Lower scores than nonmaltreated group - only for those who experienced combined verbal and physical abuse	• No sexually abused children identified	• Lower scores than nonmaltreated group	• Scores declined dramatically from test scores at 9 months of age • Significant difference between emotionally neglected and nonmaltreated groups
	Tool-Using Tasks (with mother)	• More angry, frustrated, noncompliant, and expressed less positive affect than nonmaltreated group		• No sexually abused children identified	• More angry, frustrated, noncompliant, expressed less positive affect, and showed poorer coping strategies than nonmaltreated group	• More angry, frustrated, noncompliant, expressed less positive affect, and showed poorer coping strategies
42 months	Barrier Box (alone)	• Lower on self-esteem and self-control than nonmaltreated group • Also low on creativity, assertiveness, and were highly distractible		• No sexually abused children identified	• Lower self-esteem, self-control, creativity, assertiveness, lack of flexibility, and were distractible and apathetic	• Only differed significantly on creativity with nonmaltreated group
	Teaching Tasks (with mother)	• Lacked persistence and enthusiasm for tasks, were negativistic, noncompliant, avoidant, and showed little affection toward their mothers		• No sexually abused children identified	• Lacked persistence and enthusiasm for tasks, were negativistic, noncompliant, avoidant, and showed little affection toward their mothers	
	Preschool Observation and Teachers' Checklists	• Noncompliant, poor self-control, expressed much negative emotion (anger and/or sadness or whininess), and many behavior problems	• Too few children in this group attended preschool to allow analysis	• No sexually abused children identified	• Highly dependent, poor self-control, and behavior problems	• Highly dependent, poor self-control, much negative emotion, and presented varied and extensive behavior problems (including nervous signs and self-abusive behaviors)

Age	Measure					
54 months	Curiosity Box	• Dependent, impulsive, and negative affect	• Data not collected	• Dependent, impulsive, and negative affect	• Dependent	• Uninvolved
64 months	Wechsler Preschool and Primary Scale of Intelligence (4 subtests)	• Lower than nonmaltreated children	• Data not collected	• Lower than nonmaltreated children on Block Design subtest only	• Much lower than nonmaltreated children	• Lower than nonmaltreated children on Block Design subtest only
School-age	Kindergarten adjustment • behavior ratings • teacher interview	• Aggressive in the classroom, inattentive, impatient, little positive affect, dependent, unpopular, poor comprehension of classroom activities, varied emotional problems, including nervousness, and compulsive behavior • Almost 50% were recommended for retention or referred to special education	• Data not collected	• Strong need for approval, closeness, and help; anxious and withdrawn, disruptive in the classroom, unpopular, poor comprehension of classroom activities, and varied emotional problems	• Same as Physically Abused plus anxious, withdrawn, lacking initiative, strong need for approval and encouragement, lacking a sense of humor • Lowest on all groups on academic skills, work habits, and social competency • Almost 65% were recommended for retention or referred to special education	• Aggressive, disrespectful, disruptive behavior in the classroom, unpopular, poor academic skills • Similar to nonmaltreated group on majority of the other measures

*Adapted from "A Developmental View of the Psychological Consequences of Maltreatment," by M. F. Erickson and B. A. Egeland, 1987, *School Psychology Review, 16(2),* pp. 159-160. Reprinted with permission.

All have difficulty meeting task demands of school, all seem to have an abiding anger, all are unpopular with their peers, and all have difficulty functioning independently in school and laboratory situations. The common problems these children have exhibited in varied situations over the years can be tied to the lack of nurturance central to each pattern of maltreatment we have observed in these families. (p. 161)

SOCIAL AND PHYSICAL CONTEXTS OF CHILD SEXUAL ABUSE

Although sexual abuse occurs in all demographic strata, intrafamilial sexual abuse and nonincestuous sexual abuse are not randomly distributed. Results from a survey of 795 college students, conducted by Finkelhor (1979), indicated that the strongest predictors of child sexual victimization were:

- presence of a stepfather in the home
- mother never finished high school
- mother sexually repressive/punitive
- no physical affection from father
- child not close to mother
- child lived without his or her mother for some period of time during childhood
- family income under $10,000
- two friends or fewer during childhood

These risk factors were found to be cumulative; each additional factor increased the child's vulnerability between 10% and 20%. Other research studies have also found that the presence of a stepfather or surrogate nonbiological father (i.e., foster) and a poor mother-daughter relationship increase the child's risk for sexual abuse (Gruber & Jones, 1983; Paveza, 1987). Sexual abuse of children also occurs in many families where other types of abuse are present, such as spouse battering and/or physical and emotional abuse of children (Paveza, 1987).

CONCLUSION

Assessment of allegations of child sexual abuse must utilize a developmental framework. Children are heterogeneous in their individual characteristics, their interpretation of events, their family characteristics and resources, the social and cultural world in which they live, and the specific characteristics of the abuse which they endure.

Children's interpretation of and response to their sexual abuse will be influenced by their cognitive and moral development. Infants and toddlers, who may be sexually exploited under the guise of nurturance, most likely will not interpret the sexual behaviors as bad. Furthermore, they may not show any more fear of the perpetrator than of adults who engage them in physical, nonsexual contact. However, if a child was physically hurt or injured while being sexually abused, we would expect the same type of fear response from the child victim that would be present if he or she was the victim of physical abuse.

Nightmares, fears, temper tantrums, and other problems in self-regulatory behaviors are not necessarily symptoms of sexual abuse. Normative data on child behavior problems indicate that it is not unusual for toddler and preschool-age children to exhibit eating problems, sleep problems, nightmares, mood swings, oversensitiveness, specific fears, and temper tantrums as a normal course of development. Therefore, these behaviors or emotions cannot be used solely as markers to identify a sexually abused child. Family characteristics are also poor discriminative markers of child sexual abuse. Children from high risk populations who live in families where they are physically abused, sexually abused, verbally abused, or neglected look more similar than dissimilar in their behaviors.

Preliminary research suggests that although a certain group of victims of child sexual abuse will suffer long-term and/or short-term psychological consequences, a significant number of children will not show short-term psychological consequences or endure long-term psychological effects. This heterogeneity of the population of sexually abused children makes the differentiation of victims from nonvictims a very difficult clinical endeavor.

GUIDELINES
Considerations and Cautions

- Children's understanding of their sexual exploitation will be related to their cognitive and moral developmental stage.
- Children are not miniature adults and do not interpret their experiences as such.
- Very young sexually abused children may not show any signs of distress because they may not understand that the sexual behaviors are bad or wrong.
- Fear of a specific adult may be based on classical conditioning in which there is a pairing of the adult with physically painful experiences caused by the adult or a pairing of the adult with fear and anxiety exhibited by another person.
- Nonsexually abused children display a wide range of problem behaviors throughout normal development.
- Sleeping and eating problems, mood swings, tantrums, fears, and so on are behaviors found in a high percentage of presumably nonsexually abused preschool children. Some of the problem behaviors are found to extend into late childhood.
- Sexual behaviors exhibited by children must be interpreted within a developmental context.
- Masturbation is a common behavior found throughout the course of development and is considered aberrant when it significantly interferes in the child's daily activities, causes physical injury, or interferes in the child's interpersonal relationships.
- Children who are sexually abused are a heterogenous, rather than homogeneous, group. Therefore, they will be affected differently, and as a result, may demonstrate either different behavioral symptoms or an absence of symptoms.
- Attempts to predict or identify the effect of child sexual abuse must include consideration of the family context that mediates the experience of sexual abuse.
- The stability of the child's family and how the child interprets the sexual abuse experience may greatly mitigate the effects of the sexual exploitation.
- Children from physically, sexually, and emotionally abusive and neglectful families are more alike than different. They typically have poor coping skills, poor peer relationships, and perform poorly in school.

CHAPTER 4

Children's Memory and the Issue of Suggestibility

This chapter reviews the literature on children's development of memory. The processes of children's acquisition of information, storage of information into memory, and recall of information are examined. This chapter also presents the topic of children's suggestibility. The possible conditions which cause conscious and unconscious distortions of children's recall of personally experienced events are reviewed.

* * *

Historically, infants were considered to be passive organisms who were deficient in their cognitions and memory. In contrast to this view, present data show that very young children are not cognitively deficient but instead are actively involved in making sense of their world. Furthermore, they are not memory deficient. While research indicates that even infants show memory for stimuli, the developing child's capacity for memory storage and memory retrieval is still not fully understood. The multiple factors that interact with acquisition, storage, and retrieval of memory continue to be investigated.

DEVELOPMENT OF COGNITIVE ORGANIZING STRUCTURES

SCHEMATA - SCRIPTS AND STEREOTYPES AS ORGANIZING STRUCTURES

Bauer and Mandler (1990) found 16-month-olds remembered events for up to 2 to 6 weeks when the event was experienced only one time. As discussed by Nelson (1993), toddlers' memories for events they have experienced typically do not seem to endure for longer than about 6 months, unlike the memories of older children and adults, which in some cases last for decades. However, Fivush and

Hamond (1990) found that by the age of 2½, some children can retain memory for an event up to a year and a half. Research by Hudson and Fivush (1987) found 5-year-old children could store memory for an event they experienced for up to 6 years.

Hertsgaard and Matthews (1993) proposed that there may be a biological basis for rapid forgetting in young children. They suggested that because infants' and very young children's brains have more synapses and connections than do the brains of adults, the synaptic loss and selective neuronal loss that take place throughout the first years of life (Goldman-Rakic, 1987) might provide the basis for loss of memory of the early years. Another perspective on the inaccessibility of early memories has been that impoverished encoding may result in poorly established traces of earlier experiences that then are exceptionally vulnerable to fading (Brainerd, Kingma, & Howe, 1985).

Quantitatively, older children remember more, while younger children remember less and are also more "schema-bound." According to information-processing theorists, humans organize information about the world in the form of schemata. These schemata are interconnected items which tend to be remembered in conjunction with one another (Chi & Ceci, 1987). Two organizing structures for schemata are scripts and stereotypes, defined as follows:

Scripts -   The organization of familiar routines and events. A script is the representation of a temporally organized, habitual routine rather than a memory of a particular single incident.

Stereotypes - The organization of experience that directs a person to look for certain types of information and influences the interpretation of this information. Stereotypes summarize memories or judgments about a person or a category of people.

The following example demonstrates a toddler's script development:

> Two-year-old Rebekah and her mother ate lunch at Wendy's and then went for a visit to the museum. Two months later, Rebekah and her mother met Rebekah's father for lunch at Wendy's. Rebekah (then 2 years and 2 months) inquired of her parents if they were going to the museum after lunch.
>
> *Comment: Rebekah had not eaten at Wendy's since her trip to the museum and appeared to have developed a schematic representation of Wendy's restaurant as connected to the museum.*

Nelson (1993) proposed that the very young child first constructs scripts for repeatedly experienced events. Once the child develops a sufficient body of script knowledge, the child is then able to use that knowledge as a background from which to remember a specific event. As the child develops the capacity to remember a specific event, memories of both repeated events as well as one-time events become entered into autobiographical memory (i.e., a type of episodic memory that is made up of one's personal past).

MEMORY - A COGNITIVE PROCESS EMBEDDED IN SOCIAL TASKS

Nelson (1986) observed that the usual age of learning to talk about what is remembered is consistent with the age of onset of autobiographical memory (i.e., ages 2 to 4). As discussed by Hudson (1990a, 1990b), one factor which may contribute to improvement in recall at any age, and particularly at an early age when memories are fragile, is verbal rehearsal. She proposed that sharing memories with others through verbal means may become a form of reinstatement of the memory that enables a specific memory to persist in the very young child for a more extended period of time.

Research by Hudson (1990a) indicates memories that are repeatedly recalled are later remembered in more detail than memories that are seldom discussed. Tessler (1986) found that children could more accurately remember an experience when their mothers talked with them about the experience in a narrative style (i.e., elaborating on an experience and asking questions that encouraged the child to contribute information to the conversation). Conversely, children demonstrated less accurate memories when their mothers simply pointed out objects or responded to the child's comments. These findings show the significance of the social context in the development of memory; sharing memories of experiences appears to be related to memory storage. Hudson (1990a) proposed that through parent-child "memory talk" children are learning "how" to remember rather than "what" to remember.

In addressing amnesia for childhood events, Nelson (1990) reported that older children and adults do not normally remember specific life events that occur before the age of 3 years. She gave the following qualifications: (a) the cutoff point can be as late as 8 years; (b) a few individuals have occasional memories from the age of 2 years or younger; and (c) the age of earliest memory negatively correlates with IQ, language ability, and social class. Additionally, females tend to have earlier memories than males.

According to Nelson (1990), the significant age variability regarding children's earliest memories cannot be solely explained by maturation functions but must also be explained by the variability of the children's experiences. Thus, children's engagement by their parental figures in memory talk is thought to account for both age and gender variability. Nelson further reported that adults teach children to remember in different ways. Therefore, as shown by Tessler's (1986) research, how children are engaged in "memory talk" affects what and how children remember. Because early childhood experiences of sexual abuse are rarely disclosed, let alone repeatedly discussed, infant, toddler, or early preschooler's sexual abuse memories may not be reinforced through "memory talk" for later access.

MEMORY AND CHILDREN'S EYEWITNESS TESTIMONY

Fully understanding children's acquisition of memories and retrieval of memories is critical to understanding children's statements regarding what they have experienced in their past. Ornstein, Larus, and Clubb (1991) report that children's ability to remember salient experiences over long periods of time is determined by factors, such as

- the individual's prior knowledge of the event
- the quality of the initial representation of the event to be recalled
- the interval between storage and subsequent recall
- the type of prompt used to elicit information
- the events that occur in the delay interval before recall is tested

While these factors are necessary to the understanding of children's recall of events, the developmental level of the child will impact each of these areas.

MEMORY STORAGE

ACQUISITION OF A MEMORY

How do children develop a memory for an event? Acquisition is the first phase in remembering. During acquisition of information, the child must perceive and attend to the event; at this stage, the organism appears to be selective in what information it stores. In conceptualizing how information is chosen for storage, Nelson (1990) wrote that memory for a single episode is less functional in a basic sense than memory for repeated events, based on the organism's need to guide action and predict the future. Therefore, retaining memories for single events may be less useful than retaining memories for repeated events. Nelson proposed that if memory acts as a guide for action, it would be important for the developing child to remember salient features of a single event for a time-limited period in case the event was repeated. However, if the event was not repeated within a specific time period, the memory would be deleted.

In support of this theory, Nelson (1990) cited research with infants conducted by Rovee-Collier and Hayne (1987) and research with 3- and 4-year olds conducted by Fivush and Hamond (1990). In both studies, children given one reminder of an experience produced memories of that experience. However, over the identical time period, when children were not given reminders of the experience, that experience was forgotten. Thus, this research indicates that while specific memories may be held by young children for a period of time, these memories will be subject to automatic deletion if not repeated.

Furthermore, not all experiences are put into memory because young children have difficulty conceptualizing complex events, identifying relationships, recognizing feelings, and attributing intention. These factors all have an effect on the child's encoding and storage of information into memory (Perry, 1992). This memory acquisition research may indicate that if a toddler or preschool child is sexually abused a single time, the child does not understand the experience, and if the child was not frightened or hurt, the child's memory for this single event may never be stored or may be deleted over time.

CHILD'S PRIOR KNOWLEDGE

A child's prior knowledge regarding the experience in which he or she is interacting or observing appears to influence how events are interpreted, coded, and put in memory (Chi & Ceci, 1987; Ornstein & Naus, 1985). Research investigating the development of expertise has demonstrated that highly specialized knowledge held by the individual permits him or her to encode and recall information more effectively than a nonexpert (Glaser & Chi, 1988).

This research on prior knowledge suggests that children's understanding of the sexually abusive events they experience may have an important impact on what enters into memory storage and how it is organized. Regarding the connection between children's specific information base and children's cognitive processing of their involvement in adult sexual activities, Ornstein et al. (1991) concluded, "One implication of the literature is that a child who does not understand what is happening to him or her may have little basis for subsequently remembering what they (sic) experienced" (p. 153). For example, if an 18-month-old infant's arms, legs, back, or vagina were rubbed, these actions would have the same meaning to the infant if they were pleasurable and did not involve pain.

INTEREST VALUE

The interest value of a stimuli with which a child is presented also affects what is stored in memory (Renninger & Wozniak, 1985). Activities, people, and materials that hold interest for the child are more likely to be encoded and stored in memory than those stimuli that are of less interest. For example

Four-year-old Demi was observed engaging her male peers at daycare in sex play. When authorities were called to investigate, Demi was able to describe in detail her uncle's penis, including how it got "big and little," could wave at her, and "spit at her." She even described the mole on his penis.

Comment: Demi had been engaged in sexual activity by her uncle through play. Because of her developmental level, she was not frightened by the events. Instead, she was curious and interested in her uncle's penis which he had introduced to her as a type of toy.

INTENSITY OF STRESS

The impact of stress has been of interest to researchers in their study of the connection between increased arousal and memory acquisition. However, current research findings are inconsistent regarding the impact of stress on children's memory. (See Davies, 1993, for an extensive review.)

Several research studies using child subjects suggest that high levels of stress and increased arousal enhance children's ability to focus and, as a result, facilitate the storage of information into memory. For example, in research conducted by Goodman (1993), children were subjected to a highly aversive medical procedure called "voiding cystourethrogram" or VCUG. This procedure entails a urinary tract catheterization, followed by filling the child's bladder with contrast fluid. The child's bladder is filled to an extremely uncomfortable level and the child then is instructed to urinate while the child is simultaneously observed by the physician(s). Goodman found that this painful and potentially embarrassing medical procedure was associated with enhanced recall.

Research by Steward (1992) showed that the majority of 3- to 6-year-old children who were distressed by painful medical procedures were highly accurate in their spontaneous recall of the locations on their bodies where they were touched by medical staff although these children only reported one-fourth of the touches they experienced. While older children were found to exhibit greater completeness and consistency in their reports, age did not influence the accuracy of reports. Goodman, Hirschman, et al. (1991) also found that children's stress, created through painful medical procedures, was associated with more complete recall of events as well as greater resistance to suggestion by interviewers.

In contrast to the research by Goodman (1993), Steward (1992), and Goodman, Hirschman, et al. (1991) suggesting a facilitative effect of stress, D. P. Peters (1987) and S. D. Peters (1991) argued that high levels of stress impede storage of information into memory. In a study of 3- to 8-year-old children's visits to a dentist, D. P. Peters (1987) did not find strong evidence for a facilitative effect of stress. In a second study conducted by S. D. Peters (1991), while 3- to 9-year-old children's stress, created through painful medical procedures, was associated with less accuracy for remembering peripheral details (e.g., recognition of rooms), accuracy for remembering central details (e.g., recognition of nurse) was not impaired.

In studies concerning children's memories for traumatic events such as homicides of loved ones and sniper attacks on schools (Pynoos & Eth, 1984; Pynoos & Nader, 1988), children who maintained greater distance from the danger were found to have more complete recall and less memory distortion than children who were closer in proximity to the danger. The research on children's memories for life-threatening or life-terminating events also indicates that children's memory for peripheral details may be less accurate than for central details.

Lamb, Sternberg, and Esplin (1994) argue that the research suggesting children's memories are enhanced by stressful events cannot be used to conclude that children's memories are enhanced by incidents of sexual abuse. These researchers note that not all incidents of sexual abuse are painful or traumatic, and, therefore, the potentially facilitative effects of arousal on the process of encoding information cannot be assumed. They further suggest that the context in which the child is asked to retrieve the information about the sexual event may be stressful regardless of whether the actual sexual event was stressful and, thus, may inhibit rather than enhance recall.

STRENGTH OF THE MEMORY TRACE

A memory trace is defined as the record which is encoded into memory and consists of pattern recognition and the interpretive analyses of the record. The strength of a memory trace that is stored in long-term memory has been found to be influenced by a number of factors. Research findings indicate that the strength of a memory trace is primarily affected by both the amount of exposure to a particular event and the age of the witness (Baker-Ward, Hess, & Flanagan, 1990; Brainerd et al., 1985). The longer the duration and the greater the number of exposures to the particular event, the stronger the memory trace will be. Other things being equal, older children and adults learn more from comparable exposure to a particular event than younger children.

Research findings are equivocal as to whether memory is enhanced by active participation, as opposed to passive observation (Baker-Ward et al., 1990; Foley & Johnson, 1985). Ornstein et al. (1991) suggest that if memory traces for an event in which the child participates are stronger than those traces for an observed event, this difference may be due to the greater focal attention directed to the details of the event when the child is engaged in participation.

The following example, in which Rebekah was an observer, shows Rebekah's detailed memory of her mother's response to 3-month-old Rachel's convulsion. This example reflects the complexity of memory acquisition.

> Rebekah, age 2 years and 11 months, observed her 3-month-old sister go into convulsions for approximately 30 minutes. During Rachel's convulsions, Rebekah also witnessed her mother call 911 and run down the street with Rachel in her arms to the

entrance of their apartment complex to meet the ambulance. Although the incident involving Rachel had not been discussed with Rebekah, 2 months after this incident, when Rebekah saw an ambulance, she queried her mother, "Mommy, why were you running down the street?" Her mother responded, "What do you remember?" Rebekah then gave a detailed account of her mother's running to meet the ambulance so that "it wouldn't miss their house," Rachel's being sick and being put in the ambulance by a man, the ambulance siren and lights screaming and flashing, and Rachel's being transported to the hospital.

Comment: In this incident, Rebekah was under 3 years old, an observer, and exposed to the event only a single time. However, factors confounding the effect of Rebekah's participant/observer role include Rebekah's superior intelligence and the stress of the event, as well as Rebekah's engagement in mother-daughter memory talk throughout her development. Thus, all three of these additional factors may have impacted Rebekah's memory trace.

MEMORY STORAGE OF A
SEXUAL ABUSE EXPERIENCE

Just what information enters the memory system may vary. In incidents of sexual abuse, the information that children store in memory may depend on their understanding of what was happening to them, their knowledge of anatomy and sexual behavior, whether the event was a single episode or repeated events, interest in the activity, and the stress accompanying the event (Ornstein et al., 1991). For example

Three-year-old Danny's sexual molestation by the 16-year-old babysitter was interrupted by Danny's mother, who arrived home early. The mother found the babysitter engaged in the sexual act of fellatio. When Danny was asked by authorities what the babysitter did to him, Danny stated that they played games, describing the sucking of his penis. Danny was unable to describe the clothes that the 16-year-old wore or any statements the adolescent had made to him. However, Danny was able to repeat verbatim what his emotionally distraught mother screamed at the babysitter upon discovery of the teenager molesting Danny.

Comment: Danny may have been too young to understand the meaning of fellatio. However, because pain was not involved, the activity may have held interest for him, and his focus then may have been centered on the genitals rather than the clothes of the babysitter. Because Danny did not understand the meaning of the sexual behavior, the act of fellatio may not have been stressful to him. Conversely, when his mother accidentally discovered the event, Danny may have become stressed by his mother's response and, consequently, stored in memory her statements to the babysitter.

MEMORY RETRIEVAL

In order to report their experiences, children must retrieve acquired and stored information. This retrieval of information occurs in three ways: recognition, reconstruction recall, and free recall (Perry, 1992).

RECOGNITION

Recognition is the most basic form of memory retrieval, in that the child only needs to identify an object or person as having previously been experienced (Perry, 1992). Recognition as a form of memory retrieval is present in infants. Cernoch and Porter (1985) found newborns could recognize the smell of their own mother's breast milk. Although there exist fewer age differences in recognition than in free recall forms of memory retrieval (Ceci, Ross, & Toglia, 1987a, 1987b; Saywitz, 1987), recognition memory improves with age.

Recognition in preschoolers can be very accurate; preschoolers have been found to remember as much as adults when the task did not require free recall (Nurcombe, 1986). Ceci et al. (1987a, 1987b) found 3-year-olds to be as accurate as 12-year-olds in recognizing familiar pictures.

RECONSTRUCTION RECALL

A second type of retrieval, labeled reconstruction recall, involves the mental reconstruction of the event. Reconstruction recall is the process of mentally reconstructing an event through the recall of segments of the event until the whole event is recalled. Reconstruction recall may be aided by the reinstatement of the context in which the original event occurred, as reflected in the cognitive interview technique (see Chapter 6). Context reinstatement is believed to assist reconstruction recall by attempting to present cues during retrieval that were present during the acquisition of information.

FREE RECALL

Free recall is the most complex form of memory retrieval. This form of recall requires the child to retrieve information from memory storage with few or no prompts (Perry, 1992). Research has shown that children demonstrate good recall for meaningful events, such as genital examinations (Saywitz et al., 1991), inoculations (Goodman, Aman, & Hirschman, 1987), dental examinations (D. P. Peters, 1987), and class trips (Fivush, Hudson, & Nelson, 1984).

Related to developmental differences, children are less skillful than adults in reproducing events using free recall. Young children tend to give less information than adults to free recall questions (Hamond & Fivush, 1990). In reference to young children's problems with providing detailed recounts during free recall, Lamb et al. (1994) point out that "it is important to distinguish between *competence* - the ability to provide information about one's past experience - and *credibility* - the accuracy or truthfulness of those accounts" (p. 257). For example, sexually abused children who are very young, developmentally delayed, or who have learned English as a second language may provide recounts of their abuse during free recall that may appear less than credible due to their limited verbal skills. Another problem with free recall is that suggestions from prior directive questioning at times infiltrate subsequent free recall. In one study, 9-year-old children who were exposed to a suggestive interview repeated 21% of the suggested details during subsequent free recall questioning (Warren & Lane, 1995).

RECALL PROBLEMS - SCRIPTS, FUSION, AND DEFAULT ASSIGNMENT

Children are aided in recall by their development of generalized event representations (i.e., scripts) for events that have become routines (Hudson, 1990b). A child may anticipate that her morning routine is to wake up, bathe, get dressed, eat breakfast, brush teeth, and watch cartoons on television. The child's development of generalized event representations then allows the child to use these schemas (scripts) to guide his or her recall of events (Hudson, 1990b).

Based on the development of a script memory, preschool children's retrieval of information can be very accurate (Todd & Perlmutter, 1980). However, children's reliance on "scripts" as memory guides also has been found to distort recall. For example, in one study, 5- and 7-year-old children embellished recall of stories they were read with items and events that were part of their own personal scripts (McCartney & Nelson, 1981).

Although novel events and familiar events involving a novel incident may be retained as specific memories because something unusual occurs (Hudson, 1988), it appears that a specific event involving a highly routine pattern may become difficult to recall because it becomes "fused" with previous and future events. It then is no longer available to recall as a distinct event (Hudson & Nelson, 1986). Lamb et al. (1994) suggest that, based on this cognitive process of blurring distinctions, memories involving complex and recurrent incidents of sexual abuse may be more vulnerable to distortions than memories involving simple or single incidents.

Script research also provides a theoretical framework for predicting that children will be more influenced by interference effects during long retention intervals as the memory for an event begins to fade (Snyder, Nathanson, & Saywitz, 1993). When memories for specific events begin to fade, children may rely on scripted memory to fill in gaps in memory. The phenomenon, in which the scripted memory fills in for the faded memory trace, is referred to as "default assignment." Snyder et al. (1993) suggest that default assignment may offer an explanation for the types of errors and confusion exhibited by some children during forensic interviews.

Lengthy delays between the event and questioning have been found to affect children's recounts when memory retrieval is elicited through open-ended questions. Flin et al. (1992) and Poole and White (1993) found when children were forced by open-ended questions to provide a detailed sequence of events from memory after long delays between the event and questioning, their inaccuracies increased. Children in the Poole and White study were found not only to make errors in recounting peripheral details but also were found to make errors in recounting the actions of two of the primary actors in the event. Poole and White proposed that when memory traces are strong, children may be competent to provide a credible sequence of events. However, over time, as memory traces fade, children may not be competent to provide a credible sequence of events when asked open-ended questions.

DEVELOPMENTAL DIFFERENCES RELATED TO RECALL

Researchers have investigated whether developmental differences found in the quantity of details of younger and older children's recall of events are due to the fact that older children are linguistically more sophisticated or whether they have memory representations that are more elaborate. Ornstein et al. (1991) reported that research findings show both to be true. Preliminary research suggests, at least in part, the amount of detail in older children's reports is a function of a memory representation that is more elaborate. Additionally, older children appear to have stronger memory traces than younger children.

Fivush and Hamond (1990) studied the consistency of preschool children's autobiographical recall over a 1-year period and found young preschool children (ages 2 years and 6 months to 2 years and 11 months when study commenced) were very inconsistent in what they recalled across interviews. However, the young preschool children, although inconsistent, were not inaccurate - they just gave different segments of accurate information during three different interviews that took place over a year's duration. Approximately 90% of what the children recalled during the three interviews was accurate. Fivush and her colleagues proposed that at least part of the variability in preschool children's recall may be due to the variability in the questions that are posed to them (Fivush et al., 1991).

Other research suggests that young children's recall of information can be highly consistent over long durations of time. Hudson and Fivush (1987) asked children to recall a trip to a museum that they took when they were in kindergarten. The children were interviewed immediately following the trip to the museum, 1 year after, and 6 years after the trip. When only central activities were considered, consistent information recalled was 89% at the 1-year interview and 97% at the 6-year interview. The different findings of Fivush et al. (1991) and those of Hudson and Fivush (1987) may be attributed to the age differential of the subjects in their studies. It appears toddler and young preschool-age children are less consistent, but not necessarily less accurate, than kindergarten and elementary school-age children in what they access from memory over time.

CHILDHOOD AMNESIA

As discussed by Hudson (1990a), research suggests that preschool-age children do not suffer from the phenomenon of childhood amnesia found in adults (i.e., adults are found to rarely recall personally experienced events that occurred before the age of 3 and can rarely remember events that occurred when they were ages 3 and 4 [White & Pillemer, 1979]). Rather, 3-year-old children show memory for the events they have experienced during their toddler years (Fivush & Hamond, 1990; Hudson & Nelson, 1986). This memory then appears to deteriorate over time. Research indicates that it is unlikely that memories for events which occurred in the first year of life can become consciously accessible in adulthood (Usher & Neisser, 1993). Even in childhood, such memories may become quickly lost to consciousness. In a study of documented childhood traumatic events, including childhood sexual abuse, Terr (1988) found that individuals did not have consciously accessible memories for traumatic events as they matured when the traumatic events occurred prior to the age of 3 years.

QUESTIONING – FACILITATING OR CONTAMINATING

A variety of experiences can have strong impact on the strength and organization of stored information as well as the retrieval of information. Perry (1992) summarized children's retrieval abilities by writing

It is important to understand that "forgetting" may be caused by a variety of problems: failure to perceive an event, lack of attention, difficulties in encoding or storing material, or problems in recalling the event. In addition, how the child is interviewed is likely to have a profound effect on the child's ability to recall and report information from memory. (p. 15)

Snyder et al. (1993) propose that research on children's disclosures of sexual abuse during interviewing supports two competing perspectives: (a) children's recounts of past events are enhanced by adult questions, and (b) children's recounts of past events are interfered with by adult questions, especially if the adult introduces suggestive false information (Melton & Thompson, 1987). As discussed earlier in this chapter, through "memory talk," caregiver questioning helps children learn what information is expected to be shared during recounts of past events and how it is to be presented to the listener. The implication of this finding is that young children must rely on adults' questions to assist them in their recounts because they do not have sufficient word knowledge to organize their own hierarchy of retrieval cues and have not mastered conversational form (Snyder et al., 1993). However, research also indicates that the facilitative effects of questioning are mitigated by the false information that may be introduced into early recounts of past events. Research by Ceci, Crotteau, et al. (1994) and Ceci, Loftus, et al. (1994) showed that repeated pre- and post-event inaccurate information presented to preschool-age children impacted the accuracy of children's memories for events. Tucker, Mertin, and Luszcz (1990), studying the effects of multiple interviews, found that although early interviews had a facilitative effect, during subsequent interviews, the children retained erroneous information integrated during initial interviews.

In order to address these competing problems, Saywitz (1995b) developed an interview technique called the Narrative Elaboration (see Chapter 6). This interview technique is used to teach children how to organize their recounts of events so that suggestive questioning by the interviewer can be minimized.

MOTIVATION TO
RETRIEVE MEMORIES

Saywitz (1995b) proposed that within a "social-motivational framework," the factors that affect the child's memory recount include (a) an appraisal of the task (in which the child assesses the consequences of error and the amount of effort required), (b) an appraisal of strategy effectiveness of possible outcomes and consequences (i.e., rewards and penalties), and (c) a cost-benefit analysis to determine if the expected outcome is worth the effort required. Also affecting the memory product is whether the retrieval tasks are viewed by the child as interesting and challenging or stressful and unpleasant. Thus, expectations, beliefs, emotional states, and coping patterns are thought to play a prominent role in determining the quality of information a child may provide during the forensic interview. According to Saywitz (1995b), the child's memory product is affected by the following:

INTERVIEW ENVIRONMENT FACTORS   **CHILD FACTORS**

Support	- Cues Feedback Encouragement	**Perceptions of Self-Efficacy** -	Insecurity Grandiosity
		Emotions -	Ambivalence Fear Anxiety
Interference	- Time Pressure Discouragement		
		Coping Patterns -	Denial Avoidance Mastery

Saywitz (1995b) wrote

> A social motivational framework is well suited to understanding children's testimony because it explains situations of inadequate information processing when children do not perform at their highest level of functioning. Within this framework, there are many reasons why children might not apply the most effective strategy known to them. For example, less effective, but familiar and well practiced, strategies may be chosen because they are easier to implement with less risk of failure. This may be especially true when consequences for failure are perceived to be high, incentives for investing effort are perceived as few, and the environment is perceived to be unfamiliar and unsupportive. (p. 133)

A number of studies identify factors that may interfere with a sexually abused child's motivation to provide information regarding sexual exploitation. In one such study conducted by Saywitz (1989), children ages 4 to 14 were interviewed about their knowledge of the investigative and judicial process. In the 4- to 7-year-old age range, some children thought court was "the room you pass on your way to jail." Some young children also believed that children went to jail if they made a mistake when testifying. Furthermore, many children between 4 and 7 years of age assumed the individuals in the jury box were "friends of the defendant, rather than impartial decision makers" (Saywitz, 1995b, p. 134). As discussed by Saywitz and Goodman (in press), within a social motivational framework, children's understanding of the various people and the functions of these people can have a profound effect on their memory retrieval during forensic questioning.

THE ISSUE OF SUGGESTIBILITY

REDEFINING SUGGESTIBILITY

Children's suggestibility is believed to be another source of variability in children's recounts of past events. Ceci and Bruck (1993) defined suggestibility as "the degree to which children's encoding, storage, retrieval, and reporting of events can be influenced by a range of social and psychological factors" (p. 404). This broad definition of suggestibility contrasts with the traditional narrower view of suggestibility in the following ways (Ceci & Bruck, 1993):

BROAD	**NARROW**
• Information that is divergent from an originally perceived event can be accepted while the person is fully aware of its divergence.	• Information that is divergent from an originally perceived event is accepted unconsciously.
• Suggestibility can result from information preceding or following an event.	• Suggestibility can only result from information following an event.
• Suggestibility is related to social as well as cognitive factors.	• Suggestibility is related to cognitive factors - it is memory-based as opposed to a social phenomenon.

According to Ceci and Bruck (1993) this broader definition of suggestibility takes into account forms of suggestibility that both include and do not include the alteration of the individual's memory. Thus, forms of suggestibility are thought to involve cognitive as well as social factors that impact the unconscious, as well as the conscious. For example, social factors that may impact children's conscious alteration of their recounts of past events include threats, bribes, and other forms of inducements. Cognitive factors that can impact children's unconscious alteration of their recounts can result from the provision of information preceding the event (i.e., information providing a positive or negative stereotype) or following the event (i.e., subtle suggestions and leading questions) (Ceci, 1994).

Ceci and Bruck (1993) noted that suggestibility is an extremely complex phenomenon involving situational, social, and memory factors. Suggestibility varies across all ages and also appears to be related to individual personality characteristics. The individual personality characteristics that render some children more suggestible than others are a continuing area of research focus. Thus, suggestibility should not be considered a "trait" that remains constant for an individual regardless of circumstances (Saywitz & Snyder, 1993).

The Underlying Mechanisms of Suggestibility. While research has consistently found age-related differences in children's suggestibility, the underlying mechanisms responsible for these differences remain unknown. Several theories have been proposed. One theory involves the strength of the memory trace. As previously stated, a memory trace is defined as the record which is encoded into memory and consists of pattern recognition and the interpretive analysis of the record.

As discussed by Leichtman and Ceci (1995), some trace theorists hypothesize that the incorporation of post-event information into the original memory trace occurs as a function of the trace strength, with weak, loosely integrated traces being vulnerable to greater intrusion from external sources (Brainerd et al., 1990; Ceci, Toglia, & Ross, 1988). This "blending" process is thought to occur less frequently when the memory trace is strong and the trace's features are tightly integrated. Some theorists propose that another process also exists in which the incorporation of the erroneous memory trace coexists, rather than blends, with the accurate original memory trace (McCloskey & Zaragoza, 1985a, 1985b). Therefore, original memory trace remains intact and is not overwritten.

Some theorists propose that age differences in suggestibility occur because younger children encode weaker memory traces, which are more vulnerable to disintegration, blending, or overwriting than the stronger memory traces of older children (Brainerd et al., 1990; Ceci et al., 1988). However, Howe (1991) proposed that while trace strength may be related to how quickly children forget an experience and the quantity of erroneous information included in children's recounts of events, weaker memory traces do not necessarily impair recall of accurate details.

Another theory on the underlying mechanisms of suggestibility is source misattribution (Leichtman & Ceci, 1995). Source misattribution occurs when children become confused in distinguishing whether they performed an activity or only imagined performing the activity. Source misattribution theory contends that the effect of repeated suggestive questions induces young children to create images of the suggested events which, at a later time, may be difficult to distinguish from actual experiences (i.e., memory based on direct perception versus memory based on internally generated imagery) (Leichtman & Ceci, 1995).

These memory trace theories are of interest in relation to young nonsexually abused children who are interviewed and provided erroneous information about a nonexistent abuse experience for which they do not have a memory. The gathering of empirical data over time, hopefully, will answer questions, such as: "Do nonexistent abuse experiences overwrite or become blended with the original accurate memory traces of experiences with an alleged perpetrator?" "Are children's memories resilient to this contamination?" "Do children who have experienced sexual abuse have memories that are more resilient to contamination of abuse-related suggestions than children who have not experienced sexual abuse?"

Increasing Ecological Validity. Although research has found strong evidence of age differences in suggestibility, much of this research cannot be used to prove similar levels of suggestibility in "real-world" cases of alleged child sexual abuse (Ceci, Loftus, et al., 1994). Whether the suggestibility effects reported in the existing research represent an underestimate or an overestimate of children's distortions in recounts of events under real-world forensic interviews remains unknown. In comparison to the child subjects in research studies, alleged child victims of sexual abuse may be more vulnerable to errors in their recounts of events because of repeated interviews over long time delays. Conversely, compared to the child subjects in research studies, children who have experienced sexual abuse may be less vulnerable to errors in their recounts of events due to the salience of the sexual abuse experience.

Critics of the research on children's suggestibility have focused on the lack of ecological validity (i.e., degree to which the conditions in the research study replicate the real-world situation) and the inappropriate generalizations of some of these research findings (Ceci, 1991; Yuille & Wells, 1991). In order to more closely approximate the conditions under which child sexual abuse occurs and the conditions under which children alleged to have been sexually abused are interviewed, researchers have designed more realistic and externally valid paradigms in which children personally participate.

Ceci (1993) has cited the following problems with research studies on children's suggestibility:

- Children who come to court are frequently questioned weeks, months, or even years after the occurrence of an event (as opposed to the very brief delays that are common in memory studies).
- Unlike in most research studies, it is rarely the case that actual child witnesses are interviewed only one time by one interviewer, under relaxed conditions . . . some children have been interviewed weekly for years about the same event prior to testifying in court (e.g., they may have been involved in suggestive practices in therapy sessions).
- In actual forensic situations, children are questioned by parents, therapists, and legal officials; adults who carry status and power in their eyes. In such situations, children may be more likely to comply with the suggestions of the interviewers than in analogous experimental situations, where interviewers are generally less important to them and less imposing. (p. 9)

While Raskin and Esplin (1991) concur with Ceci (1993), Saywitz (1995a) has cautioned that, to date, there is no empirically derived evidence that validates the existence of a national epidemic of poorly conducted interviews. Although it is correct to state that there is no evidence to validate the existence of extensive poor interviewing, there also is no evidence to validate its absence. To date, there is an absence of descriptive data on the quality of the interviews that the majority of alleged sexually abused children undergo. This lack of empirical information makes it difficult to draw broad conclusions on the quality of interviewing that is conducted in contemporary practice.

Repeated Post-Event Pressured Interviewing. Studies considered to be the most ecologically realistic incorporate procedures that involve actual physical touching between the child and an adult and include settings with high levels of stress, feelings of possible loss of control, and embarrassment (Goodman et al., 1990). A number of studies have investigated one or more of these factors. Clarke-Stewart, Thompson, and Lepore (1989) investigated children's suggestibility when repeatedly questioned with a pressured suggestive interviewing style. In their study, eighty-eight 5- and 6-year-old children interacted with a man posing as a janitor. The janitor followed one of two scripts. In both scripts, the janitor cleaned the room. He then either cleaned the toys, including a doll, or handled the doll roughly and suggestively. In both cases, the child was invited to join in the activities of the janitor. A dialogue also was produced by the janitor that reinforced either the idea that he was cleaning the doll (e.g., "This doll is dirty; I better clean it") or playing with the doll roughly and suggestively (e.g., "I like to play with dolls." "I like to look under their clothes; I like to bite them and twist their arms and legs").

An hour after the child's interaction with the janitor, an interviewer, who the child was told was the janitor's boss, questioned the child about the janitor's activities. The three interview conditions were (a) neutral and nonsuggestive, (b) accusatory - suggesting the janitor was inappropriately playing with the toys instead of working (i.e., "Maybe he pretended to clean it, but really he was playing"), and (c) exculpatory - suggesting the janitor was cleaning the toys and not playing ("Maybe he pretended to play with the doll, but really he was cleaning"). In the latter two conditions, the interview questions became increasingly stronger as the interview progressed (i.e., "I just want you to tell the truth. Chester wasn't really cleaning the toys was he?", or "I just want you to tell the truth. Chester wasn't really playing, was he?"). After these suggestions were presented to the children, the interviewer asked the child to give an open-ended free report and asked 17 factual and 6 interpretive questions (i.e., "Was he doing his job or was he being bad?").

Following the first interview, each child was reinterviewed by a second interviewer. This second interviewer provided either the same suggestive questions provided to the child during the first interview or contradictory suggestive questions. After this second interview, the children were asked by their parents to recount what the janitor had done.

When children were not given misleading information (neutral and nonsuggestive interviewing), their narrative recounts were brief but accurate, and their answers to factual questions were also accurate for what they had witnessed. Conversely, two-thirds of the children who were given misleading information during their first interview contradicted what they had witnessed and provided answers in line with the interviewer's suggestions on the interpretive questions. At least four of the six interpretive questions were answered by 90% of the misled children in agreement with the interviewer's suggestion and in contrast to what they actually had witnessed. However, the misled children continued to correctly answer the factual questions. When the second interviewer contradicted the first interviewer, the majority of the children altered their answers to the interpretive questions to fit the suggestion of the second interviewer. When interviewed by their parents, the misled children made reports to their parents that were consistent with the suggestions of the interviewers rather than consistent with what they witnessed.

Clarke-Stewart et al. (1989) ruled out several hypotheses that could be used to explain their results, including memory alteration or social pressure. They proposed that if the suggestion actually altered the children's memory, the misled children would not have continued to correctly answer the factual questions. They further postulated that if the misled children had altered their stories because of social pressure, the children would have narrated the accurate scenario of what they actually witnessed when they were questioned in a neutral manner by their parents. Rather, these researchers argued for the consideration of a third hypothesis that in a situation in which there is ambiguity in interpretation or which the child has not understood well in the first place, the child is prone to accept the adult's version of the event as the "truth."

Furthermore, some children were found to be more susceptible to interviewer's interpretations based on personality factors and parenting factors. Children who were more suggestible to misleading questions were found to have parents who placed less value on self-direction and were less strict about lying than other parents. The more suggestible children also were found to be more suggestible in many contexts and less knowledgeable about the social value placed on not telling lies.

In summary, whether children accurately remember and interpret an event is a complex issue. In order to predict when children are more susceptible to suggestions, the interaction between multiple variables must be better understood. Children's personalities may interact with the interview setting, the interviewer's style, and the structure of the questions in ways that as yet are not fully understood.

Events That Involve the Child's Own Body. It has been proposed that research relevant to children's recounts of past sexual abuse events should include events which involve the children's own bodies. Related to the issue of children's suggestibility in sexual abuse cases, Goodman et al. (1990) proposed that children may be more resistant to suggestion in cases in which

- the event involves the child's own body
- the event is somewhat stressful
- the event is predictable

Several studies have examined whether children's memories are more resilient to alteration when the events in question involve children's bodies. In the review by Ceci and Bruck (1993), four studies investigating body contact were reviewed. These same studies will be reviewed here. (See Ceci & Bruck, 1993 for an extensive historical review.)

In a study by Ornstein, Gordon, and Larus (1992), 3-year-old and 6-year-old children's memories were immediately assessed following a pediatric examination. Half of the children were then assessed 1 week later, and half were assessed 3 weeks later. Several misleading questions were presented to the majority of the children. The results showed high rates of errors of omission were present within both groups of children when interviewed with open-ended questions. Results further indicated the younger the children, the poorer their recall to open-ended questions (i.e., a higher number of omissions of factual details) and the poorer their resistance to misleading questions (i.e., a higher number of commissions of false details) when the initial interview took place after a short time delay. Furthermore, the greater the time delay between the event and questioning, the poorer the performance for both age groups (i.e., an increased number of omissions and commissions).

In another study involving body contact, Oates and Shrimpton (1991) examined children's memory for events. One group of 4- to 12-year-old children received a blood test, and a second group of 4- to 12-year-old children encountered a friendly stranger in the school library who put a loose cotton shirt over their clothes and then removed it. Children's memories of the events were assessed 4 to 10 days or 3 to 6 weeks following the event. When age was not considered, the type of interaction (i.e., blood test group and friendly stranger group) did not influence memory for the event, and both groups performed comparably. Therefore, it appears that stress was not a factor in children's memories for the events. However, the age of the children was found to differentiate groups. Older children (ages 7 to 12) performed significantly better than the younger children (ages 4 to 6) on both free recall and direct nonmisleading questions.

Similar to the Ornstein et al. (1992) results, Oates and Shrimpton (1991) found that younger children were less resistant than older children to misleading questions when there was a short time delay between the initial interview and the event. However, the greater the time delay between the event and questioning, the poorer the performance for both younger and older children. When interviewed after a long delay (3 to 6 weeks), both older and younger children were susceptible to misleading questions related to actions that took place during the event.

The research by Ornstein et al. (1992) and Oates and Shrimpton (1991) suggests that children were not resistant to erroneous suggestions about events that involved their own bodies. However, in both studies, children were resistant to being misled about the person with whom they interacted. Results also indicated younger children were more susceptible to suggestion than older children when questioned shortly after the event. However, when time between the event and questioning was longer in duration, differences in suggestibility between younger and older children decreased. In contrast, research by Rudy and Goodman (1991) and Saywitz et al. (1991) indicated that very young children were quite resistant to erroneous suggestions about events that involved their own bodies, especially if the misleading information included abuse-related suggestions.

In a study by Rudy and Goodman (1991), memory for an event was examined by pairing 4-year-old and 7-year-old children who then were left with an adult stranger. The stranger asked one child to dress in a clown's costume, lifted up the child, photographed the child, and asked the child to tickle him and touch his nose; the other child was encouraged to carefully watch this activity. The children were then asked misleading and nonmisleading questions 10 days after the event. Some of the misleading questions concerned actions that might lead to an accusation of sexual abuse (i.e., "He took your clothes off didn't he?"). When age was not considered, children who participated in the activity with the stranger did not evidence better memory than those who only observed the activity performed. While Rudy and Goodman reported the participants and observers were found to differ significantly on their susceptibility to misleading questions, results based on reanalysis of Rudy and Goodman's data by Ceci and Bruck (1993) showed no significant differences.

Related to age effects, 7-year-old children gave more correct answers than 4-year-olds to nonmisleading questions and to misleading questions that were not abuse related. However, 4-year-old and 7-year-old children did not perform differently on their resistance to misleading abuse-related questions. Only one false report of abuse was made by a 4-year-old child (observer) who claimed that he and the other child (participant) had been spanked.

In another study addressing the issue of children's suggestibility, Saywitz et al. (1991) investigated 5-year-old and 7-year-old girls' memories of their medical examinations. Half of the 5-year-old and 7-year-old children were given a scoliosis examination, while the other half of the girls were given a medical examination which included examination of their genitals. The children were questioned about their examination 1 or 4 weeks following the examination. At that time, they were asked suggestive and nonsuggestive questions that were categorized by the researchers as not related to sexual abuse or related to sexual abuse (i.e., "How many times did the doctor kiss you?"). Seven-year-old children gave more correct answers to misleading nonabuse related questions and to nonmisleading abuse-related questions. After a time delay (4 weeks), age differences began to disappear with 7-year-olds becoming less accurate.

With both age groups, omission errors (not reporting information that did occur) were more likely than commission errors (adding information that did not occur). For example, the children who were administered the genital examination frequently did not disclose the genital touching by the doctor unless specifically asked. Furthermore, when the children who were examined for scoliosis were asked leading questions about genital touching by the doctor, the incidence of false reports was low. Although there were age differences on suggestive abuse-related questions, only a few children actually made commission errors. Specifically, 7-year-old children never made a false report of abuse, while only three of two hundred and fifteen 5-year-olds made a false report of abuse.

Although the four studies cited previously were designed to include events that involved the child's own body, their ecological validity has been criticized. Some researchers argue that interview procedures of traditional laboratory studies are qualitatively different from the forensic interviews that some alleged child victims undergo. Ceci et al. (1993) observed that the child subjects in research designs similar to the four previously cited studies are not repeatedly interviewed for extended periods of time with high levels of suggestive questioning. As a result, in these studies where children are not repeatedly interviewed and provided repeated erroneous suggestions, conscious rather than unconscious alteration of memory recall may underlie children's inaccurate recounts. In addressing the low rates of children providing erroneous information in the Saywitz et al. (1991) study, Ceci et al. (1993) conclude, "Why ought one expect errors of commission (claiming the doctor took her [sic] clothes off and kissed them while they were naked)? To do so would only bring embarrassment to them as such behavior is 'naughty' " (p. 122).

Events Involving Repeated Pre- and Post-Misinformation. Ceci and Bruck (1993) argued that although research that examines children's recounts of past events involving touch to the body have greater ecological validity than previous laboratory research, these studies lack examination of the multi-factored forces that are present in child sexual abuse cases. Ceci (1994) proposed that research on children's suggestibility must examine the effect of multiple interviews over extended periods of time. The need to examine the effect of erroneous suggestions on memory as the memory trace for the event in question begins to deteriorate, is seen as critical. Examination of the negative stereotyping of an individual and the phenomena of source misattribution are also thought to be of relevance in understanding children's suspectibility.

Stereotyping. Leichtman and Ceci (1995) investigated the effect of both pre-event "stereotyping" of the adult with whom the child would interact and repeated post-event misleading suggestions. This research has been referred to as the "Sam Stone Study." During the study, a stranger named Sam Stone paid a 2-minute visit to 176 preschoolers, ages 3 years to 6 years old, in their daycare setting. The four experimental conditions in this study included (a) control group, (b) stereotype information only group, (c) suggestive interviewing only group, and (d) combined suggestive interviewing and stereotype information group. The stereotyped information provided to the children prior to Sam Stone's visit occurred once a week over a 4-week period. Sam Stone was stereotyped to the children through verbal narratives as a clumsy person who always got into trouble and broke things.

Following Sam Stone's visit, children in all four groups were interviewed four times over a 10-week period. In the stereotype information group, children were only presented pre-event stereotyped information; post-event questioning was nonsuggestive. In the suggestive interviewing group, children were not presented pre-event stereotyping information but were only presented post-event suggestive questions. In the combined stereotype information and suggestive questioning group, children were presented both pre-event stereotyped information and post-event suggestive questioning. Children in the control group were not presented either pre-event stereotyped information or post-event suggestive interviewing.

Following the fourth interview, at the end of the 10-week period, the children were interviewed a fifth time by a new interviewer who used forensic procedures, including first eliciting a free narrative, then using probes, urging the children to acknowledge when they did not remember, and so on. During the fifth interview, the interviewer also asked the children if they remembered two fictitious events during which Sam Stone, reportedly, soiled a teddy bear and ripped a book.

The results showed that the group of children (control group) who were not provided pre- or post-event misleading information were very accurate in their recounts of the past events about which they were questioned. The majority of control subjects, when given a suggestive probe by the interviewer, did not provide false information regarding Sam Stone. Conversely, a large percentage of children (experimental groups) who were given repeated pre- and post-event misleading information claimed that Sam Stone ripped a book or soiled a teddy bear when presented with a suggestive probe. In all experimental groups, the error rates of the younger children were significantly higher than the error rates of the older children. After a gentle challenge, the percentages of errors for all ages in the three experimental groups decreased. However, in the combined stereotyped information and suggestive interviewing group, 21% of the 3- and 4-year-old children continued to maintain that they saw Sam Stone do the misdeeds even after their statements were challenged. Eleven percent of the 5- and 6-year-olds in the combined stereotyped information and suggestive interviewing group maintained that they saw Sam Stone do the misdeeds. Leichtman and Ceci (1995) further reported that a number of children embellished the nonevents with convincing false perceptual details. For example, one child claimed that Sam Stone took the teddy bear into the bathroom and soaked it in hot water before smearing it with a crayon.

Source Misattributions. In order to examine source misattributions, research by Ceci, Crotteau, et al. (1994) used a replication of one of the techniques that has been used by some therapists who interview children alleged to have been sexually abused. This technique involves the repeated encouragement of a young child by a therapist to think about a possible event that the therapist believes may have occurred sometime in the child's past but is being "denied" or "repressed" by the child. One hundred and twenty-two 3- to 6-year-old children were interviewed individually and provided a list of both real (parent supplied) and fictitious (experimenter-contrived) events. The children were asked to judge which events on the list actually had happened to them. All lists contained two actual salient events each child had experienced and two fictitious events. One of these fictitious events concerned getting one's hand caught in a mouse trap and having to go to the hospital to get it removed. The other involved going on a hot air balloon ride with classmates.

This study has been referred to as the "Mouse Trap Study." Each week, for 10 consecutive weeks, the children were individually interviewed by a trained adult who asked the preschoolers to think hard about whether they had experienced a number of fictitious or actual events. For example, a child might be asked about the following fictitious event with the interviewer query, "Have you ever gotten your finger caught in a mouse trap and had to go to the hospital to get the trap off?" The children were also given prompts to visualize the scene.

After 10 weeks, an unfamiliar adult conducted a forensic interview with each child. During this interview, the child was asked about whether he or she had ever experienced the actual or fictitious events that the child had previously been asked to think about. For example, the interviewer would ask the child, "Think real hard, and tell me if this ever happened to you. Can you remember going to the hospital with the mouse trap on your finger?" Following the child's reply, the interviewer would ask for additional details ("Can you tell me more?"). The interviewer would also ask follow-up questions based on the child's answer, such as, if the child said he or she did go to the hospital to get the mouse trap off, the interviewer asked how he or she got there, who went with him or her, and what happened at the hospital.

Results indicated that true events were almost always recalled accurately. However, false events were recalled by 44% of the 3- and 4-year-old children at the first interview and by 36% of this age group at the seventh interview. False events were recalled by 25% of the 5- and 6-year-old children at the first interview and by 32% of this age group by the seventh interview. Although the majority of the children's false assents did not consistently increase across sessions as they continued to be interviewed, when they did produce false narratives the children were observed to provide an internally coherent account of the context, as well as the affect associated with it. The children's narratives of the fictitious events were described as "elaborate." Ceci, Crotteau, et al. (1994) provided the following example of one such narrative:

> My brother Colin was trying to get Blowtorch (an action figure) from me, and I wouldn't let him take it from me, so he pushed me in the wood pile where the mouse trap was. And then my finger got caught in it. And then we went to the hospital and my mommy, daddy, and Colin drove me there, to the hospital in our van, because it was far away. And the doctor put a bandage on this finger. (pp. 399-400)

The preceding study was replicated by Ceci, Loftus, et al. (1994). In the Ceci, Crotteau, et al. (1994) study, children were only instructed to think about whether they may have experienced the fictitious events, while in the Ceci, Loftus, et al. (1994) study, preschool children were informed each week by the interviewer that they had actually experienced the fictitious events. In this second study, when forty-eight 3- to 6-year-olds were presented erroneous information over a 12-week period, there was a reliable increase in children's claims that they remembered experiencing the fictitious event. However, an important finding in this study was that neutral nonparticipant events resulted in the most false assents, whereas negative events resulted in the fewest false assents.

At the twelfth and final interview, children were informed that the interviewer who had questioned them over the past 11 sessions had made a number of mistakes including telling them that they had experienced events that they had not. Following this new information, when the children were asked if they had actually experienced the fictitious events, the majority of the children reduced their false assents. However, the false assent rate was still greater than 50% for neutral nonparticipant and positive events.

In the Ceci, Loftus, et al. (1994) study there was some evidence that children's erroneous reports increased in their vividness over time. The children's narratives during their final sessions were found to include insertions of appropriate affect, inclusion of low frequency details, and spontaneous corrections. Conversely, there were few changes in the true-event memories; vividness increased little after the third interview for true-event memories.

In further research by Poole and Lindsay (1995), 59% of the children in their study who were read a book by their parents that described how Mr. Science had put something "yucky" in their mouths later reported that they had actually experienced this event. The children in this study were also found to deliver their erroneous recounts with "a degree of spontaneity and contextual detail often considered 'diagnostic' of experienced events" (Poole & Lindsay, 1995, cited in Poole & Warren, 1995, p. 5).

The studies by Leichtman and Ceci (1995), Ceci, Crotteau, et al. (1994), and Ceci, Loftus, et al. (1994) indicate that some young children may be highly suggestible when repeatedly given pre-event biasing information and/or repeated post-event suggestive questioning that includes telling children to try to remember events that never occurred. However, Saywitz and Goodman (in press) argue against using these studies to draw conclusions about the risk of suggestibility when interviewing alleged child victims of sexual abuse. They state that the events presented to the children in these studies are not germane to the experience of sexually abused children.

Events Involving the Child's Own Body With Repeated Interviews Over Lengthy Duration. In an attempt to create greater ecological validity, Bruck, Ceci, Francoeur, and Barr (1995) used a research design in which the child subjects experienced physically painful bodily contact, followed by interviews thought to closely replicate forensic child sexual abuse questioning. In the first phase of the study, 5-year-olds were examined by a male pediatrician and given a polio vaccine and Diphtheria Pertussis Tetanus (DPT) inoculation. They were immediately given suggestive feedback by a research assistant about how much the shot hurt them. A week later, they were interviewed by a second research assistant and asked to use a rating scale of how much they cried after receiving the shot and how much the shot hurt. Results indicated the children's reports were not significantly influenced by the one suggestive feedback intervention. These phase one findings suggest that if young children are questioned immediately after their participation in an event which involves some direct contact to their body, they may be more resistant to interviewer error.

Phase two of the Bruck, Ceci, Francoeur, and Barr (1995) research involved reinterviewing the same preschool children three more times, approximately 1 year after the shot. During the three (time delayed) interviews, the children were provided with repeated suggestions regarding how they had acted a year earlier when they received their inoculations. Erroneous information also was provided to the children, such as, falsely reminding them that the research assistant performed the behaviors the doctor actually had performed (i.e., given them a shot and an oral vaccine), and the doctor had performed the behaviors the research assistant actually had performed (i.e., given them a treat, read them a story, etc.).

Results from phase two indicated large suggestibility effects. In the fourth interview, when asked to tell what happened to them when they had visited their doctor a year earlier, almost half of the children presented erroneous information. Approximately 40% of the children in the misled group reported that the research assistant gave them the shot, while only 10% in the group that was not given erroneous information incorrectly reported the research assistant gave them the shot. These findings on the interaction between repeated suggestions and duration of time suggest the combination of these factors may cause some children to be highly susceptible to memory distortions involving both central and peripheral details, even when the experience involves physical pain, if the event is a routine life event (i.e., shots).

In analyzing the effects of stress and IQ on suggestibility, Bruck, Ceci, Francoeur, and Barr (1995) found suggestibility was associated with higher stress at the time of the inoculation. Degree of stress was defined as the length of time it took to calm the child after the inoculation. Differences in intelligence, as measured by the Peabody Picture Vocabulary Test, were not associated with suggestibility.

Bruck, Ceci, Francoeur, and Barr (1995) also examined the type of questions presented to subjects, in order to differentiate children who were not misled but who gave inaccurate reports. In 27 out of 28 cases of nonmisled children providing erroneous information, these children only provided inaccurate information when asked a directed "Who" question following an open-ended request to tell everything they remembered about getting a shot a year earlier. Specifically, these nonmisled children were asked questions, such as "Who gave you the shot?" or "Who gave you a treat?"

The different results found in the studies by Ceci, Crotteau, et al. (1994); Ceci, Loftus, et al. (1994); Poole and Lindsay (1995); and Clarke-Stewart et al. (1989) appear to be multi-factored. One such factor may be due to the differences in whether the children actually did or did not previously experience the event under question. Whether the fictitious event was positive or negative also appeared to influence children's suggestibility. The preschool children in the Ceci, Crotteau, et al., and the Ceci, Loftus, et al. studies may have been more vulnerable to alterations in their recounts of memory for the event because they had not participated in an actual experience, an experience that could provide them information to contradict the researchers' false suggestions. In the Ceci, Loftus, et al. study, children's false assents were significantly greater for the nonparticipant positive events. In the Clarke-Stewart et al. study, children were more resistant to the researchers' false suggestions regarding the factual details of the event they experienced. However, they were more vulnerable to alterations in their recounts of memory for the event when the false information related to subjective judgments rather than to factual details.

The differences in the results between the Clarke-Stewart et al. (1989) research and the Bruck, Ceci, Francoeur, and Barr (1995) research also appear to be multi-factored. One such factor may be the difference in time delay between the events and interviews. The preliminary empirical findings on children's suggestibility indicate that the length of time delay between the event and suggestive questioning may be a critical factor in understanding children's vulnerability to changes in their recounts of memory for events. In addition, the Bruck, Ceci, Francoeur, and Barr (1995) results suggest that children may be more vulnerable to confusion when presented false information about the components of an event (e.g., getting a shot) if in the past the event has been repeatedly experienced and the components of those experiences have been variable (e.g., who gave the shot, placement of the shot, etc.).

In considering the implications of these findings, professionals must be especially cautious when interviewing children alleged to have been sexually abused when there has been a lengthy time delay between the alleged event(s) and the interview. Furthermore, professionals should question the effect on children of being kept from all contact (even supervised) with a parent accused of sexual abuse during the investigation. Lengthy separation from a parent may, in some cases, provide fertile soil for stereotyping the absent parent as a "bad" person and possibly increase the child's risk for contamination. However, the effect of positive stereotyping of an offender by a mother who is protective of the offender must also be considered.

CONSCIOUS DISTORTION
OF THE TRUTH

Research also has focused on children's conscious distortions of their recounting of past events. Ceci et al. (1993), investigating children's motivations to lie, have defined lying as "the deliberate, conscious production of a response that the child knows to be incorrect for the purpose of achieving a goal" (p. 128).

When a child alleges sexual abuse, the child may be accused of intentionally lying. To date, research has not supported a finding that young children are at risk to provide detailed lies about being victims of sexual abuse. Goodman and Hegelson (1985) reported that children are found to have limited knowledge of explicit adult sexual behavior from which to invent plausible, detailed sexual events unless personally exposed to adult sexual behavior (R. Goldman & J. Goldman, 1982; Gordon, Schroeder, & Abrams, 1990). It appears in some cases that in contrast to children independently creating false stories of sexual abuse, adults, rather than children, have created the false allegations through inappropriate questioning and poor interviewing.

As discussed by Steward et al. (1993), in their excellent review of child development and interviewing, children do not always tell the truth (i.e., error of commission) or at least not all of the truth (i.e., errors of omission). By age 4, children know that it is wrong to tell a lie.

Research shows that it is not until age 4 to 4½ that children understand the concept of false belief and are capable of intentional deception (Bussey, 1992). Although children are capable of intentional deception, children typically do not tell lies claiming they have participated in events that they believe are bad and will get them into trouble. Instead, they usually lie to get themselves out of trouble. Children also may lie to keep loved ones out of trouble.

Ceci et al. (1993) have identified the following factors as motivations for children to lie:

- personal aggrandizement
- sustaining a game
- protecting a loved one
- avoiding embarrassment

A number of preliminary research studies have investigated these motivations. In a study conducted by Ceci and colleagues (cited in Ceci & Leichtman, 1992) examining personal aggrandizement as a motivator for lying, preschool children were asked by a "loved one" to pick up the blocks with which they were playing. The adult left the room immediately following this request. An adult confederate then came into the room and picked up the blocks for the children. In the questioning of the children, following the "loved one's" return, the children were informed this adult was very pleased with whomever had picked up the blocks and wanted to give this child or children a gift. Some children were found to be susceptible to these manipulations.

Another study conducted by Ceci and colleagues (cited in Ceci & Leichtman, 1992), investigated sustaining a game as a motivator to lie. Preschool children were shown a watch by a "loved one" and then told they were going to make a game out of hiding it from the teacher. The children were told the game was a secret and they should not tell anyone, even if asked. During the interview that followed, the children were asked if they knew who had taken the watch. Only 10% of the children in this study lied to the teacher by telling her they did not know where her watch was hidden or who had hidden it.

Researchers have studied the question of whether children will lie about adult transgressions they observe if the adult asks them not to tell. Research results indicate developmental factors and the child's relationship to the adult influence the child's response. Bottoms et al. (1990) found that the younger the preschool children, the more likely they were to give the interviewer accurate information regardless of whether they were told to keep an adult's transgression a secret or they received no directions. Conversely, older preschool-age children were more likely to collude with an adult who was a parent, and even leading questions did not elicit their report about the parent's transgression. In further research investigating consciously made omissions, both older and younger preschool children, when threatened, were less likely to divulge their observation of a transgression made by an adult who threatened them (Bussey, 1990).

Preliminary research conducted by Ceci and colleagues (cited in Ceci and Leitchman, 1992) also indicated that young children can be manipulated into lying to protect a loved one. Using a parent-child paradigm, the evening before children (ages 3 and 4 years) were interviewed, they were kissed by a parent while they were being bathed and dressed. During an interview the following day, the children were told that it was very bad to let someone kiss them when they did not have clothes on. The children were then asked whether anyone had ever kissed them in such a situation. The majority of the children responded to the interviewer that they had never been kissed without their clothes on. However, at a later time, when informed it was not bad to be kissed by a parent when naked, these same children revealed that they had been kissed by their parent when nude.

In other research conducted by Ceci and colleagues (cited in Ceci & Leichtman, 1992), young children were found to be vulnerable to being manipulated into lying through the presentation of a prize. In this study, 3- and 4-year-old children, attending a nursery school, played a game of musical chairs and hot potato. Prior to the commencement of the games, a confederate who had previously developed an affectionate relationship with the children pretended to break the tape recorder that was required for the games. Following the games, the children were individually interviewed in a room containing a large gumball machine. The children were told they could have a penny for the gumball machine only if they had won the game. The children did not receive a penny if they answered that they had not won the game. The children were also asked if they knew who had broken the tape recorder. Over 50% of the children lied about winning the game when offered a prize for winning. The performance of the control subjects who were not offered a prize (i.e., penny for a gumball machine) demonstrated that they remembered who had won the games; thus, memory failure was ruled out as an explanation of the false claims. The majority of children in this study were also found to lie to protect the adult who broke the tape recorder and with whom they had a positive relationship.

In yet another study of consciously made omissions and commissions, Steward (1993) studied one hundred and thirty, 3- to 6-year-old children's memories of their visit to an outpatient clinic. During the visit to the clinic, each child had experienced a wide range of potentially painful and stressful medical procedures. Approximately 15% of these children denied that any of the body touches given to them by the medical staff were painful. These children were not repressing the incident as they were found to remember many other details of the clinic visit.

These findings on suggestibility and children's conscious distortion of their recounts indicate that when young children are cognitively mature enough to understand the negative consequences to a loved one that may result from disclosure of a transgression, they are at greater risk to keep the secret. However, very young preschool children may be less motivated to keep the secret to protect someone based on their limited cognitive knowledge of the potential consequences to others (e.g., the "game-like" quality of hiding the watch may have been more confusing to the young preschoolers than the concreteness of breaking the tape recorder). Furthermore, young children appear to be vulnerable to manipulations by adults that include both threats and rewards. Finally, children may not disclose experiences that they interpret as having negative connotations to themselves or others.

CONCLUSION

Children at different ages have different memory skills. Children's acquisition of information, storage of information into memory, and recall of information is determined by an interacting matrix of factors. The factors include the quality of the initial representation of the event, the individual's prior knowledge regarding such events, the interval between storage and recall, the experiences that occur between storage and recall, and the type of prompt used to elicit recall. Factors that may weaken memory storage include the child's possessing little or no knowledge about similar events, the event holding little interest, the child not actively participating in the event, and/or the event not producing a negatively or positively excited state. As previously indicated, these factors appear to interact with each other in a complex matrix.

While young children are capable of accurately perceiving straightforward, factual occurrences, they have difficulty conceptualizing complex events or using abstract reasoning, such as attributing intention. These developmental limitations may also interfere in storage of information into memory.

Even very young children can remember events. Sixteen-month-old children have been found to remember events for up to 6 weeks. Two-and-a-half-year-old children may retain a memory for an event for up to a year-and-a-half duration. Five-year-old children have been found to retain memories for as long as 6 years. Memories for events that were experienced prior to the age of 3 or 4 years old are not retained by the majority of adults. Research on the phenomena of infantile amnesia indicates that it is unlikely that memories for events that occurred in the first year of life can become consciously accessible in adulthood.

Retrieval of information stored in memory occurs through recognition, reconstruction recall, or free recall. Recognition is the simplest form of retrieval and is present in infants. There exist fewer age differences in recognition memory than in the other forms of memory retrieval. Preschoolers have been found to remember as much as adults when the task requires recognition of stimuli that are not complex. Young children are not as proficient as adults at retrieval of information when stimuli are complex or when the retrieval task requires free recall. Free recall is the most complex form of memory retrieval.

General event representations or "scripts" may aid preschool children in their recall of events. However, young children's reliance on "scripts" as memory guides may distort memory of the actual event. Because memory is at least partly reconstructive, at times it is difficult to determine when an individual is remembering the actual details of an autobiographical memory or reconstructing what he or she believes must have occurred based on general event knowledge.

Researchers continue to investigate the conditions under which children's recall of personally experienced events can be influenced. Suggestibility presently is viewed as a complex phenomenon involving situational factors, social factors, and memory factors. Some researchers have proposed that young children's susceptibility to suggestibility is reduced when the event involves the child's body. Current research suggests that while suggestibility proneness may be reduced for bodily events, it is not negligible.

Preliminary research indicates that repeated suggestive questions over a series of intervals, as well as a lengthy time lapse between the experienced event and recall, may increase a child's risk to be influenced by later suggestive interviewing. Additionally, pre-event information "stereotyping" an individual may increase a child's risk to be influenced by later suggestive interviewing about the stereotyped individual. Personality factors may also make some children more prone to be influenced by misleading information, and younger children may be more suggestible than older children.

Ceci and Bruck (1993) observed that methodological differences between studies, including differences in age of the subjects, the number of subjects used in the study, the number of misleading questions presented to the children, and the variability in the linguistic complexity of the misleading questions, have made it difficult to draw firm conclusions on the degree of children's suggestibility based on the current research. To date, none of the suggestibility studies alone or together provide a definitive answer to the question of children's suggestibility.

Further complicating the quality of information children provide during forensic interviews are children's misconceptions. Many children hold misconceptions about adult figures in the forensic arena. Children also may have misconceptions regarding who is to blame for the sexual activities and/or fear the consequences that will befall them for recounting their sexual experiences. These misconceptions also may have a profound effect on children's narrative recounts during forensic questioning.

The current research suggests that when children are interviewed soon after the event, in supportive environments by interviewers who have not drawn preconceived conclusions and do not present misleading information nor pressure the child for answers, both preschool-age and school-age children can provide accurate recounts of their past experiences.

GUIDELINES
Considerations and Cautions

- Cases of recovered memories of sexual abuse experienced in the first year of life may justifiably lead the evaluator to question the validity of the report.
- Children and adults possibly do not have memories for events experienced in infancy because as infants, they have not developed a body of scripts for familiar events to use as a background to remember a specific event.
- Older children and adults possibly do not have memories for events experienced before the age of 3 due to synaptic pruning and neuronal loss that takes place throughout the first years of life.
- Preschool-age children may remember personally experienced events that cannot be remembered at a later time in development. Specifically, 3- and 4-year-old children may remember events that took place when they were age 2 that will then be lost to memory as they age.
- Recall of specific memories by very young children is often dependent on extensive external cuing.
- Preschool-age and school-age children's memories are generally accurate if not influenced by pre- and post-event inaccurate suggestions.
- Preschool-age children may be less consistent, although not less accurate, than kindergarten and school-age children when recalling events to nonmisleading questioning.
- Children's specific memories of familiar, repeated events are subject to fusion, confusion, and loss of detail.
- Some early memories may confuse real experience with repetitions of what others have reported, or may distort what actually happened. Early memories seem to be more vulnerable to these effects than later memories.
- Suggestibility is related to social, as well as cognitive, factors and can result from information preceding or following an event.
- Preschool-age children are more vulnerable to suggestibility than school-age children.
- Source misattribution may be an underlying mechanism of suggestibility. Source misattribution occurs when children become confused in distinguishing whether they performed an activity or only imagined performing the activity.
- Children who are repeatedly interviewed over a lengthy time period may be at greater risk to acquiesce to inaccurate abuse-related suggestions.
- School-age children may intentionally lie to protect a loved one, whereas very young preschool-age children may not be cognitively sophisticated enough to lie to protect a loved one if they do not understand the wrongfulness of the event.
- Both preschool-age and school-age children may intentionally lie when their personal safety is threatened.
- Both preschool-age and young school-age children may intentionally lie in order to receive a reward.
- Children's motivations to recount their memories may be influenced by their perceptions of the environment, consequences for failure, and the incentives for investing effort in recall.

- Children's personalities may interact with the interview setting, the interviewers' interview style, and the structure of the questions to influence accuracy of narrative recounts in ways that are as yet not fully understood.

CHAPTER 5

The Structure
of the Interview

This chapter describes two approaches to assessing allegations of child sexual abuse - the "indicator" approach and the "standards" approach. Structural issues to consider when interviewing children alleged to have been sexually abused are reviewed. How to obtain information prior to the interview and how to record the interview are discussed. Four evaluation formats are also presented.

*　*　*

Professionals involved in evaluating cases of alleged child sexual abuse are inherently concerned with the accuracy of their professional judgments. In the attempt to increase the accuracy of professionals' judgments in child sexual abuse cases, two approaches have been developed (Berliner & Conte, 1993). One approach is the "indicators" approach, which focuses on identifying markers for discriminating between sexually abused and nonsexually abused children. The "indicator" approach is described in detail in Chapter 7. The second approach is the "standards" approach, which has focused on developing protocols and guidelines for conducting evaluations and interviews with alleged child sexual abuse victims. The standards approach is described in this chapter and Chapter 6.

The standards approach specifies the conduct of the professional who evaluates allegations of child sexual abuse. As previously noted, the two professional organizations in the United States that have disseminated guidelines for evaluating allegations of child sexual abuse are the American Academy of Child and Adolescent Psychiatry (AACAP; 1990) and the American Professional Society on the Abuse of Children (APSAC; 1990). The APSAC guidelines are generally consistent with those of AACAP. The recommendations of these guidelines include

AACAP	APSAC
• The evaluator should be a psychiatrist or PhD. An MD or PhD should supervise an evaluator possessing less training	• The evaluator should have specialized training in child development, sexual abuse, and forensic practice
• Obtain case histories from relevant persons	• Obtain collateral information
• Interview both parents in cases of intra-family abuse	• Consider conducting interviews with the alleged offender

AACAP *(Cont'd)*	APSAC *(Cont'd)*
• Videotape the interviews • Minimize the number of interviewers and child interviews • Utilize children's drawings as one form of assessment technique • Use anatomical dolls cautiously • Conduct medical examination of the child • Conduct psychological testing on both parents	• Video or audio recording are optional • Conduct two to six interviews of the child • Use assessment aids cautiously (e.g., dolls, drawings, and psychological testing) • Provide detailed written documentation with specific attention to questions and responses

In addition to these guidelines, numerous specific interview protocols exist. Most of these interview protocols attempt to improve the validity of professional judgments by incorporating relevant social science knowledge (Berliner & Conte, 1993). These guidelines and protocols generally draw upon the research on children's social, emotional, and cognitive development. By being knowledgeable of the research, following guidelines, and utilizing structured interview procedures, evaluators may be at less risk of compromising their external or internal independence. As a result, they may be less likely to misinterpret or contaminate information derived during the evaluation process.

Despite the development of guidelines and protocols for evaluating allegations of child sexual abuse, these are only recommendations and are not endorsed as a standard of practice. Professionals continue to debate the types of structure that are best for acquiring accurate information in child sexual abuse cases. Topics of debate include (a) the amount of background information to which the evaluator should have access prior to interviewing the child, (b) whether the interview should be audio or video recorded, and (c) the format (model) of the evaluation.

CONDUCTING THE INTERVIEW: ACQUIRING PRIOR INFORMATION VERSUS THE "BLIND" INTERVIEW

Because the evaluator's behavior and the structure of the evaluator's questions can influence the child's responses, some professionals have recommended that the evaluator conduct a "blind" interview. The "blind" interview is structured so that the evaluator has no information about the alleged abuse or the identity of the alleged perpetrator prior to his or her contact with the child. The advantage of such an interview is that the evaluator is not biased by information and, therefore, is less likely to lead the child during the interview.

In criticizing the "blind" interview approach, some professionals have argued that interviews cannot be conducted nor interpreted in a vacuum (Berson, 1994). These professionals recommend that, in order to guide the evaluation and obtain useful information, the evaluator must be provided detailed information about the child, the identity of the alleged perpetrator, and the alleged incidents of abuse.

They further argue that while the "blind" interviewer may be less likely to ask leading questions, this interviewer is handicapped from formulating appropriately focused questions when he or she has no information. Thus, while a "blind" interviewer is more likely to ask open-ended questions and less likely to ask possibly contaminating questions, very young children, due to their cognitive limitations, may be unable to provide any relevant information to interviewers who are not somewhat directive. The National Center for the Prosecution of Child Abuse (1993) cautions, "Interviewing a child without knowing any of the details revealed to others is analogous to performing a medical examination without knowing the patient's history or looking for an unfamiliar destination without a road map" (p. 59).

The court's responses to the question of whether the interview should be "blind" have been mixed. In at least one case (*State v. Wright,* 1989) a sexual abuse conviction was overturned on the grounds that the doctor who testified about the alleged abuse was provided information about the sexual abuse allegation prior to evaluating the child. The doctor's questioning was assessed to be leading and thought to impact the credibility of the child's report. Despite this legal ruling, few experts would currently support the "blind" interview approach. To date, clinical observations, rather than empirical research, are the basis of these opinions.

Limiting the information the interviewer is provided will not solve the problem of obtaining reliable information. There exist interview factors other than the interviewer's knowledge of the specific allegations regarding the sexual abuse which impact the reliability of children's statements. For example, although the interviewer may be "blind," the interviewer may ask highly inappropriate questions due to limited knowledge of children's developmental needs and limitations. However, a thorough knowledge of child development still does not ensure that the evaluator, whether "blind" or informed, will conduct a good interview.

Since limiting the case information the interviewer is provided does not ensure adequate interviewing, the utility of multidisciplinary interview centers staffed by highly skilled interviewers has been explored. Preliminary research supports the use of comprehensive interviews - conducted by specially trained child interview specialists at centers physically designed for children - followed by interdisciplinary team reviews (Saywitz, 1994). Findings suggest that with the use of a multidisciplinary interview center, the number of interviews, interviewers, and settings per case can be significantly reduced. When children are given fewer interviews conducted by skilled interviewers rather than "blind" interviewers, the elicitation of reliable information from children may be enhanced.

DOCUMENTATION
OF THE INTERVIEW

Another structural issue that is debated is whether videotaping interviews with the child should become a standard of practice. This has become an important issue since some evaluators have been accused of contaminating children's accounts through the use of leading questions. It has also become an important issue as the psychological effect of multiple interviews on both victims and nonvictims is considered.

The typical child witness is officially interviewed between 3.5 and 11 times before appearing in court (Gary, 1993; McGough, 1994). Because of the possible negative effects that multiple interviews may have on a child, videotaping a child's initial interview is considered to be a means of precluding or at least minimizing repeated interviews.

A number of researchers (Lamb et al., 1994; Perry & Wrightsman, 1991; Yuille et al., 1993) and this author recommend videotaping child sexual abuse interviews. The videotaped interview provides

- an accurate record of the interview
- visual documentation of the child's gestures and facial expressions accompanying the child's verbal statements
- a visual and verbal record for other professionals to review, possibly years later
- a reduction of interviews by other professionals
- a form of ongoing training for the interviewer
- professional protection for the interviewer
- an effective aid in obtaining a confession by the perpetrator
- an effective tool for helping the nonoffending parent or the accusing parent to understand what did or did not happen

In a 3-year study conducted by the California Attorney General under the direction of an interdisciplinary panel of experts, professionals (including law enforcement officials, mental health professionals, prosecutors, and defense attorneys) reported that videotaping promoted justice by (a) preserving evidence of abuse, (b) promoting proper interview techniques, (c) inducing confessions that avoided costly trials, and (d) promoting better-informed decisions by law enforcement, social services, and legal counsel (Saywitz, 1994).

When child sexual abuse allegations have been ongoing for years within custody cases, videotaping also may assist the evaluator, who becomes involved at a later date in the case, by preserving baseline data. In these very complex cases, it is helpful to review the initial questions that were presented to the child and his or her initial responses to those questions. Direct observation of the child's affect during the interview may also provide the evaluator with important information. Videotaping further assists in documenting spontaneous demonstrations of the child's experiences that could not be as graphically captured in case notes. For example

Molly, a 10-year-old girl whose parents are divorced, lives with her single parent mother. She visits her father, stepmother, and two adolescent stepbrothers every other weekend. One day, when the mother was packing Molly's clothes for the weekend visit with her father, Molly began to cry and said she didn't want to go. Molly then disclosed to her mother that her 16-year-old stepbrother had been having sex with her. Following Molly's disclosure, she was taken by her mother for an evaluation because, according to the mother, "Molly has a history of telling lies." The interview was videotaped.

Initially, Molly presented as an anxious child. When questioned by a psychologist with nonleading questions, Molly disclosed that she was sexually abused by one of her teenage stepbrothers. However, her narrative report was somewhat fragmented and difficult to understand. When she told the psychologist that "I bent down, and then he did it to me, and I cried," the examiner stated that she was not clear exactly what Molly meant. Molly then stood up, placed the palms of her hands on her chair, stuck her buttock out and stated, "He made me go like this, and he stuck his wiener in my butt, and it hurt so bad it made me cry." The videotaping provided a permanent document of Molly's entire verbal and physical demonstration.

Additionally, presenting the video documentation may assist in obtaining a perpetrator's confession, or it may also assist in helping a worried parent understand that his or her child is not a victim of sexual abuse. The following is one such example:

Andy is an 8-year-old girl whose parents separated and divorced when she was 5. She was seen by a mental health professional following fears by the mother that Andy's father was sexually abusing their daughter. Andy had complained to her therapist that her mother repeatedly asked her if her father was sexually abusing her. The therapist referred Andy to a child sexual abuse expert for further evaluation. Andy was videotaped while interviewed.

Throughout the interview, Andy denied that she was the victim of any form of physical or sexual abuse. When asked focused questions regarding sexual initiations perpetrated by her father, Andy assertively stated, "That's so gross, my dad would never do that to me." She then stated, "My mom's always asking me questions like that, and she never believes me when I tell her he's not doing anything to me."

Comment: This videotape was used with the mother in order to help alleviate the mother's fears.

Opponents of videotaping argue that a videotaped interview can be used to discredit the interviewer (Berliner, 1992). In the wake of the McMartin case and other well-publicized cases where interviewer techniques were criticized, professionals have questioned recording their interviews for fear of having one's work publicly evaluated. Opponents of videotaping the child interview delineate the following disadvantages:

- the process is intrusive and the child may be reluctant to disclose information
- logistical complications of obtaining equipment and an interview room may prohibit use
- technical quality of the videotape may be poor

- loss of interview data through equipment malfunction may occur
- videotaped interview may be used to impeach the child
- the interviewer's technique may become the focus of the case rather than the sexual abuse allegation
- the videotape may be released to inappropriate people, such as the media

Opponents of videotaping further argue that because a child's disclosure of sexual abuse may be a gradual process rather than a single event, the use of a single videotaped interview in court can be very misleading. For example, when an alleged victim does not disclose his or her sexual abuse during the videotaped interview, this may be misinterpreted as substantiation that the sexual abuse did not occur. Stern (cited in Berliner, 1992) argues that whatever advantages might exist to support a policy to videotape the initial investigative interview, the advantages are substantially outweighed by the disadvantages. He points out that because the investigative interview with the child is only one point along a continuum of disclosure, no matter how skilled the interviewer, there is no reason to believe that a single interview session will provide the most complete or accurate disclosure of abuse that the child could provide.

While there are advantages and disadvantages to videotaping interviews, the guidelines from the American Professional Society on the Abuse of Children (APSAC, 1990) recommend the following:

- Audio or video recording may be preferred practice in some communities. Professional preference, logistics, or clinical consideration may contraindicate recording of interviews. Professional discretion is permitted in recording policies and practices.
- Detailed written documentation is the minimum requirement, with specific attention to questions and responses (verbal and nonverbal) regarding possible sexual abuse. Verbatim quotes of significant questions and answers are desirable. (p. 3)

Stephenson (cited in Berliner, 1992) argues that it may be more difficult for the interviewer to defend statements made by the child if the interviewer attempts to rely on handwritten session notes made during the session rather than utilizing a videotaped interview. For example, during cross-examination, the interviewer may be questioned about the child's physical gestures, facial expressions, and specific interviewer questions and child responses. Stephenson suggests that these factors would more clearly be presented to the court through videotaping.

It is the opinion of this author that if the professional is following the recommended APSAC (1990) guidelines and accurately keeping verbatim quotes of interviewer questions and child responses, these notes, most likely, will also be scrutinized. Therefore, if one can defend case notes, such as explaining why a child was inconsistent or recanted, one can also explain why a child exhibits these same behaviors if recorded on videotape rather than in case notes.

The Specialty Guidelines for Forensic Psychologists (Committee on Ethical Guidelines for Forensic Psychologists, 1991) address the obligation of forensic evaluators to adhere to a high standard when documenting their evaluations. The Guidelines delineate that the standard applied to forensic documentation is higher than that applied for general clinical practice. In addressing the issue of documentation of the interview, Yuille et al. (1993) state, "Our goal should not be to hide poor interviews for it is important that the adequacy of the methods used to obtain children's evidence be assessed" (p. 101).

If the professional chooses to videotape his or her interviews, the parents should be informed that the interview will be videotaped. Some professionals require the parents sign a consent statement that their child can be videotaped. While there is no uniform professional agreement on written parental consent, there does exist professional consensus on the need to inform the child that he or she is being videotaped during the interview. If the child is 12 years old or older, his or her written consent or assent to release information should be obtained as well as the legal guardian's written consent. The release of information should specifically include the videotape if this piece of documentation is to be released to other professionals.

EVALUATION MODELS

A third structural issue for the evaluator involves that of the format of the evaluation and, consequently, the information that will be gathered. Four primary models have emerged which structure and guide the format of evaluations. These models are referred to as (a) the Comprehensive Model, (b) the Child Interview Model, (c) the Parent/Child Observation Model, and (d) the Child Observation Model (Everson, 1993). Table 5.1 (pp.116-117) summarizes the components, assumptions, strengths, and weaknesses of the four models.

COMPREHENSIVE MODEL

If the underlying assumption held by the evaluator is that allegations of child sexual abuse are complex and require examination of multiple sources of information, the evaluator would utilize a Comprehensive Model for conducting the evaluation. Collateral sources of information involve immediate and extended family members, as well as family friends, babysitters, teachers, and professionals representing various agencies involved with the family. Additionally, interview data derived from interviews with the child and observations of the child with the alleged offender are perceived as important pieces of data. The strength of the Comprehensive Model is found within its format, which allows the information that is derived from the child interview to be examined against relevant background mate-

TABLE 5.1
Child Sexual Abuse Evaluation Models*

	MODEL			
	Comprehensive	Child Interview	Parent/Child Observation	Child Observation

Key Components	• **Collateral interviews**
	  - caregivers (accused and nonaccused)
	  - other relevant individuals (social service, police, babysitter, daycare, school, etc.)
	• **Review of records**
	  - police
	  - social service
	  - previous interviews
	• **Child interview**
	  - two or more
	• **Parent/Child interaction observation**
	• **Medical examination**
	• **Comprehensive assessment of alleged perpetrator**
	• **Comprehensive assessment of both parents**
	  - if custody/visitation involved
		• **Primary caretaker interview**
		  - developmental data on child
		  - child's overall functioning
		  - assess ability of caretaker to protect
		• **Child interview**
		  - one or more interviews
		• **Medical examination**
			• **Child interview**
			  - one time
			• **Observation of child's play**
			  - one or two sessions
			• **Interview parent - nonaccused**
			  - interview conducted with child present
			  - parent discusses allegation with child present
			• **Interview parent - alleged perpetrator**
			  - interview conducted with child present
			  - parent discusses allegation with child present
			• **Observation of alleged perpetrator and child**
			  - evaluator leaves room
			  - alleged perpetrator asks the child about the allegation
				• **Interview parent - nonaccused if incest allegation**
				  - developmental data on child
				  - child's overall functioning
				• **Long-term observation of child's play**
				  - look for symbolic play behaviors
				  - look for reenactment of sexual exploitation

Assumptions	• Empirically based data must be considered when drawing a conclusion about child sexual abuse • Child's statements during the interview are an important source of information	• Child's statements during the interview are the most important data • False allegations are rare	• The affect of the subjects and nature of the interactions are analyzed • Behavioral actions of the child with parental figures are more important than what the child reports verbally • The play situation is a rich source of information about family dynamics and parental role-taking abilities • False allegations can be identified by looking at the quality of the relationship between the child and parent	• Observation of the content of child's play will yield the most important data • Play allows for the natural expression of the child's thoughts, feelings, perceptions, and beliefs • As a projective technique, it bypasses the need for direct questioning

*Adapted from *Evaluating Young Children for Suspected Sexual Abuse,* by M. D. Everson, 1993, unpublished paper presented at American Professional Society on the Abuse of Children San Diego Conference on Responding to Child Maltreatment, San Diego, CA.

MODEL			
	Comprehensive	**Child Interview**	**Parent/Child Observation**	**Child Observation**
Strengths	• Child's statements are evaluated within the total context • Both the nonaccused and accused parent are included in the evaluation process • Information derived from child interview and collateral sources are examined against the research	• Time efficient • More immediate decisions can be made regarding protection of the child • Can be utilized when there is no access to the parents	• Both the nonaccused and accused parent are included in the evaluation process • The present quality of the relationship between the parent and child is analyzed • Child's statements regarding his or her feelings about the accused parent is evaluated through observation of parent/child interaction	• Avoids the anxiety and defenses engendered by direct questioning • Child's expression of thoughts through play may provide information regarding family roles and family dynamics
Weaknesses	• Empirical data in the area of child sexual abuse remains limited • Professionals disagree on the weight that should be given to the child's statements • Professionals disagree on the interpretation of information derived from the child and collateral sources - citing the limitations of empirically based knowledge • Extremely time-consuming and costly	• Professionals disagree on the weight that should be given the child's statements • Professionals disagree on the ability of the interviewer to contaminate a child and create a false memory • Professionals disagree on the prevalence of false allegations	• No empirical data to support the diagnosis of child sexual abuse by the observation of the child and alleged perpetrator • Children may exhibit strong attachment to a sexually abusive parent • Sexual behavior is a low-frequency behavior with a low probability that sexualized behavior will occur during observation of child and alleged perpetrator • Children may be traumatized by questioning in front of an abusive parent	• Acceptable levels of reliability and validity are difficult to obtain • Empirical studies have not identified specific markers in children's play that are diagnostic of sexual abuse • Accused parent is not included in the evaluation process

rial and against empirical research (Everson, 1993). The American Professional Society on the Abuse of Children (1990) utilizes a Comprehensive Model as its prototype for child sexual abuse evaluations. APSAC lists the following criteria as important factors in conducting evaluations:

- Review of all relevant background material as part of the evaluation.
- Documentation of all the materials used and demonstration of objective review of materials in the evaluation process. (p. 3)

Provided below is a list of sources of information involved in the evaluation of a 4-year-old child alleged by her mother to have been sexually abused by her father:

- Interview to collect developmental history - child's father, Robert Wilson - 7/28/90
- Interview to collect developmental history - child's mother, Barbara Wilson - 7/29/90
- Videotaped interview of Cindy Wilson on (a) 8/2/90, (b) 8/5/90
- Videotaped observation of Cindy alone in playroom playing with doll house and other toys - 8/8/90
- Videotaped observations with Cindy Wilson and her mother, Barbara Wilson, on (a) 8/12/90 and (b) 8/24/90
- Videotaped observations of Cindy Wilson with her father, Robert Wilson, on (a) 8/17/90 and (b) 8/22/90
- Stanford Binet Intelligence Scale, Fourth Edition - Administered 8/6/90
- Grunes Interview Procedure - 8/2/90
- Bene Anthony Family Relations Test - 8/5/90
- Children's Apperception Test (CAT) - 8/5/90
- Burks' Behavior Rating Scales - completed by Barbara Wilson
- Child Sexual Behavior Inventory - completed by Barbara Wilson
- Burks' Behavior Rating Scales - completed by Robert Wilson
- Child Sexual Behavior Inventory - completed by Robert Wilson
- Burks' Behavior Rating Scale - completed by Kathleen Meadows, Cindy's preschool teacher
- Child Sexual Behavior Inventory - completed by Kathleen Meadows, Cindy's preschool teacher
- Collateral telephone interview with Susan Jones - Mental Health Counselor - 8/14/90
- Collateral telephone interview with Bob Dooley - Police Detective - 8/14/90
- Collateral telephone interview with Sarah Long - State Child Protection Team Investigator - 8/14/90
- Collateral telephone interview with Robert Wilson's mother, Martha Wilson - 8/15/90
- Collateral telephone interview with Barbara Wilson's mother, Sharon Wallace - 8/15/90
- Collateral telephone interview with Mrs. Kathy Sims - supervisor of visitation between Mr. Wilson and his daughter - 8/16/90
- Collateral interview of Sally Roberts - babysitter for Cindy from age 18 months through age 3 years and one month - 8/16/90
- Collateral interview of Kathleen Meadows, Cindy's preschool teacher - 8/20/90
- Review of Police and State Child Protection agency records
- Review of case notes of Susan Jones, Mental Health Counselor
- Review of handwritten notes, authored by Barbara Wilson
- Review of videotapes of Cindy and her father at home and at play prior to the sexual abuse allegation
- Review of medical examination report authored by Dr. Sklaren
- Review of psychological evaluation of child's mother, Barbara Wilson
- Review of psychological evaluation of child's father, Robert Wilson

The data from various sources will have to be carefully interpreted within the context of each specific case. For example, a preschool-age child's session with a parent accused of perpetrating the sexual abuse will have to be analyzed in relation to whether the child has been allowed visitation with this parent, and the amount of negative information the child has been provided by others about this parent. For example

Kaci, age 5, had not seen her father in over a year upon the recommendation of her therapist. The therapist had informed the court that Kaci would be traumatized if she continued to visit with her father following the disclosure of Kaci's sexual abuse. However, during Kaci's last visit with her father prior to the termination of visitation, Kaci was observed to interact in a positive and affectionate manner with her father. When Kaci and her father were observed together over a year later by the forensic evaluator, Kaci appeared anxious and hypervigilant throughout the session.

Comment: *Whether Kaci's anxious behavior resulted from a history of child sexual abuse or negative stereotyping of the father to Kaci by Kaci's therapist and mother could not be determined.*

CHILD INTERVIEW MODEL

In contrast to the Comprehensive Model, if the primary underlying assumption held by the evaluator is that the child's statements during the interview are the most critical pieces of information from which to draw a conclusion, the evaluator would utilize a Child Interview Model. The assumption of this model is that false allegations are rare, and the statements made by a child are generally reliable. No attempt is made by the evaluator to gather collateral pieces of information.

During the 1960s and 1970s, the Child Interview Model was the primary model utilized by the professional community and most likely derived its origins from the mental health model, which utilized interviews with the symptomatic person. This model was also used with adult rape victims. With rape victims, when an allegation of sexual abuse surfaced, the alleged adult victims were typically interviewed by a crisis counselor, social service caseworker, or some other professional. Similarly, children who were alleged to have been sexually abused were interviewed about their abuse during one session, typically by a crisis counselor or social service caseworker.

Several decades ago, little information about child sexual abuse had been dispersed to the public; therefore, children's statements about sexual victimization were not attributed to parents' deviant coaching or to the children's intentional attempts to harm the alleged perpetrator. During this earlier time period, children were believed by some to "never lie," while others attacked children's statements as "fantasy-based."

During the late 1970s and early 1980s, movement away from this model began to occur as the professional community struggled with the issues of parents possibly contaminating children's memories or coaching children to make false allegations, and children possibly initiating false allegations in order to hurt someone or to manipulate people. By the early 1980s, the public had become aware of the magnitude of the problem of child sexual abuse and, as a result, a child's knowledge of adult sexual acts perpetrated on children could no longer solely be attributed to the child's experience.

Presently, the greatest weakness of this model is the almost exclusive reliance on the alleged sexually abused child's statements and the absence of recommendations for gathering a broad spectrum of collateral information. Due to its limited scope, the Child Interview Model does not meet the Specialty Guidelines for Forensic Psychologists (Committee on Ethical Guidelines for Forensic Psychologists, 1991) which recommend the forensic evaluator actively seek collateral sources of information.

Currently, this model may be appropriately used when the evaluator does not have access to collateral sources of information, and the evaluator's conclusions and recommendations focus on treatment interventions for the child victim rather than criminal prosecution of the alleged perpetrator.

PARENT/CHILD
OBSERVATION MODEL

The Parent/Child Observation Model was originally created to evaluate the physically abused child. Based on attachment theory and research, the Kempe Institute in Denver developed one of the first structured formats for the Parent/Child Observation Model. Attachment research indicates that relationships are demonstrated in observable behaviors exhibited by the child within the parent-child dyad (Ainsworth & Bell, 1970; Egeland & Farber, 1984). Therefore, the underlying assumption held by the evaluator utilizing this Parent/Child Observation Model is that when the parent is the alleged abuser, the observations of the child and parent interactions are the most critical pieces of data. The Kempe International Assessment format has recently been developed as a protocol to evaluate child sexual abuse, as well as physical abuse, by observing the behavioral interactions between parent and child (Haynes-Seman & Baumgarten, 1994).

Research suggests the use of a Parent/Child Observation Model with physically abusive parents and their children may provide useful information. Physically abusive parents have been found to use fewer positive interactions than nonabusive parents, particularly in response to their children's attempts at initiating positive interactions. Physically abused children also spend less time interacting with their parents because abusive parents initiate and respond much less than nonabusive parents (Fagot & Kavanagh, 1991; Kavanagh et al., 1988). These findings may be useful when evaluating children whose allegations include physical abuse accompanying sexual abuse. However, there is no empirical support for the assumption that the observation of a child and an offending parent can be used to reliably differentiate a sexually abused from a nonsexually abused child.

The Parent/Child Observation Model format also includes the questioning of the alleged child victim with the perpetrator present. This questioning format appears to be used infrequently by professionals evaluating alleged child sexual abuse victims. In a national survey of 212 sexual abuse specialists, Conte et al. (1991) found that 96% of these specialists typically did not interview the alleged victim in the presence of the accused individual.

Rather than endorse the direct questioning of the child in the presence of the accused perpetrator, many clinicians endorse the observation of the alleged child victim with the alleged perpetrator. However, few professionals suggest relying on these observed sessions as the criteria for drawing conclusions. The policy statement from the American Academy of Child and Adolescent Psychiatry (1990) reads

> The possibility of false allegations needs to be considered, particularly if allegations are coming from the parent rather than the child, if parents are engaged in a dispute over custody or visitation, and/or if the child is a preschooler. Under such circumstances, the clinician should consider observing the child separately with each parent. Before these observations, the clinician should meet alone with the child to establish trust and ensure that the child will feel some degree of control over the interview with the alleged offender. If the child is too upset by the proposed visit, and there is risk of traumatizing the child, the clinician may decide that the visit with the alleged offender should not occur. Persistence from the parent alone is not reason to avoid this part of the evaluation. (p. 3)

Conversely, researchers and clinicians such as Faller, Froning, and Lipovsky (1991) call into question the practice of using the parent-child interview in the assessment process. Faller and her colleagues state that there are both practical and ethical considerations for not utilizing a strategy that requires an alleged child victim to encounter his or her alleged abuser. Their considerations include

- preceding the individual child interview with a conjoint session with the perpetrator will inhibit disclosure by the child when interviewed alone
- during the conjoint session, the likelihood that the child will disclose is improbable, while the likelihood that the parent will manipulate the child into saying the abuse did not occur is probable
- the conjoint session may not yield information that either confirms or disconfirms sexual abuse
- the parent-child relationship may appear to be appropriate in cases in which there has been sexual abuse
- sexualized interaction is a low-frequency behavior and is unlikely to occur during the conjoint session
- a conjoint session is potentially abusive and may make the child feel betrayed if the child has disclosed abuse during a prior individual session

- even when the child's allegation may be false, the child is further enmeshed in the conflict between the parents if the accused is allowed to confront the child

In making decisions about whether to utilize the accused parent-alleged child victim conjoint sessions, the best interests of the child must prevail. While it is never in the best interest of a child to place him or her in a threatening situation where the child may recant a true allegation, neither can it be in a child's best interest to be kept from an innocent family member or person with whom the child has had a positive relationship. Although there is no standard of practice, the guidelines from the American Professional Society on the Abuse of Children (APSAC; 1990) may provide some direction. The guidelines suggest

> Joint sessions with the child and the non-accused caretaker or accused or suspected individual may be helpful to obtain information regarding the overall quality of the relationships. The sessions should not be conducted for the purpose of determining whether abuse occurred based on the child's reactions to the accused or suspected individual. Nor should joint sessions be conducted if they may cause significant additional trauma to the child. A child should never be asked to confirm the abuse statements in front of the accused individual. (p. 40)

The following examples underline the complexity of determining how the child will be affected by the interview:

> Juanita is an 8-year-old child who disclosed to her teacher that her stepfather was molesting her. During the evaluation process in a joint session with her stepfather, when confronted by her stepfather, she agreed that she lied. Years later, when in therapy as a teenager, she disclosed to the therapist that her stepfather had sexually abused her, but the session with him confronting her had frightened her into recanting.

> **Comment:** *The case of Juanita reflects the vulnerability of a young child and her inability to stand up to a powerful authority figure.*

The following example depicts another type of problem:

> Sharon is a 3½-year-old child who screamed and cried when told she was going to see her father, whom she had not seen in 6 months. Father-daughter visitation had been terminated until further evaluation. Termination of visitation was based on Sharon's alleged statement to her mother, "Daddy hurts my pee pee." The therapist chosen by Sharon's mother did not conduct a formal evaluation regarding the sexual abuse allegation nor did the therapist refer Sharon for such an evaluation. Despite the absence of such formal evaluation, the therapist concluded it would be extremely traumatic for Sharon to be seen by her father. Eventually, the court ordered an evaluation, and the chosen therapist elected to observe Sharon and her father together. The therapist made this decision after receiving information from collateral sources that Sharon had not appeared fearful of her father prior to the alleged sexual abuse disclo-

sure. Immediately preceding the scheduled conjoint session between Sharon and her father, Sharon's mother reported that Sharon had nightmares and begged not to have to go to the session. However, when Sharon was led back into the room to be reunited with her father, once she saw her father, her face lit up in a smile, and she released the evaluator's hand and ran with outstretched arms to her father.

Comment: *This last example suggests that Sharon's "fear" of her father was based on dynamics other than those related to the sequelae of child sexual abuse. Sharon only showed fear of her father when not in his presence; when interacting with her father, fear and anxiety were absent. Although Sharon's behavior with her father cannot be used to determine whether Sharon is or is not the victim of sexual abuse, her behavior can be used to assess the quality of the relationship with her father.*

CHILD OBSERVATION MODEL

The primary assumption held by the evaluator using the Child Observation Model is that reexperiencing a traumatic phenomena may be evidenced in the child's play. Winnicot (1971) has described children's play as the interface between a child's intrapsychic reality and the outer world in which the child attempts to control outer objects. As described by Nader and Pynoos (1991), a child's traumatic play includes the reenactment of episodes of the traumatic event or repetition in the child's play of traumatic themes. The child's play is considered to give description to the details of the event that remain in the child's active mind. The observation of a child's play is viewed as an avenue to access information that the child might otherwise not reveal.

While observation of the child's play may offer the evaluator important clinical data, a child's play cannot be used as a sole source of data to draw a conclusion about whether a child is the victim of sexual abuse. Comparative studies analyzing the play of sexually abused and nonsexually abused children have not found "markers" of sexual abuse that consistently differentiate these two groups. Everson and Boat (1994) suggest that while children's play with nonanatomical dolls can be used to make inferences about whether a child perceives a parent or caretaker as harsh and rejecting, this play cannot be used to draw conclusions about whether a child has or has not been sexually abused by the parent or caretaker. The following example offers insight into clinical data that might be provided through a child's play:

Five-year-old Teryn was the focus of a contested custody case involving allegations of sexual abuse allegedly perpetrated by her father. During observation of Teryn's play, Teryn had the mother doll angrily tell the female child doll that boys are bad. The child doll then was engaged in play with a male child doll, during which the mother doll angrily interceded and demanded to know if her daughter was kissing the boy.

Comment: Teryn's play theme may reflect the conflict in which she is caught by a hypervigilant mother. However, a determination of whether Teryn is or is not a victim of sexual abuse cannot be made based on this doll play.

CONCLUSION

There are no easy answers for the complex problem of evaluating allegations of child sexual abuse. There continue to be ongoing debates regarding the structural issues of the child interview. While "blind" interviews offer the advantage of minimizing leading/contaminating questions, these interviews have the disadvantage of not providing the evaluator with information to develop focused questions that may assist young children in organizing their memory and narrative. Most experts do not support use of the "blind" interview. Lamb et al. (1994) argue that obtaining information about a case prior to the interview with the child does not imply that the interviewer has made a decision about the validity of the child's allegation.

Although videotaping is recommended by many experts, some clinicians fear videotaping their interviews because of the potential for scrutiny in the adversarial legal arena. However, the positive aspects including specific documentation of the actual interview, reduced interviews for the child, and the possible reduction of further trauma for the child may far outweigh the negative factors. Detailed documentation also allows the forensic evaluator's assessment methods to be fully reviewed. Because the information that evaluators provide to the court may permanently alter a child's or an adult's future, evaluators' methods must be thoroughly reviewed.

Currently, there does not exist a national standard of practice regarding the structural format to utilize when evaluating child sexual abuse allegations. During the 1960s and 1970s, when the problem of child sexual abuse was beginning to receive greater attention from professionals and from society in general, the Child Interview Model was utilized as the structured format for evaluating allegations of child sexual abuse. However, because of the growing complexity of child sexual abuse allegations, many professionals have moved toward the utilization of a Comprehensive Model. The strength of the Comprehensive Model is found within its format, which allows the information that is derived from the child interview to be examined against relevant background material, third-party information, and research findings.

GUIDELINES
Considerations and Cautions

- The Comprehensive Model, which provides the evaluator with the fullest range of information, should be utilized when possible.
- The interview should be thoroughly documented, at the very minimum, with case notes, including verbatim evaluator questions and child answers. The dialogues need to be recorded at the time of questioning and not after the session.
- Videotaping or audiotaping should be considered as it allows complete documentation of the session without the interference of writing dialogues.
- Verbal or written consent by the parent should be obtained prior to videotaping or audiotaping the child. The child should also be made aware that he or she will be videotaped.
- Observation of the alleged perpetrator-alleged child victim dyad may be utilized to assess the relationship. Observation of the dyad should not be used to "identify" sexual abuse.
- In all alleged cases of child sexual abuse, prior to evaluating the child, parents should be instructed to terminate questioning the child about possible sexual abuse.
- The individual interviews with the child should be conducted prior to observing the accused parent-alleged child victim dyad.
- The accused parent should not be allowed to confront the child about the sexual abuse allegation because it (a) may further confuse the child who may not have been abused but now thinks he or she was or (b) may frighten the child who has been abused.
- If the child refuses to meet with the alleged perpetrator, maintain multiple hypotheses regarding the cause of the child's refusal.
- Due to the complexity of child sexual abuse cases, professionals should not rely solely on children's statements alleging sexual abuse to form an opinion.
- Children's play has not revealed "markers" that consistently differentiate sexually abused from nonsexually abused children.
- Conclusions cannot be drawn from one source of data. Conclusions regarding the probability of whether a child is the victim of sexual abuse should be based on multiple sources of data.

CHAPTER 6

Child Interview Techniques

This chapter discusses important developmental factors that must be considered prior to interviewing children and then describes the actual process for conducting interviews.

* * *

While researchers and clinicians attempt to collect empirically derived information on the various evaluation models, they also are gathering empirically based data on the various techniques used to evaluate children who allege sexual abuse. Currently, the most widely used technique is verbal questioning. Corwin (1990) writes, "Reliable and effective verbal interviewing of children in cases of suspected child maltreatment is one of the most important challenges in the field today" (p. 1).

THE ACCURACY OF CHILDREN'S REPORTS

Children's lack of competence in eloquent communication skills does not indicate that they are unable to be accurate reporters.* Both younger and older children alleged to have been sexually abused may not fully or consistently communicate their complete memories for an event because the demands of the forensic system may be poorly matched to the child's stage of language development (Saywitz & Goodman, in press). Snyder et al. (1993) wrote

> . . . their recounts may be compromised by their limited syntactic production and narrative production skills. They may remember more than they can produce, interpret adults' questions differently, and as a result, occasionally respond in ways that may seem unreliable or inconsistent to their listeners. (p. 49)

---

*Within the legal arena the term "reliability" is synonymous with the term "accuracy." This legal definition of reliability is not synonymous with psychology's definition, which defines reliability in terms of consistency rather than validity.

Some professionals argue against questioning very young children. They postulate that children below the age of 4 are very poor sources of information and are extremely suggestible (Gardner, 1992).

FACTORS THAT INFLUENCE ACCURACY

Although under some conditions very young children may be poor sources of information, young children's memories may be as accurate as adults' memories under some conditions. Research indicates that the following factors influence the child's responses and, as such, impact the accuracy of the child's statements (Ceci & Bruck, 1993; Saywitz, 1995b):

- age of the child
- verbal rehearsal of an event
- specificity of details
- the amount of information that a child has about an event
- interviewer's position of authority and interviewer's style
- structure of the questions
  - repeated questions
  - grammatical construction and word choice
- sociocultural influences
- personality factors

Age of the Child

> *Note -*   *When interviewing young children, it is important to remember that both preschool-age and school-age children can provide accurate information if you do not pressure them and you do not present them with suggestive questions.*

Young children's memories can be accurate between the event and subsequent recall if the subject matter makes sense to them or involves a personally meaningful event (Fivush & Hamond, 1990). Nelson (1990) noted that young children often remember more than they can tell. While children are less skillful than adults in describing past events when asked open-ended questions, they do not provide more incorrect information; they typically provide less information. However, open-ended questions used with young preschool-age children after a lengthy time delay between the event and their questioning may produce increased inaccuracy in their recount (Poole & White, 1993).

Age is also related to children's susceptibility to suggestibility. In their review of the literature, Ceci and Bruck (1993) found that in 14 out of 17 of the recent developmental studies in which preschoolers were compared with older children and adults, preschoolers were more suggestible.

Grammatical Construction and Word Choice

> _Note -_   _Be knowledgeable about children's language development and know the language ability of the child you are interviewing. Informally or formally determine the child's cognitive ability. Also, consider cultural factors, such as English as a second language and the child's mastery of English language concepts._

Walker (1993) reported that there are certain types of grammatical constructions presented in forensic questioning which have not been mastered by young children and, thus, can affect the reliability of children's statements. Saywitz (1995b) proposed that when forensic interviewing does not match the developmental capabilities of the child, inaccurate responses are more likely to be given by the child. Because children may try to answer questions they do not fully understand, they "may contradict themselves because they are stretching to try to explain something they do not understand" (Saywitz, 1995b, p. 122). As a result, these children may appear incompetent.

Research indicates that the less developed the child's language, the greater the risks that the child's statements will be misinterpreted or that the child will misinterpret the interviewer's questions. Therefore, taking into account children's language development during forensic interviews may help improve children's communications. The following information on children's language development is taken from an extensive literature review conducted by Saywitz (1995b):

- **Between 18 and 22 months of age**

    - **Children have developed approximately a 50-word vocabulary**
    - **Children use noun and verb content words**
    - **Children typically do not use adjectives and adverbs as modifiers - their statements are brief and sparse**

- **During preschool-age years**

    - **Expressive language is greatly expanded in comparison to the toddler**
    - **Children are capable of accurately describing past experiences; however, their use of past tense and their concept of time is not well developed**
    - **Children have limited understanding of auxiliary verbs - such as have, can, do, and may**
    - **Children have problems with "yes-no" questions because these questions involve auxiliary verbs**
    - **Children cannot consistently answer why, when, or how questions**

- **Between the ages of 5 and 10**

    - Children gradually develop the ability to understand and use multi-syllabic words, longer sentences, more complex grammatical constructions, and implicit conversational rules

- **Prior to 10 years old**

    - Legal terms used with children in court may be misinterpreted by children
    - If children are asked abuse-related questions in "legalese," error rates increase substantially (i.e., lengthy compound sentences with independent and embedded clauses)

Saywitz (1995b) cautions interviewers to be aware of the following issues:

- **Problems for the young child often arise when one question contains a number of previously established facts** (e.g., "When you went to visit your uncle and aunt over your last summer vacation, did your uncle take you by yourself to their beach house, and if so tell me what happened there?").

    - In order to be manageable for the young child and to heighten the accuracy of the child's response, these compound sentences need to be broken down into several short questions. A more manageable question for the child would be "Tell me about your uncle's beach house."

- **Questions that allow multiple answers and interpretations but restrict answers to "yes" or "no" without qualification also are problematic** (e.g., "Did he take you into the bedroom and take off your clothes and have you touch him?").

    - With questions that allow multiple answers, the interviewer is unable to interpret whether the response refers to the location (bedroom), the first activity (taking off clothes), or the second activity (touching him). A more manageable question for the child would be "Were your clothes on or off?"

- **Children are found to require transitional comments during questioning to signal a change of topic and to signal them to switch frames of reference.**

    - "The cumulative effect of rapid switching of topics without proper introduction leaves children disoriented with little understanding of how and why the questions are being asked" (Saywitz, 1995b, p. 120). An example of how to transition to a new topic would be "We were talking about your friends; now I want to ask you some questions about your mom and dad."

Specificity of Details

> *Note -*   *The younger the child, the more cautious you must be when asking for details. Be knowledgeable regarding the child's ability to provide details for time, place, number of times, and intentions.*

The accuracy of information provided by children decreases when extensive detail is required (Rabinowitz, 1985). As discussed by Saywitz (1995b), forensic questions often require witnesses to give specific facts, such as time, date, and location of occurrence. Concepts of time and geography are learned gradually over the course of the elementary school years.

Young children may not possess the cognitive skills to accurately answer many of the specific content-type questions that are asked of them during forensic inteviews. For example, when children are asked how many times the alleged sexual activity occurred, in order to answer this question, children must be able to count abstract events. The following developmental milestones on children's concepts of time and quantity are from the literature review conducted by Saywitz (1995b):

- **Prior to 6 to 7 years old**

  - **Children have not mastered telling time**
  - **Children have trouble with calendar dates and determining something happened before or after something else**
  - **Some children may be able to count by rote (1, 2, 3, 4 . . .)**
  - **Most children cannot count events, which are abstract and do not have discrete boundaries**

- **By 8 years old**

  - **Children can identify and refer to days of the week and the seasons accurately**
  - **Children can use reasoning to identify a period of time. For example, they can reason that if there was snow outside when they were involved in sexual activities, the sexual abuse must have occurred when it was winter**

- **Prior to 10 years old**

  - **Children continue to have difficulty reporting events in exact chronological order**

The following example depicts the difficulty a preschool-age child may have when asked questions that are too advanced for his or her cognitive development.

An allegation of child sexual abuse was made by Rachel's mother, naming Rachel's father as the abuser of Rachel. The father's visitation was temporarily terminated. At the time of Rachel's forensic evaluation, Rachel, then age 3, had not seen her father in 2 months. When asked by the evaluator how long it had been since she had seen her father, Rachel replied, "Two days." At a later time in the interview, when asked how many times her father had touched her, Rachel reported, "A hundred."

Comment: Rachel's inaccurate responses reflect the inappropriateness of the questions asked of this young child. Her answers to these questions should not be used to determine the veracity of the sexual abuse allegation.

Saywitz (1995b) observes,

> Many preschoolers may be able to recite the numbers from 1 to 10, but this does not
> mean they understand the underlying number concepts or that they can count events
> in time. For them, counting can be a rote skill, like reciting words to a song. Even
> counting predesignated objects does not ensure that children can count events that do
> not have discrete boundaries. (p. 121)

Young children also have difficulty answering questions about another person's
intentions. The following developmental milestones on children's concepts are
taken from the Saywitz (1995b) review:

- **Prior to 6 to 7 years old**

  - **Preschoolers have difficulty answering "why" questions, such as "why" an-
    other person performed some task or "why" another person asked them to
    perform a task (e.g., "Why did he make you get on your knees?")**
  - **Children have difficulty taking another person's perspective**
  - **Children generalize in ways that seem illogical when they attempt to create
    explanations for what they observe**

The following example depicts lack of logic, typical of a very young child:

> Three-year-old Sharon, during a forensic interview, was asked if the alleged perpe-
> trator of her sexual abuse was nice or mean. Sharon reported that he was mean.
> When further queried as to the basis of her decision, Sharon reported that he was
> mean "because he smoked cigarettes."

> *Comment: Although Sharon uses faulty logic, this should not be used to negate the
> accuracy of factual statements made by Sharon. Children can report facts accurately
> even when they misinterpret the causal relations or draw implausible inferences
> (Goodman & Clarke-Stewart, 1991).*

Further complicating the forensic interview is young children's reluctance to
provide an "I don't know" response when asked to disclose details that they do not
understand or remember. Young children may answer questions they do not understand or remember because they feel that any question by an adult requires a
definitive answer. They may believe that an "I don't know" answer is not acceptable (Raskin & Yuille, 1989) or consider "not knowing" to be a sign of failure
(Moan-Hardie, 1991). Furthermore, children may have detailed memories for events
they have experienced, but when asked questions that are beyond their cognitive
abilities, they may provide bizarre answers that are misinterpreted as indicating
they are unable to provide a reliable, coherent recount of their experiences. Therefore, special care must be taken to ensure that questions are posed to children at an
appropriate developmental level. For example

Jana, age 4, was questioned, during a forensic evaluation, by a mental health professional regarding the specific sexual acts that were alleged to have been perpetrated by her father. Prior to questioning about the sexual abuse allegation, Jana was asked to demonstrate her knowledge of concepts, including "inside." Jana demonstrated her knowledge of inside by putting a ball inside a box. When asked if the perpetrator's "pee pee went *inside* her pee pee," Jana answered in the affirmative. When asked for further details, Jana reported that she knew his pee pee went inside because "he tickled my tummy," and "it felt silly."

Comment: Whether a penis went "inside the pee pee" is a question someone unfamiliar with intercourse may not be able to accurately answer (Lamb et al., 1994). Although a preschool-age child may be able to demonstrate knowledge of the concept "inside" by placing a familiar discrete object (e.g., ball) inside another familiar discrete object (e.g., box), this knowledge does not imply that the child can adequately answer questions about a part of her body for which she has no experience in inserting objects.

Repeated Questions

Note -   Do not repeat questions that have a yes-no answer because the child may think the first answer he or she gave you was incorrect.

Repeated questioning may decrease the reliability of young children's statements under certain circumstances. In a study using 4-, 6-, and 8-year-old subjects, the 4-year-old children were found to be the most likely to change their responses, both within and across sessions, when they were presented repeated yes-no questions. However, repeated questioning, using open-ended questions, did not change their responses when questioned after a short time delay (Poole & White, 1991). Ceci and Bruck (1993) suggest that repeating open-ended questions may only signal a request for additional information; however, repeating specific questions that have a limited number of possible answers (e.g., yes or no) may indicate to the young child that his or her first response was incorrect. For example

After sexual abuse was alleged by the maternal grandmother, 3½-year-old Doreen was interviewed by a social services caseworker and two policemen simultaneously over a 1 hour period of time. Doreen was repeatedly asked what her father did to her. She was repeatedly questioned, "Did your daddy touch your pee pee?" and "Did you touch your daddy's pee pee?" During the first half hour, Doreen denied any sexual abuse. During the second half hour, Doreen changed her responses and began to answer "yes" to the abuse questions.

Pronouns, Negatives, and Referents

Note -   Be cautious in forming questions with pronouns, negatives, and referents when questioning developmentally immature children.

The following developmental milestones on children's use of negatives, pronouns, and referents are provided by Saywitz (1995b):

- **Prior to 6 to 7 years old**

  - Children have not mastered the use of pronouns (e.g., he, her, they) although they use pronouns in their speech (e.g., "What did you do with Mr. Price?" is less confusing than "What did you do with him?")
  - The use of negatives and double negatives can be confusing to young children (e.g., "Is that true?" is less confusing than "Is that not true?")
  - Children have not mastered the use of referents (e.g., this, that, here, there) although they use referents in their speech (e.g., "Were you at the Brown's house?" is less confusing than "Were you there?")

Auditory Discrimination Skills and Word Knowledge

> *Note -*   *Be aware that children confuse unfamiliar words for familiar words which sound similar.*

During an evaluation a child may appear to understand what is being asked of him or her but actually may be interpreting the words and questions inaccurately. The following information on children's development of auditory discrimination skills and word knowledge are provided by Saywitz (1995b):

- **Prior to 8 years old**

  - Children tend to make auditory discrimination errors because auditory discrimination skills are not fully developed
  - Children tend to mistake unfamiliar terms for a similar sounding word (e.g., the child might mistake "jury" for jewelry)
  - Children think they understand the meaning of a word when, in fact, they are thinking of a different meaning than the interviewer (e.g., when asked, "Do you know what an allegation is?", the young child may respond affirmatively but may be thinking about alligators)
  - Children also often assume a familiar definition is the only definition of a word (e.g., the child might interpret a legal "hearing" as something you do with your "ears")

Children typically do not anticipate multiple meanings for words, nor do they ask adults for clarifications when they are confused. The following example depicts young children's difficulty in anticipating multiple meanings for words:

Jackie, age 3, was asked by her mother to get ready for bed. Jackie informed her mother that she did not want to remove her socks because she was a "socker" (soccer) player. After a brief period of time Jackie informed her mother that she needed to put on her shoes because she now was a "shoe" player.

Young children's tendency toward literal interpretations can create problems for the forensic interviewer (T. H. Blau & R. M. Blau, 1988), as the following example demonstrates:

> Following 5-year-old Daven's disclosure that his uncle engaged him in oral sex, he was interviewed by a state child-protection investigator. Daven was asked, "Did your Uncle Larry have his clothes on or off when he put his penis in your mouth?" Daven responded, "On." When asked to describe how the alleged perpetrator's pants were on, the child described the pants as pulled down around the perpetrator's feet.
>
> ***Comment:*** *If clarifying information had not been sought, the child's literal interpretation of the perpetrator's pants being "on" would have made the child's story appear unreliable.*

The interviewer's choice of language can also shape children's responses to be more consistent with the interviewer's hypothesis. For example, 4- and 5-year-old children provide more false recognition to questions with definite articles (e.g., "Did you see the car?" than indefinite articles - e.g., "Did you see a car?") (Dale, Loftus, & Rathbun, 1978).

The Amount of Information
That a Child Has About an Event

> ***Note -*** *Be cautious in asking direct questions about a child's involvement in sexually abusive activities so that you do not provide the child with erroneous information or pressure the child to create erroneous information.*

Younger children's responses may not be reliable when they have only a small degree of knowledge about an event (Ceci et al., 1987a, 1987b). Children who are uncertain of the accuracy of the information contained in the adult interviewer's question are found to be at risk to acquiesce to suggestions by an interviewer. The following developmental milestones are taken from the Saywitz (1995b) review:

- **Prior to 6 to 7 years old**

  - **Children are more likely to "guess" the correct answer based on information contained in the question**
  - **Children are more likely to fill in information when they have incomplete knowledge**

Verbal Rehearsal of an Event

> ***Note -*** *It is important to know how many times the child was questioned and by whom the child was questioned prior to your interviewing the child.*

Memories that are repeatedly recalled are later remembered in more detail than other memories that are seldom discussed or considered (Hamond & Fivush, 1990; Hudson, 1990a). While there is evidence that repeated verbal recall improves later recall, the critical issue when questioning children about sexual abuse is whether verbal recall strengthens the original memories or simply creates new memories about imagined fictitious events (Ceci & Bruck, 1993; Snyder et al., 1993). Therefore, it is important to examine both quantity and quality of previous questioning of the child in order to determine whether the child's current statements contain suggestions from previous interviews.

Interviewer's Position of Authority and Interviewer's Style

> Note - *When interviewing a child, it is important for you to build rapport with the child prior to interviewing the child about the sexual abuse allegation.*

When young children are interviewed by an authority figure, they tend to be more yielding to suggestion. Very young children tend to be more vulnerable than older children and adults to the interviewer's misleading questions and suggestions (Ceci & Bruck, 1993). In a study by Ceci et al. (1987b), 3-year-old children were more likely to acquiesce to misleading questions presented by an adult interviewer than when the same information was presented by a 7-year-old child.

Children may, at times, agree with erroneous suggestions contained in the interviewer's misleading questions in order to please the adult. For example

> Five-year-old Marla, who was developmentally delayed, was questioned by an interviewer who initially asked, "Did any person touch your pee?" Marla responded, "May" (her 1-month-old sister). She was then asked if anyone else touched her vagina, to which she responded with a different family member's name to each new question. The interviewer then queried, "Does your teacher, Mrs. Cohen, touch your vagina?", to which Marla responded, "Yes."

> **Comment:** *Marla's response to this final question does not disprove or prove sexual abuse. Marla may have been a victim of sexual abuse by at least one of the individuals named but may also have falsely identified at least some people in perhaps an attempt to please the interviewer. Conversely, Marla may not have been a victim of sexual abuse but was acquiescing to the interviewer's questions and giving information that falsely named all individuals.*

When examining the effects of authority figures on children's responses, Goodman et al. (1990) found that the negative effect of authority on suggestibility can be diminished by establishing supportive and friendly rapport with the children. Goodman and her colleagues presented a series of factual questions (e.g., "Did the doctor look at your feet?") and a set of misleading abuse questions (e.g., "Did the doctor kiss you?"). Based on the results of their interviews with 3- to 7-year-old children after they were inoculated, younger children were found to give fewer false reports to "nice" interviewers who gave them positive reinforcement than to "neutral" interviewers.

In a study by Geiselman, Saywitz, and Bornstein (1991), the interviewing style of an authority figure was found to produce a differential effect on the children's recount of the events they had experienced. In this study, the researchers observed authority figures' interviewing styles and categorized the interviewer's style as ambivalent, condescending, or positive. Ambivalent interviewers were described as bored and disinterested. They spent little time developing rapport with the child. These ambivalent interviewers elicited the smallest number of both accurate and inaccurate facts from the children.

Condescending interviewers were described as conveying to the children that they did not have faith in the children's responses. These interviewers questioned the child's responses (e.g., How do you know. . . ?). The condescending interviewers also frequently repeated questions, rapidly posed questions, and interfered with the child's responses by interrupting the child. These interviewers asked the most questions and elicited more information from the child than did the ambivalent interviewers. However, the condescending interviewers not only elicited a greater degree of accurate facts, they also elicited a greater degree of inaccurate information compared to the ambivalent interviewers.

Positive interviewers appeared to develop good rapport, showed interest in what children were saying, maintained good attention, praised the children for their efforts, and used open-ended questions to generate expanded responses. They asked fewer questions than the condescending interviewers and generated more information. These interviewers obtained the most information, including the greatest number of accurate facts as well as a greater quantity of inaccurate information. Regardless of interview style, it appears that the more information sought, the greater the quantity of both accurate and inaccurate information that is acquired.

Sociocultural Influences

> _Note -_   _Identify the child's cultural background and determine the cultural factors that might affect a child's willingness or ability to disclose his or her sexual abuse experience(s) to you._

Children's ability and willingness to narrate past events are affected by sociocultural factors. Snyder et al. (1993) provide an excellent discussion on several of these cultural factors. For example, these researchers propose that because some Native American groups consider it inappropriate to hold a conversation with a stranger about events, a child from this cultural group would most likely be inhibited from providing any information during a forensic interview. Similarly, they identify that the Asian culture's emphasis on respect for elders might make it difficult for Asian children to testify about another member of their culture, particularly an adult. They further suggest that children from sociocultural groups that do not frequently use the narrative recount in communication may be less adept at producing cohesive, credible narrative accounts during forensic interviews.

These observations are consistent with the findings of Elliott and Briere (1994) which showed developmentally delayed children and children who learned English as a second language were less likely to be identified as confirmed victims of sexual abuse based on their verbal statements. Rather, these children were more likely to be identified as confirmed cases of sexual abuse based on external evidence, such as medical findings. Future research may substantiate that sexually abused children from specific cultural groups also may be less likely to be identified through their verbal statements due to their cultural inhibitions.

Personality Factors

> *Note -*   *Take into account the child's unique personality and how the child's personality might assist or inhibit a disclosure to you of a true case of sexual abuse. Also consider personality factors that might create increased vulnerability to suggestibility through the presentation of erroneous information.*

The child's personality is another variable that must be added into the complex matrix of interacting interview variables. Steward's (1993) research, involving children's memories of potentially stressful medical procedures, found two clusters of responses when children were asked to remember and report experiences that were judged to be very distressing. For the majority of the children in the study, the more negative the experience was judged, the more complete the report. However, for a small number of children, while the children were able to provide an accurate narrative of where their experience took place and who was present, they were unwilling to disclose what happened to them during the procedure. Since they were questioned immediately after the medical procedures, it clearly had not been forgotten. Thus, personality factors appeared to influence disclosure.

SUMMARY OF FACTORS
THAT INFLUENCE ACCURACY

In summary, research suggests that the accuracy of children's reports depends largely upon the ability of the interviewer to ask questions in a nonthreatening manner, in language children can comprehend, and about concepts they can understand. Accuracy is also affected by a matrix of interacting factors (physical, social, cultural, and emotional) in which the interview transpires. Myers (1992) reported that despite the problems with the quality and reliability of a child's statement and the professional debate over the weight that should be given to the child's statement, the courts currently consider the verbal interview with the child an important factor in making judicial decisions.

INTERVIEWING THE CHILD

DEFINING THE JOB
AND BUILDING RAPPORT

During the initial phase of the interview, the interviewer should introduce himself or herself and define his or her job in simple terms that are not confusing to the child. For example, the interviewer might state, "My name is Dr. Kaye. My job is to talk to children. I'm going to try to learn all about you. I want to learn about things you like. And I want to learn about things you don't like. Your job is to help me learn about you."

The initial phase of the interview should also include a period of rapport building with the child during which the interviewer can also collect baseline data on the quantity and quality of information the child can provide. The following guidelines for rapport development are offered:

- Ask simple questions about the child and provide some personal information about yourself
- Empathize with a nervous child's feelings
- Do not ask questions that could be regarded as coercive, such as "Do you want to be my friend?"
- Use positive, open-ended questions, which are likely to promote expanded conversation: "What are your favorite TV shows?"

This initial period of interaction and observation may include the evaluator and child or include the evaluator and parent-child dyad. However, every effort should be made to have the child separate from the parent prior to interviewing the child regarding the question of sexual abuse. The following is an example of building rapport with a child who was unable to separate from his mother:

Over the course of a week, every morning before the evaluator's first patient, 3-year-old Bertie and his mother would come to the evaluator's office to play for 15 minutes. Each day, the evaluator observed Bertie's communication with his mother. Each day, the evaluator increased her own interaction with Bertie. Bertie, after 5 days, was able to separate from his mother. He also was assessed to have adequate language concepts for a verbal interview.

ASSESSING LANGUAGE CONCEPTS

A child's understanding of basic concepts is essential if a verbal interview will be used to collect accurate information. Assessment of the quantity and quality of details the child is capable of providing may be done through observation or directed, structured questions. Boat and Everson (1986) suggest utilizing structured, neutral questions to evaluate the child's understanding of the concepts of "who, what, where, and how." They provide the following examples for assessing the child's understanding of these terms.

- *Who:*   Can the child identify people who provide different functions?

    - Who lives in your house?
    - Who helps you get dressed?

- *What:*   Can the child distinguish among activities or behaviors initiated by others?

    - What do you and mommy like to play?
    - What do you and daddy like to play?

- *Where:*   Can the child discriminate and name different locations?

    - Where do you sleep?
    - Where does your mommy sleep?
    - Where does your daddy sleep?

- *How:*   Can the child articulate differences?

    - How do you feel when you go to school?
    - How do you feel when you fall down?
    - How do you feel when you get a present?

If the child cannot accurately demonstrate the basic concepts of who, what, where, and how, caution must be used when interpreting any information the child reports regarding his or her alleged sexual experiences. A child who does not possess knowledge of these basic concepts most likely is not appropriate for an interview.

Further assessment must also address whether the child's concepts and language are well developed enough to articulate past events, basic concepts of time and frequency, and so forth. The following questions are examples that address the child's cognitive ability to answer questions related to details of sexual abuse. During this phase of the assessment, the child is not asked any direct questions about the alleged abuse.

- *Time*   Whether the child may be able to answer questions regarding
  of Day: the time of day when the alleged sexual abuse occurred is addressed by the following general questions:

    - "Let's look out the window. Is it day time or night time now?"

- "Do you take a nap?"
- "Is it day time or night time when you take a nap?"
- "When you go to sleep at night, is it light or dark outside?"

If the child cannot answer these questions, the child may not be able to provide details about the time of day the alleged sexual abuse occurred.

- **Number of Times:** Whether the child may be able to answer questions regarding the number of times the alleged sexual abuse occurred is addressed by the following general questions:

  - The child is given a sheet of stickers and directed - "Put three stickers on me."
  - "Put five stickers on you."
  - "Do you take a bath or a shower?"
  - "How many times did you take a bath yesterday?"

  If the child cannot answer these questions, the child may not be able to answer questions about the number of times the alleged sexual abuse occurred.

- **Position of Clothing:** Whether the child may be able to answer questions regarding the position of clothing during the alleged sexual abuse is addressed by the following general questions:

  - The child is presented a standard doll with her clothes on, "Does this doll have her clothes on or off?"
  - The child is presented a standard doll with her shirt on and pants off, "Does this doll have her clothes on or off?"
  - "Do you take a bath or a shower?"
  - "Are your clothes on or off when you take a bath?"

  If the child does not understand the concepts "on" and "off," the child may not be able to answer questions about whether his or her clothes or the perpetrator's clothes were on or off during the alleged sexual abuse.

- **Position of Bodies:** Whether the child may be able to answer questions regarding the position of the child's and the perpetrator's bodies during the alleged sexual abuse is addressed by the following general questions:

- The child is directed "Let's hop like a bunny."
- The child is directed "Let's sleep on the floor like a kitty."
- "Were we standing up or lying down when we hopped like a bunny?"
- "Were we standing up or lying down when we slept like a kitty?"
- "When you go to sleep in your bed, are you standing, sitting, or lying down?"

If the child cannot answer these questions, the child may not be able to provide details about the child's or the perpetrator's physical position during the alleged sexual abuse.

If the child does not possess the developmental concepts or language to answer these questions, such questions should be avoided when interviewing the child about the sexual abuse allegation. Asking for details that are beyond the child's developmental level will only access unreliable and possibly inaccurate information. Unreliable information can only confuse rather than assist the evaluator. The child's inability to answer detailed questions does not indicate the child is not a victim of sexual abuse, but instead presents information on the child's cognitive immaturity.

The child's verbal skills may sometimes be so limited that the interview cannot proceed. The following is an example of a session that was terminated after the child's concepts were determined to be too limited to provide any accurate information:

Jessie, age 2, spontaneously stated to his mother when she was bathing him, "Kiss pee pee." Jessie also was observed on several occasions to put his penis up to the family dog's mouth and state, "Kiss pee pee." Jessie was taken by his mother to a therapist in order to determine if Jessie was the victim of sexual abuse. During the initial part of the first session, Jessie's understanding of basic concepts was assessed. Jessie was queried, "Jessie, who lives at your house?" Jessie responded, "House." Jessie was then questioned, Jessie "Who sleeps at your house?", to which Jessie responded, "Sleeps." Jessie was asked, "Who hugs you?" Jessie responded, "Hugs." Jessie then was shown a photograph of his father, mother, and stepbrother. Jessie was told, "Point to your mommy." Jessie took the palm of his hand and patted the photograph of all three individuals. At this point, questioning was discontinued because Jessie did not possess the basic verbal language and concepts to provide any reliable information during a verbal interview.

Children under the age of 3 rarely have developed verbal skills that provide them the ability to communicate their experiences with any degree of detail. Terr (1988, 1990) found that children who experienced a traumatic event when they were younger than 28 months old, did not retain a memory for the event that they could report in verbal narrative. Rather, Terr found children retained a sensory memory of the trauma and typically demonstrated the memory through their behavior rather than through a spontaneous verbal report or, if questioned, an understandable verbal recount.

ESTABLISHING A NARRATIVE RESPONSE SET

The interviewer must help the child understand that he or she is interested in receiving detailed and complete descriptions of events. To establish the type of detailed response that the interviewer wants from the child, the child should first be asked to describe some recent meaningful event, such as his or her last birthday party (Lamb et al., 1994). For example, the interviewer might initiate the following dialogue: "How old are you?" (Child replies she is 6 years old.) "Tell me everything about your birthday when you were 6."

Following the child's initial description, the interviewer should continue to encourage the child to describe the birthday in more detail in order to train the child to provide detailed accounts. For example, the following dialogue demonstrates how the child might be asked by the interviewer to elaborate: "You said you played games at your birthday party. Tell me everything you remember about the games you played at your party." Saywitz (1995b) has developed a procedure labeled Narrative Elaboration that is described in a later section of this chapter. The Narrative Elaboration technique further develops the narrative response set.

STRUCTURING QUESTIONS

When the interview is used to gather information on the question of sexual abuse, Boat and Everson (1986) suggest

> The evaluator may use the form of questioning deemed necessary to elicit information on which to base an opinion. Highly specific questioning should only be used when other methods of questioning have failed, when previous information warrants substantial concern, or when the child's developmental level precludes more nondirective approaches. However, responses to these questions should be carefully evaluated and weighed accordingly. (p. 5)

As reflected in the Boat and Everson (1986) guidelines, open-ended questioning during the initial part of the interview is recommended. A problem with open-ended questioning is that when children are asked to simply describe an event that has occurred, their accounts are often very brief (Goodman et al., 1987; King & Yuille, 1987). Open-ended questioning generally does not elicit much relevant information related to a sexual abuse allegation. When asked open-ended and nondirective questions, most young children do not disclose information about any form of touching. Keary and Fitzpatrick (1994) found many young children who had previously disclosed sexual abuse did not repeat this information during the formal investigation in which "nonleading" interviews were used. The two scenarios, with 4-year-old Janie, demonstrate the dilemma of how to obtain accurate and detailed information to ensure the legal protection of a sexually abused child while also ensuring the information elicited from the child is accurate:

Scenario #1

Evaluator:	"Janie, tell me about your family."
Janie:	"My mom and dad and Bobby; he's my little baby brother."

Comment: *Janie's answer is a developmentally appropriate response that we would expect to this open-ended, nondirective question.*

Scenario #2

Evaluator:	"Janie, tell me about your family."
Janie:	"My dad, and he touches my pee pee with his finger, and he does it every night, and I'm in the bedroom when he does it."

Comment: *Rather than an accurate, uncontaminated statement, this kind of detailed response to an open-ended, nondirective question might suggest either coaching of the 3-year-old child or previous repetitive questioning. Young children typically do not provide multiple details regarding their sexual abuse in response to nondirective questioning.*

When open-ended, nondirective questions do not produce information upon which the evaluator can draw conclusions regarding the allegation of sexual abuse, the evaluator may need to gradually introduce more directed, focused questions. Based on preliminary research findings (Lawson & Chaffin, 1992; Sorenson & Snow, 1991), which show a number of sexually abused children exhibit denial and minimization of their sexual abuse when first formally interviewed, the use of more directive questioning is considered by many professionals to be necessary and justified.

Boat and Everson (1986) have designed a conceptual framework for interviewing children. This conceptual framework is based on four levels of escalation of increasingly directive questions. The first level involves questions about critical events or times in the child's life when the sexual abuse most likely occurred (e.g., bath time, visits to Uncle Bob's, etc.). If the child does not disclose sexual abuse at this level, the interviewer proceeds to the second level and asks the child in general terms about the particular individual(s) who is (are) suspected of perpetrating the sexual abuse. Direct reference to the sexual abuse is avoided. (It is also necessary to ask questions about other individuals in the child's life in order to minimize undue focus on any one person.) At this level the use of photographs may assist the evaluator in asking open-ended questions about family members and the alleged perpetrator if this person is a family member or known to the child. Photographs can be presented to the child with prompts such as "Who is this person?" and "Tell me about this person." As with any tool, photographs should be used with caution. Photographs of the alleged perpetrator should be presented with photographs of other individuals known to the child so that undue attention is not directed toward the alleged perpetrator.

If the child does not offer specific information to substantiate sexual abuse or provide substantial information to confirm that the alleged sexual abuse did not occur, the interviewer proceeds to the third level of questioning. At this level, the child is asked directly about several types of abuse - but only in general terms. The alleged perpetrator is not mentioned by the evaluator at this level (Boat & Everson, 1986).

Boat and Everson (1986) propose that there are special circumstances when a fourth level of questioning may be necessary in order to protect a child. While a fourth level of questioning may be necessary for protecting some children, this level of questioning may signal to the child that the interviewer wants a particular response. There is a risk at this fourth level that this type of questioning may contaminate very young children's memories with inaccurate information. Therefore, this type of questioning, if conducted, must be undertaken with great caution. To substantiate the information provided by children to these more directive questions, these questions should be followed by attempts to elicit elaboration (e.g., "Tell me more about that.") or justification (e.g., "What makes you think that?").

The challenge remains how to gather information about an event that the child has experienced, but is reluctant to disclose or does not have the language to disclose, without leading the child and obtaining inaccurate information. Saywitz and Goodman (in press) address the debate regarding interviewers' contaminating children's memories by concluding, "Discussions regarding the use of specific or leading questions are often cast in extremes, pitting the notion that everything a child says is accurate against the notion that one misleading question invalidates a child's entire report."

"Directive" questions are not synonymous with "leading" questions, yet these terms may be used interchangeably within the legal community. Legal and mental health professionals often use the terms "directive questions" and "leading questions" differently. As discussed by Myers (1992), while mental health professionals may think of a question, such as "What else did you do?" as "directive" but not "leading," legal professionals may argue that such questions are overly "suggestive." Although there appears to be agreement on the avoidance of highly coercive, strongly leading questioning due to their potentially detrimental effects, the use of interviewing or directive questions remains a gray area in which there is not consensus regarding the drawbacks versus the benefits of such interviewing.

Reed (1993) reminds us that it is as conceivable that sexually abused children can be misled to minimize, deny, or recant their abuse, as it is that nonsexually abused children may be misled to falsely claim abuse. Therefore, when structuring questions, the interviewer should be aware that children can be influenced in either direction.

Faller (1993) has created a conceptual framework for examining the structure of interview questions. In so doing, she has designed a continuum of structured questions, moving from open-ended, nondirective questions to close-ended, directive questions. While open-ended questions may offer the most accurate information, leading questions typically offer the least accurate information. Table 6.1 (p. 147) presents examples of the continuum of structured questions utilizing Faller's conceptual framework.

Faller (n.d.) suggests that it is important for the interviewer to separate the behavior and circumstances in question from the person alleged to have initiated the behavior. This separation allows for focused but nonleading questions. For example

- A *person* focused question would be "What do you and your dad do together?"
- A *behavior* focused question would be "Does anyone at your house yell?"
- A *circumstance* focused question would be "What happens when you visit your mom's house?"

During the forensic interviewing with a young child alleged to have been sexually abused, it may be prudent for the evaluator to assess how the child has come to know what he or she is reporting. The following dialogue is an example of how this questioning might occur with a 7-year-old boy:

Evaluator:	"My car is red." "Steven, what color is my car?"
Steven:	"Red."
Evaluator:	"How do you know my car is red?"
Steven:	"Because you told me."
Evaluator:	"Now I want to find out about how you know some other things. You said your dad does something bad to your sister. What does he do?"
Steven:	"He touches her private."
Evaluator:	"Do you know your dad touched your sister because you saw it with your own eyes? Or do you know your dad touched your sister because someone told you?"
Steven:	"I saw it."
Evaluator:	"Tell me about what you saw."
Steven:	"My dad touched my sister's private and then he pushed her down the stairs."
Evaluator:	"Where were you when your dad touched your sister's private and pushed her down the stairs?"
Steven:	"I was in my room reading."
Evaluator:	"If you were in your room reading, how did you see this?"
Steven:	"I could imagine it in my mind."

In order to educate the courts about the positive and the negative aspects of utilizing directive questions, the forensic interviewer must understand the research findings on interviewer influence and children's susceptibility to suggestibility. The interviewer must rely on these findings to structure his or her interview, to

TABLE 6.1 Continuum of Structured Questions - Open-Ended to Leading*			
QUESTION	FORMAT	EXPLANATION	EXAMPLES
Open-Ended	*General*	• Most nondirective form of questions • Least useful with cognitively immature (i.e., toddler, preschooler, or young elementary school-age) children when attempting to gather information about a specific topic • Children typically do not disclose contextual details and other details that support the veracity of an allegation when asked general questions • It would be very unusual to gain enough information through this format of questioning to draw any conclusions regarding the veracity of an allegation, especially with preschool-age children	E: "Why did you come to see me today?" C: "I don't know."
Directive	*Focused*	• Questions become more focused • Three areas of focus include environment, person, and body parts	Person Directed - <u>Alleged Perpetrator</u> E: "What's your brother's name?" C: "Tom." E: "What does Tom do that's nice?" C: "He buys me candy and gives me horsey rides." E: "What does Tom do that's not nice?" C: "He makes his pee pee poke at me." Body Part Directed - <u>Genitals</u> E: "What are pee pees for?" C: "For licking."
	Multiple Choice	• Child is given a number of possible answers to a question • The interviewer should include the correct answer as one of the alternatives	E: "When you licked Tom's pee pee, what room were you in?" C: "The bedroom." E. "Were you in your bedroom, Tom's bedroom, or your mom's bedroom?" C. "Tom's bedroom."
Most Directive	*Yes-No*	• Some researchers and clinicians believe yes-no questions - should not be used because they are too leading - will elicit responses that the child thinks the interviewer wants to hear rather than accurate information - are necessary to get children to disclose their abuse	E: "Did Joe touch you on your ding-a-ling?" C: "Yes."
Leading	*Coercive*	• Consensus of the professional community is that leading questions are inappropriate under any circumstances • The question format makes it clear to the child what response is desired by the evaluator • Leading questions may have a coercive quality	E: "Your daddy made you touch his pee pee, didn't he?" C: "Yes."

*Adapted from *Evaluating Young Children for Possible Sexual Abuse,* by K. C. Faller, 1993, unpublished paper presented at the American Professional Society on the Abuse of Children San Diego Conference on Responding to Child Maltreatment, San Diego, CA. Reprinted with permission.

make decisions about the weight to be given the child's responses to the directive questions, and to then clearly convey these facts to the court.

ENHANCING RESISTANCE
TO INTERVIEWER INFLUENCE

As discussed by Saywitz and Moan-Hardie (1994), when the forensic setting, tasks, and stimuli are unfamiliar, verbal, and complex, young children may display comprehension problems based on the following facts:

- Listeners assume that a speaker's utterances are sincere, germane, reliable, and intelligible - until 9 to 13 years of age, children are gradually developing an appreciation for the conditions that violate these postulates of conversation.
- Children perceive adults to be trustworthy and cooperative, if not supportive, conversational partners who seek to clarify rather than confuse. Children may assume that adults would not be purposefully deceptive conversational partners.
- Children tend to consider adults to be highly credible sources of information, and more credible than children . . . children assume that adults rarely make mistakes and that an adult interviewer knows more than the child about what happened.
- Children acquiesce to leading questions in order to please adults, to avoid anger, or to protect self-image from humiliation . . . [because they possess] limited perspective-taking skill, [a] relatively egocentric viewpoint, and limited knowledge of the interviewers' motivations. (Saywitz & Moan-Hardie, 1994, p. 412)

Because of these problems, mental health professionals have developed techniques to improve children's ability to respond accurately during forensic interviews. While the forensic interviewer may not know whether any inaccurate post-event information has been encountered by the child prior to the forensic interview, strategies may be utilized to enhance children's narrative recounts and to increase resistance to the present interviewer's influence. In a literature review on enhancing children's resistance to misleading questions, Reed (1993) delineated seven basic strategies for reducing interviewer influence. These strategies have practical utility and face validity; the strategies are described in Table 6.2 (p. 149).

Strategies for enhancing the quality and accuracy of children's statements are aimed at providing children with a supportive interview atmosphere and with a clear understanding of what is expected of them. Children are less negatively influenced by the interviewer if their psychological discomfort is decreased. For example, if the child interview is conducted by two very serious looking, gruffly speaking police officers in uniforms, the child's psychological discomfort may be significantly increased. This may be especially relevant if children perceive themselves as having done something wrong, such as having caused their sexual abuse.

Preliminary research has shown that by encouraging children to be assertive with the adult interviewer, children are better equipped to resist misleading questioning by the interviewer. For example, the accuracy of children's statements may

TABLE 6.2
Strategies for Enhancing Children's Resistance to Interviewer Influence and Misleading Questions*

STRATEGY	IMPLEMENTATION OF THE STRATEGY	CAUTIONS	RESEARCH RELATED TO USE OF STRATEGY
1. Be friendly rather than authoritarian with the child.	Interviewer acts friendly and exhibits behaviors such as smiling, complimenting the child, initiating a play activity, or giving a snack. A snack or any tangible gift should be presented to the child before formal interviewing.	When selectively reinforcing only the child's responses that affirm the interviewer's hypothesis, the information derived from the child may be inaccurate.	Goodman, Bottoms, et al., 1991
2. Explain to the child that you are naïve, especially regarding the facts of the case.	Interviewer makes informative statements to the child, such as "I don't know what happened to you. I need you to tell me what happened because I wasn't there."	Because the child may mistakenly believe that the interviewer knows more about what happened than the child knows, the child may acquiesce to suggestions that directly contradict his or her memory of the event.	Saywitz and Synder, 1993 Saywitz and Moan-Hardie, 1994 Moan-Hardie, 1991
3. Advise the child that if questions are repeated, this does not mean the child's previous response was incorrect.	Interviewer makes informative statements to the child, such as "If I ask the same question more than once, keep giving me the answer you know is right." "If I ask you the same question more than one time, it's not because you gave me the wrong answer the first time."	The child may alter a response if his or her confidence regarding the accuracy of the response is undermined or if the child feels he or she has displeased the interviewer. Young children are at risk to change their response when they are repeatedly asked yes-no questions.	Moan-Hardie, 1991 Saywitz, Geiselman, and Bornstein, 1992 Poole and White, 1991
4. Give the child permission to decline answering questions that are too difficult to discuss at the moment.	Interviewer makes informative statements to the child, such as "If you don't want to answer a question, you don't have to answer."	It would be counterproductive to overemphasize the child's difficulty in talking. The child may then choose to not discuss any aspect of the alleged sexual abuse.	No empirical studies available
5. Encourage the child to admit lack of memory or knowledge rather than to guess.	Interviewer makes informative statements to the child, such as "I'll be asking you lots of questions today. If you don't know the answer, or if you forgot the answer, don't guess; instead say, 'I don't know' or 'I forgot.' "	The concepts of saying "I don't know" should be role-played with the child by asking the child questions of which he or she has no knowledge or memory (e.g., "How old am I?"). During role-playing, the child should be praised for admitting "I don't know" and given corrective feedback for guessing.	Moston, 1987 Moan-Hardie, 1991 Raskin and Yuille, 1989 Saywitz, Geiselman, and Bornstein, 1992 Saywitz and Moan-Hardie, 1994 Warren, Hulse-Trotter, and Tubbs, 1991
6. Encourage the child to admit confusion rather than to guess.	Interviewer makes informative statements to the child, such as "Some of the questions I ask you may be very hard and may get you mixed up. If I say something that makes you feel mixed up, don't guess; instead say, "I don't know what you mean."	The concept of saying "I don't know what you mean" should be role-played with the child by presenting the child with confusing questions (e.g., "If I said you were up and I was down, who would do it?")	Saywitz and Synder, 1993 Saywitz, Geiselman, and Bornstein, 1992 Saywitz and Moan-Hardie, 1994 Warren, Hulse-Trotter, and Tubbs, 1991
7. Encourage the child to disagree with you and to correct you when you misstate the facts.	Interviewer makes informative statements to the child, such as "Sometimes I may say something that you know is incorrect. If I say something that you know is wrong, will you please tell me?" "Just tell me, 'That's not right' or 'You made a mistake.' "	The concept of correcting the interviewer should be role-played with the child by asking the child innocuous, nonabuse-related, misleading questions. The misleading questions need to be formulated for the child's developmental level. Otherwise, these questions may make the interviewer appear incompetent to the child.	King and Yuille, 1987 Moan-Hardie, 1991

*Adapted from "Enhancing Children's Resistance to Misleading Questions During Forensic Interviews," by D. L. Reed, 1993, *The Advisor*, 6(2), pp. 5-8. Reprinted with permission.

be assisted by teaching children to correct the interviewer when the interviewer makes a misstatement (Saywitz & Moan-Hardie, 1994), to notify the interviewer when they are confused (Warren, Hulse-Trotter, & Tubbs, 1991), and to admit when they do not know or do not remember an answer (Saywitz & Moan-Hardie, 1994).

In research conducted by Saywitz et al. (1992), children participated in a staged event and were interviewed 2 weeks later. The children in the preparation group were warned that some of the questions they would be asked during the interview might suggest an answer that reflected the interviewer's guess. These children were also informed that the interviewer was not present at the event and could not know what really happened. Children in the preparation group then practiced resisting misleading questioning by stating the answer when they knew it or by stating "I don't know" when they did not know the answer. The preparation group resisted significantly more misleading questions than the group of children given no preparation.

Strategies for enhancing children's resistance to suggestibility may be less effective with preschool-age children, especially 3- and 4-year-olds. Currently, more research is needed to thoroughly understand the variables that help children take advantage of the interviewer's directions and strategies for minimizing the effect of misinformation presented by the interviewer.

The following example illustrates how the seven basic strategies for reducing interviewer influence are applied. These strategies were implemented following an initial play session, at which time the interviewer established rapport and evaluated 7-year-old Betty's concepts and verbal fluency.

1. Betty had first been offered a lollipop when she came into the session. No further treats were offered once questioning about the sexual abuse began so that Betty would not misinterpret the treat as a reward.
2. Betty was told, "I'm not with you everyday, so I don't know about things you do or things that happen to you. I need you to tell me about the things you do and things that happen to you."
3. Betty was then advised, "If I ask the same question more than once, keep giving me the answer you know is right. If I ask you the same question more than one time, it's not because you gave me the wrong answer the first time." This strategy was practiced with Betty to ensure that she understood the directions and concepts.
4. Betty was given permission to decline answering questions that were too difficult for her to talk about. She was told, "If some of the questions make you too uncomfortable, you don't have to answer them right now."
5. Betty was encouraged to say that she did not remember or did not know rather than to guess. She was told, "If you don't know the answer to any of the questions I ask, or if you forgot the answer, don't guess - just say, 'I don't know' or 'I forgot.'" This strategy was practiced with Betty to ensure that she understood the directions and concepts.
6. Betty was encouraged to admit when she was confused. She was told, "Some of the questions I ask may make you mixed up and confused. If I say something to

make you feel mixed up, don't guess at the answer, just say, 'I don't know what you mean.' " This strategy was practiced with Betty to ensure that she understood the directions and concepts.

7. Betty was encouraged to disagree with or correct the evaluator. She was told, "Sometimes I may say something that you know is wrong. If I say something that is wrong, please tell me. Just tell me, 'That's wrong' or 'You made a mistake.' " This strategy was practiced with Betty to ensure that she understood the directions and concepts.

INTERVIEW PROTOCOLS AND GUIDELINES

To date, there does not exist a specific method or an empirically based protocol for interviewing children that is accepted as a "standard of practice" in the field. Although a number of protocols exist, none have empirical validation. Several of these protocols include

- The Stepwise Interview (Yuille et al., 1993)
- Using Anatomical Dolls: Guidelines for Interviewing Young Children in Sexual Abuse Investigations (Boat & Everson, 1986)
- Clinical Guidelines for Interviewing Preschoolers with Sexually Anatomically Detailed Dolls (White et al., 1987)

THE USE OF MEMORY STRATEGIES

A number of contemporary researchers are beginning to investigate techniques that compensate for children's weaknesses in narrating their memories and capitalize on their strengths. Under investigation are memory strategies that enhance completeness of children's initial narratives, reduce the need for leading questions, and strengthen resistance to suggestive questions. One technique under investigation has focused on the use of imagery and memory organization strategies.

THE COGNITIVE INTERVIEW

A structured technique that utilizes memory strategies has been developed by Geiselman and his colleagues (Geiselman et al., 1984). This approach, known as the cognitive interview, involves a collection of memory-enhancement techniques. Originally, the cognitive interview was designed to assist in forensic questioning of adult crime victims. Because Geiselman and his colleagues' cognitive interview technique used the type of memory aids that were likely to benefit children, this technique was modified to assist children in their reports of sexual abuse (Saywitz et al., 1992). The cognitive interview technique is purported to maximize the completeness of children's reports without incurring increased error.

Fisher and McCauley (1995) described the cognitive interview as consisting of the following six steps:

1. The individual mentally recreates the environmental, cognitive, physiological, personal context, and affective states that existed at the time of the original event. (The more cognitive overlap there is between the originally encoded event and retrieval, the better the retrieval.)

   Saywitz (1992) provides the following example of how the child is directed to reinstate the context at this first stage:

   > Children are asked to describe the environmental and personal context aloud. Before giving narrative accounts, children are asked to "Picture that time when . . . , as if you were there right now. Think about what it was like." Following this instruction, interviewers prompt children with questions like "What did the room look like? What things were in the room? Who was there? How were you feeling when you were in that room?" and so forth. Interviewers avoid words like "imagine" or "pretend." (p. 10)

2. The individual reports everything, even partial information, regardless of the perceived importance of the information.

   Saywitz (1992) provides the following example of how the child is directed at this stage:

   > Next, children are told, "Now I want you to start at the beginning and tell me what happened, from the beginning to the middle to the end. Tell me everything you remember, even the little parts that you don't think are very important. Tell me everything that happened." (p. 10)

3. The interviewer gains access to information through several retrieval paths - recounting the events in a variety of orders, such as in chronological order and then in reverse order. (This reverse order retrieval technique is not used with young children.)

4. The interviewer minimizes distractions that interfere with the child's retrieving or describing information from memory; the interviewer asks open-ended questions and does not interrupt when the child is responding.

5. The interviewer encourages the child to close his or her eyes and use mental imagery to induce recall of more detailed sensory representation rather than representations that reflect more abstract interpretations of the event.

6. The interviewer does not ask a standardized checklist of questions; the interviewer tailors questions to the unique representation of the particular child.

Preliminary research on the cognitive interview technique with children has shown positive results. Studies by Geiselman and Padilla (1988) and Geiselman et al. (1991) found that in comparison to the standard interview, the cognitive interview increased the number of correct facts by greater than 20% without increasing the amount of incorrect information reported.

McCauley and Fisher (1992) used a modification of the cognitive interview, which was structured toward overcoming children's tendency to provide very brief descriptions. The researchers taught 7-year-old subjects to provide extensive and elaborate responses rather than their typical brief responses. In comparison to the standard interview group, the children who received the cognitive interview recalled a greater number of correct facts without increased errors. In a second study, there was no decrease in the amount of accuracy of information recalled by the children during their first interview, which was implemented several hours after the event, and the second interview that was implemented after a 2 week delay (Fisher & McCauley, 1995).

However, as cautioned by Geiselman and Padilla (1988), the younger the child, the less effective the technique. The cognitive interview technique has not been as useful with very young children because of its complexity. It is believed to be most useful with children 7 years and older (Saywitz, 1992; Saywitz et al., 1992). Furthermore, Ceci, Loftus, et al. (1994) found that a large percentage of preschool-age children subjected to some of these same memory strategy techniques, when repeatedly interviewed about fictitious events, created detailed disclosures of the false events. As previously discussed, the underlying mechanism believed to be responsible for these erroneous memories is source misattribution, which occurs when children become confused in distinguishing whether they performed an activity or only imagined it.

NARRATIVE ELABORATION

Another innovative questioning technique developed to increase the quantity and detail of information children provide during a forensic interview is Narrative Elaboration (Saywitz & Snyder, 1993). This technique seeks to maximize children's free recall by using pictorial cues and organizational strategies to trigger memory (Saywitz, 1995b). It is designed to avoid the use of specific questions during the interview. Before being asked to provide an account of what happened, children are taught by the interviewer that their narrative recount should include details regarding the following categories:

- participants
- setting
- actions
- conversation
- affective states

During this teaching process, the child is given simple drawings on five cards depicting each category. The cards are to be used as mnemonic devices during the interview. For example, the participant category is represented by the *Who* card, which depicts a stick figure. Saywitz (1995b) reports that her development of categorical cues was based on developmental research which suggests that children develop scripts for mental representations of episodes. Children's scripts are found to be organized on the schema-based categories: participants, setting, actions, and conversation/affective states.

When implementing the Narrative Elaboration technique, prior to the forensic questioning, children practice using the cards. With the cards as reminders, the children practice narrating details from each category when describing routine activities. After practicing, the children are then asked to describe the event under investigation.

In a study conducted by Saywitz and Goodman (in press), 6- to 11-year-old children trained in the Narrative Elaboration technique provided 53% more accurate information in a free recall narrative of a past school activity than did children in a control group who received no preparation. Saywitz and Goodman caution that the Narrative Elaboration technique has not been tested on preschoolers. They further report that this technique has not been tested on reports of traumatic events, on events children are hesitant to report, or over long delays between the event and the narrative recount.

ADDITIONAL ASSESSMENT TECHNIQUES

When open-ended questions and focused questions do not provide enough information to draw conclusions about the veracity of the allegation of child sexual abuse, other assessment techniques may be utilized in order to gather information on the child (see Chapters 8 and 9 for discussions of additional techniques).

CONCLUSION

Interviewing children can be a complex task. Procedures should always be understood and applied with an awareness that children are not homogeneous; rather, they differ from each other on many dimensions. Personality factors, memory skills, and expressive and receptive language capacity, as well as the child's cognitive and moral development all impact the interview. The difficulty in interviewing children is that there exist a diversity of children - including those children who have experienced sexual abuse and those who have not. Some of these children may be vulnerable to tell about an experience that never happened while others may be reticent to disclose any information no matter how skilled the interviewer. The National Center for the Prosecution of Child Abuse (1993) proposes

> The most sensitive, informed, and experienced interviewer will not elicit meaningful responses from every child. Each case and each child will be unique. Because your style and questions must be tailored to fit the needs of the individual at a particular time, there is no script that guarantees success. (p. 81)

Children's recall of events is subject to a variety of known problems. For example, very young children typically do not disclose detailed information on specific topics to open-ended questions. Specific questions are more likely to elicit specific detailed information. However, the more details that are sought from a very young child through highly directive questioning, the greater the risk that the young child's statements may become inaccurate due to suggestibility factors.

In order to insulate children from interviewer influence and leading questions, a number of strategies have been developed. These strategies have focused on reducing the status differential between the child and adult interviewer and informing the child of the specific responses he or she should utilize during the interview. While the full extent of children's ability to benefit from these strategies is unknown, preliminary research suggests that these strategies are helpful in reducing interview influence and suggestibility with school-age children. However, these strategies generally have not been found to be useful with preschool children. Further research examining strategy effectiveness with different age groups is needed.

To date, there does not exist an interview protocol that serves as a standard of practice in the field. A number of protocols exist but are not empirically validated. Currently several new interview techniques show promise for forensic interviewing with school-age children. The Cognitive Interview may hold some promise in maximizing the completeness of children's reports while minimizing the need for leading questions. However, this technique is not appropriate for toddlers or preschool-age children. Furthermore, this technique requires specialized training for the interviewer to become proficient. Saywitz et al. (1992) found that experience and classroom-style training were not sufficient to develop an interviewer who was reliably effective when questioning children with this technique. Narrative Elaboration is another technique that has been developed to enhance the completeness of children's reports while reducing the need for directive questioning. Although this technique has been found to enhance the quantity of accurate details provided by school-age children, it has not been validated on preschool-age children.

While memory enhancement techniques may enhance children's narratives, these techniques need to be used with caution. Preliminary research by Ceci, Loftus, et al. (1994) indicates that when young children are repeatedly asked to think about experiencing events that have not occurred, erroneous disclosures may result.

> # GUIDELINES
> ## *Considerations and Cautions*

- Begin the interview with alternate hypotheses regarding why the child may be a victim or may not be a victim of sexual abuse.
- Do not begin the interview with a predetermined conclusion.
- When assessing toddlers, do not use the verbal interview as a primary source of information.
- Do not utilize a verbal interview if the child does not possess adequate verbal language and basic concepts.
- Prior to utilizing an interview to assess the question of sexual abuse, develop rapport with the child.
- Assess the child's understanding of basic concepts (i.e., who, what, where, how).
- Assess the child's mental age together with ethnic, educational, cultural, and experiential background to assist in framing appropriate questions.
- Match the child's language, and use the child's terminology.
- Verbally present and role-play with the school-age child strategies to reduce acquiescence to misleading questions.
- Allow free recall of the event without interruption. Withhold specific questions entirely until the child has exhausted his or her free recall.
- Begin questioning with open-ended questions. Move to directed questions when necessary. When using directive questions, along the continuum of focused, multiple choice, and yes-no questions, begin with focused questions; once a detail is established, move to more directive questioning to obtain clarification, then move back to focused questions.
- Be especially cautious in using directive questions with preschool-age children to avoid providing the child false suggestions.
- Do not use leading questions.
- Do not use language such as "imagine" and "pretend."
- Do not use the word "story" to ask for a description of what happened to the child. In the child's family, the word "story" may mean "make believe."
- Pronouns (he, she, they), auxiliary verbs (have, can, do), and prepositions (in, on, around) may be difficult for the younger child to understand. Do not ask a very young child a question he or she cannot answer (i.e., "Did he put his pee pee inside your pee pee?").
- The word "touch" may be used by younger children only to describe what is done with hands. If you ask the child if the alleged perpetrator touched her when he performed cunnilingus or fellatio, the child may say "no."
- Do not over respond to contradictions. Accept them and attempt to ask clarifying questions later.
- With young children, be prepared to work in 15 minute segments with rest and play between segments.
- Memory enhancing techniques, such as the Cognitive Interview, should not be introduced until the child has made a clear disclosure of sexual abuse. There is concern that this technique used with a nonsexually abused child could elicit a false disclosure.
- Do not use techniques such as the Cognitive Interview on preschool-age children or without specialized training.

CHAPTER 7

Development of Criteria for Assessing the Veracity of the Child's Statements

This chapter focuses on the indicator approach for evaluating allegations of child sexual abuse. This approach is based on the identification of variables that can be used to differentiate between sexually abused and nonsexually abused children. The components of children's statements that have been used by mental health professionals as validation criteria are presented.

* * *

As previously described, the "standards" approach and "indicators" approach represent two recent efforts to improve the accuracy of evaluators' judgments. While the standards approach focuses on improvements in practice procedures, the indicator approach focuses on discriminating variables that can be used for classification of cases. As such, the indicator approach relies on identification of verbal, emotional, and behavioral characteristics that differentiate sexually abused from nonsexually abused children. These characteristics are then used by the evaluator to form an opinion about the veracity of the allegation. As discussed by Berliner and Conte (1993), fundamentally, the indicator-based assessment strategies suffer the same validity problems as the standards approach. For most of the criteria, there is little, if any, empirically based evidence that the criteria discriminate sexually abused from nonsexually abused children.

Professional debates have yet to lead to a consensus on the components within a child's statement that strengthen or weaken the veracity of the child's sexual abuse allegation. Based on clinical observations, Klajner-Diamond, Wehrspann, and Steinhauer (1987) postulate that there are three important areas to explore when determining the veracity of a child sexual abuse allegation:

- whether the child has the cognitive capacity to recollect an experience of sexual abuse
- the child's story in its interpersonal and social context
- the quality of the story narrated directly by the child

Currently, there is a developing consensus within the courts regarding which components of the child's statement are to be accorded greater weight when attempting to determine the veracity of sexual abuse allegations. Myers (1992) reports that the statement components and supporting factors that are given the greatest consideration in judicial assessment of reliability include the following:

- spontaneity [of the statement]
- use of developmentally appropriate terminology
- consistency [of the statements]
- developmentally unusual knowledge of sexual acts or anatomy
- idiosyncratic details about sexual abuse
- child's belief that disclosure might lead to [his or her] punishment
- child's state of mind and emotion
- child's correction of the interviewer
- play or gestures that support the child's description of abuse
- child's or adult's motive to fabricate
- quantity and quality of previous questioning (pp. 46-50)

While these factors have been derived from preliminary research results and the clinical experience of mental health professionals, there are inherent problems in applying lists of criteria to children who are variable in their cognitive abilities, personalities, coping styles, and personal experiences (Myers, 1992). Due to individual differences, the presence of statement components will be influenced by the child's developmental level and the child's personal interpretation of his or her sexual involvement. The presence of these statement components also may be influenced by the relationship between the child and the perpetrator as well as whether the child's disclosure was intentional or accidental. The following example reflects several of these differences:

> Kary, age 17, and Katey, age 14, had been sexually abused by their stepfather over a 10-year period of time. The sexual abuse was chronic, occurring several times a week and involving intercourse. The stepfather bought the girls lavish clothes and almost anything the girls desired. However, he also set consistent rules and consequences. As a result, the girls saw him as a fair and loving father. The girls were honor students, cheerleaders, and well liked by teachers and peers. The disclosure by Kary of the sexual abuse was precipitated by the stepfather not allowing Kary to date. When her stepfather informed her that she could not go to her senior prom with a boy, Kary became enraged and disclosed the abuse to her school guidance counselor. Katey was angry that Kary had disclosed the abuse and remained protective of their stepfather. When the statements of the two girls were analyzed, the statement components were very different, and at a first superficial glance, Kary appeared to be fabricating the sexual abuse allegation.

In an effort to create a framework for assessing allegations of child sexual abuse, Faller (1993) organized key validation indicators that she derived from nine publications which addressed child sexual abuse validation criteria. Based on Faller's work, Table 7.1 (pp. 162-164) presents a review of the literature and utilizes an organizational system in which eight criteria are delineated for assessing the veracity of a child's statement of sexual abuse. These eight criteria include:

1. timing and circumstance of disclosure
2. language congruent with developmental level
3. quantity and quality of details
4. appropriateness of sexual knowledge based on developmental level
5. repetition over time: internal and external consistency
6. description of offender behavior
7. plausibility of abuse
8. emotional reaction of the child during the interview

Within each of these eight categories, seven publications addressing statement analysis are reviewed. Five out of the seven authors presented in Table 7.1 (pp. 162-164) have derived the key indicators from clinical observations. The criteria suggested by these clinical observations have consensus validity, as they are widely used by professionals in the United States, Canada, and Europe. Only the work by Raskin and Esplin (1991) and Faller (1984) have attempted to establish empirical validity; however, the research findings validating the credibility factors are only preliminary.

TIMING AND CIRCUMSTANCES OF DISCLOSURE

Note -   *Sexual abuse of toddler and preschool-age children is most likely to be revealed through accidental discoveries rather than premeditated disclosures. Elementary-school-age children's sexual abuse is as likely to be revealed through accidental discovery as through premeditated disclosures. While many sexually abused children first disclose sexual abuse to their mothers, children with mothers who deny the possibility of sexual abuse are less likely to disclose. Children who are sexually abused by a natural parent or who experience penetration or intercourse with aggression are also less likely to disclose their abuse.*

The following criteria are thought to be important in the timing and the circumstances of the disclosure:

• Initial disclosure is spontaneous
• Absence of undue influence or ulterior motives to fabricate
• Anxiety or hesitancy regarding divulgence of the sexual abuse

An example of a spontaneous statement precipitated by a memory trigger follows:

TABLE 7.1
Criteria for Determining the Veracity of a Sexual Abuse Allegation*

Analysis of Child's Statements: Criteria for Determining the Veracity of an Allegation	Benedek and Schetky (1987)	Corwin (1988)	Faller (1984, 1988)	Gardner (1992)	Helman (1992)	Raskin and Esplin (1991)	Wehrspann et al. (1987)
1 Timing and circumstance of disclosure	• Child makes statements in the absence of the accusing parent (incest) • Absence of secondary gain, no ulterior motives	• Avoidance and anxiety regarding questions about sex	• Initial disclosure is spontaneous	• Hesitancy regarding divulgence of the sexual abuse	• Child makes specific statements about being abused	• Initial disclosure is a spontaneous statement • Motivation to report • Context of the report	• Spontaneity of disclosure
2 Language congruent with developmental level	• Told from a child's viewpoint • Uses own vocabulary	• Age-appropriate language	• Told from a child's viewpoint • Age-appropriate language and description	• Descriptive terms appropriate to idiosyncratic terms used in child's home	• Events told from the child's perspective	• Age-appropriate language • Unstructured production with spontaneous digressions	• Story told from the child's point of view • Choice and combinations of words coupled with the child's naïve attempts to describe events not fully understood

3   Quantity and quality of details
 • Explicit detail of sexual involvement
 • Contextual information:
   - Where
   - When
   - Where others were
   - Clothing
 • Dynamics of the sexual relationship
   - engagement
   - progression
	• Idiosyncratic event
	 • Good recall of details including sensory motor
	 • Increasingly progressive sexual acts over time
		• Explicit description and demonstration of what occurred
		   - Where it happened
		   - Who did it
			• Idiosyncratic event
			 • Explicit account
			   - Where it happened
			   - When it happened
			   - Where other people were
			   - What child was wearing, what offender was wearing, what was taken off
				• Degree of specificity of sexual abuse details because child can refer to an internal visual image
				 • Details include the time, place, appropriate time of day, presence or absence of other individuals, what was worn
					• Explicit sexual details
					 • Engagement and progression of activities
					 • Distinguishing of idiosyncratic details
					 • Affective details
						• Details characteristic of the offense
						 • Superfluous or peripheral details
						 • Unusual details
						 • Descriptions of interactions with sequences of actions and reactions
						 • Spontaneous corrections
						 • Logical consistency
							• Response triggered by a memory stimulus
							 • Details including what the participants were wearing, what they took off, where other family members were
							 • Idiosyncratic details

#	Category							
4	Appropriateness of sexual knowledge based on developmental level	• Precocious knowledge of sexual matter	• Premature eroticization • Precocious • Seductive behavior	• Demonstrates knowledge of sexual anatomy and functions beyond that expected for child's developmental stage	• Advanced sexual knowledge for age • Sexual vocabulary beyond chronological peers • Experience of adult sexual excitement	• Sexual details that exceed the child's developmental level	• Unusual details that are meaningful	• Details clearly beyond the child's developmental level
5	Repetition over time: External and internal consistency	• Child makes statements in the absence of the accusing parent (incest) • Vocabulary may change but the events stay consistent	• Consistency in reporting major facts of sexual victimization (minor details may vary)	• Child's statements to others are consistent	• Description does not vary over time • Internal consistency • Description as a whole "hangs together"	• Consistency of reporting salient details	• Consistency with other statements	• Repeating approximately the same story to more than one person • Repeating the same basic theme through more than one medium (drawings, doll play) • Consistency in the face of challenge
6	Description of alleged perpetrator's behavior	• Psychological coercion - threatened to keep secret	(Not addressed in this article)	• What offender said to obtain participation • Statements about telling or not telling	• Threats and bribes	• Indications of secrecy • Threats, coercion, and pressure • Bribes or rewards	• Reproduction of conversations with the perpetrator • Attributions of thoughts, feelings, or motivations to the perpetrator • Pressures to recant	• Direct bribery or threat by the alleged perpetrator or nonoffending parent associated with child changing or withdrawing allegation
7	Plausibility of description of abuse	(Not addressed in this article)	• Circumstantially congruent description of being sexually abused	(Not addressed in this article)	• Credibility of description versus borrowed scenario	• Description recounted in a varied and rich manner as opposed to a rehearsal litany	• Logical structure - consistent with the laws of nature • Admissions of memory deficits	(Not addressed in this article)

*Adapted from *Evaluating Young Children for Possible Sexual Abuse*, by K. C. Faller, 1993, unpublished paper presented at the American Professional Society on the Abuse of Children San Diego Conference on Responding to Child Maltreatment, San Diego, CA. Reprinted with permission.

TABLE 7.1 (Continued)
Criteria for Determining the Veracity of a Sexual Abuse Allegation

	Analysis of Child's Statements: Criteria for Determining the Veracity of an Allegation	Benedek and Schetky (1987)	Corwin (1988)	Faller (1984, 1988)	Gardner (1992)	Helman (1992)	Raskin and Esplin (1991)	Wehrspann et al. (1987)
C R I T E R I A								
8	Emotional reaction of the child during interview	• Emotional reaction consistent with accusations	• Overdetermined denial/avoidance and anxiety in response to specific questions about sexual behavior	• Emotional response consistent with account: fear, anxiety, disgust, anger, sexual arousal	• Exhibits significant fear when asked to discuss the abuse • Affect appropriate to content of what is said	• Affect congruent with allegation	• Presence of appropriate affect • Self-depreciation or assumption of blame • Pardoning or excusing the perpetrator	• Emotional state consistent with the abuse - state of mind at the time of the abuse - emotional state when telling what occurred

Four-and-a-half-year-old Karen had been living in a foster home for several weeks. Karen had been removed from her biological parents after she had been partially submerged in boiling bath water for wetting her pants. Karen had suffered third degree burns over most of her lower body. There was no suspicion of sexual abuse when Karen was removed from her home. One evening during dinner, the foster father, while consuming his dinner of macaroni, jokingly said to his wife, "You know dear, I hate macaroni - it makes me gag." Spontaneously, Karen responded to her foster father's statement, "I gag too when my other daddy puts his wee wee in my mouth and the icky stuff comes out."

Although some young children may spontaneously disclose their sexual abuse when a stimulus triggers a memory, many young children do not spontaneously disclose their abuse. Furthermore, although some young children may reveal their sexual abuse through a premeditated disclosure, some children may not disclose their abuse due to misguided loyalty or fear of repercussions. Gardner (1992) states that children who have been sexually abused are often quite hesitant to reveal abuse. He speculates that children are reluctant to disclose their abuse because they may feel guilty or ashamed about their participation in the sexual act. This argument by Gardner seems more appropriate for elementary-school-aged children rather than preschoolers.

Cognitive immaturity may be a significant factor in the absence of spontaneous statements with preschool-age children who are functioning at the pre-operational stage of development (refer to Chapter 3, Table 3.1, p. 51). At this stage, children do not possess the cognitive sophistication needed for logical, abstract thought. As a result, young children may not comprehend the complexity of the sexual behavior in which they are engaged (de Young, 1987). Thus, young children do not feel compelled to talk about sexual acts that they do not understand. Additionally, many young children are not hesitant or anxious when questioned about sexual abuse. In some cases, the most anxious children are not victims who disclose their abuse for the first time, but rather, are nonvictims who have been repeatedly interrogated at home by a worried or malicious parent.

As such, while spontaneity of disclosure can be a strong criterion for validating sexual abuse, for many sexually abused children the mode of disclosure is not a spontaneous verbal statement. In young children, disclosure is more likely to take the form of an accidental discovery (Sorenson & Snow, 1991). Thus, a young child's sexual exploitation may be first suspected through the diagnosis of a sexually transmitted disease (Lawson & Chaffin, 1992) or through a child's demonstration of repeated, significantly aberrant sexual behaviors. As a result, while a spontaneous disclosure can add further credibility to a child's statement, its absence should not necessarily be viewed as lessening credibility. The following is an example of an accidental discovery of sexual abuse, wherein the child did not make a spontaneous statement:

Mary, age 4, attended a public preschool program near her home. Her teachers were becoming concerned about her sexualized interaction with her peers. On several occasions, when playing house, she was found lying on top of a peer and moving her hips in a "humping" manner. During nap time, Mary would repeatedly put a peer's hand down her underpants, appearing to rub her vagina with the peer's hand. The teachers appropriately advised the mother to take the child for an evaluation. During the evaluation, Mary disclosed that her brother was involving her in sexual activity at home. Mary's statements were corroborated by her mother's disclosure that a year earlier she had caught her teenage son molesting Mary.

LANGUAGE CONGRUENT WITH DEVELOPMENTAL LEVEL

Note -   _Toddler, preschool, and young elementary-school-age children will not pro-_
            vide you with eloquent narratives of their sexual abuse. Young children
            also at times are difficult to understand because they do not think sequen-
            tially, their narratives are fragmented, and they are limited by immature
            verbal fluency.

Age-appropriate words and concepts are factors also cited by the majority of experts as important criteria in assessing the reliability of the child's statements. The following are criteria thought to support language congruency:

- Description based on the child's point of view or perspective
- Use of age-appropriate vocabulary and speech

Descriptions of the sexual abuse based on the child's point of view, as well as vocabulary that is congruent with age and speech patterns, are viewed as critical components in support of veracity. When a child uses adult words and concepts to describe his or her abuse, the statements become suspect. However, a child who has been taught appropriate adult names for body parts, such as penis and vagina, should not be confused with a child who has been coached or led into making a sexual abuse allegation that is untrue. The following example is a statement that is developmentally consistent with the language of the 3-year-old interviewed:

Brittany, age 3, was interviewed after she was found lying on the floor with the family dog licking her vagina. During her interview, when asked, "Who puts their tongue on your cooter (vagina)?", Brittany reported, "Mickey and Steven lick my cooter."

Comment: Mickey is the family dog, and Steven is the teenage nephew of Brittany's mother. When questioned, Brittany's answer was not a long, detailed narrative, which would be atypical for a 3-year-old child. Rather, Brittany's statements were short and specifically related to the interview question. Furthermore, her language and the terminology were age appropriate.

Conversely, the following is an example of a statement made by a 3-year-old girl that does not represent age-appropriate language and concepts. It should be noted that Sarah would have been age 2 at the time of the alleged abuse.

Sarah, age 3 years and 1 month, was interviewed 1 year after her mother had fled with her daughter from their home state. The mother had fled after state officials and a therapist determined that Sarah's father had not sexually abused Sarah. When interviewed 1 year after the abuse was first alleged, 3-year-old Sarah reported that this sexual molestation took place "at the First National Bank." She further reported that while her father put objects in her vagina, an "artist" who also was present touched her vagina.

Comment: In this example, the word "artist" would be beyond the vocabulary skills of most 2 year olds, as would the knowledge that she was sexually abused at the First National Bank.

QUANTITY AND QUALITY OF DETAILS

<u>*Note -*</u>   *Toddler, preschool, and young elementary-school-age children's narratives typically do not include many details. While very young children may provide specific details of a sex act they have experienced, they may not be able to provide details involving time, frequency, or intention, due to their cognitive immaturity.*

The quantity and quality of details are thought by the experts to be an important factor in assessing the reliability of a statement. The following are criteria thought to support the quality and quantity of details:

- Explicit, detailed account including contextual details (e.g., where, when, what one was wearing, where others were during the abuse)
- Unusual or superfluous details
- Idiosyncratic and sensorimotor details
- Increasingly progressive sexual acts

While children can provide some degree of specificity of sexual abuse details based on their referral to an internal visual image, their ability to provide details will be influenced by their developmental level (refer to Chapter 6). Specificity of details would include explicit and contextual information, such as where and when the abuse happened, what clothing was on or off, and where others were during the abuse. Specificity would also include idiosyncratic details, such as knowledge of sexual acts or anatomy that are so significantly beyond the normal understanding of the alleged victim's chronological or mental age that there exists a high probability that the child must have experienced what is described. These details might be disclosed through reproduction of conversations with the perpetrator, descriptions of interactions with the perpetrator, or sensorimotor details. An example of an idiosyncratic detail is found in the following example:

Jenny, age 8, told her mother that the mother's boyfriend was sexually abusing her. Jenny's mother did not report the abuse, but the mother's friend, unbeknownst to the mother, made a report. Jenny was interviewed by the state caseworker and then sent to a psychologist for further evaluation. Jenny reported to the psychologist that the mother's boyfriend touched her vagina with his hand. She added that the boyfriend required her to touch his penis. When given the anatomical dolls and asked to demonstrate how she touched the boyfriend's penis, the child put the tips of her fingers on the scrotum, and rapidly moved the tips of her fingers up and down the scrotum. She then stated he said, "Tickle it, tickle it, baby."

Comment: *In this example, the child demonstrated a behavior (i.e., fondling the scrotum) that is generally unknown to young elementary-school-age children. Furthermore, Jenny disclosed information about the verbal statement made by the alleged perpetrator that was highly plausible given the sexual behavior described.*

When the episode of the sexual abuse is novel, the child utilizes his or her autobiographic memory to remember the details. However, the more repetitious the abuse, the more the details may blend together for any one specific event, and the child then may utilize a schema-driven memory. When memory is schema driven, it may be difficult for the child to remember a specific sexual abuse encounter unless something novel took place.

Children also may not divulge many details and minimize their involvement due to their sense of shame. The following is an example involving twin sisters whose sexual abuse was initially unsubstantiated due to their minimization of their involvement in sexual activities. During an interview by state caseworkers, they reported having been sexually abused at the same time. They both stated it occurred only one time, yet they provided different stories of this event.

Beth and Bonnie were 10-year-old twins whose friend told a teacher that Beth was being sexually abused by her stepfather. When interviewed separately by the state caseworker, the girls both acknowledged that they were being sexually abused by their stepfather. They both, independently, stated that they were abused on one occasion and that the other sister was present. They then both described different events. Beth described her stepfather making her perform oral sex on him while her sister was made to masturbate herself. Bonnie, however, described her stepfather making her and her sister roll his naked body across the floor and then wrestle with him and fondle him. Both girls described detesting their stepfather. The case was classified as Unfounded.

Comment: *Beth and Bonnie were later found to have been repetitively sexually abused by their stepfather for a number of years. However, out of shame, they both stated the abuse had only occurred on one occasion. During their initial interview with the caseworker, both girls had given truthful descriptions of sexual activities in which their stepfather had engaged them. Because the girls initially both stated it only happened one time and then gave different stories of the sexual abuse, the girls were thought to be lying.*

Statements from very young children may present yet another problem concerning the use of details to determine the veracity of a child's statements. While the quantity and quality of details in children's reports has consensus validity as one of the indicators of an accurate memory, Ceci (1994) suggests caution when using details as a criterion for determining credibility, especially with very young children. As previously reported, in research conducted by Ceci and his colleagues (Ceci, Crotteau, et al., 1994; Ceci, Loftus, et al., 1994), the presence of an explicit and detailed account of an event was no assurance the report was accurate. Rather, Ceci's research showed that young nonsexually abused children (ages 3 to 6 years) could produce elaborate, internally coherent accounts of a fictitious event, as well as demonstrate affect associated with the fictitious account, when interviewed with erroneous suggestions over a several month period of time.

APPROPRIATENESS OF SEXUAL KNOWLEDGE BASED ON DEVELOPMENTAL LEVEL

Note -   _Preschool and elementary-school-age children frequently masturbate and engage their peers in activities in which they show each other their genitals. They also may play doctor and mimic taking a rectal temperature by inserting a pencil or another object representing a thermometer in a peer's rectum. However, when young children begin to mimic adult sexual activities, it can be assumed that they have had some type of exposure to these sexual activities._

Advanced sexual knowledge is identified as a factor which supports the credibility of a child's statement. The following are criteria thought to identify sexual knowledge that is advanced for a child's developmental level:

- Sexual knowledge that exceeds the child's developmental level
- Precocious knowledge of sexuality
- Premature eroticization

Young children who are engaged in sexual activity may develop knowledge about human anatomy and sexual anatomy functions earlier than their peers. While young children are curious about the anatomy of themselves and others, this curiosity takes the form of looking and comparing. Although children may visually examine and touch the body part of another person, they typically do not touch another person's body parts in a sexualized way. Furthermore, most young preschool and early elementary-school-aged children do not have knowledge that a penis fits inside an anal or vaginal opening unless they have observed or experienced this sexual act.

When the young child begins to imitate or verbally describe adult sexual acts, this suggests that the child has unusually advanced sexual knowledge. The following example portrays advanced sexual knowledge:

Four-year-old Jamie was found by his teacher in back of the playhouse attempting to anally penetrate 4-year-old Jeff. When later questioned about his behavior by a therapist, Jamie reported, "We're fuckin." When asked what people do when they are "fuckin," Jamie reported, "They stick their dick in the poop hole."

Comment: Four-year-old Jamie's demonstration of the knowledge that a penis goes inside of an anus is very unusual behavior for a preschool child. However, without further information, it is unknown if Jamie learned this through a sexually abusive experience or if he learned this information from exposure to individuals engaging in anal sex.

A second example portrays advanced sexual knowledge for a preschool-aged child:

Susan, age 3½, was playing at Tommy's house. Tommy also was 3 years old. While the children were playing in Tommy's room, Tommy's mother overheard Susan instructing Tommy, "If you rub it back and forth - like this - it will stick out." Tommy's mother walked into the room and discovered Susan and Tommy with their clothes off with Susan rubbing Tommy's penis. When Susan was asked by Tommy's mother where she had learned this behavior, Susan happily reported that her grandfather had taught her when she went to visit him over the summer.

Comment: Susan's behavior, coupled with her verbal disclosure, supports the criteria of advanced sexual knowledge, possibly learned from a sexual experience with her grandfather.

Conversely, the following example does not represent advanced knowledge; however, the child was inaccurately identified as sexually abused because of his developmentally appropriate understanding of bodily functions. This is an example of a case that was incorrectly substantiated because of the interviewer's limited knowledge of child development and her lack of knowledge regarding the appropriateness of the child's statement:

Johnny, age 5, exposed himself at his after-school daycare. On several occasions, he also called out "penis" and "penis breath." A daycare worker then interviewed Johnny because she suspected that he was the victim of sexual abuse. Johnny was asked specifically about each of his family members. When Johnny was asked if he ever put his mouth on his 16-year-old sister's vagina, he stated, "No, I'd get pee in my mouth if I did that." The daycare worker concluded that Johnny was the victim of sexual abuse that was perpetrated by his sister, based on his advanced sexual knowledge (i.e., understanding that he would get urine in his mouth if he put his mouth on his sister's genitals).

Comment: Johnny's knowledge that urine comes out of female and male genitals is age-appropriate knowledge for preschool and elementary-school-aged children. Johnny's understanding that if he put his mouth on the body part from which urine is released, he would get urine in his mouth reflects Johnny's excellent reasoning skills rather than sexual abuse.

When drawing conclusions about advanced sexual knowledge, the source of this potential knowledge must be carefully evaluated. Further assessment must investigate whether the child's knowledge is based on (a) an experience of sexual abuse, (b) accidental exposure to sexual activity, (c) education through repetitive questioning, or (d) education through peer talk and/or activity.

The author is reminded of a childhood experience that may illustrate this fourth area. According to my cousin, who is 4 years my senior, I, at age 5, informed her that babies were made by "the man going pee inside of the woman." As an adult, my cousin still vividly remembers this statement because she was "horrified" to be informed of this news. In currently discussing this incident with my parents, they had no knowledge of my accidental exposure to adult intercourse nor any memory that they had provided me any information at age 5 regarding procreation. Thus, I can only speculate that I had overheard this news from a school or neighborhood playmate.

REPETITION OVER TIME - EXTERNAL AND INTERNAL CONSISTENCY

Note -   *A child's exhaustive description of his or her sexual abuse typically does not occur during the initial disclosure. For many children disclosure is a process that occurs over time. What a child discloses during one interview may be expanded upon in a later interview. Furthermore, younger children are found to provide different segments of information based on dissimilar questions posed by different interviewers.*

Both external and internal consistency have been considered by some experts to be indicators of credibility. External consistency is defined as the consistency of the story repeated across interviews. The definition of internal consistency is the consistency of details that are disclosed within the story. The following are criteria thought to support external and internal consistency:

- Consistency of core elements
- Consistency of reporting salient details
- Consistency with other statements

For internal consistency criteria to be met, the child's statements over multiple interviews are required to contain the same central features, such as who, what, where, and when. Although, across interviews, the child may provide additional information that includes other perpetrators, sexual acts, times, and places, the original elements should remain constant. However, each core element may not necessarily be articulated at each interview.

Currently, support is eroding for the use of external consistency of statements as a determining criterion for reliability. Rather, some experts believe that actual victims of sexual abuse tend to be inconsistent in their statements due to normal memory functions (Ornstein, 1993). Memory researchers propose that memory for an event is not captured in a videotape format. Rather, memory is stored and retrieved from long-term memory in fragmented pieces (Loftus & Ketcham, 1991).

Thus, when a child discloses information about an event, he or she may add details at a later time that were not retrieved from memory during initial interviews. Furthermore, memory researchers state that if a child has experienced repeated sexual abuse, the incidents may blend together and confusion may result regarding which incident is related to a specific time or date (e.g., the last incident, the incident at Christmas, etc.). An example follows of a case that shows both external and internal consistency:

> Saul, age 5, was found performing fellatio on his 3-year-old foster brother. Saul was interviewed by a state caseworker. Saul told the caseworker that Tim (his teenage foster brother) "sucks my peter." Saul further reported that "I suck Tim's peter," and that this behavior occurred in Tim's bedroom when Tim was left to babysit the younger foster children. Saul was then evaluated by a well-trained mental health professional on three separate occasions about this allegation. His statements remained consistent regarding who was involved, what happened, where it happened, and when it happened. Tim confessed and validated Saul's disclosures.

Conversely, an example follows of inconsistency in statements from children who were victims of sexual abuse:

> Gretchen, age 5, and her brother Danny, age 7, were removed from the care of their biological parents due to physical abuse. At the time of their removal, there was no suspicion of sexual abuse. During their second week in a foster home, Gretchen and Danny were found by their foster mother engaged in intercourse. When a state caseworker questioned the children, they denied that they had seen sexual intercourse performed by anyone and further denied that they had ever been sexually abused. The children were then sent to a child psychologist who spent two sessions - as part of the evaluation - playing with the children individually, prior to conducting an interview. Each child, during these play sessions, was asked benign questions. They were not asked any questions about abuse, nor were they given any materials such as anatomical dolls. After building rapport, a structured interview addressing sexual abuse was conducted with each child. At that time, 5-year-old Gretchen disclosed, "The man with the guitar sucked my wee wee." She further disclosed, "The man with the guitar sucked Danny's wee wee, too." Gretchen then disclosed that her mother and father would have Gretchen and her brother stand by their bed and watch them "touch each other's wee wees." Gretchen reported that "Daddy got on top of Mommy and jumped up and down." Danny, who was seen independent of his sister, disclosed that his uncle, who his parents call the "guitar man," sucked Danny's penis and made Danny suck his penis. During questioning by the psychologist, Danny denied that he had ever seen any adults have sex.

Finally, the following case lacks both external and internal consistency:

Janet, age 12, had lived with her father since the age of 6. On different occasions, her father had cohabitated with five women in the 6 years that Janet had resided in his custody. Janet's father rarely spent time with his daughter while she was in his care. Janet did not do well in school, either socially or academically. Janet, over the past two summers, had resumed contact with her mother. At the end of her second summer vacation with her mother, Janet stated that she did not want to go home because her father was sexually abusing her. When interviewed by the state caseworker, Janet reported that she was first sexually abused by her father when she was 6 years old. She stated that her father was drunk, came into her room while nude, got on top of her, and performed intercourse. Janet stated that no one was home when this first incident occurred. When Janet was interviewed a week later by a therapist, Janet reported that she was 7 years old at the time of the first incident. She stated, at the time of the first incident, her father came into her room, he was fully clothed, and he took off his clothes and her clothes prior to mounting her. Janet reported to the therapist that she screamed, and her father's girlfriend then came running into the room. This scenario was not confirmed by the girlfriend identified as the rescuer by Janet.

Comment: Because a child is at risk to blend together multiple sexual abuse incidents, if abuse occurs repeatedly, it is not implausible for a child, when describing a specific incident, to state to one interviewer that her father was naked while describing him as partially clothed to another interviewer. However, something as significant as a person attempting to rescue the child would be unlikely to be confused across interviews. Although improbable, it is also possible the girlfriend lied. As is evident, these cases are the most difficult to judge.

When examining inconsistency in a child's statements, the issue of recantation must be addressed. Recantation is not uncommon among children who are identified as victims of sexual abuse (Sorenson & Snow, 1991). The process of recantation may best be understood within an operant conditioning model (i.e., a model based on reinforcers and punishers). The following reinforcers and punishers may influence the withdrawal of a sexual abuse allegation:

Positive Reinforcement for Recanting True Allegations

1. Child makes false statements by denying sexual abuse that did occur.

   If allegation is true, may recant to (a) keep perpetrator out of jail, (b) keep family together, or (c) come home (from foster care or relative placement).

   • *Although the child may be identified by authorities as a liar, the child remains with the family and the family remains intact.*

2. Child makes statements in an attempt to please the interviewer (social desirability response).

   If allegation is true, may recant because of repeated interviewing.

- *The young child may change the story in order to please the interviewer. Younger children may be vulnerable to interviewer influence both for agreeing to something that never took place, as well as to agreeing that something that actually happened did not take place.*

Negative Reinforcement for Recanting True Allegations

1. Child is intimidated by interviewer and lies that nothing happened in order to end the session and terminate the aversive interviewing.

   If allegation is true, may recant because of coercive interviewing.

   - *Child may recant because he or she is intimidated by the interviewer. Children may be vulnerable to interviewer pressure both for agreeing to something that did not happen, as well as agreeing that something that actually happened did not take place.*

2. The child fears the perpetrator and recants the allegation in an attempt to protect himself or herself.

   If allegation is true, may recant because of fear.

   - *Child may recant because of fear that the perpetrator will retaliate. Children may fear for their safety even when the perpetrator is incarcerated.*

Punishment for Recanting False Allegations

1. If the motivation for the allegation was revenge, recanting the allegation would put the child/adolescent at a greater disadvantage with the falsely accused individual.
2. If the motivation was for increased social status or attention, the child/adolescent's status would diminish because he or she now would be identified as a liar.
3. If the motivation was escape from another type of abusive situation, the route of escape would be blocked.

   It has been the experience of the author of this book that children who fabricate allegations of sexual abuse rarely recant false allegations due to the serious consequences.

   If allegation is false, may not recant based on fear of consequences.

   - *Children who fabricate false allegations may be motivated by revenge, by a desire for nurturing/attention/status, or as a way to escape another type of abusive environment.*

Thus, recantation is not synonymous with inconsistency. Instead, whether children restate to authorities that their initial allegations were false appears to be a function of the consequences they anticipate.

DESCRIPTION OF THE ALLEGED PERPETRATOR'S BEHAVIOR

Note -   *Many children who have been sexually abused, possibly the majority of children, are not threatened by the perpetrator with harm. Some children's statements that perpetrators have threatened to kill them or their parents may be the result of previous leading questioning. Although some perpetrators may frighten the child into secrecy, many children are manipulated into secrecy through "friendship" and "love."*

The child's description of the behavior of the alleged perpetrator is another factor thought to give credibility to the child's statement. The following criteria are thought to reflect important aspects of offender behavior:

- Coercion and threats
- Bribes or rewards
- Element of secrecy
- Statements about telling or not telling
- What the offender said to obtain participation
- Pressure to recant

While many experts cite the child's disclosure of coercion and threats as an indicator of credibility, many victims of sexual abuse are not frightened into silence. Rather, many children may be tricked or manipulated into silence. For example, the Finkelhor et al. (1990) retrospective national prevalence study indicated that over 80% of the identified victims of childhood sexual abuse did not experience life-threatening force and intimidation during their abuse. As previously delineated, younger children are not developmentally sophisticated enough to understand that sexual abuse is wrong nor do they understand the need to disclose the sexual activities. An example follows that depicts the manipulation of the relationship, rather than threats of harm, that resulted in secrecy:

Doris was sexually abused by her father throughout her childhood and adolescent years. Doris speculates the abuse began during her preschool years. Doris' relationship with her mother was estranged; her father was her closest companion. Doris had few friends during her childhood and adolescence; she mainly did things with her father. As an adult, Doris entered therapy due to marriage problems. She disclosed her sexual abuse for the first time during therapy. She had never been amnestic of the abuse. She had not previously told anyone because she had wanted to protect her father.

Conversely, children can be terrorized into not disclosing their abuse. When sexually abused children witness violence exhibited by their abusers, they understand on an implicit level the danger in disclosing their sexual abuse. An example follows of a child who was never explicitly told she would be harmed if she disclosed her sexual abuse:

> Fredrique, age 9, was engaged in oral sex and fondled by her mother's boyfriend, Rick. The boyfriend also allowed his male friends to engage Fredrique in sexual activities. Fredrique was witness to Rick's physical fights with other male adults as well as his physical battering and sexual abuse of her mother. Rick never told Fredrique not to tell about her sexual abuse. Fredrique stated that when her school teachers would put on demonstrations about disclosing sexual abuse, she would pray that they would not be able to identify her as a victim. Although Fredrique believed she would be hurt or killed by Rick if the abuse was disclosed, he never threatened her.

PLAUSIBILITY OF DESCRIPTION OF ABUSE

Note -   _The child's developmental level, verbal fluency, and quality of questioning will affect the plausibility of the child's narrative. Children who are developmentally immature may provide illogical answers when complex details are sought by the interviewer. Young children repeatedly interviewed by vigilant parents may also be at risk to create improbable stories. However, these illogical or implausible statements cannot solely be used to determine that a child has not been sexually abused._

The following criteria are thought to support the plausibility of sexual abuse allegations:

- Description recounted in a varied and rich manner as opposed to a rote recitation
- Circumstantially congruent description of being sexually abused

Experts suggest that if the child's statements are plausible, the behaviors described should be "consistent with the laws of nature." For example, the following statements by Jennifer are accurate descriptions of physical anatomy:

> Ten-year-old Jennifer stated that her teenage uncle would rub her vagina and put his tongue on her vagina. She stated that on one occasion, he tried to put his penis in her vagina, but "it wouldn't fit."

Statements that are not plausible are sometimes referred to as confabulated (i.e., made up) responses. Statements that are created in an attempt to provide information in order to please an interviewer are, at times, confabulated responses. Gardner (1992) states that younger children have few reality experiences, and as a result, if they make something up, they do not appreciate the absurdity in what they are saying. An example follows of a statement that represents a possible confabulated story:

> After repeated interviewing by her mother, 4-year-old Stacy stated her father, when bringing her back from a visit, would completely undress her, lick her vagina, and put his penis in her vagina - all while continuing to drive. She further stated that on one occasion, her father undressed her and molested her in a fast-food restaurant drive-through lane.

Everson (1995) has issued a caution to the evaluator who attempts to determine if a statement is plausible. He proposed that what may seem implausible to the average observer may be misperceptions due to developmental limitations, psychological trauma, bizarre and distorted memories created through drug effects, or deliberate attempts by the perpetrator to confuse the child. He also proposed that the implausible statements may be created through suggestive questioning or coaching, attempts to gain approval, or deliberate exaggeration or fantasy. Everson (1995) has developed the following list as possible explanations for unusual, bizarre, or fantasy-like elements in children's accounts of abuse:

- Accurate description of reality
- Misperception or miscommunication due to developmental limitations
- Distortion due to attempts to assimilate novel events into existing schemata
- Misperception or memory distortion due to psychological trauma
- Miscommunication due to interviewer error
- Misperception due to drug effects
- Deliberate attempts by perpetrator to discredit or confuse child
- Threat incorporation
- Dream incorporation
- Media influences
- Fantasy in the service of mastery over anxiety
- Misreports by child to deflect blame or deny victimization
- Exaggeration to gain attention or approval
- Incorporation of drawing errors
- Distortion due to confabulation
- Distortion due to interview fatigue
- Impact of leading or suggestive questioning techniques
- Distortion due to successive misapproximations
- Snowballing of an innocent lie
- Deliberate exaggeration
- Fantasy lying
- Delusions due to psychotic processes

EMOTIONAL REACTION OF THE CHILD DURING INTERVIEW

<u>Note -</u>   *The characteristics of the sexual abuse, the child victim-perpetrator relationship, and the child's interpretation of who is to blame for the sexual abuse will affect the child's emotional reaction during the interview. Furthermore, the number of times the child has been interviewed will influence his or her emotional response.*

The emotional reaction of the child during the interview is believed by experts to be an important factor in assessing the reliability of the child's statements. The following criteria are thought to add support to the veracity of sexual abuse allegations:

- Emotional reaction consistent with accusations
- Emotional state consistent with the abuse

  - state of mind at the time of the abuse
  - emotional state when describing what occurred

The emotional reactions of the child should be consistent with a sexual abuse allegation. For example, the evaluator would not expect the child to exhibit fear of the alleged perpetrator when the sexual abuse was alleged to be game-like and the child was manipulated through play rather than threats. However, this dynamic will be influenced by the child's developmental level (refer to Chapter 3).

While some victims of sexual abuse may fear their perpetrators, others may continue to have a strong attachment to them. The following is an example of an emotional reaction that is consistent with the victim-perpetrator relationship of a 14-year-old victim:

> Holly was interviewed after her older sister disclosed that their father had sexually abused her and Holly since their early elementary school years. Holly was angry at her sister for betraying their father. She was tearful and hostile toward the interviewer and protective of her father. Although she acknowledged the sexual abuse, she stated that it had only occurred because "their mother didn't take care of him."

Conversely, the next example does not reflect an emotional reaction consistent with the allegation of sexual abuse made by a 6-year-old child. This allegation, reportedly, first was made by the child to her mother:

> Danya described to the evaluator how, when visiting her father, he would come into her bedroom, rip off her nightgown, pull her hair, pinch her breasts and vagina, get on top of her, and put his penis in her. She made good eye contact with the evaluator and maintained a smile throughout her description of these events. She did not appear anxious nor fearful. When observed in a session with her father, she did not show any fear of him.

A CASE STUDY UTILIZING
CRITERIA FOR ASSESSING THE
VERACITY OF THE CHILD'S STATEMENTS

The following case study of 6-year-old Louise illustrates an evaluation in which the indicator approach was used.

CASE STUDY: LOUISE

Louise was born on May 23, 1985, in the state of Florida to Mark and Leslie Nelson. The pregnancy with and delivery of Louise were without complications. Louise's father is a building contractor, and her mother is a full-time homemaker. Both parents were in their late 20s at the time of Louise's birth. Louise's parents maintained a close relationship with their parents and siblings who live in the same town. Louise is the oldest of two children born to her parents. Her younger brother, David, is 2 years her junior.

Louise suffered from colic during the first 4 months of her life. She was described by her parents as a happy and active toddler, but somewhat shy. Louise's mother reported that she has a close relationship with both Louise and her brother. The mother observes Louise to be a child who feels free to ask many questions; Louise is observed to typically disclose things she worries about to her mother.

At age 3, Louise was put in a preschool four mornings a week for socialization experiences. She made a positive adjustment and was well liked by her peers and teachers. During her kindergarten school year, she attended public school where she again was observed to do well socially and academically. During her first grade school year, she was placed by her parents in a private Catholic school. Louise's parents believed the smaller classes and accelerated curriculum at the private school would benefit Louise.

Louise engages in dance lessons, roller skating, and bike riding with her peers in the neighborhood. She attends church every Sunday with her parents. She is a compliant child at home and described by her parents as an easy child to parent.

During Louise's infancy, toddler, and preschool years, extended family members typically gathered for family dinners several times a month. Louise was always provided babysitting by a relative when her parents went out. There were no traumatic experiences, either medical or psychological, that Louise experienced during the first 6 years of her life.

When Louise was 6 years and 8 months old, Louise spent the weekend with her paternal grandfather, who was caring for his sick mother. Louise had, on other occasions, been cared for by her grandfather and enjoyed being with him. The mother reported that on Sunday, when she (Louise's mother) arrived at the grandfather's home to bring her daughter home, the grandfather appeared "agitated." He told Louise's mother that he had discovered Louise had a rash and, consequently, he then talked to Louise about "personal hygiene."

According to the mother, she did not think anything unusual about the grandfather's statement other than thinking that his agitated behavior was uncharacteristic. In the car on the way home, the mother then asked Louise if she had a nice time with her grandfather. Louise spontaneously stated, "Pop Pop touched my private, and I wasn't supposed to tell you." Louise then stated to her mother that her grandfather gave her a bath and made her look at her genitals with a mirror. When the mother inquired if her grandfather had done anything else, Louise reported that during the weekend, on one occasion, when her grandfather was standing in the kitchen, he pulled his penis out of his pants and stated, "Hey girlie, how about looking at this?"

The mother discussed Louise's statements with Louise's father. The parents reported that they were both shocked. The father then telephoned his sister, who tearfully disclosed that their father had sexually abused her as a child. The parents reported that they were extremely upset with this information but did not talk about any of these events in Louise's presence. The following day, Louise was taken to her pediatrician who conducted a medical examination. There was no medical evidence of penetration. The pediatrician then reported the allegation of sexual abuse to the Social Services Child Abuse Registry. Louise was interviewed the following day by a state child abuse investigator. The State Investigative Summary reads

Department received a report alleging that the paternal grandfather touched Louise on vaginal area. Child is alleged to have told mom about incident. Paternal grandfather advised mom he took a mirror and held it to child's vagina and "instructed her on proper hygiene." Bio daughter now 40 y/o came forward and also advised that father also molested her when she was a child. Louise stated to investigator paternal grandfather touched her privates twice when she was visiting, both times in his bedroom when no one around. She said he asked her to touch his private and she did. She said she didn't want to but he made her. Paternal grandmother was out of town when it happened. Mom and Dad stated child after spending night with paternal grandfather told them he touched her privates. Mom advised she called the doctor who examined Louise and did not believe child was penetrated but did believe HRS should look into issue. Paternal grandmother and paternal grandfather were seen. Paternal grandfather initially agreed to talk to HRS but not police. He called attorney who advised him not to speak to anyone so he pled the fifth. Grandmother, interviewed prior to grandfather, advised that grandfather had bothered her children when they were little, she filed for divorce and then "let him come back" after counseling. She stated, "he has a split personality," and he can "be good for awhile" he used to be a minister. She also said he likes "porno" and "exposed" himself to neighbor children in the past. Grandmother said she was out of town when the "misunderstanding" with Louise transpired. She said he "was only touching the child and showing her the area with a mirror to teach her proper hygiene." Molly J, adult daughter of grandfather, stated he started fondling her at age 7 and began forced sexual intercourse when she was age 12, and continued 5 years. She said he made threats to her. She stated that her mother had been aware of the sexual abuse and father's exposing himself to neighbor children. Louise's pediatrician reported parents are very appropriate and did not allow the child to see paternal grandparents after daughter's disclosure. Pediatrician verified mom did bring child in after all allegations made and exam found no medical evidence of sexual abuse but family was traumatized by all info surfaced regarding paternal grandfather and appear to have coped well with situation, appearing appropriate and protective.

One month after the state child abuse investigator interviewed Louise, the child was referred to a psychologist for further evaluation. Louise, at that time, was refusing to talk to the State Attorney; her behavior had become unmanageable at home, her grades were dropping, and she was becoming emotionally distant from her father.

The psychologist noted Louise was an attractive blond-haired, blue-eyed, 6-year-and-9-month-old female. Height and weight were average. Manner of dress was appropriate, and hygiene was good. Gait and motor behavior were normal, while posture was somewhat tense. She separated with some hesitation from her mother. Primary facial expression was sad. Speech quality was soft, while speech quantity was normal. Speech impairments were absent. Affect was restricted, and mood was depressed. Unusual or bizarre thinking was not observed. Attention and concentration were normal. Estimated range of intellectual ability was informally assessed to be above average.

During the session with the psychologist, Louise was asked about friends, school, and other general topics. When asked why she was brought to see the psychologist, she said she did not know why she was there. Louise then was asked to draw a happy face and to name something that made her happy when she was with her father and mother. Louise reported that swimming with her father and mother made her happy. Louise was asked to name something that made her happy when she was with her "Maw Maw" and "Pop Pop." Louise stated that she was happy when she used to go to visit her Maw Maw and Pop Pop at their house. Louise was then asked to draw a sad face and to name something that made her sad when she was with her father and mother. Louise stated that she felt sad when her mother and father yelled at her or spanked her. When asked to name something that made her sad when she was with her Maw Maw and Pop Pop, Louise stated that she felt sad because "my Pop Pop did something wrong to me." Louise was asked what her grandfather did that was wrong, and she responded that he touched her genitals. The psychologist noted that Louise's eyes focused on the floor, and her body slumped forward when she made this statement.

Louise was then administered a series of structured questions using anatomical drawings to structure the format of questioning. Questions that were not abuse-related were presented first. Louise was shown the drawing of a nude, white preschool female child. The following dialogue occurred:

Psychologist:	"This is a picture of a little girl who gets hugged. Who gives you hugs?"
Louise:	"My mom, dad, and brother."

In order to clarify Louise's names of body parts, Louise was shown a second drawing, identical to the first drawing, of a nude preschool female child. Louise was asked to name the body parts and their functions.

Psychologist:	"What do you call this body part?"
Louise:	"Eyes."
Psychologist:	"What do you do with eyes?"
Louise:	"Look and cry."

Louise proceeded to name additional body parts and to identify their functions. She named the genitals a "private" and reported that its function was to go to the bathroom. The following dialogue then took place:

Psychologist:	"Tell me about the last time you went to visit your Pop Pop."
Louise:	"My Pop Pop touched my private."
Psychologist:	"Tell me about your Pop Pop touching your private."
Louise:	"I was visiting him, and he made me look at my private in a mirror."
Psychologist:	"What else happened when you were visiting your Pop Pop?"
Louise:	"He said my private was pretty, and he kissed it."
Psychologist:	"Where were you?"
Louise:	"His room."
Psychologist:	"Did he take his clothes off, or did he leave them on?"
Louise:	"He left his shirt on, but not his shorts."
Psychologist:	"Tell me about your clothes when Pop Pop took off his shorts."
Louise:	"He made me take them off at first to take a bath."
Psychologist:	"Did he say anything to you?"
Louise:	"He said not to tell anybody, even my mom or dad - but I did. I don't ever want to go back to stay with him."

In order to further clarify Louise's names of body parts, Louise was shown a drawing of a nude, adult male. Upon inquiry, Louise reported that she calls the penis a private:

Psychologist:	"Whose private have you seen?"
Louise:	"My Pop Pop's and my brother's."
Psychologist:	"Tell me about that."
Louise:	"I see my brother's when he's in the bathroom taking a bath."
Psychologist:	"Tell me about seeing Pop Pop's private."
Louise:	"He showed me his private when I visited him, and he made me touch it. But I didn't want to."
Psychologist:	"Did he say anything to you when he showed you his private?"
Louise:	"He said, 'Hey girlie, how about looking at this' - but I didn't want to look."

Psychologist:	"Do you still like your Pop Pop?"
Louise:	"Not anymore."
Psychologist:	"Did you use to like your Pop Pop?"
Louise:	"Yeah, a whole lot."

Louise was interviewed a second time, 1 week later. At her second interview, Louise was presented anatomical dolls and asked to show the psychologist what her grandfather had done to her. Louise's statements were externally and internally consistent.

ANALYSIS - CASE STUDY OF LOUISE

Evaluation Model. Comprehensive Model: sources of data include history from the parents, history from paternal aunts alleging childhood sexual abuse, State Child Abuse Investigative Report, private school and Sunday school teachers' observations of behaviors (pre- and post-event), verbal interview with Louise, observation of Louise with her parents.

Putting the Puzzle Together. History from parents, which was confirmed by relatives and teachers, characterizes Louise as a compliant, affectionate child. She is a shy child, but not a fearful or attention-seeking child. She exhibits good social skills and coping skills. This is not a child who wants to be the center of attention.

Louise's observed behaviors are consistent with the behaviors of children who have secure attachments with parental figures. Louise, prior to the allegation, had never experienced any medical or psychological traumas, such as serious illnesses, losses, or natural disasters. Basically, her family life was stable and somewhat sheltered.

There is no evidence of the allegation being due to secondary gains for Louise or her parents. For example, pre-allegation Louise was observed to have a close, affectionate relationship with her paternal grandfather. She looked forward to her visits with him. Post-allegation Louise was fearful of her grandfather and did not want to see him again. Louise's parents had a positive relationship with both of their families. The parents had no motive to create a false allegation.

Louise's initial statements to her mother and her statements made during the verbal interview with the psychologist met the following criteria for strengthening statement veracity:

Timing and Circumstances of Disclosure

There is no evidence that Louise's allegation was a result of prompting or leading questioning. Louise's allegation to her mother was made spontaneously after her mother had asked a question seeking positive information about Louise's visit with her grandfather.

Language Congruent With Developmental Level

Louise's language was congruent with that of a 6-and-a-half-year-old child. Louise reported that in her family, a vagina is called a "private," and a penis is called a "private." Louise never used any adult terminology to describe the sexual abuse she alleged. Consistent with disclosures of young children, Louise gave more details when questions were more directive.

Quantity and Quality of Details

Louise's statements to her mother and to the psychologist included several unusual details. Her initial statement to her mother that her grandfather made her look into a mirror at her genitals was the first example. The second example was Louise's statement that her grandfather exposed his penis and stated, "Hey girlie, how about looking at this?" The third example was Louise's response to the psychologist's question, "Did he take his clothes off, or did he leave them on?" Louise responded, "He left his shirt on, but not his shorts."

Repetition Over Time - External and Internal Consistency

Because disclosure is a process and not an event, Louise's external consistency (statements to different adults) was not strong. Although Louise disclosed both the same details to the mother, state investigator, and psychologist, she did so in pieces rather than in one detailed narrative. Her internal consistency, however, was strong. Louise consistently reported her grandfather made her look at her genitals in the mirror, exposed his penis to her, touched her vagina, and had her touch his penis. The more focused the questions, the more details Louise provided.

Description of the Alleged Perpetrator's Behavior

Louise's description of her grandfather's behavior was consistent with descriptions of the sexual abuse he was alleged to have demonstrated with his daughter during her childhood. For example, Louise's aunt reported that when her father began to sexually abuse her at about age 7, the sexual behavior initially involved fondling and not intercourse. The grandfather also had a history of exposing himself to other children. Louise's allegation involved all of these elements.

Plausibility of Description of Abuse

Louise's description was very plausible.

Emotional Reaction of the Child During the Interview

The mother observed that Louise was upset when disclosing the information. Louise stated she did not want to go back to stay with her grandfather "ever again." The psychologist noted that Louise made poor eye contact and was visibly upset when answering questions. Louise told the psychologist she would not talk to the judge or State Attorney about what had happened to her.

Case Outcome

Louise was placed in therapy. Louise refused to speak to authorities, and Louise's aunt refused to testify against their father. As a result, Louise's grandfather was never prosecuted. Louise's grandfather acknowledged to the family that he "may have" performed the behaviors alleged by Louise and agreed to pay for her therapy. Louise's parents chose to terminate their contact with the grandfather.

CONCLUSION

Based on clinical rather than empirical work, a number of researchers have attempted to identify criteria that strengthen the veracity of a child's statement. Only two researchers, to date, have studied these key indicators empirically. While the criteria derived from clinical observations are less definitive than methodically sound research, criteria derived from clinical observations by multiple well-respected professionals have consensus validity.

The criteria identified in this chapter offer the evaluator some direction and structure for the assessment of the veracity of a child's statements alleging sexual abuse. However, the skilled evaluator must consider these criteria within the total gestalt (i.e., developmental history, family, environment, motivation to disclose, etc.) in order to understand a specific case and draw scientifically based conclusions. When standing alone, a single indicator does not have much meaning.

To date, there does not exist robust empirical support for definitive markers within a child's statement that can consistently identify sexual abuse victims from nonvictims. Furthermore, because each child is unique, the components of a child's statement will be influenced by the child's developmental level, his or her personal interpretation of the sexual experience, and the child's relationship with the perpetrator.

GUIDELINES
Considerations and Cautions

- Understand the difference between validation of criteria derived from empirical research versus clinical observations. While criteria derived from clinical observations are less definitive than methodically sound research, criteria based on consistent observations by multiple well-respected professionals have consensus validity.
- The interactions between the key indicators and the child's developmental level, the child's interpretation of the alleged abuse, and the child victim-alleged perpetrator relationship must be considered.
- When examining a child's statement for validating factors, the same standards cannot be applied across developmental levels (i.e., numerous details in the narrative of a 2½-year-old versus an 8-year-old).
- The presence or absence of any single key indicator cannot be used to substantiate that a child is sexually abused or is not sexually abused.
- A single novel episode of sexual abuse may create a more detailed memory of the abuse than repetitive abuse where the details of multiple incidents may become blended together.
- While absurd statements may reflect confabulation, these statements may also reflect developmental limitations or memory distortions induced through other means.
- When a child discloses information about an event, he or she may add details at a later date that were not retrieved from memory during the initial interviews.
- Spontaneous disclosures may be more likely with preschool-age children than with elementary-school-age children or adolescents because they are naïve to the repercussions of disclosure. However, a spontaneous disclosure with any age child appears to be a low-frequency behavior.
- Intentional disclosures may be more likely with elementary-school-age children and adolescents versus preschoolers based on the older children's understanding of the complex meaning of their sexual involvement.
- Internal, rather than external, consistency may support credibility.
- Recantation is not synonymous with inconsistency. Instead, whether children state to authorities that their initial allegation was false appears to be related to the consequences they anticipate.
- The emotional reaction of the alleged victim should be examined within the context of the allegation (i.e., physical aggression versus gentle manipulation).
- Education from peers may provide children with some rudimentary principles of sexual behavior and procreation.
- Repetitive, coercive questioning may provide the child with education regarding advanced sexual knowledge (e.g., "Did he stick it inside your pee pee?").

CHAPTER 8

Child Interview Props - The Anatomical Dolls

This chapter reviews the use of the anatomical doll as an interview tool.
Professionals' judgments regarding children's behaviors with the dolls
are presented. Normative studies on nonsexually abused children's be-
haviors with the dolls and comparative studies of nonsexually abused
and sexually abused children's behaviors with the dolls also are reviewed.
Although anatomical dolls can facilitate the verbal reports of preschool-
and school-age children, children's play with the dolls cannot be used to
identify sexually abused children.

*　　*　　*

Central to the protection of a child is the child's ability to communicate what
has happened to him or her. As previously discussed, verbal questioning has traditionally been the method for increasing the amount of information children recall
when they are interviewed about their memory of an event. This presents a problem with very young children and mentally handicapped children who possess limited verbal skills. In an attempt to assist the verbal reports of these children, concrete interviewing props have been employed by many clinicians when interviewing children alleged to have been sexually abused. Because play is an avenue for
children to communicate their understanding of and experiences with the world,
toys have naturally been chosen as a tool to assist children in narrating their memories. Over the past several decades, materials utilized to facilitate children's verbal
reports of sexual abuse have included anatomical dolls, anatomical drawings,
nonanatomical dolls, puppets, and model homes with replicas of floor plans.

The manipulation of objects that were present during a critical event are thought
by some professionals to trigger memories of past events and to assist the child in
overcoming language problems. These tools are also thought to help overcome
children's embarrassment and reluctance to verbally disclose their abuse.

THE DEBATE OVER
THE USE OF PROPS

The use of props as interview tools has been debated by researchers and clinicians. Currently debated is whether these props help the child to provide a more detailed description of what the child experienced or whether the props stimulate embellishment or misunderstanding of the child's experience.

Several studies support the claim that presenting the child with actual items and objects involved during an event may facilitate more complete recall of the events (Pipe, Gee, & Wilson, 1993; Saywitz et al., 1991). These studies indicate that context cues and props appear to assist children when they are questioned, specifically, if the questions are not leading or misleading and/or relate directly to the cued items. Results from a number of other studies do not substantiate the claim that props enhance recall of events, especially for children ages 3 and younger (Goodman & Aman, 1990; Gordon et al., 1993).

Several studies using anatomical dolls as interview aids have found that the dolls increase the recall accuracy of young children (3 to 7 years) with little or no increase in false assertions of genital touching (Katz et al., 1995; Steward & Stewart, in press).

However, a study by Bruck and her colleagues found a high rate of false assertions and false denials of genital touching by very young children (3½ years and younger) when anatomical dolls were used as interview aids in conjunction with direct, leading, and misleading questions (Bruck, Ceci, Francoeur, & Renick, 1995).

While the research is inconclusive as to whether the presentation of actual items and objects to which a child was exposed during an event may facilitate recall, research results suggest that younger children may be most susceptible to increased inaccuracy when they provide information stimulated by object cues if repeatedly interviewed (Pipe et al., 1993). Pipe and her colleagues caution

> Interviewers must, of course, always be aware of the risk that these retrieval techniques might reduce the accuracy of reports. The effect on accuracy appears to depend on the nature of the cues and props, the way they are presented, and how children are instructed to use them. (p. 43)

Researchers are presently investigating children's responses when they are presented with an array of irrelevant items that the interviewer assumes to be relevant. Presently, there is an absence of research to answer questions about how these irrelevant items might influence children's narratives.

THE ANATOMICAL
DOLL AS A PROP

Anatomical dolls have been widely used by clinicians who investigate and evaluate child sexual abuse allegations. Boat and Everson (1988), in their 1985 survey of nearly 300 professionals in North Carolina, found 94% of the child protection agencies, 67% of mental health clinicians, and 40% of law enforcement professionals used the dolls. In a 1988 national survey, 92% of mental health clinicians involved with child sexual abuse reported using the dolls (Conte et al., 1991). Sixty-two percent of Boston law enforcement professionals and 80% of mental health clinicians in a 1989 survey also reported using the dolls (Kendall-Tackett & Watson, 1992).

In the absence of normative base rate data, clinicians using anatomical dolls in sexual abuse evaluations have relied on their own judgment in deciding whether a child's interactions with the dolls represent (a) age-appropriate curiosity and play, (b) a demonstration of sexual interactions the child has observed, or (c) a reenactment of the child's own sexual victimization. As previously discussed (see Chapter 2), there are serious problems with this subjective method of decision making. Decision making based on subjective clinical judgment is less reliable than decision making based on actuarial methods, thus increasing the chance of making either a false-positive or a false-negative identification.

The American Psychological Association (1991), the American Academy of Child and Adolescent Psychiatry (1990), and the American Professional Society on the Abuse of Children (1995) recommend that clinicians using anatomical dolls should possess the training and experience required to conduct investigations or evaluations with alleged child victims of sexual abuse.

Presently, there is general agreement that the dolls cannot be used as a "diagnostic test" for determining whether a child has or has not been sexually abused. In an attempt to provide professionals guidance in their use of the dolls, the American Professional Society on the Abuse of Children (1995) has developed comprehensive guidelines for the use of anatomical dolls.

Anatomical dolls were first marketed for public use in the late 1970s by Migima Designs. The doll maker proposed that the dolls were to be used by children to identify body parts and to demonstrate or clarify what had happened to them. Since the creation of the anatomical doll, several other companies have produced these dolls. While there is no uniform set of standards that govern the features of anatomical dolls, features that are now considered standard include vaginal, anal, and mouth openings, fingers, and pubic hair on the sexually mature dolls.

One criticism of anatomical dolls has been that their genitalia appear disproportionately large. In response to this criticism, Bays (1990) measured the genitalia and breasts of 17 doll sets and extrapolated her findings to human adult size. The penis, scrotum, vulval slit, and breasts of the dolls measured by Bays were not exaggerated.

ANATOMICAL DOLLS -
FANTASY AND CONTAMINATION

The anatomical dolls have been the subject of frequent legal challenges in court. These dolls have been criticized as too sexually suggestive and stimulating, thus causing the child to fantasize and make false allegations. According to critics, the anatomical novelty and sexual explicitness of the dolls may induce even nonsexually abused children to have sexual fantasies and to act out sexually (Gardner, 1992), which may be misinterpreted as evidence of sexual abuse.

Further questions have been raised in the legal arena regarding the possible contaminating effect of anatomical dolls. Some clinicians argue that the sexual details of the dolls may focus the child on sexual anatomy and, as a result, create a demand for sexual information (Gardner, 1992; Yates & Terr, 1988a, 1988b). Based on this assumption, Gardner (1992) cautions against any use of anatomical dolls:

> The child cannot but be startled and amazed by such a doll. The likelihood of the child's ignoring these unusual genital features is almost at zero level. Accordingly, the dolls almost demand attention and predictably will bring about the child's talking about sexual issues. . . . Again, the contamination here is so great that the likelihood of differentiating between bona fide and fabricated sex abuse has become reduced considerably by the utilization of these terrible contaminants. (p. 277)

Despite the claims of Gardner (1992) and others, research does not confirm the notion that exposure to anatomical dolls induces children who have not had prior sexual experiences or prior exposure to the dolls to engage in sexual fantasies with the dolls (Boat & Everson, 1993; Everson & Boat, 1990; Glaser & Collins, 1989; Sivan et al., 1988). While children's exposure to anatomical dolls creates a heightened interest in a child's own genitals or the genitals of others, exposure to the dolls has not been found to cause sexual acting out (Boat, Everson, & Holland, 1990). Currently, a number of jurisdictions will not admit into evidence information derived from interviews with alleged child sexual abuse victims when anatomical dolls have been utilized to acquire information from the children.

Possibly the problem with the use of anatomical dolls has been misidentified. The source of the problem may not be related to the dolls' contaminating effect but rather to the evaluator's misuse of the dolls and misinterpretation of the child-doll interactions. Criticism regarding evaluator error with the anatomical dolls holds greater validity than the charge that children, if presented with the dolls, will develop sexual fantasies.

The following example demonstrates inappropriate use of the dolls as a projective test and the inappropriate interpretation of child-doll behavior:

Janie, age 3, was given a nude child female doll and a nude adult male doll. Initially, Janie avoided the dolls and played with other toys in the office. Janie eventually returned to the dolls and examined the child female doll, inserting her finger into the doll's vagina. She then placed the child doll face down on top of the male doll which was lying face up. Janie then took the male doll's penis between her fingers and pulled on the penis. Following this session with the dolls, the therapist, based on Janie's doll play, identified the child as a victim of sexual abuse.

Comment - This therapist erred by using the dolls as a projective test. A child's interaction with the dolls cannot be used as the sole or major determinant in confirming sexual abuse.

PROFESSIONAL STANDARDS OF "NORMAL BEHAVIOR" FOR DOLL USE

To make judgments about alleged child victims' behaviors with the dolls, clinicians must have a standard of "normal" behavior. The questions arise (a) Do professionals use a consistent standard of what constitutes normal behavior with the dolls? and (b) Are professionals' judgments about children's behaviors with the dolls valid? Two studies, to date, have addressed these issues. Boat and Everson (1988) had law enforcement, child protection workers, mental health workers, and physicians rate the "normalcy" of behaviors with the dolls demonstrated by nonsexually abused, preschool-age children. The professionals responded to the following question: "With the anatomical dolls, what would you consider to be normal play behavior by children ages 2 to 5.9 years who have *not* been sexually abused?" Opinions of the professionals as to the normalcy of various behaviors demonstrated by nonsexually abused preschool children with the anatomical dolls are presented in Table 8.1 (p. 194).

Within each professional group, visual and manual explorations were considered more common than demonstration of explicit sexual acts with the dolls. Over 90% of child protection workers, mental health practitioners, and physicians agreed that touching the dolls' genitals, breasts, and anal areas would be normal. Law enforcement officers were less likely than other professionals to view this behavior as normal. Fewer than 15% of the child protection workers, mental health practitioners, physicians, and law enforcement officers reported that demonstrations of more overt sexual acts (i.e., vaginal/anal penetration, oral/genital penetration, genital/genital contact) were normal behaviors for nonsexually abused children. Within each professional group, there was approximately a 50/50 split regarding whether avoiding the dolls or anxious behavior in response to the unclothed dolls constituted normal behavior. There was not one behavior that professionals unanimously agreed upon as indicative of normal interaction with the dolls for young

TABLE 8.1
Judgments About Normalcy of Behaviors of
2 to 5 Year Olds With Anatomical Dolls*

NONSEXUALLY ABUSED CHILD'S BEHAVIOR WITH THE DOLLS	CHILD PROTECTION WORKERS (N = 63)	MENTAL HEALTH PRO-FESSIONALS (N = 17)	PHYSICIANS (N = 13)	LAW ENFORCE-MENT (N = 16)
	All numbers in percentages (% normal)			
Undressing the dolls	98	94	100	100
Staring at the dolls' genitals	95	94	85	94
Touching dolls' breasts**	98	100	92	75
Touching dolls' genitals	97	100	92	88
Touching dolls' anal area***	94	100	92	63
Showing dolls kissing	89	82	77	75
Avoiding dolls or anxious behavior	48	59	46	50
Placing dolls on top of each other (lying down)****	48	29	39	6
Showing fondling - digital penetration	14	12	23	21
Showing vaginal penetration	9	6	15	13
Showing anal penetration	9	6	15	13
Showing oral-genital contact	9	6	15	6
Showing genital-genital contact	9	6	15	6

**$p < .01$.
***$p < .01$.
****$p < .02$.

*Table reproduced from "Use of Anatomical Dolls Among Professionals in Sexual Abuse Evaluations," by B. W. Boat and M. D. Everson, 1988, *Child Abuse & Neglect, 12,* p. 176. Reprinted with kind permission from Elsevier Service Ltd., The Boulevard, Langford Lane, Kidlington OX5 1GB, United Kingdom.

nonsexually abused children. Not even undressing the dolls received unanimous consensus as a normal behavior.

Kendall-Tackett (1992) replicated Boat and Everson's (1988) study with mental health clinicians and law enforcement professionals and reported similar results. Professionals agreed that highly sexualized behaviors were abnormal for nonsexually abused children. However, the professionals did not agree about less explicit sexual behaviors, such as touching the breasts or genitals of the doll. Profession, gender of the professional, and years of experience were all related to variability in the ratings of the more ambiguous, less explicit behaviors. Law enforcement professionals, women, and those with the least amount of professional experience were more likely to view ambiguous behaviors as abnormal.

NORMATIVE RESEARCH ON CHILDREN'S INTERACTIONS WITH ANATOMICAL DOLLS

NONSEXUALLY ABUSED CHILDREN'S BEHAVIOR WITH ANATOMICAL DOLLS

The development of behavioral norms for nonsexually abused children's behavior with anatomical dolls has been the focus of several research studies. These normative studies indicate that when exposed to anatomical dolls, some children without known histories of sexual abuse inspect the dolls by touching the dolls' genitals and breasts (Everson & Boat, 1990; Glaser & Collins, 1989). While the majority of children without known histories of sexual abuse do not exhibit sexually explicit behaviors such as vaginal or anal intercourse, fellatio, or cunnilingus, a small number of these children do exhibit overtly explicit sexual behaviors when playing with anatomical dolls. Table 8.2 (pp. 196-197) summarizes four studies that examined presumably nonsexually abused children's interactions with the anatomical dolls.

Findings from these normative studies are inconsistent. While some studies have found nonsexually abused children do not show sexually explicit behavior (i.e., vaginal or anal intercourse) with the dolls (Sivan et al., 1988), other studies have found a small portion of nonsexually abused children do show explicit sexual behavior with the dolls (Everson & Boat, 1990). Everson and Boat's research suggests that although the rates of sexually explicit play are low in middle class SES children, these rates increase in more diverse samples. Male children from lower SES families are more likely to exhibit explicit sexualized behavior with the dolls in front of others. These atypical demonstrations of explicit sexual acts by presumably nonsexually abused young children appear to be related to some form of prior sexual exposure (Everson & Boat, 1990; Glaser & Collins, 1989).

As suggested by Everson and Boat (1990), the dolls appear to provide sexually knowledgeable children with implicit permission to reveal their knowledge of sexuality in play. While anatomical dolls may be used as an aid to communicate sexually abusive experiences, anatomical dolls may also be utilized by children to communicate their sexual knowledge. For example, a child who has witnessed an adolescent sibling engaging in sex with girlfriends or boyfriends may have sexual knowledge about intercourse, fellatio, or cunnilingus without having been sexually molested. This raises a serious problem for evaluators who attempt to assign a causal link to the sexually explicit behaviors demonstrated by children with the dolls.

TABLE 8.2
Behavior of Nonsexually Abused
Children With Anatomical Dolls

FACTORS	Everson and Boat (1990)	Gabriel (1985)	Glaser and Collins (1989)	Sivan et al. (1988)
Subjects	• 209 nonsexually abused children • SES - Upper to lower class • Ages 2 years to 5 years and 11 months	• 16 nonsexually abused children • SES - No information • 2½ years to 5 years	• 91 nonsexually abused children • SES - Middle class • Ages 2 years to 6 years	• 144 nonsexually abused children • SES - middle class • Ages 3 years to 8 years
Procedure	• 30 minute doll interview presented in the following format with interviewer present: - Free play with clothed dolls - Body part/body functions inventory - Free play with unclothed dolls - While dolls still unclothed, child prompted with "Show me what the dolls can do together" • 3, 4, and 5-year-olds were observed playing with dolls when alone (2 to 6 minutes) - this last procedure was added later in the study and therefore not every subject was observed in this manner • No other toys were presented	• Free play with dolls, adult present (30 minutes) • Other toys present • After 15 minutes of play "a number of inquiries were made by the observer about the dolls"	• Children's parents interviewed in the home • Informal session in preschool, with adult and one or more other children present (25 minutes): - Free and directed doll play - Body parts/functions interview	• Family of four dolls (2 adults, 2 children) presented to each child while seated in a playroom • Observations of childrens' interactions with the dolls under three free play conditions in the following format: - Free play, adult present - Body parts/functions interview (doll's clothes taken off during interview) - Free play, adult absent, doll left undressed

Findings	• Suggestive intercourse positioning
	- Interviewer present:
	  0% of 2 year olds
	  10% of 3 year olds
	  9% of 4 year olds
	  18% of 5 year olds
	- Child alone:
	  No 2 year olds
	  3% of 3 year olds
	  5% of 4 year olds
	  7% of 5 year olds
	• Clear intercourse positioning
	- Interviewer present:
	  0% of 2 year olds
	  2% of 3 year olds
	  2% of 4 year olds
	  4% of 5 year olds
	- Child alone:
	  No 2 year olds
	  3% of 3 year olds
	  7% of 4 year olds
	  12% of 5 year olds
		• 94% of child subjects showed overt interest and interaction with genitals of the dolls
		• None of the child subjects demonstrated sexual intercourse
			• 44% of the children showed reticence or avoidance to the dolls
			• 71% of children touched male doll's genitals
			• 4% of children touched female doll's vaginal opening
			• 2% demonstrated clear sexual intercourse (penis inserted into vagina)
			• 3% demonstrated suggestive sexual intercourse (penis not inserted into vagina)
			• Three children showed some aggressive behaviors with the dolls (two boys, one girl)
				• Inspection of sexual body parts was common
				• None of child subjects exhibited explicit sexual activity with the dolls
				• Female and older children interacted most with dolls
				• Only 25% of play time spent with dolls - children found dolls no more interesting than other toys
				• <1% of behaviors considered aggressive

FACTORS	Everson and Boat (1990)	Gabriel (1985)	Glaser and Collins (1989)	Sivan et al. (1988)
Weaknesses	• Some statistics weak due to small cell sizes	• Small sample size • Developmental differences not identified • Types of inquiries made by observer are unkonwn	• Sample not representative of general population based on SES • Observations completed with adult present • Some children played in groups with dolls • Subjective behavior ratings • Developmental differences not identified	• Involved only middle class subjects • Significant differences were found in all but a few of the Chi-Square tests - possibly an artifact of the large number (7,302) of observations considered • Developmental differences not identified
Strengths	• Sample representative of general population of nonsexually abused children • Definitions of observation categories clear and concise • Overall good statistical analyses	• One of the first studies to collect normative data on this important behavior	• Good sample size • Interviewed parents within their own homes with both parents present in most cases • Study carried out in child's own familiar preschool or playground	• Pilot tested the observation categories

CHRONOLOGICAL AGE AND SEXUALLY EXPLICIT DOLL PLAY

Boat and Everson (1994) further analyzed their original normative data on nonsexually abused children's interactions with anatomical dolls. (Refer to Table 8.2 [pp. 196-197] for a description of this research.) Tables 8.3 through 8.5 present the research results from the second analysis by Boat and Everson (1994).

Table 8.3 (p. 198) and corresponding Graphs 8.1 to 8.4 (p. 217) present the percentage of 2- to 5-year-old males and females who demonstrated spontaneous undressing of the dolls. This table also presents the percentage of 2- to 5-year-old males and females who engaged in manual exploration of the doll's genitals, anus, and breasts.

A large number of presumably nonsexually abused toddler and preschool-age children spontaneously undressed the anatomical dolls when the dolls were presented to the child by the interviewer. The majority of toddlers and preschool-age children, when presented with the anatomical dolls, explored the doll's genitals, anus, and breasts. Furthermore, the younger the child, the more likely the child was to exhibit this exploratory behavior. When the children were left alone with the dolls, their manual exploration of the breasts and genitalia decreased. Boat and Everson (1994) suggested that this decrease may have occurred because the novelty of the dolls had worn off by the time the interviewer had left the room.

TABLE 8.3
Percent of Nonreferred Children by Age and
Gender Demonstrating Spontaneous Undressing of Dolls
and Manual Exploration of Genitals, Anus, and Breasts*

	AGE							
	2 years		**3 years**		**4 years**		**5 years**	
	Male (N = 28)	Female (N = 27)	Male (N = 24)	Female (N = 27)	Male (N = 26)	Female (N = 27)	Male (N = 28)	Female (N = 22)
Interviewer Present	All numbers in percentages							
Spontaneous Undressing	36	48	29	22	31	11	29	27
Exploration of Genitals and Anus**	86	85	79	70	65	63	43	55
Exploration of Breasts***	61	63	54	48	35	26	25	18

	2 years		**3 years**		**4 years**		**5 years**	
	Male (N = 0)	Female (N = 0)	Male (N = 17)	Female (N = 16)	Male (N = 20)	Female (N = 21)	Male (N = 23)	Female (N = 17)
Child Alone	All numbers in percentages							
Exploration of Genitals and Anus	—	—	18	31	40	52	35	47
Exploration of breasts	—	—	6	6	25	14	13	29

** Age effect $p < .001$.
*** Interviewer gender effect $p < .05$ and age effect $p < .001$.

---

*From "Exploration of Anatomical Dolls by Nonreferred Preschool-Aged Children: Comparisons by Age, Gender, Race and Socioeconomic Status," by B. W. Boat and M. D. Everson, 1994, *Child Abuse & Neglect, 18*(2), p. 145. Reprinted with kind permission from Elsevier Service Ltd., The Boulevard, Langford Lane, Kidlington OX5 1GB, United Kingdom.

Table 8.4 (p. 199) and corresponding Graphs 8.5 to 8.20 (pp. 218-220) present the number of 2- to 5-year-old males and females who, while playing with the dolls, engaged one doll with another doll in sexualized behavior. Doll play was labeled "suggestive" intercourse when the positioning of the dolls mimicked intercourse but did not include insertion of the doll's penis into the vagina, mouth, or anus of the other doll, a verbal description of intercourse, or sexual movement between the dolls. Doll play was labeled "clear" intercourse when it included the preceding behaviors.

During a free play period, which was devoid of directions from the evaluator, 2-year-old children did not engage two dolls in symbolic sexual play, other than to have the dolls kiss each other. When the evaluator was present, several presumably nonsexually abused males and females in each of the 3-, 4-, and 5-year-old age groups showed suggestive vaginal intercourse between two dolls. The highest frequency of suggestive vaginal intercourse was found with 5-year-old males, 25% of whom engaged in such behavior when the interviewer was present.

TABLE 8.4
Percent of Nonsexually Abused Children by Age and Gender Demonstrating Doll-to-Doll Enactment of Sexualized Behavior*

	AGE							
	2 years		**3 years**		**4 years**		**5 years**	
	Male (N = 28)	Female (N = 27)	Male (N = 24)	Female (N = 27)	Male (N = 26)	Female (N = 27)	Male (N = 28)	Female (N = 22)
Interviewer Present	All numbers in percentages							
Kissing	11	11	8	11	15	11	36	23
Touching breasts	0	0	0	0	0	0	4	0
Touching genitals	0	0	4	0	4	0	0	0
Suggestive vaginal intercourse**	0	0	13	7	12	7	25	9
Suggestive oral intercourse***	0	0	0	0	4	0	7	0
Suggestive anal intercourse***	0	0	4	0	0	0	0	0
Clear vaginal intercourse	0	0	4	0	4	0	7	0
Clear oral intercourse	0	0	0	0	0	0	0	0
Clear anal intercourse	0	0	4	0	0	0	4	0

	2 years		**3 years**		**4 years**		**5 years**	
	Male —	Female —	Male (N = 17)	Female (N = 16)	Male (N = 20)	Female (N = 21)	Male (N = 23)	Female (N = 17)
Child Alone	All numbers in percentages							
Kissing***	—	—	6	6	5	19	13	12
Touching breasts	—	—	6	6	5	0	9	6
Touching genitals	—	—	0	0	10	5	0	12
Suggestive vaginal intercourse	—	—	4	0	0	5	9	6
Suggestive oral intercourse	—	—	0	0	0	5	0	0
Suggestive anal intercourse	—	—	0	0	0	0	0	0
Clear vaginal intercourse	—	—	0	0	5	5	4	12
Clear oral intercourse	—	—	0	0	5	5	0	0
Clear anal intercourse	—	—	0	0	0	5	0	0

** Age effect when suggestive vaginal, oral, and anal intercourse combined, $p < .01$.
*** Age effect $p < .01$.

*From "Exploration of Anatomical Dolls by Nonreferred Preschool-Aged Children: Comparisons by Age, Gender, Race, and Socioeconomic Status," by B. W. Boat and M. D. Everson, 1994, *Child Abuse & Neglect, 18*(2), p. 146. Reprinted with kind permission from Elsevier Service Ltd., The Boulevard, Langford Lane, Kidlington OX5 1GB, United Kingdom.

Additionally, when the evaluator was present, one or two males in each of the 3-, 4-, and 5-year-old age groups demonstrated clear vaginal intercourse. When the evaluator was not present, suggestive vaginal intercourse with the dolls decreased with males and females in each of the 3-, 4-, and 5-year-old age groups.

TABLE 8.5
Percent of Nonsexually Abused Children by
Age and Gender Demonstrating Child-to-Doll Enactments of
Sexualized Behavior by Age and Gender of Child*

	AGE							
	2 years		3 years		4 years		5 years	
	Male (N = 28)	Female (N = 27)	Male (N = 24)	Female (N = 27)	Male (N = 26)	Female (N = 27)	Male (N = 28)	Female (N = 22)
Interviewer Present	All numbers in percentages							
Kissing	7	7	0	4	0	0	7	0
Suggestive vaginal intercourse	0	0	0	0	0	0	4	0
Suggestive oral intercourse	0	0	0	0	0	0	0	0
Suggestive anal intercourse	0	0	0	0	0	0	0	0
Clear vaginal intercourse	0	0	0	0	0	0	0	0
Clear oral intercourse	0	0	0	0	0	0	4	0
Clear anal intercourse	0	0	0	0	0	0	0	0

	2 years		3 years		4 years		5 years	
	Male —	Female —	Male (N = 17)	Female (N = 16)	Male (N = 20)	Female (N = 21)	Male (N = 23)	Female (N = 17)
Child Alone	All numbers in percentages							
Kissing	—	—	0	6	5	0	9	0
Suggestive vaginal intercourse	—	—	0	0	0	0	0	0
Suggestive oral intercourse	—	—	0	0	0	0	0	0
Suggestive anal intercourse	—	—	0	0	0	0	0	0
Clear vaginal intercourse	—	—	0	0	0	0	4	0
Clear oral intercourse	—	—	6	0	0	5	4	0
Clear anal intercourse	—	—	0	0	0	0	0	0

*From "Exploration of Anatomical Dolls by Nonreferred Preschool-Aged Children: Comparisons by Age, Gender, Race and Socioeconomic Status," by B. W. Boat and M. D. Everson, 1994, *Child Abuse & Neglect, 18*(2), p. 147. Reprinted with kind permission from Elsevier Service Ltd., The Boulevard, Langford Lane, Kidlington OX5 1GB, United Kingdom.

Conversely, demonstrations with the dolls of clear vaginal intercourse increased for female 4- and 5-year-old children when the evaluator was not present, although these were very low frequency behaviors. Demonstrations of suggestive oral and anal intercourse or clear oral and anal intercourse were also very uncommon.

Table 8.5 (above) and corresponding Graphs 8.21 to 8.32 (pp. 221-222) present the percentage of 2- to 5-year-old males and females who, while playing with the dolls, engaged their own bodies with a doll in sexualized behavior.

These data in Table 8.5 (above), which are also displayed in graph form, indicate that presumably nonsexually abused children rarely use the anatomical dolls to engage themselves in sexual acts. During a free play period which was devoid of directions, 2-, 3-, and 4-year-old males and females did not use the dolls with their own bodies in suggestive or clear vaginal or anal intercourse positions with or without the evaluator present. However, one presumably nonsexually abused 5-year-old, low SES male used his mouth on the dolls in suggestive oral intercourse when the evaluator was present. When the evaluator was not present, two 3- and 5-year-old, low SES males and one 4-year-old female used their mouths on the dolls in clear oral intercourse, while one 5-year-old male placed his genitals to the doll and "humped" the doll.

These normative data indicate that suggestive intercourse positioning through the placement of doll to doll in the missionary position, without attempts at penile insertion, may be common play behavior with the dolls among preschool-age children ages 3 and older. Additionally, although not common, some nonsexually abused children demonstrate explicit sexual behaviors with the dolls.

The present normative data suggest that the anatomical details of the dolls may assist the evaluator in differentiating displays of physical affection and casual knowledge of sex from explicit knowledge of the mechanisms of sexual intercourse. However, Everson and Boat (1990) caution

> Because of the occurrence of such sexual knowledge in presumably non-sexually abused samples, explicit sexualized play with anatomical dolls, including enactment of apparent sexual intercourse, cannot be considered a definitive marker of sexual abuse in the absence of a clear verbal account of abuse by the child. (p. 741)

COMPARATIVE RESEARCH
ON CHILDREN'S USE
OF ANATOMICAL DOLLS

NONSEXUALLY ABUSED
VERSUS SEXUALLY ABUSED
CHILDREN'S BEHAVIOR
WITH ANATOMICAL DOLLS

The previously described normative data show that at least some presumably nonsexually abused children do demonstrate explicit knowledge of sex when playing with the dolls. As a result, researchers have attempted to examine the quantitative and qualitative differences in interactions with the dolls between sexually abused and nonsexually abused children. Table 8.6 (pp. 202-203) summarizes six studies, conducted since 1985, that compare the behavior of sexually abused and nonsexually abused children with anatomical dolls.

Research on the quantitative and qualitative behavior differences in the doll play of sexually abused and nonsexually abused children remains inconclusive. Cohn (1991) found no differences between these two groups in the demonstration

TABLE 8.6
Behavioral Differences Between Sexually Abused and Nonsexually Abused Children With Anatomical Dolls

FACTORS	August and Forman (1989)	Cohn (1991)	Jampole and Weber (1987)	Kenyon-Jump, Burnette, and Robertson (1991)	McIver, Wakefield, and Underwager (1989)	White et al. (1986)
Subjects	• 16 females - suspected of sexual victimization • 16 females - presumably nonsexually abused • Ages 5 years to 8 years	• 35 children (12 males and 23 females) referred for assessment of sexual abuse • 35 matched children presumably nonsexually abused • Ages 2 years to 6 years	• 10 children (2 males and 8 females) sexually abused • 10 matched children presumably nonsexually abused • Ages 3 years to 8 years	• 9 children (5 males and 4 females) sexually abused • 9 matched children presumably nonsexually abused • Ages 3 years to 5 years	• 10 children (2 males and 8 females) sexually abused – ages 3 years to 5 years • 50 children (22 males and 28 females) presumably non-sexually abused – ages 2½ years to 7 years	• 25 children (12 males and 13 females) referred for sexual abuse evaluation • 25 children (9 males and 16 females) presumably non-sexually abused • Ages 2 years to 5¼ years
Procedure	• Subjects were observed interacting with the dolls after being directed to change the dolls' clothes, child alone (5 minutes) • Directed storytelling about dolls, adult present (3 minutes)	• Child instructed to play with any toy in the playroom (3 minutes) • Focused play with dolls, adult present (5 minutes) • Free play with dolls, adult present (3 minutes) • Free play with dolls, child alone (3 minutes)	• Free play with any toy or doll in playroom, adult present (10 minutes) • Free play with dolls after child informed dolls had genitals, adult present (10 minutes) • Body parts interview • Free play with dolls, child alone (15 minutes) • Free play, adult present (remainder of hour)	• Free play with dolls, adult present (10 minutes) • Free play with dolls after child informed dolls had genitals, adult present (10 minutes) • Body parts interview • Free play with dolls, child alone (10 minutes)	• Structured interview with adult present (ranged from 8 to 46 minutes) • 22 children interviewed in an office while 38 were interviewed in their homes	• 7 dolls were presented to each subject (2 adult males, 1 adult female, and 4 children) • Free play for rapport building (10 minutes) • Structured doll interview, adult present
Findings	• Children suspected of sexual victimization showed more avoidance than did the nonreferred children when interacting with dolls in the presence of an adult • Children suspected of sexual victimization made more genital references with the dolls than did the nonreferred children when left alone with the dolls • Children suspected of sexual victimization showed more aggression than the nonreferred children when left alone with the dolls	• Children suspected of sexual victimization versus nonreferred children did not differ in their frequency of sexually explicit behavior • 5% of the children suspected of sexual victimization inserted fingers into doll's genitals • 5% of nonreferred children inserted their fingers into doll's genitals • No difference between children suspected of sexual abuse and nonreferred children in general discomfort, aggressive behavior, curiosity, and humor in reaction to dolls • Aggressive behavior with the dolls was a low frequency behavior for both groups	• 90% of sexually abused children demonstrated sexually explicit behavior with the dolls • 20% of the nonsexually abused children demonstrated sexually explicit behavior with the dolls • Finger penetration not considered a sexual behavior	• No difference between sexually abused and non-sexually abused children in manual exploration of dolls • No significant difference between groups in display of explicit sexual behaviors (vaginal, oral, and anal intercourse with thrusting motions between doll to doll or child to doll and masturbation by the child) • Significant difference found between groups when explicit behaviors combined with suspicious behaviors (putting hands between legs, touching own genitals, kissing the breasts of a doll, and straddling a clothed doll)	• 50% sexually abused children displayed sexual behavior or aggressive behavior • 62% nonsexually abused children displayed sexual behavior or aggressive behavior	• The majority of children suspected of sexual victimization were categorized in low to medium suspicion category versus majority of nonsexually abused children were categorized in the low suspicion category • Children suspected of sexual victimization versus nonsexually abused children showed more unusual behaviors during the doll interview relative to sexualized doll play and the description of sexual abuse situations

Weaknesses	• Small sample size • No validation of diagnostic categories (i.e., abused versus nonsexually abused categories (i.e., abused versus nonsexually abused children were categorized based on their referral or lack of referral for formal investigation by state authorities) • The raters not blind • Male subjects not included • Developmental and gender differences not taken into account • Definition of sexualized behavior included giggling at doll's genitals and playing with the doll's underwear	• Small sample size • No validation of diagnostic categories (i.e., abused versus nonsexually abused) children were categorized as sexually abused based on an assessment of sexual abuse) • 12 children suspected of sexual abuse versus 3 nonreferred children previously exposed to dolls • Majority of children suspected of sexual abuse - low SES • Majority of children nonreferred - middle SES • Developmental and gender differences not taken into account • Study design only left the children alone with dolls for a period of 3 minutes	• Small sample size • No validation of diagnostic categories (i.e., abused versus nonsexually abused) • Sexually abused children previously interviewed by state authorities • Sexually abused children previously had been or were in the care of the State versus one-half of the control group children from intact families • Developmental and gender differences not taken into account • The length of session may have impacted children's play with dolls (many tired after ½ hour) • Very broad units of analysis	• Small sample size • No validation of diagnostic categories (i.e., abused versus nonsexually abused) • Two subjects in the sexually abused group were unsubstantiated victims but suspected to have been abused • Some children actively participating in therapy • The length of the session may have impacted children's play with the dolls • Developmental and gender differences not taken into account	• Small sample size • No validation of diagnostic categories (i.e., abused versus nonsexually abused) • Sample sizes of sexually abused children versus nonsexually abused children skewed • Sexually abused children and nonsexually abused children not matched • Developmental and gender differences not taken into account • Categories of sexual behavior and aggressive behavior not well defined or differentiated • Observers not blind • Not published in a peer review journal	• No validation of diagnostic categories (i.e., abused versus nonsexually abused) • Majority of sexually abused children from nonintact families versus majority nonsexually abused children from intact families • Groups not matched on parental marital status, race, or gender distribution • Children were not observed in play with the dolls without the interviewer present • Categories of sexualized doll play and unusual behaviors relative to descriptions of sexual abuse situations were not clearly defined • Developmental and gender differences not taken into account
Strengths	• Groups matched on age and race • Behavior checklist to observe play was designed; reliability of behavior scale good • Clear definition of categories • Children not previously interviewed by authorities	• Rater blind to status of subjects • Groups matched on age, sex, and race • Large sample size • Good research design	• Rater blind to status of subjects • Groups matched on age, sex, and race • Narrow definition of sexualized behavior (finger penetration not considered a sexual behavior)	• Observers blind to status of subjects • Groups matched on status: intact versus nonintact family socioeconomic status, age, gender, and race • Clear definitions: oral-genital contact, anal-genital contact, clearly expressed intercourse defined as explicit sexual behavior	• Researchers raise the questions: - whether children identify with the dolls as family members - the role of directive interviewing on children's reactions	• The raters were blind to the status of the subjects • Children not previously interviewed by authorities • More dolls available to differentiate between those individuals in the child's life and the perpetrator

of sexually explicit play behaviors with the dolls. An equal percentage of children from both groups inserted their fingers into the dolls' vaginal and anal openings. Additionally, aggressiveness with the dolls was found to be a low-frequency behavior for both groups. Among other problems, a critical flaw in this study was the method used to identify subjects as sexually abused.

In a study conducted by McIver et al. (1989), both sexually abused and nonsexually abused subjects showed sexual behaviors with anatomical dolls. However, in contrast to Cohn's (1991) findings, McIver and his colleagues found aggressive doll play to be a fairly frequent behavior demonstrated by both groups of children. Problems with the design of this study were numerous and, consequently, the results must be considered with caution. This study was not published in a peer review journal. This suggests that the research design and methodology were not rigorous.

Kenyon-Jump et al. (1991) also collected data that showed preschool children identified as sexually abused did not display a greater number of explicit sexual behaviors with anatomical dolls than did a matched control group. However, when individual cases were analyzed, differences were noted. Reportedly, one of the suspected sexually abused male preschool-aged subjects removed his pants and underwear and demonstrated genital-to-genital intercourse between himself and a doll on four separate occasions. Although two children in the nonsexually abused group placed a male and female doll on top of one another and pushed or rubbed the dolls together, they did not insert the penis into the vagina. The researchers speculated that penetration appeared to be a critical factor for differentiating sexually explicit doll play of sexually abused and nonsexually abused children. However, this conclusion is not supported by the Boat and Everson (1994) research. Rather, Boat and Everson (1994) speculate that knowledge based on visual exposure to explicit sexual behavior may also account for explicit demonstration of intercourse.

In contrast to the preceding studies, White et al. (1986) found significant differences in the doll play of sexually abused children and nonsexually abused children. Sexually abused children showed greater interest in the dolls' anatomical parts and also demonstrated sexual acts with the dolls. White and her colleagues found that nonsexually abused children showed no unusual sex play with the dolls. Wolfner, Faust, and Dawes (1993) noted that the White et al. study suffered from methodological problems which confound the results.

Jampole and Weber (1987) also found that sexually abused children engaged anatomical dolls in sexual activity more frequently than did nonsexually abused children. However, while 90% of the sexually abused children engaged the dolls in sexual activity, 20% of the nonsexually abused children also did so.

August and Forman (1989), using slightly older subjects of 5 to 8 years old, examined differences in aggressive behavior, avoidant behavior, and genital reference. Sexually abused children showed more aggressive behavior with the dolls and made more genital references when the interviewer was not present. Genital references were defined as pointing at or touching genital areas or breasts, giggling while looking at genitals or breasts, and removing, looking, or playing with doll's undergarments. Sexually abused children were more avoidant of the dolls when asked to tell a story in the presence of the interviewer. A problem with this study was the researchers' exceptionally broad definition of sexualized behavior, which included giggling at the doll's genitals and playing with the doll's underwear. Based on the empirically derived normative data collected on nonsexually abused children's doll play, it is questionable to include in a definition of sexualized behavior children's touching or giggling when looking at dolls' genitals or breasts. Furthermore, whether removing, looking, or playing with the doll's underwear is sexualized behavior when the children, as part of the study procedure, were instructed to change the doll's clothing is debatable.

METHODOLOGICAL
PROBLEMS WITH THE
COMPARATIVE RESEARCH

One problem with these comparative studies is the confounding factor of observers' knowledge of the status of the children (i.e., sexually abused or nonsexually abused), a condition that may have influenced their observations. A second confounding factor was the method used to identify subjects as sexually abused or nonsexually abused. For example, in some studies, children assigned to the sexually abused category were only "suspected" of being sexually abused and may not have been sexual abuse victims. Additionally, a number of children in the nonsexually abused group were identified as nonvictims because they had never been referred for a sexual abuse evaluation.

The differences in definitions regarding what constitutes sexually explicit behaviors with the dolls also makes comparisons between studies difficult. Kenyon-Jump et al. (1991) defined explicit sexual behaviors as vaginal, oral, and anal intercourse with thrusting motions between doll to doll or child to doll. Conversely, August and Forman (1989) defined sexualized behaviors as including giggling when viewing the dolls' genitals and playing with the dolls' underwear.

In Jampole and Weber's (1987) study, finger penetration was excluded as a sexually explicit behavior, while in the Cohn (1991) study, finger penetration was included.

Currently, the data do not support a conclusion that the doll play of sexually abused and nonsexually abused groups can accurately differentiate these groups. One problem is that the differential sexualized doll play may be reflecting background variables. As demonstrated by Boat and Everson's (1994) research with nonsexually abused children, low SES males were more likely to exhibit suggestive and clear vaginal intercourse than females or higher SES males.

PROFESSIONAL ACCURACY
IN CLASSIFYING CHILDREN
BASED ON DOLL PLAY

Wolfner et al. (1993) identify two distinct questions when studying children's play with the anatomical dolls: (a) Do sexually abused and nonsexually abused children respond differently to anatomical dolls?, and (b) Can mental health clinicians accurately discriminate between such children based on children's anatomical doll play?

Realmuto, Jensen, and Wescoe (1990) addressed the accuracy of clinicians' identification of sexually abused and nonsexually abused children when anatomical dolls were used. In their study, a child psychiatrist conducted blind interviews with six sexually abused children and nine nonsexually abused children. The nine nonsexually abused subjects consisted of five subjects who were not being provided any mental health services and four subjects who were being provided mental health counseling. The interviewer followed a standardized protocol (i.e., identical procedure) for all subjects. Accurate classification of the children as sexually abused and nonsexually abused was 53%; this overall accuracy rate did not surpass chance expectations. Wolfner et al. (1993) concluded

> We are left with the conclusion that there is simply no scientific evidence available that would justify clinical or forensic diagnosis of abuse on the basis of doll play. The common counter is that such play is "just one component" in reaching a diagnosis based on a "full clinical picture." Anatomically Detailed Doll play cannot be validly used as a component, however, unless it provides incremental validity (validity that adds to the predictive accuracy of existing methods), and there is virtually no evidence that it does. (p. 9)

In response to the conclusions cited by Wolfner et al. (1993), Everson (1994) argues that the question of whether mental health clinicians accurately discriminate between sexually abused and nonsexually abused children, based on their doll play, incorrectly assumes that the major use of anatomical dolls is as a "diagnostic test." Rather, current accepted practice in conducting evaluations of child sexual abuse allegations is to avoid using the dolls as a "test" because these tools lack psychometric properties required of test instruments.

GUIDELINES FOR DOLL USE

Unlike Wolfner et al. (1993), Everson and Boat (1994) argue that a blanket condemnation of the use of anatomical dolls in child sexual abuse evaluations is unjustified. Rather, they propose that the skills of the individual interviewer must be considered. Additionally, decisions for using anatomical dolls must be based on the relevancy of the specific functional use of the dolls within the context of the particular evaluation.

FUNCTIONAL USES FOR
ANATOMICAL DOLLS

In an effort to develop a comprehensive list of the possible relevant functions of anatomical dolls, Everson, Boat, and Sanfilippo (1993) analyzed 20 anatomical doll guidelines and protocols. They identified seven relatively distinct uses of anatomical dolls for sexual abuse evaluations that were consistently proposed by clinicians and researchers. The seven identified functions for the dolls have been titled

1. Comforter
2. Icebreaker
3. Anatomical Model
4. Demonstration Aid
5. Memory Stimulus
6. Diagnostic Screen
7. Diagnostic Test

The American Professional Society on the Abuse of Children (APSAC; 1995) has incorporated five of these seven functional uses within their guidelines on the use of anatomical dolls. The use of the doll as a "Comforter" was a category dropped for use by APSAC. The use of the dolls as a diagnostic test is not appropriate under any circumstances and therefore was not included in the APSAC guidelines. The functional use of the dolls and the need for a protocol related to use of anatomical dolls are described in Table 8.7 (p. 208). The use of the dolls as a diagnostic test is also addressed in this table.

THE RELATIONSHIPS
BETWEEN FUNCTIONAL USE
AND THE NEED FOR A
STANDARDIZED DOLL PROTOCOL

While the development of a standard protocol for interviewing children with the dolls has been attempted by several researchers (Boat & Everson, 1986; Friedemann & Morgan, 1985; White et al., 1987), a standardized procedure has not been universally adopted.

Everson and Boat (1994) suggest that the importance of a protocol is directly related to the functional use of the dolls during an evaluation. Table 8.7 (p. 208) lists the heuristic rating that Everson and Boat assigned to the doll's various uses. As the table shows, a standard protocol is unnecessary if the dolls are to be utilized as a Comforter or an Icebreaker since the purpose of these functions is not to collect assessment data. Conversely, a standard protocol is indicated with the Ana-

TABLE 8.7
Functional Uses for Anatomical Dolls*

FUNCTIONAL USE	DEFINING CHARACTERISTIC	EXAMPLE	NEED FOR PROTOCOL
Icebreaker The dolls can serve as a conversation starter and convey permission for the child to talk about sexual material.	• Dolls are used to first introduce the topic of sexual body parts. • Typically, interviewer makes a specific reference about the sexual body parts of the dolls or provides an opportunity for the doll(s) to be undressed, exposing the sexual body parts.	"Under their clothes, these dolls have all their body parts, just like you and me. They even have private parts."	None
Anatomical Model The dolls serve as anatomical model for assessment of the child's sexual knowledge, understanding of bodily functions, and knowledge of the mechanisms of sexual intercourse.	• Dolls are undressed by evaluator and child or presented undressed. • Evaluator uses the doll(s) as a visual aid in asking the child direct questions about body parts, body functions, and sexual knowledge.	"What is this part called?"	Minimal
Demonstration Aid The dolls serve as tools which enable the child to "show" rather than to "tell" what happened. The dolls are used to clarify the child's statement after a verbal disclosure has been made.	• The child's experience and not his or her knowledge of body functions is the focus. • Evaluator directs the child to use the dolls to reenact what the child has observed or experienced.	"You told me that Daddy makes you rub his bottom; show me how you rubbed Daddy's bottom."	Moderate
Memory Stimulus/(overlapping functions) Diagnostic Screen The dolls may act as a memory stimulus in that they may trigger the child's recall of specific events of a sexual nature.	• Evaluator provides an opportunity for the child to explore freely and manipulate the dolls while the evaluator observes the child's play, reaction, and remarks.	Child mouths doll's penis in the course of play: "I wonder where you learned how to do that."	Minimal
_ _ _ _ _ _ _ _ _ _ _ _ _ _ _ _ _ Dolls may be used to screen for precocious sexual interest or atypical developmental knowledge.	_ _ _ _ _ _ _ _ _ _ _ _ _ _ _ _ _ • Explicit sexual behavior, unusual emotional responses, and suspicious statements by the child are noted and used to guide the focus of the interview, through follow-up questions to the child.	_ _ _ _ _ _ _ _ _ _ _ _ _ _ _ _ _	_ _ _ _ _ _ _ _ _ _ _ _ _ _ Minimal
Diagnostic Test Sexually abused children interact and play with the dolls in significantly different ways from nonsexually abused children. (*Note* - no empirical proof.)	• Explicit sexual behavior with the dolls is used to diagnose sexual abuse. (*Note* - no general acceptance in the scientific community.)	• Child inserts penis of male doll into vagina of female doll. (*Note* - normative data do not suggest that behavior can be used to diagnose sexual abuse.)	Diagnostic test cannot be used

*Adapted from *Functional Uses of Anatomical Dolls in Sexual Abuse Evaluations*, by M. D. Everson, B. W. Boat, and M. Sanfilippo, 1993, unpublished paper presented at the American Professional Society of the Abuse of Children San Diego Conference on Responding to Child Maltreatment, San Diego, CA. Also adapted from "Putting the Anatomical Doll Controversy in Perspective: An Explanation of the Major Uses and Criticisms of the Dolls in Child Sexual Abuse Evaluations," by M. D. Everson and B. W. Boat, 1994, *Child Abuse & Neglect*, 18(2), pp. 113-129. The latter reprinted with kind permission from Elsevier Science Ltd., The Boulevard, Langford Lane, Kidlington OX5 1GB, United Kingdom.

tomical Model when using the dolls in gathering data on a child's labels for body parts, understanding of bodily functions, and knowledge of sexual behavior. Everson and Boat (1994) further suggest that a standard protocol for using the dolls as a Demonstration Aid, as a Memory Stimulus, or for screening purposes is not imperative but might be useful in discouraging the use of leading questions.

THE RELATIONSHIP BETWEEN
FUNCTIONAL DOLL USE
AND RISK OF EVALUATOR ERROR

Related to the utilization of anatomical dolls during an evaluation, Everson and Boat (1994) also address children's susceptibility to suggestions and risk of interviewer error. Table 8.8 presents heuristic ratings of risk related to doll use based on Everson and Boat's assessment.

The research does not support the argument that the dolls are highly suggestive to sexually naïve, nonsexually abused children. Rather than creating sexual thoughts in naïve children, the dolls have been found to assess the extent of sexual knowledge in sexually knowledgeable children. Everson and Boat (1994) argue that anatomical dolls should be used in assessments for their stimulus value in that they "stimulate, disinhibit, and provide an easy vehicle" for children to reveal their sexual knowledge (p. 120).

Interviewer error may be the greatest risk in anatomical doll use. The primary concern regarding interviewer error is the possibility of presenting overly suggestive or leading questions when utilizing the dolls. However, Everson and Boat (1994) suggest that the use of the anatomical dolls may prevent as many errors as

TABLE 8.8 Risk Factors Related to Anatomical Doll Use*		
FUNCTIONAL USE	**SUSCEPTIBILITY FOR CHILD'S SUGGESTIVENESS**	**SUSCEPTIBILITY FOR INTERVIEWER ERROR**
Comforter	Low	Minimal
Icebreaker	Low	Minimal
Anatomical Model	Low	Low
Demonstration Aid	Low to Moderate	Moderate
Memory Stimulus	Moderate	Low
Diagnostic Screen	Moderate to High	Moderate
Diagnostic Test	Very High	High

*From "Exploration of Anatomical Dolls by Nonreferred Preschool-Aged Children: Comparisons by Age, Gender, Race and Socioeconomic Status," by B. W. Boat and M. D. Everson, 1994, *Child Abuse & Neglect, 18*(2), p. 119. Reprinted with kind permission from Elsevier Service Ltd., The Boulevard, Langford Lane, Kidlington OX5 1GB, United Kingdom.

the dolls promote. They argue that the dolls may help to reduce the level of leading and suggestive questioning by providing structure to the interview and providing a nonverbal method for clarification of the child's verbal statements.

DEVELOPMENTAL FACTORS AND SYMBOLIC REPRESENTATIONAL MATERIALS

As the debate regarding the discriminating value or contaminating potential of the dolls continues, anatomical dolls are used with the basic premise that children can and will easily identify with the doll and treat it as a representation of themselves. A number of clinicians propose that the dolls are especially helpful to young children, enabling them to reenact through a medium what they are unable to describe with words. Kendall-Tackett and Watson (1992) found that over 90% of surveyed professionals thought the dolls were helpful with children ages 3 to 5½ years old, and over 80% of the professionals thought that dolls were helpful with children ages 6 to 9 years old.

It is widely believed that very young children with limited verbal abilities are the most appropriate candidates for utilization of anatomical dolls as an interview tool. However, findings from several studies indicate that representational materials, such as the dolls, do not facilitate toddler and younger preschool-age children's attempts to narrate their experiences. For example, research conducted by DeLoache (1987) indicates that 2- and 3-year-old children fail at tasks that require understanding of symbolic representations.

DeLoache and Marzolf (1993), with a sample of 72 children, compared 2-, 3-, and 4-year-old children's ability to use anatomical dolls as a symbolic representation of themselves. All of the children reported less information using the dolls than they did through statements or gestures to their own bodies. The children never spontaneously used the dolls in response to the interviewer's questions, even to support or elaborate their verbal disclosures. The children only used the dolls at the request of the interviewer and the children were not very competent at using the dolls, even when prompted to do so. Additionally, Goodman and Aman (1990) compared 3- and 5-year-old children's memory performance with and without anatomical and nonanatomical dolls. While results suggested that the dolls facilitated reports for the 5-year-old children, the facilitative effect was not present for the 3-year-old children.

DeLoache (1993) proposed that when an object, such as a doll, is used as a representational object, the child must deal with the dual nature of the object: the doll as a salient object and the doll as a symbol that represents something other than itself. Because young children's attention and interest are directed to properties of the object itself, DeLoache postulated that it may be difficult for young children to view it as a representation of themselves.

Gordon et al. (1993) found some support for the assumption that very young children may benefit when anatomical dolls are used as symbolic representations of themselves. These researchers compared the memory performance of 3- and 5-year-old children who were interviewed after a routine physical examination with and without anatomical dolls. Data showed that use of the dolls provided no facilitative benefit to memory performance for the 3-year-old children although there was a slight facilitative benefit to memory performance for the 5-year-old children. However, 3-year-old children were more resistant to misleading questions when interviewed with the anatomical dolls. Gordon and his colleagues (1993) suggest that the anatomical dolls may facilitate the quality (accuracy) of the report, if not the quantity of details.

In contrast to the previous findings, Bruck, Ceci, Francoeur, and Renick (1995) found that use of the anatomical dolls with 3 year olds appeared to elicit errors of commission rather than provide a facilitative benefit to accurate memory performance. Immediately following a medical exam, thirty-five 3-year-old girls who were examined vaginally and thirty-five 3-year-old girls who were not examined vaginally were asked to describe where the doctor touched them. During the verbal inverview, the majority of the girls who were not touched vaginally correctly refrained from stating they were touched on their genitals. However, following this free narrative, when the children were presented anatomical dolls and asked to describe where the doctor touched them, 60% of these nonvaginally examined children indicated genital insertions and other incorrect acts. Bruck, Ceci, Francoeur, and Renick (1995) speculate that the use of the dolls may actually reduce the validity of reports with 3-year-old children.

CONCLUSION

Interview tools utilized in child sexual abuse evaluations need to be used judiciously and cautiously. Research has not proven the mnemonic value of various props such as anatomical dolls. Furthermore, the effect of presenting children with irrelevant props is unknown.

Research does not support the claim that anatomical dolls cause children to fantasize about adult sexual experiences or to act out sexually with the dolls. However, some sexually abused and nonsexually abused children do exhibit explicit sexual behaviors when interacting with the dolls. Rather than fantasy, these behaviors appear to be representations of the children's physical involvement or visual exposure to adult sexual acts.

Some clinicians postulate that if a child actively avoids the anatomical dolls, shows distress if the dolls are undressed, shows unusual preoccupation with the dolls' genitalia, or positions the dolls on top of each other, the child has been sexually abused. However, research does not support this presumption. Preliminary normative data indicate that it is not uncommon for nonsexually abused preschool-age children to play with the dolls' genitalia and to place the dolls in suggestive sexual positions.

Everson and Boat (1994) suggest that clinicians who use anatomical dolls for purposes of assessment have been inappropriately influenced by traditional psychodynamic play therapy approaches. They suggest that while the child's play with nonanatomical dolls can be used to make inferences about whether a child perceives his or her father as harsh and rejecting, the child's play with anatomical dolls must be used with great caution in making inferences about whether a child has been sexually abused by his or her father. Steward et al. (1993) maintain that the appropriate controlled use of props as tools to help the child describe the who, what, and where of an event is in sharp distinction to the use of these props in therapeutic play where they may be used to express feelings and fantasies.

Normative and comparative research, focused on nonsexually abused and sexually abused children's anatomical doll play, has produced inconsistent findings. Comparison of these studies is difficult due to methodological problems, including lack of validation of sexually abused and nonsexually abused subjects and incomparability of groups on factors, such as SES and living situation. Thus, the differences in sexualized behavior found between "sexually abused" and "nonsexually abused" children in these studies may reflect nothing more than the background variables and types of behaviors that led to the initial referral and suspected abuse (Ceci & Bruck, 1993).

While some of the variability in the findings may be attributed to the methodological differences between studies (e.g., differences in age groups studied, demographic characteristics of the children, and procedures used), this does not fully account for the divergent findings. Ceci and Bruck (1993) propose that a problem that has been overlooked when analyzing the findings from the anatomical doll studies involves the confounding factor of previous exposure to the dolls. Ceci and his colleague bring attention to previous exposure problems, noting that within the experimental studies, some children who were identified as sexually abused were repeatedly exposed to the anatomical dolls prior to the child's participation in the research study. Additionally, identified victims in these studies may have been questioned by parents about a number of sexual themes prior to their participation in the studies. The nonsexually abused children most likely were not subjected to previous experiences with the anatomical dolls nor were they previously questioned by parents or interviewers about sexual abuse. Therefore, findings that sexually abused children exhibit higher levels of explicit sexual activity with the dolls when compared to nonsexually abused children may reflect the sexually abused children's prior questioning and experience with the dolls rather than the effects of sexual abuse.

One large normative study conducted by Everson and Boat (1990), while not flawless, appears to have controlled for many of the methodological problems found in other studies and, thus, offers the best preliminary normative data on nonsexually abused children's play with anatomical dolls. Manipulation of the dolls' genitals was found to be common behavior among toddler, preschool, and young elementary school-aged, nonsexually abused children. The normative data from this research also showed that some nonsexually abused children engaged in explicit sexual positioning of the dolls; however, it was a low-frequency behavior. Additionally, a few presumably nonsexually abused children were found to engage themselves with the dolls in explicit sexual acts.

Boat and Everson (1993) note their concern regarding the ongoing debate on whether sexually abused and nonsexually abused children interact differently with anatomical dolls in a manner that is "diagnostically" significant. They report "this line of questioning is problematic because it is often based on the naïve conceptualization of the dolls as a diagnostic test" (p. 63).

Little is known about the effects of interview procedures with the dolls on children's responses to the dolls (e.g., how and when the dolls are presented to the child). The impact on children's responses of previous questioning about sexual acts or previous doll presentation also is unknown. For ethical reasons, it is impossible for research to recreate the repeated questioning to which a child may be subjected in an actual child sexual abuse investigation. Thus, some of these problems may never be fully addressed.

The American Professional Society on the Abuse of Children (1990) cautions that when utilizing the anatomical dolls to evaluate child sexual abuse allegations, it is essential that the evaluator fully document and describe in detail his or her use of the dolls. Recently, the American Professional Society on the Abuse of Children (1995) published Practice Guidelines for the use of anatomical dolls in child sexual abuse assessments. The guidelines are offered to encourage appropriate use of the dolls but are not intended to establish a legal standard of care.

Ceci and Bruck (1993) warn, "Until such time that research is available, the dolls ought to be used with great caution" (p. 425). Wolfner et al. (1993) strongly advise against any use of anatomical dolls for assessment purposes. Based on the absence of accurate base rates of behavior, Wolfner and his colleagues argue that the use of the dolls cannot be justified.

At the present time, there is no known behavior demonstrated with the dolls by children that is a definitive marker of sexual abuse. In the absence of other evidence, under no circumstances can a child's play with dolls be used to identify a child as sexually abused, no matter how sexually explicit the play. If used judiciously, anatomical dolls may be useful for their stimulus value in providing a vehicle for children to report their sexual knowledge or as a prop to assist them in demonstrating the sexual experiences they have verbally reported to the evaluator. However, preliminary research suggests that anatomical dolls should not be used by young preschool-age children as a demonstration aid.

GUIDELINES
Considerations and Cautions

- When props or other retrieval techniques are used during interviews with children, interviewers should be aware that, in some cases, these retrieval techniques may reduce the accuracy of children's reports.
- The effect of props on the accuracy of children's disclosed information appears to depend on the type of cues and props utilized, the way they are presented, and how the children are instructed to use them.
- Empirical data do not confirm that anatomical dolls elicit fantasizing or sexual acting out in children. The problem is not with the child's behavior elicited by the doll stimulus but rather with the interviewer's interpretation of the child/doll behaviors.
- The limitations on the use of the dolls should be considered - the dolls are an interview tool and not a test for sexual abuse.
- The developmental level of the child should be considered prior to using the dolls.
- Children 3 and younger may not be able to utilize the dolls as a symbolic representation of themselves or the alleged perpetrator.
- Anatomical dolls used with very young children (3 years and under) may increase reports of sexual interactions that did not occur and, thus, reduce the validity of these young children's reports.
- The functional use of the doll should be considered prior to presenting the doll to the child.
- The dolls should not be presented to the child as a demonstration aid before the child makes a verbal statement to the interviewer regarding sexual victimization.
- Dolls should be presented only once over the course of several interview sessions.
- When the dolls are used in an interview, a description of how and why the dolls were utilized and the procedures used with the child should be recorded.
- Evaluators cannot assign a causal link to sexually explicit behavior demonstrated by the child with the anatomical dolls, no matter how sexually explicit the behaviors, unless other incremental evidence substantiates the link.
- The dolls should never be utilized as a projective measure to "diagnose" sexual abuse from the child's doll play.

Graphs Representing
Data on the Use
Of Anatomical Dolls

Graphs 8.1 to 8.4 Representing Data
From Table 8.3 *(Child-to-Doll)*

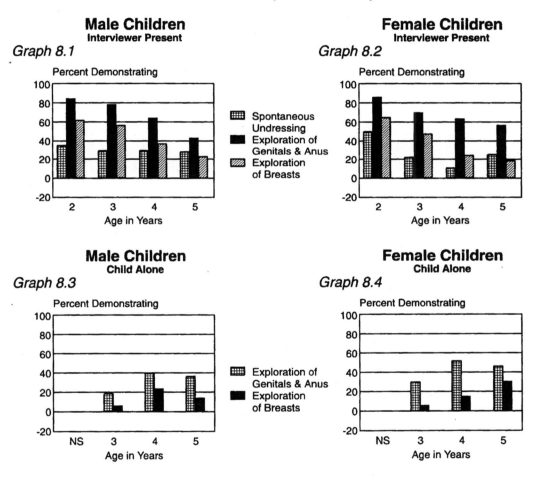

Graphs 8.5 to 8.10 Representing Data
From Table 8.4 *(Doll-to-Doll)*

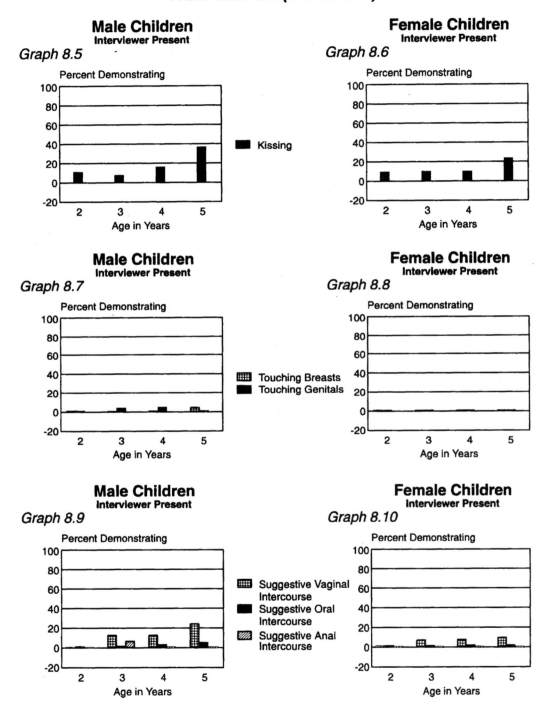

Graphs 8.11 to 8.16 Representing Data
From Table 8.4 *(Doll-to-Doll)*

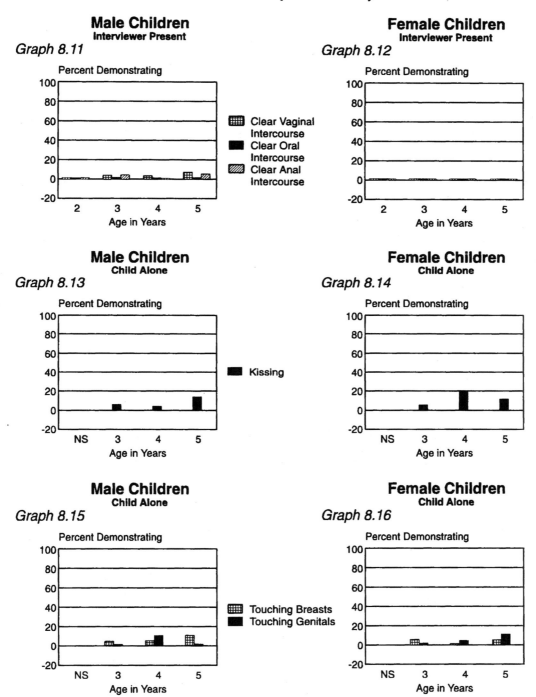

Male Children
Interviewer Present

Graph 8.11

Percent Demonstrating

Clear Vaginal Intercourse
Clear Oral Intercourse
Clear Anal Intercourse

Age in Years

Female Children
Interviewer Present

Graph 8.12

Percent Demonstrating

Age in Years

Male Children
Child Alone

Graph 8.13

Percent Demonstrating

Kissing

Age in Years

Female Children
Child Alone

Graph 8.14

Percent Demonstrating

Age in Years

Male Children
Child Alone

Graph 8.15

Percent Demonstrating

Touching Breasts
Touching Genitals

Age in Years

Female Children
Child Alone

Graph 8.16

Percent Demonstrating

Age in Years

Graphs 8.17 to 8.20 Representing Data From Table 8.4 *(Doll-to-Doll)*

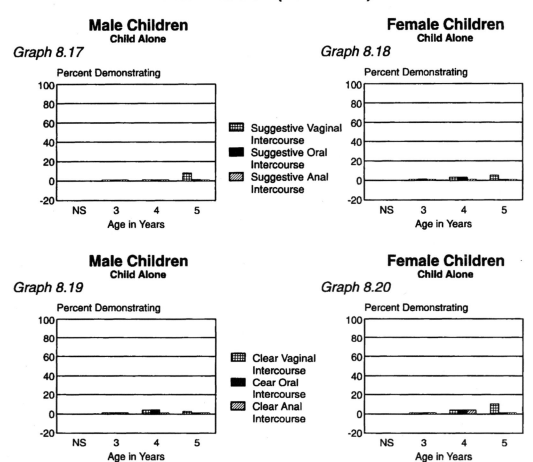

Male Children
Child Alone

Graph 8.17

Female Children
Child Alone

Graph 8.18

Percent Demonstrating
100
80
60
40
20
0
-20
NS
3
4
5
Age in Years
Suggestive Vaginal Intercourse
Suggestive Oral Intercourse
Suggestive Anal Intercourse
Percent Demonstrating
100
80
60
40
20
0
-20
NS
3
4
5
Age in Years

Male Children
Child Alone

Graph 8.19

Female Children
Child Alone

Graph 8.20

Percent Demonstrating
100
80
60
40
20
0
-20
NS
3
4
5
Age in Years
Clear Vaginal Intercourse
Cear Oral Intercourse
Clear Anal Intercourse
Percent Demonstrating
100
80
60
40
20
0
-20
NS
3
4
5
Age in Years

Graphs 8.21 to 8.26 Representing Data
From Table 8.5 *(Child-to-Doll)*

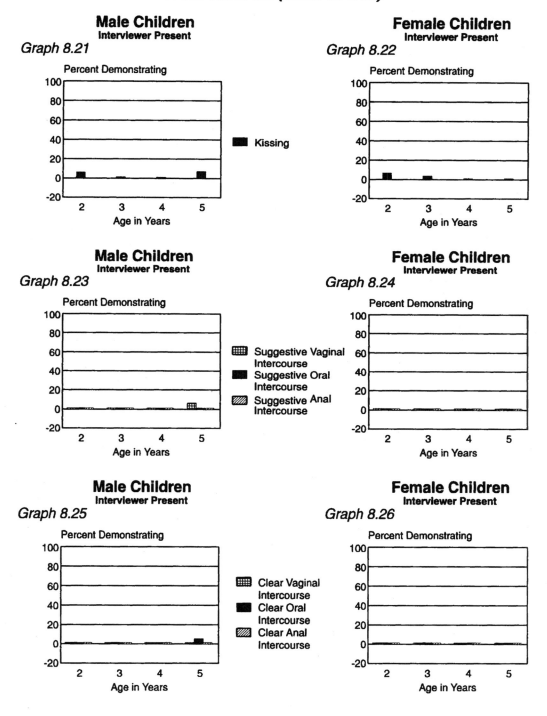

Graphs 8.27 to 8.32 Representing Data
From Table 8.5 *(Child-to-Doll)*

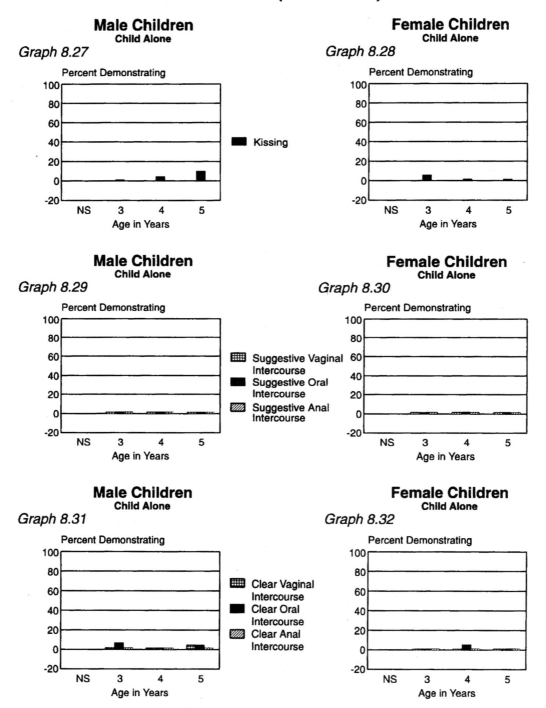

CHAPTER 9

The Use of Standardized Observation Systems, Behavior Rating Scales, and Projective Techniques in the Evaluation of Child Sexual Abuse

This chapter reviews a number of assessment devices, including standardized observation systems, forced choice behavior rating scales, projective personality techniques, and children's drawings. Discussion focuses on the sensitivity versus specificity of these assessment tools. Assessment tools that have adequate predictive diagnostic validity with respect to reliably differentiating sexually abused from nonsexually abused children currently do not exist.

* * *

Since the evaluator must draw upon multiple sources of data in the assessment of a sexual abuse allegation, observation systems, behavior rating scales, and projective techniques are, at times, utilized as further sources of data. Information derived from the case history and from interviews with collateral sources may be combined with these data to develop an integrated evaluation of the child.

PSYCHOMETRIC PROPERTIES

In discussing the use of assessment instruments within the evaluation process, the psychometric properties of the instruments must be considered. Psychometric information informs us whether an assessment instrument consistently measures what it purports to measure and how accurately it measures the identified entity. When an instrument consistently yields substantially the same results for the same person over repeated administrations, the instrument is said to be a *reliable* assessment instrument. When an instrument accurately measures what it purports, the instrument is said to be a *valid* assessment instrument. The reliability and validity of an instrument are critical factors to consider when using test data to develop a more comprehensive understanding of a child.

If an assessment instrument does not have adequate psychometric properties, the data derived from the instrument are suspect. Professionals who base their conclusions on data from assessment tools that are not reliable and valid instruments are at a higher risk to make false-positive and false-negative errors.

For example, if we were to use anatomical dolls as a "diagnostic" test for sexual abuse, we could not show statistically significant reliability and validity for the "doll test." When children are given anatomical dolls to manipulate, their interactions with the dolls have not consistently been found to discriminate sexually abused from nonsexually abused children; therefore, the validity of the "doll test" has not been established. Secondly, there is no data to indicate that sexually abused children, over repeated administrations, interact with anatomical dolls in a consistent, quantifiable way; therefore, reliability has also not been established. Without this psychometric information, we have no way of clearly interpreting the meaning of a child's behavior on the "doll test." Similar problems have been found when nonstandardized checklists and projective techniques, such as children's drawings, are utilized as "diagnostic" instruments with children alleged to have been sexually abused.

This chapter will attempt to review a number of assessment devices, including standardized observation systems, forced choiced behavior rating scales, and projective instruments. Utilization of behavior rating scales in child sexual abuse evaluations range from standardized, general problem checklists to specific child sexual abuse checklists. Projective techniques used in the evaluation of child sexual abuse range from standardized and nonstandardized inkblot tests and projective storytelling tests to nonstandardized interpretation of children's drawings.

STANDARDIZED PARENT-CHILD OBSERVATION SYSTEMS

If the evaluator chooses to observe the alleged perpetrator-alleged child victim dyad, a structured observation system may greatly aid in the analysis of the interaction. A large number of parent-child assessment systems exist that employ a behavioral paradigm. While naturalistic settings, such as the home, may possibly enhance the external validity of the results (Campbell & Stanley, 1963), this may not be possible or practical when conducting an evaluation of child sexual abuse.

Most observational approaches observe the parent and child in a clinical playroom setting that is organized in a standardized manner and is amenable to nonintrusive observation via one-way mirrors or videotaping. The structured observation system is a measurement instrument subject to the same considerations of reliability and validity as traditional standardized psychometric instruments. One instrument designed as a standardized observation system is:

- The Parent-Child Interaction Play Assessment
  (Refer to Appendix G, p. 311 for a review of this instrument.)

BEHAVIOR RATING
SCALE FORMATS

Several different formats are used in the design of behavior rating scales. Some scales utilize a checklist format, in which the respondent endorses the presence or absence of a behavior. Other devices utilize a Likert response format, in which a statement is followed by a continuum on which anchoring points are indicated (e.g., "almost always," "often," "never"). The administration of the rating scale to parents and others, such as teachers, allows for standardized assessment of the child's behaviors across multiple settings.

As discussed by Martin, Hooper, and Snow (1986), there are four important sources of variation that should be considered when utilizing behavior rating scales; these include Source Variance, Setting Variance, Temporal Variance, and Instrument Variance. Martin et al. define the sources of variance:

- *Source variance* involves the accuracy of the respondent. Rater biases, such as the halo effect, leniency or severity biases, and central tendency biases, can effect accuracy of results. The halo effect occurs when a specific group of children are over- or underrated for positive or negative characteristics. Leniency or severity bias occurs when a parent or teacher uses one extreme or the other of the rating scale to rate the child. Central tendency bias occurs when the rater restricts his or her range to the central range of the rating scale.
- *Setting variance* occurs when the child is affected differently by the various environments in which he or she interacts. For example, a child may act out at home but be well behaved at school.
- *Temporal variance* is caused by variance in behavior produced by the passage of time. Because the behavior rating scales are designed to measure raters' impressions summed over a period of a few months or sometimes longer, the rating scale process tends to average out daily temporal variance.
- *Instrument variance* refers to the resulting difference in test outcome from two comparable instruments, such as two rating scales. Method variance refers to the utilization of multiple instruments, such as a rating scale and a projective instrument.

A number of different behavior rating scales exist and can be categorized by specificity of purpose. Behavior rating scales also can be grouped according to whether the rating scale provides normative data and meets the requirements of reliability and validity associated with standardized psychometric tests.

STANDARDIZED PROBLEM
BEHAVIOR RATING SCALES

Behavior rating scales utilized to identify the nature and extent of a child's overall behavior problems and which meet the standards of reliability and validity include

- Burks' Behavior Rating Scales
- Child Behavior Checklist (CBCL)
- Conners' Rating Scales
- Louisville Behavior Checklist
- Personality Inventory for Children (PIC)
  (Refer to Appendices H-M, pp. 313-325 for a review of these instruments.)

These behavior rating scales utilize the primary caretaker as the respondent in an attempt to identify specific behavior problems. Additionally, the Child Behavior Checklist, Louisville Behavior Checklist, Conners' Rating Scales, and the Burks' Behavior Rating Scales also utilize the child's teacher as a respondent. The teacher as a respondent provides the evaluator with another source of important data. For example, in cases of alleged incestuous child sexual abuse, the behavior rating scale results from the teacher can be compared against the behavior rating scale results from the father and/or the mother.

Both the Child Behavior Checklist (on the parent form only) and the Louisville Behavior Checklist include several questions that directly address sexual behavior problems. However, due to the small number of sexual-referent questions, the information obtained is limited. Furthermore, on the CBCL teacher's form, the sexual-referent questions are not presented.

ACCURACY OF BEHAVIOR
RATING SCALES WITH
SEXUALLY ABUSED CHILDREN

Although checklists can be useful in identifying the presence of specific emotional and behavioral problems, these checklists do not assess the inner experiences of the child. Rather, checklists assess the severity of problems as perceived by an outside person (e.g., parent or teacher). As a result, checklists are subject to the problem of respondent bias which could influence the validity of the results.

In an attempt to assess the accuracy of behavior rating scales completed by mothers of sexually abused children, Everson et al. (1989) compared the mothers' scores on the Parental Reaction to Incest Disclosure Scale (PRIDS), mothers' descriptions of their sexually abused children's behavior on the CBCL, and the children's self-descriptions of behavior problems. For mothers of sexual abuse victims who provided ambivalent or minimal support to their children, there was little concordance between descriptions of their children's behaviors on the CBCL and their children's self-descriptions of problems they were experiencing. In contrast, there was substantial concordance between the supportive mothers' descriptions of their children's behaviors on the CBCL and the children's self-reports of problem behaviors.

RESEARCH ON THE DISCRIMINATIVE POWER OF BEHAVIOR RATING SCALES WITH SEXUALLY ABUSED CHILDREN

In a review of the recent empirical studies on the impact of sexual abuse on children, over one-fourth of the sexually abused children were found to show no significant behavior problems on broad-based child behavior rating scales (Kendall-Tackett, Williams, & Finkelhor, 1993). While standardized behavior rating scales may be useful in identifying the presence of emotional and behavior problems, they lack both specificity and sensitivity regarding behaviors that may be markers of child sexual abuse. The presence or absence of specific emotional and behavior problems in isolation cannot be used to identify a child as having been sexually abused.

The following example demonstrates how checklists may provide data to assist the evaluator in the development of a more comprehensive evaluation of a child alleged by a parent to be the victim of sexual abuse:

> Jolene's father alleged that his 4-year-old daughter was the victim of sexual abuse perpetrated by Jolene's stepfather. The parents had been divorced for a year. Jolene's father attempted to stop visitation between Jolene and her mother. The father reported that Jolene was exhibiting serious psychological problems, including symptoms of depression, anxiety, and disturbed thinking. On the Burks' Behavior Rating Scales, all scales were significantly elevated with the father as the respondent; all scales were within the normal range with the mother as the respondent; and all scales were within the normal range with the teacher as the respondent.

> *Comment: This information suggests several possibilities: (a) the child is either behaving differently when she is with her father, in contrast to her behavior at school or with her mother, (b) the father is exaggerating the child's behavior, or (c) the*

mother is underreporting behavior problems that the child exhibits at home but may not exhibit at school. These checklist results can only be used as one segment of information and cannot be used to determine whether the child is or is not the victim of sexual abuse.

NONSTANDARDIZED PROBLEM BEHAVIOR RATING SCALES

In order to provide more precise behavior checklists for identifying sexually abused children, lists of behaviors identified as symptoms of sexual abuse have been developed by practitioners. These symptoms have included eating and sleeping disturbances, fears and phobias, depression, guilt, shame, anger, and school problems (Browne & Finkelhor, 1986; Sgroi, 1982). Also included were toileting problems; psychosomatic symptoms, such as headaches, aches, and pains; gastrointestinal disturbances (D. S. Everstine & L. Everstine, 1989; Foreward & Buck, 1978); self-destructive behaviors; and sexualized behaviors (Finkelhor & Browne, 1985; Sgroi, 1982). It should be noted that the identification of these symptoms within the literature was primarily derived from the clinical observations of mental health professionals rather than from empirically based normative or comparative studies.

The checklists of behaviors identified as behavior symptoms are now sometimes referred to as "laundry lists." The problem with these lists of behaviors is the lack of empirical evidence validating the behaviors as "markers" of sexual abuse. Rather, these "symptoms of sexual abuse" are not unique markers of sexual abuse but are symptoms of regression in adaptive functioning that can be precipitated by many childhood stressors, including but not limited to child sexual abuse (Browne & Finkelhor, 1986; Conte & Schuerman, 1987). The behaviors typically found on these lists included

- oppositional and defiant
- overly passive and accommodating
- emotionally labile
- enuretic
- encopretic
- sleep disturbances
- nightmares
- masturbates excessively

- engages other children in sex play
- fear of men
- fear of strangers
- overly dependent
- emotionally isolating (avoidant)
- drop in grades
- eating disorders

Empirical studies have generally confirmed that these clusters of symptoms are not unique to sexually abused children. However, one symptom that is an exception, and appears to be related to child sexual abuse trauma, is a child's sexual preoccupation and initiation of adult sexual activity with other children or adults (Friedrich, 1988; Friedrich et al., 1986).

STANDARDIZED CHILD SEXUAL ABUSE BEHAVIOR RATING SCALES

CHILD SEXUAL BEHAVIOR INVENTORY

Because highly sexualized behavior in children was found to be a discriminating behavior in some child sexual abuse victims, Friedrich (n.d.) developed a checklist that would assess sexual behaviors with enough specificity to be useful; the name of this checklist is the Child Sexual Behavior Inventory (CSBI). The parents are the respondents on the CSBI. The findings from the Friedrich et al. (1992) normative CSBI study showed a significant relationship between the CSBI score and (a) type of abuse, (b) number of perpetrators, and (c) use of force. Children who demonstrated higher levels of sexualized behavior were found to have experienced more severe abuse, a greater number of perpetrators, and the use of force or threat of death. Furthermore, the Friedrich et al. (1992) study found an association of sexual abuse with greater levels of familial distress and fewer educational and financial resources in the family.

CSBI results of eight hundred eighty 2- to 12-year-old presumably nonsexually abused children were compared with CSBI results of two hundred seventy-six 2- to 12-year-old children identified as sexually abused. Sexually abused children were found to exhibit higher levels of sexual behavior than nonsexually abused children on the majority of 35 sexual behaviors identified on the CSBI. Specifically, 27 of the 35 sexual behaviors were found to differ significantly between the two groups in terms of frequency of parent endorsement. However, a total of 21 of the 35 sexual behaviors also were endorsed by at least 5% of the parents of the nonsexually abused children. Furthermore, none of the sexual behaviors had a zero occurrence rate for either the nonsexually abused or the sexually abused group (Friedrich et al., 1992).

According to Friedrich (1993), there were eight sexual behaviors on the CSBI that were endorsed by 40% of parents for both nonsexually abused males and females 2 to 6 years of age. These included

- scratches anal or crotch area, or both
- touches or tries to touch the mother's or other women's breasts
- touches sex parts when at home
- kisses adults not in the family
- undresses self in front of others
- sits with crotch or underwear exposed
- kisses other children not in the family
- if a boy, plays with girls' toys, and if a girl, plays with boys' toys

In 1993, Friedrich revised the CSBI into the current 36-item CSBI-R. To date, the CSBI-R checklist continues to be developed. The CSBI and the CSBI-R have been standardized and meet acceptable reliability and validity criteria for psychometric tests (Friedrich, 1993). On the CSBI-R, Friedrich (1993) retained 30 of the 35 original items from the CSBI. Six new items were included, bringing the total items for the CSBI-R to 36. Additionally, new - albeit small - clinical and normative samples were used with the revised checklist. One hundred forty-one 2- to 12-year-old, presumably nonsexually abused children were compared to one hundred thirty-three 2- to 12-year-old children identified as sexually abused.

The original CSBI data on 1,156 subjects (Friedrich et al., 1992) are presented in Table 9.1 (p. 231). The table shows the frequency of sexual behaviors reported to have occurred with the study subjects at least once within the 6 month time span during the study. These numbers do not include the intensity or relative frequency of incidents within this time span.

Methodological problems with the CSBI normative study (Friedrich et al., 1992) included not matching nonsexually abused and sexually abused subjects on background variables. A greater percentage of nonsexually abused subjects came from intact families, were better educated, had higher SES status, and experienced fewer stressful life events. Additionally, there was a very low frequency of nonwhites in the nonsexually abused subject group compared to a much higher percentage of nonwhites in the sexually abused subject group.

The Boat and Everson (1994) normative study of presumably nonsexually abused children's behavior with anatomical dolls is relevant when examining Friedrich's normative data. Boat and Everson's (1994) finding that nonwhite, low SES, nonsexually abused children exhibit significantly higher levels of sexualized behavior with the dolls suggests that the Friedrich et al. (1992) findings of significant differences between nonsexually abused and sexually abused groups may be confounded by background variables. Similar to the comparative doll studies, the differences in sexualized behaviors found by Friedrich et al. (1992) between sexually abused and nonsexually abused children, at least in part, may reflect background variables rather than sexual behaviors that are the result of sexual abuse. As such, the sexual behavior scores of the nonsexually abused children may not be truly representative of the broad spectrum of all nonsexually abused children. Because of these problems, Friedrich (1993) has continued to revise his instrument and to collect new normative data.

CSBI normative data indicate that as a child matures, there is a steady decrease in overall sexual behavior. The CSBI group mean score for presumably nonsexually abused children, 2 to 6 years old, is approximately 11, while for children 7 to 10 years old, the mean score is approximately 5. Table 9.2 (p. 233) presents the mean scores for the nonsexually abused and sexually abused groups.

Higher Child Sexual Behavior Inventory scores do not necessarily equate with a higher probability that the child has been sexually abused. The evaluator must compare the child's score against the mean scores of nonsexually abused and sexually abused groups in order to draw a meaningful conclusion. For example, a 4-year-old female's CSBI score of 59 would put the child two standard deviations

TABLE 9.1
Clinical/Normative Male and
Female Endorsement Contrasts, CSBI-V.1*

ITEM (ABBREVIATED)	GIRLS AGE 2-6		GIRLS AGE 7-12		BOYS AGE 2-6		BOYS AGE 7-12	
	(Data listed in percentages)							
	Normative (N = 252)	Clinical (N = 74)	Normative (N = 174)	Clinical (N = 113)	Normative (N = 248)	Clinical (N = 41)	Normative (N = 206)	Clinical (N = 48)
Puts mouth on sex parts	.0	12.2	.0	4.4	.4	17.1	.0	16.7
Asks to engage in sex acts	.0	10.8	.6	14.2	1.2	22.0	.0	20.8
Masturbates with object	.8	21.6	1.7	7.1	.8	17.1	.0	4.2
Inserts objects in vagina/anus	2.8	28.4	.6	3.5	.0	19.5	.0	10.4
Imitates intercourse	.4	21.6	1.1	8.0	.8	19.5	2.4	16.7
Sexual sounds	.8	17.6	.6	8.0	.4	14.6	3.9	25.0
French kisses	4.0	21.6	1.7	5.3	1.6	19.5	2.4	10.4
Undresses other people	4.4	21.6	.0	14.2	4.4	22.0	.5	16.7
Asks to watch explicit TV	1.6	6.8	3.4	15.0	.0	19.5	6.8	18.7
Imitates sexual behavior with dolls	4.0	21.6	7.5	15.0	.8	22.0	1.5	12.5
Wants to be opposite sex	7.5	13.5	1.1	7.1	7.3	17.1	1.9	8.3
Talks about sexual acts	2.8	33.8	10.3	28.3	2.4	31.7	9.2	43.7
Dresses like opposite sex	9.5	5.4	2.9	5.3	6.0	12.2	3.4	8.3
Touches others' sex parts	5.6	36.5	4.0	13.3	8.9	41.5	4.9	27.1
Rubs body against people	8.3	39.2	4.6	17.7	8.5	24.4	4.4	25.0
Hugs strange adults	14.3	45.9	4.0	23.0	6.5	29.3	2.4	8.3
Shows sex parts to children	7.5	31.1	2.3	15.0	15.7	43.9	4.4	29.2
Uses sexual words	1.2	23.0	12.1	31.9	4.8	43.9	19.9	52.1
Overly aggressive, overly passive	17.5	47.3	8.6	38.9	8.1	29.3	6.3	29.2
Talks flirtatiously	15.9	20.3	14.9	19.5	8.5	14.6	2.9	14.6
Pretends to be opposite sex	20.6	12.2	8.0	11.5	16.9	24.4	2.9	10.4
Masturbates with hand	16.3	41.9	8.6	18.6	22.6	43.9	11.2	43.7
Looks at nude pictures	7.9	14.9	18.4	14.2	11.3	19.5	27.2	41.7
Shows sex parts to adults	17.9	28.4	6.9	9.7	25.8	26.8	9.7	16.7
Touches sex parts in public	19.0	37.8	2.9	10.6	35.5	39.0	15.5	27.1
Interested in opposite sex	20.6	31.1	32.8	46.9	21.0	29.3	19.9	47.9
Tries to look at people undressing	33.3	45.9	14.9	18.6	33.9	48.8	27.7	41.7
Touches women's breasts	48.4	58.1	9.2	11.5	43.5	48.8	11.7	22.9
Kisses nonfamily children	55.2	45.9	21.3	30.1	41.1	39.0	9.7	20.8
Kisses nonfamily adults	52.4	50.0	26.4	29.2	41.1	34.0	18.9	27.1
Sits with crotch exposed	59.1	60.8	29.9	36.3	35.1	26.5	15.5	27.1
Undresses in front of others	61.9	56.8	23.0	31.0	49.6	61.0	21.4	37.5
Touches sex parts at home	54.4	58.1	18.4	24.8	64.1	73.2	36.4	50.0
Scratches crotch	67.9	63.5	34.5	33.6	58.1	56.1	40.8	50.0
Uses opposite sex toys	71.4	43.2	42.5	26.5	63.3	56.1	30.6	31.2

*From "Sexual Behavior in Sexually Abused Children," by W. N. Friedrich, 1993, *Violence Update, 3*(5), p. 4. Reprinted with permission.

above the mean CSBI score of 21 for 4-year-old children known to have been sexually abused. Thus, the sexualized behavior reportedly exhibited by a preschool child with a score of 59 is highly unusual for both sexually abused and nonsexually abused children.

Similar to other checklists, the validity of the Child Sexual Behavior Inventory is based on the neutrality of the person filling out the checklist. This source variance may influence the accuracy of the CSBI results. If a presumably objective person, such as a preschool teacher, completes the checklist, the results may have greater validity than if the checklist is completed by a nonneutral person. Because items on the CSBI are face-valid, any respondent can deny or exaggerate the presence of sexual behavior.

The Child Sexual Behavior Inventory, similar to other checklists, is recommended to be used as part of a larger evaluation process rather than in isolation. The CSBI may be utilized in combination with other behavior rating scales when evaluating an allegation of sexual abuse.

In the following example, the child being evaluated is 5 years old:

RESPONDENT	BURKS' BEHAVIOR RATING SCALES - PRESCHOOL AND KINDERGARTEN EDITION	CONNERS' RATING SCALES	CHILD SEXUAL BEHAVIOR INVENTORY - REVISED
Susan Bennett (taught child 18 months) Faith Christian Preschool	• Nonsignificant on all 18 scales	• Nonsignificant on all 8 scales	• Score = 3
Joyce Allan (taught child 3 months) Park Elementary School	• Nonsignificant on all 18 scales	• Nonsignificant on all 8 scales	• Score = 2
Father	• Nonsignificant on all 18 scales	• Nonsignificant on all 8 scales	• Score = 5

Mother	• Significant elevations on 9 of 18 scales
	  - Excessive Anxiety
	  - Excessive Dependency
	  - Poor Ego Strength
	  - Poor Attention
	  - Poor Impulse Control
	  - Excessive Suffering
	  - Poor Anger Control
	  - Excessive Aggressiveness
	  - Excessive Resistance
		• Significant elevations on 5 of 8 scales
		  - Restless Disorganized
		  - Psychosomatic
		  - Obsessive Compulsive
		  - Hyperactive-Immature
		  - Anxious-Shy
			• Score = 59

When comparing the Child Sexual Behavior Inventory results with other standardized checklist results, the evaluator must consider both source variance and setting variance. For example, one parent may exhibit a leniency bias while another parent may exhibit a severity bias. Setting variance may occur when the child demonstrates different behaviors within the various settings, such as school and home.

Related to the utility of the Child Sexual Behavior Inventory for decision making on an individual-case basis, Friedrich (1993) states that the CSBI checklist should not be relied on in isolation as a primary indicator of sexual abuse. As with

TABLE 9.2
Total Scores for Normative and Clinical Groups on 35-Item Child Sexual Behavior Inventory*

SUBJECTS	AGE (YEARS)	NORMATIVE		CLINICAL	
		M	*SD*	*M*	*SD*
Boys 35-item	2 to 6	10.60	[7.64]	20.51	[18.18]
Girls 35-item	2 to 6	11.72	[8.32]	21.19	[18.07]
Boys 35-item	7 to 12	5.56	[5.95]	16.69	[15.37]
Girls 35-item	7 to 12	5.35	[6.14]	11.19	[12.92]

*From "Child Sexual Behavior Inventory: Normative and Clinical Contrasts," by W. N. Friedrich, P. Grambsch, L. Damon, S. K. Hewitt, C. Koverola, R. A. Lang, V. Wolfe, and D. Broughton, 1992, *Psychological Assessment, 4*, p. 308.

any other checklist, the Child Sexual Behavior Inventory should be used in the context of a thorough evaluation that includes interviews, medical exams, and other collateral sources.

BEHAVIOR RATING SCALE FOR DETERMINING SEXUAL ABUSE WITHIN CUSTODY LITIGATION

SEX-ABUSE LEGITIMACY SCALE

Due to allegations of sexual abuse arising in litigated custody and visitation cases, Gardner (1987) developed the Sex-Abuse Legitimacy Scale (SAL Scale) for differentiating true allegations of sexual abuse from false allegations. Criteria related to the accuser, accused, and the alleged child victim were designed to be rated using a three-point scale. The SAL Scale has not been standardized and, as a result, awarding points (one to three) is subjective. Because of problems with the instrument, including the subjectiveness of the scoring system, Gardner discontinued the use of the SAL Scale but continued to use criteria from the scale in a checklist-type manner. Gardner (1992) identified 30 criteria he considered useful for differentiating between true and false sexual abuse accusations. Similar to the nonstandardized lists of symptoms previously described in this chapter, Gardner's (1992) list of 30 criteria has not been standardized. Since normative and comparative data have not been collected on these criteria, forming diagnostic decisions based on the quantity of these criteria is highly questionable and, again, may increase the risk for false-positive or false-negative errors by the evaluator.

RATING SCALES DERIVED
FROM THE POST-TRAUMATIC
STRESS DISORDER CRITERIA

Dissociation has been a reported consequence of severe trauma. Similar to increased sexualized behavior found in some sexually abused children, dissociative disorders also have been found to be related to child sexual abuse. Dissociation is viewed as a complex psychophysiological process that occurs on a continuum ranging from minor normative dissociations, such as daydreaming, to psychiatric conditions in which there is a separation of mental processes that are normally integrated (Bernstein & Putnam, 1986; Putnam, 1991; Spiegel & Cardena, 1991). Currently, there is ongoing debate on how to establish criteria for determining pathological levels of dissociation in children because many normative behaviors in young children may parallel older children's dissociative behaviors. For example, daydreaming, forgetfulness, shifts in attention, and a variable sense of identity are common behaviors exhibited by young children (Hornstein & Putnam, 1992).

The essential features of dissociation in children are (a) amnestic periods and/or trance-like states and (b) marked changes in behavior and functioning (Friedrich et al., in press). Instruments designed to assess dissociative behavior and symptoms of severe trauma include

- Child Dissociative Checklist
- Children's Impact of Traumatic Events Scale - Revised
- Trauma Symptom Checklist - Children
- PTSD Reaction Index
  (Refer to Appendices N-Q, pp. 327-333 for a review of these instruments.)

RESEARCH ON DISCRIMINATIVE
POWER OF DISSOCIATION
AND SEXUAL CONCERNS

The degree to which dissociation and sexual behavior discriminate sexually abused from presumably nonsexually abused groups of children and adolescents with and without psychiatric problems has been examined by Friedrich et al. (in press). Dissociation and sexual behavior were measured with the Child Dissociative Checklist and the Trauma Symptom Checklist - Children, among other measures. Although psychiatric and nonpsychiatric groups differed significantly in their dissociative behaviors and sexual concerns, psychiatric sexually abused and psychiatric nonsexually abused groups did not differ significantly on the Child Dissociative Checklist and the Trauma Symptom Checklist - Children. Friedrich and his colleagues concluded that although the results suggest that both sexual concerns and dissociation can be assessed reliably, neither sexual concerns nor dissociation is unique to sexually abused children.

RATING SCALES DERIVED FROM CHILDREN'S ATTRIBUTIONS AND PERCEPTIONS RELATED TO THEIR SEXUAL VICTIMIZATION

Sexually abused children have been observed by clinicians to develop unique attributions and perceptions related to, and as a function of, their sexual abuse experience (Mannarino, Cohen, & Berman, 1994; Morrow, 1991; Sgroi, 1982). As discussed by Mannarino and colleagues, these attributions and perceptions include feeling different from peers, blaming themselves for the abuse, feeling that other people no longer believe what they say, and feeling reduced interpersonal trust. The child victim's attributions and perceptions are believed to reflect and influence how the sexually abused child "processes" the victimization experience and, as such, are considered to be factors that mediate symptom development (Mannarino et al., 1994). An instrument designed to assess children's attributions and perceptions related to their sexual victimization is

- The Children's Attributions and Perceptions Scale
  (Refer to Appendix R, p. 335 for a review of this instrument.)

SENSITIVITY VERSUS SPECIFICITY

Preliminary research indicates that the previously referenced rating scales assessing dissociation, sexual concerns, and children's attributions and perceptions may be sensitive to the identification of symptoms, thoughts, and perceptions of sexually abused children. However, none of these rating scales show specificity to behaviors or cognitions exhibited by sexually abused children. Therefore, these instruments do not have predictive diagnostic validity, and all results, positive or negative, must be cautiously interpreted within a larger context of a full forensic evaluation.

Empirical investigations show that although some sexually abused children may exhibit dissociative behaviors, sexual concerns, self-blame, reduced interpersonal trust, and so on, nonsexually abused traumatized children also exhibit these same behaviors and cognitions (Friedrich et al., in press). Furthermore, although several abuse characteristics (i.e., severity and duration) are related to dissociation (Friedrich et al., in press), there is strong evidence that family disruption and stress confounds the difference between sexually abused and nonsexually abused children on behavioral measures (D. A. Wolfe & Mosk, 1983). Specifically, family variables of conflict and parental support have been shown to be of greater magnitude than abuse-specific variables in understanding the impact of sexual abuse (Alexander & Lupfer, 1987; S. D. Peters, 1988).

There are several other child sexual abuse checklists on the market that will not be reviewed in this chapter. Many of these checklists lack acceptable psychometric properties.

OTHER CHECKLISTS

To assist the evaluator in organizing data when conducting evaluations of abuse or neglect, Petty (1990) developed the Checklist for Child Abuse Evaluation. Petty's checklist is a metaconstruction for assisting clinicians in organizing their data. The Checklist contains 24 sections which address topics that have been found to be relevant in child abuse and/or neglect evaluations. The evaluator is the respondent on this organizing checklist.

IDIOGRAPHIC VERSUS NOMOTHETIC INSTRUMENTS

It has been proposed that within the sexual abuse evaluation, projective techniques may have assessment utility (Leifer et al., 1991). Support for the use of projective techniques is based on the rationale that projective tests tap aspects of functioning that the child may not be willing or able to report (B. Klopfer et al., 1954). The underlying premise of the projective technique is that when presented with an ambiguous stimuli, the individual will reveal part of his or her own personality, including the way in which the world and people are perceived and thought about.

When examining the clinical utility of projective instruments, the distinction between nomothetic and idiographic data must be addressed. Nomothetic science is concerned with general lawfulness and, as such, nomothetic data present criteria that represent groups of people or syndromes. These criteria are then used to help assign a given person to a given group. Conversely, idiographic science is concerned with understanding the individual person and his or her responses in reference to other responses from the same individual. Responses are not compared to other individuals' responses and, therefore, idiographic data cannot be used for group assignment.

Some projective techniques lend themselves more readily to the nomothetic approach, while other projective techniques are based strictly on an idiographic approach. Bellak (1993) speculates that expressive methods and those scoring schemes primarily predicated upon formal characteristics (such as the Rorschach) lend themselves to valid generalizations more readily than those instruments concerned primarily with content (such as the Thematic Apperception Test). Both nomothetic and idiographic information provide us with different but equally important data.

NONSTANDARDIZED PROJECTIVE INSTRUMENTS - IDIOGRAPHIC METHODS

The Thematic Apperception Test (TAT), the Children's Apperception Test (CAT), and the Projective Story Telling Test are thematic picture techniques that may be used as assessment tools when an evaluation is conducted on a child alleged to have been sexually abused. Due to the lack of empirically based quantitative scoring systems, these nonstandardized instruments represent idiographic methods of assessment. The administration of the TAT, CAT, and Projective Story Telling Test requires the child to create stories to a picture stimulus. While these tests can provide important clinical information, because of their limited psychometric properties, they cannot be used for diagnostic purposes and for assignment of individuals to groups. (Refer to Appendices S and T, pp. 337-339, for a review of TAT, CAT, and Projective Story Telling.)

Because the thematic analysis involves an idiographic rather than a nomothetic approach to understanding the child, the evaluator is interested in the child's common themes or consistencies that emerge across an entire protocol rather than statistical probabilities and comparison of the child's responses to normative data. Hypotheses about relationship dynamics, problem-solving skills, emotional stability, perceptual distortions, or disturbances in thinking can be addressed with these instruments. However, since the differences between sexually abused and nonsexually abused children's stories are unknown, conclusions about sexual abuse from the projective data cannot be drawn. Therefore, the use of these tests to identify children who have been sexually abused is not indicated given the absence of reliability and validity data.

STANDARDIZED PROJECTIVE INSTRUMENTS - NOMOTHETIC METHODS

Historically, instruments identified as projective techniques have been excluded from the category of objective tests, not on the basis of the rules of standardized measurement but on the basis that the test stimulus is not structured to elicit a specific class of responses, such as intelligence tests and achievement tests (Exner, 1986). While some projective instruments do not have normative data or meet the psychometric criterion for validity and reliability, several projective instruments do meet psychometric standards. Based on quantitative scoring systems, the Rorschach (Exner, 1986) and the Roberts' Apperception Test for Children (RATC; McArthur & Roberts, 1990) meet the criteria for both objective and projective categorization. These instruments reflect both nomothetic and idiographic methods. (Refer to Appendices U and V, pp. 341-343 for a review of the RATC and the Rorschach.)

Although the Rorschach and the Roberts' Apperception Test for Children have clinical utility in assessing personality organization and psychological functions, these instruments cannot be used to identify whether a child has experienced sexual abuse. The Rorschach has been used as an assessment instrument in several research studies that have examined the psychological functioning of child sexual abuse victims. Table 9.3 (pp. 238-240) presents several of the current Rorschach

TABLE 9.3
The Rorschach as a Tool for Assessing Child Sexual Abuse*

	Friedrich et al. (in press)	Leifer et al. (1991)	Shapiro et al. (1990)	Zivney, Nash, and Hulsey (1988)
Subjects	Psychiatric Sexually Abused - Substantiated • 37 inpatients with documented sexual abuse • 28 outpatients with documented sexual abuse Psychiatric Sexually Abused - Suspected But Unsubstantiated • 29 inpatient on a child psychiatry unit • 8 outpatient children referred for psychological evaluation Psychiatric Sample • 88 inpatients on a child psychiatry unit referred for depression, conduct, anxiety, eating, and somatization disorders • 62 outpatient children referred for evaluations to rule out learning problems, Attention-Deficit/Hyperactivity Disorder, and depression Nonpsychiatric Comparison Group • 46 nonsexually abused children recruited from Protestant religious education groups • All nonpsychiatric subjects 8 years to 15 years • All psychiatric subjects ages 7 to 15 • All subjects from middle SES	• 79 black sexually abused females seen for an evaluation of sexual abuse at a children's hospital - Ages 5 years to 16 years - Majority low SES • Abuse characteristics: - 73% penile penetration - 15% experienced single victimization - 32% molested by more than one person - 30% abused one time every 2 weeks or less - 55% abused more frequently - Median duration of sexual abuse 5 months - 15% in foster care at time of study • 32 black females who were medical patients at a children's hospital with no known history of sexual abuse - Majority low SES - Matched by age to a randomly selected subset of the abuse sample	• 53 black sexually abused females - Ages 5 years and 16 years - Majority low SES • Abuse characteristics: - 77% penile penetration - 15% experienced single victimization - 31% molested by more than one person - 32% abused one time every 2 weeks or less - 53% abused more frequently - 15% in foster care at time of study • 32 black females who were medical patients at a children's hospital with no known history of sexual abuse - Majority low SES - Matched by age to a randomly selected subset of the abuse sample	Early Abuse Group (EA) • 37 females whose sexual abuse occurred between ages 3 years and 8 years Late Abuse Group (LA) • 43 females whose sexual abuse occurred between ages 9 years and 16 years Clinic Patient Controls (CPC) • 70 female patients referred for testing but evidenced no history of sexual abuse
Procedure	• All potential psychiatric subjects were administered the Wechsler Intelligence Scale. Only children with a Verbal IQ of ≥ 80 were included in the study • 191 of 252 children in psychiatric groups completed the Rorschach - Specific Rorschach variables scored were sex and morbid content • Each child completed the Trauma Symptom Checklist-Children (N = 298) • Adolescents completed the MMPI. Only the Sc scale was examined • Parents completed the Child Behavior Checklist (CBCL), the Child Dissociation Checklist (CDC), and the Child Sexual Behavior Inventory (CSBI).	• Rorschach Inkblot Technique - Exner Scoring System - Rorschach Content Test Anxiety and Hostility Scale - Mutuality of Autonomy Scale - Barrier and Penetration Scales • Rorschach administered by clinical psychologist or clinical psychology graduate student • Scored by two clinical psychologists blind to subject's category	• Rorschach Inkblot Technique - Exner Scoring System - Rorschach Depression Index (DEPI) - Child Behavior Checklist (CBCL) - Internalizing Scale - Children's Depression Inventory (CDI) • Rorschach administered by clinical psychologist or clinical psychology graduate student • Rorschach protocols scored by two clinical psychologists blind to the subject's category	• Authors used previously collected psychological reports, social histories, and Rorschach test data • The Rorschach and Clinical Interviews were carried out by experienced clinic staff (at least Master's degree and formal coursework in projectives) • Rorschach Structural Summaries were available for all patients (when missing values were encountered, cases were deleted from analysis)

Findings	• If there was a history of sexual abuse, correlational analyses indicated there was a greater chance of physical abuse present
	
	Rorschach Results
	• The sexually abused and probable sexually abused groups were more likely to produce sexual content in response to Rorschach
	• There were no differences on Morbid content
		Rorschach Results
		• Abused subjects showed:
		  - More disturbed thinking and impaired reality testing
		  - A high level of stress relative to their adaptive abilities
		  - Greater emotional demands
		  - Perceptions characterized by more primitive, disturbed relations between figures
		  - Higher scores on Hostility scale
		  - Significantly more overtly sexual responses
		• No differences in level of interpersonal engagements
		• No difference in measure of coping resources
		• No difference in Barrier scores; however, abused group produced higher scores on Penetration scale
		• No variance on Rorschach variables as a function of age
			Rorschach Results
			• Random selected subset of 32 abused subjects was compared to control group matched on age
			• The abused group's DEPI score was significantly higher than in the controls
			• Abused group gave more achromatic color responses than controls suggesting a higher degree of constrained affect and inhibition of impulse
			• Abused group produced greater number of Morbid responses suggesting a greater prevalence of perceptions of the self as damaged
			• No difference between groups on the egocentricity index
			• The abused group's Pearson correlations among CDI, CBCL internalizing, and DEPI were all nonsignificant
				• Over half of the girls abused before the age of 9 could be distinguished from the later-abused girls in disturbances of cognition, view of self, and relatedness
				• No significant difference between EA and LA groups on rate of abuse, number of perpetrators, and use of force
				• Duration of abuse differed significantly. EA subjects evidenced longer periods of victimization
				
				Rorschach Results
				• More disturbed thinking found in the EA group, as their responses consisted of more M-, DV, and FABCOMs
				• EAs had significantly more Morbid and Personal responses

Weaknesses	• Psychometrician administering Rorschach was aware of subjects' status • Family distress could have confounded the differences between groups on behavioral indicators	• Sample characteristics limit generalizability (low SES, race) • Groups possibly differed on variables other than sexual victimization (matched for age only) • Some subjects refused participation (subject - self selection) • Possible inclusion of false positives and false negatives in groups - no definitive criteria for how sexual abuse confirmed by State Department of Children and Family Services • No analyses by characteristics of abuse, including relationship and number of perpetrators, sexual acts and duration of abuse, violence, response of nonoffending parent, or placement in foster care	• Same weaknesses cited for Leifer et al. (1991) • Internalizing scale and CBI normative data were used as comparison, rather than a matched group	• Rorschach data taken from case files, therefore, cannot ensure clinic staff's consistency in administration of procedures or scoring of Rorschach • Possible inclusion of false positives - no definitive criteria for how sexual abuse confirmed by Texas Department of Human Resources • No analyses by characteristics of abuse, including relationship and number of perpetrators, sexual acts and duration of abuse, violence, or response of nonoffending parent • Large age range cannot accurately account for developmental differences

*Only the Rorschach test data is addressed in this table. Other test data from these studies have not been listed.

TABLE 9.3 (Continued)
The Rorschach as a Tool for Assessing Child Sexual Abuse

	Friedrich et al. (in press)	Leifer et al. (1991)	Shapiro et al. (1990)	Zivney, Nash, and Hulsey (1988)
Strengths	• Psychometricians established interscorer reliability of > .90 on Rorschach protocols • Used many measures to assess the children's behaviors (e.g., self-report, projective measures, parent reports) • Used four different groups to compare scores on multiple measures • Developmental differences were taken into account for statistical analyses	• Rorschach scored using standardized criteria (Exner) • Interscorer agreement high • Blind raters • Strong statistical analysis	• Rorschach scored using standardized criteria (Exner) • Blind raters • Strong statistical analyses • Interscorer agreement high	• Blind raters • Strong statistical analyses • Random sampling

studies that have compared sexually abused and nonsexually abused children. Studies that used adult subjects are not included in this table.

PROJECTIVE INSTRUMENTS
LACK DISCRIMINATION ABILITY

Comparison studies, using the Rorschach to differentiate sexually abused from nonsexually abused children, have found inconsistent differences between these two groups of children. In the study by Shapiro et al. (1990), sexually abused girls obtained higher Depression scores on the Rorschach compared to the girls' self-reports. Behavioral observations of the girls correlated more closely with the Rorschach results than the girls' self-reports. Therefore, the Rorschach test results may have provided more accurate data than the girls' self-reports regarding depressive symptomatology.

A later study by Leifer et al. (1991) found sexual abuse to be associated with broad psychological dysfunction as measured by the Rorschach. In relation to the comparison group, sexually abused girls showed more disturbed thinking, higher levels of depression and dysphoria, greater stress, and more preoccupation with sexuality. Interestingly, no differences were found between sexually abused girls and presumably nonsexually abused girls in the girls' coping resources or interest in interpersonal relationships.

In a study conducted by Friedrich et al. (in press), a psychiatric group of sexually abused children were found to produce significantly higher sexual content scores in their Rorschachs than the nonsexually abused psychiatric group or the nonreferred control group.

Zivney, Nash, and Hulsey (1988) found that pathology and developmental difficulties associated with sexual abuse depend, in part, on when the sexual abuse began. Using the Rorschach to measure pathology, the authors found that over one-half of the early sexually abused girls manifested disturbed cognition, damaged self-image, and impairments in interpersonal needs, while only 12% of the late sexually abused subjects displayed this same pathology. However, these findings have not been consistently replicated.

While these preliminary studies suggest that sexual abuse may result in psychological problems for some child victims, standardized tests will probably never substantiate a direct cause-and-effect relationship between sexual abuse and psychopathology since child victims' reactions are extremely diverse. However, while projective testing cannot be utilized to identify a child as having been sexually abused, projective testing has utility within a sexual abuse evaluation for assessing psychological functioning and identification of developing personality problems. For example, the following responses to the Rorschach reflect the aberrant sexual preoccupation of a sexually abused adolescent:

Beverly was a 17-year-old female who had been sexually abused by her older brother for a number of years. At the time of the Rorschach administration, Beverly was sexually active with a number of males.

Within the 10 cards, Beverly's Rorschach results contained 8 sex responses and 2 morbid responses out of a total of 38 responses. Beverly's sexual responses involved the following:

Card I	Initial Response -	"Did you ever read about subliminals? That right there says 'sex'."
	Response to Inquiry -	"The way it's embedded - the shading makes it look that way."
Card II	Initial Response -	"I don't like saying (paused) female anatomy - how's that?"
	Response to Inquiry -	"The crevice right here. I'm going to be crude. There would be the lips, and that would be the vagina. I guess the red helps too."
Card IV	Initial Response -	"I must have a sick mind; it looks like another female anatomy."
	Response to Inquiry -	"It looks like lips. I hate that word - that's the hole. You might think I look at these all the time. I don't."
Card VI	Initial Response -	"Crevice - that's the word I'm going to use instead of female anatomy."
	Response to Inquiry -	"It looks more like it - the outer part - is darker than the inner part. It's a well-used one."
Card VII	Initial Response -	"That's a crevice - they drew these didn't they?"
	Response to Inquiry -	"There's the lips and the clitoris. These are sick."
Card VIII	Initial Response -	"The whole anatomy of a crevice. It could look like that just because the way the ink is."
	Response to Inquiry -	"I don't like knowing about this; it makes me sound gay - I'm not though - I know just as much about guys. This is the uterus and the fallopian tube."
Card IX	Initial Response -	"I don't want to be crude, but here's another one. It's all swollen because it just got done."
	Response to Inquiry -	"This looks like the hole, and this part looks like the lips are swollen like it just got done."
Card X	Initial Response -	"The orange things, the way they are placed. It looks like - you know what I'm going to say? Ovaries. I hate thinking like that."
	Response to Inquiry -	"The ovaries, and these things are the fallopian tubes going down to the ovaries."

Comment: *Although Beverly's responses suggest significant sexual concerns, her responses alone cannot be used to identify Beverly as a victim of sexual abuse. However, these responses can be used as one source of data in the forensic evaluation.*

ARTWORK

Children's drawings also have been used as a projective technique in the evaluation of children. Drawings have been thought to have utility based on the premise that a child's drawings are a reflection of his or her personality. That is, the child's drawings are thought to express affective aspects of the personality. Similar to nonstandardized projective tests, such as the TAT, children's drawings represent an idiographic method of data collection.

As presented by DiLeo (1983), representational drawing begins to be developed by children between the ages of 3 and 4. Since people are a significant part of children's lives, the human figure tends to consistently be children's favorite subject (DiLeo, 1970). DiLeo reports that during the preschool years, spontaneous drawings by children tend to become more elaborate with the inclusion of significant items, such as houses, trees, suns, and other aspects of nature. Preschool children are also said to commonly draw with "intellectual realism." That is they draw what they know to be there regardless of whether it is actually visible. Utilizing this "x-ray" technique, the preoperational child will draw transparencies, such as people visible through walls (DiLeo, 1983).

At about age 7 or 8, "visual realism" will gradually replace "intellectual realism." This shift corresponds with Piaget's (1970) theory of movement from the preoperational to the concrete operational stage. DiLeo (1983) observes that these shifts express a metamorphosis in thinking from egocentricity to an increasingly objective view of the world. Table 9.4 represents DiLeo's outline of the developmental progression of children's drawing related to Piaget's stages of development.

TABLE 9.4
Development of Drawing Related to Piaget's Stages of Cognitive Development - A Synoptic View*

APPROXIMATE AGE	DRAWING	COGNITION
0 to 1 1 to 2	*Reflex Response to Visual Stimuli* • Crayon is brought to mouth; the infant does not draw • At 13 months, the first scribble appears Kinesthetic drawing	*Sensorimotor Stage* • Stage is preverbal. Infant acts reflexly, thinks motorically • Movement gradually becomes goal directed as cortical control is gradually established
2 to 3 3 to 4 4 to 7	• Circles appear and gradually predominate. Circles then become discrete *Descriptive Symbolism* • Between 3 and 4 years old, a first graphic symbol is made • Also called the "pictorial" stage *Intellectual Realism* • Draws an internal model, not what is actually seen. Draws what is known to be there. Show people through walls. Transparencies	*Preoperational Stage* • Stage marks the beginning of organized language and symbolic functions • Child begins to perceive language as a tool to get needs met • Child is perceptually oriented and does not use logical thinking. As a result, cannot reason by implication • Child's reasoning is transductive reasoning: reasoning from a particular idea to a particular idea without logically connecting them. The child's view is highly egocentric. Make-believe play is imaginative • Egocentric. Views the world subjectively
7 to 12	*Visual Realism (DiLeo, 1983)* • Subjectivity diminishes. Draws what is actually visible. No more x-ray technique (transparencies). Human figures are more realistic, proportioned. Concerned with symmetry, placement, size, and use of space. Colors are more conventional	*Concrete Operations Stage* • Thinks logically about things • Thinking is concrete rather than abstract • Child can now perform and make elementary groupings of classes and relations. Objects are classified according to the qualities of which the child is aware • Child can now see how consequences follow from actions. Reasoning ability enables the child to acquire and follow directions. Concepts of reversibility: things that were the same remain the same though their appearance may have changed
12+	• Begins to add exaggerated sexual characteristics to the human body	*Formal Operations Stage* • Views his or her products critically. Able to consider hypotheses. Can think about ideas, not only about concrete aspects of a situation

*Adapted from *Interpreting Children's Drawings* (p. 38), by J. H. DiLeo, 1983, New York: Brunner/Mazel. Copyright © 1983 by Brunner/Mazel, Inc. Reprinted with permission.

FAILURE TO STANDARDIZE DRAWINGS
AS A PROJECTIVE ASSESSMENT TOOL

Acceptance of drawings as a projective technique began to occur in the 1940s and 1950s. As reviewed by DiLeo (1983), at that time, Machover (1949) proposed the "body image" hypothesis, purporting that when a person draws a human figure, it is actually a representation of how one views oneself. Machover's hypothesis was based on clinicians' observations of relationships between an individual's human figure drawing and the person's physical handicap. For example, human figures drawn by physically impaired children included their handicaps (Bender, 1952).

As further reviewed by DiLeo (1983), attempts to standardize children's drawings as a projective instrument in the assessment of underlying psychological dynamics, failed to satisfy the standards required of psychometric tests. Koppitz (1968) attempted to develop indices and a standardized scoring procedure in the measurement of emotional and developmental factors on the Draw-a-Person Test (Goodenough, 1926; Harris, 1963). Other attempts at standardization have included the House-Tree-Person (Buck, 1970; Jolles, 1971) and Kinetic Family Drawing (Burns & S. H. Kaufman, 1972). To date, adequate psychometric properties, including interrater reliability, have not been demonstrated on children's drawings when used as projective tests. According to DiLeo, the subjective element in interpreting drawings introduces a practically uncontrollable variable, which presents a barrier to meeting psychometric test standards. This is because when interpreting drawings, the examiner, out of necessity, must rely on intuition as well as analytic skill (DiLeo, 1983).

As Anastasi (1988) has noted, when assessment results are derived from nonstandardized projective instruments, they typically become confounded with the skill level of the clinician using the instrument. In a review of the Draw-a-Person Test in Buros' Mental Measurements Yearbook, Harris (1972) warns that the examiner can "project" his interpretations of the subject's constructions, "unless well-developed criteria for classifying and interpreting the subject's responses exist" (p. 402).

ARTWORK AS
DIAGNOSTIC TOOLS

Projective drawings have frequently been administered as part of a battery of psychological tests in many evaluation settings. Over several decades, drawings have been reported to be among the most frequently used tests by psychologists in clinical settings (Lubin, Larsen, & Matarazzo, 1984; Lubin, Wallis, & Paine, 1971; Piotrowski & Keller, 1992; Wade & Baker, 1977). Projective drawings also have been among the most popular tests within the school setting (Kennedy et al., 1994; Prout, 1983). Currently, the use of drawings is endorsed by some professionals as having utility in the identification of child sexual abuse victims (Burgess & Hartman,

1993). The American Academy of Child and Adolescent Psychiatry (1990) noted that children's drawings may be suggestive of sexual abuse in the child's "depiction of genitalia or avoidance of sexual features altogether" (p. 5).

These claims reflect the assumption held by some professionals that qualitative features differ in drawings of sexually abused children versus nonsexually abused children. Empirical research does not consistently support this assumption. To date, the types of differing qualitative features identified by researchers as associated with child sexual abuse are broad in range and also are found in the drawings of other types of children. Neither an empirical nor clinical consensus has been reached regarding the identification of features that are mutually exclusive for sexually abused children. Table 9.5 (pp. 246-248) examines the current comparative research on differences between sexually abused and nonsexually abused children's drawings.

The results of these studies are variable and do not lend scientific support for the use of children's drawings as a tool to diagnose child sexual abuse. Similar to the problem with using anatomical dolls as a diagnostic test, childen's drawings do not provide incremental validity (validity that adds to the predictive accuracy of existing methods). The studies presented in Table 9.5 (pp. 246-248) will be further discussed throughout the following section.

GENITALS IN
CHILDREN'S ART

Some professionals have proposed that genitalia drawn on human figures by children are a marker of sexual abuse. There do not exist strong empirical data to support this assumption. Hibbard, Roghmann, and Hoekelman (1987) reported that children known to have been sexually abused were 5.4 times more likely to draw genitalia than were the presumably nonsexually abused comparison children. However, only 10% (5 out of 52) of the sexually abused children drew genitals on their human figures. Only 2% (1 out of 52) of the presumably nonsexually abused children drew genitalia. Thus, only 6 children out of 114 subjects drew genitalia during the drawing task. Furthermore, only 1 subject out of 114 children drew genitalia on the free drawing when asked to create a whole person. The other five children only drew genitalia when given a human figure outline and directed to complete the person by drawing in the body parts.

Although several studies have found sexually abused children's drawings may overrepresent sexual characteristics on human figures, other studies have found variable results. Yates, Beutler, and Crago (1985) found sexually abused children were more variable in both over- and underrepresenting sexual characteristics on their human figure drawings when compared to nonsexually abused children. Conversely, Sidun and Rosenthal (1987) failed to find a statistically significant differ-

TABLE 9.5
Comparison of Sexually Abused and Nonsexually Abused Children's Drawings

FACTORS	Chantler, Pelco, and Mertin (1993)	Cohen and Phelps (1985)	Hibbard and Hartman (1990)	Hibbard, Roghmann, and Hoekelman (1987)	Kaufman and Wohl (1992)	Yates, Beutler, and Crago (1985)
Subjects	*Sexually Abused Group* • 26 sexually abused children - Ages 6 years to 11 years *Clinic Group* • 37 children (referred to clinic for behavior or academic problems) - Ages 6 years to 12 years *Community Group* • 39 nonreferred children from the community - Ages 8 years to 11 years	• 89 sexually abused children • 77 presumably nonsexually abused (referred to mental health clinic for other problems) • Ages 4 years to 18 years	• 65 sexually abused children alleged to have been sexually abused (currently in therapy or receiving medical evaluations) • 66 nonsexually abused children from general pediatric clinics • Ages 5 years to 8 years • No significant differences between groups on characteristics of age, sex, race, and SES	• 57 children referred to Child Protection Services for possible sexual abuse - 36 confirmed by medical evidence, witness, or confession - 21 suspected victims - no medical or other substantiation • 55 comparison nonsexually abused children from public medical clinic and private pediatric clinics • Ages 3 years to 7 years • Data analysis performed on 52 sexually abused and 52 nonsexually abused children • Children matched by age, sex, race, and SES	• 18 child victims of sexual abuse • 18 children from the community • 18 nonsexually abused children from mental health clinic • Ages 5 years to 10 years	• 18 female incest victims referred by the court for therapy - Ages 3.5 years to 17 years • 17 females with emotional disturbance but no known incest - Ages 4 years to 17 years • Matched for age and SES
Procedure	• Two instruments administered - Louisville Behavior Checklist (LBC) - Human Figure Drawing (HFD) • HFD scored with Koppitz Emotional Indicators (EI) Scoring System • Mothers completed LBC • Each drawing scored for the presence or absence of each EI	• Subjects administered House-Tree-Person Drawing, a drawing of the family engaged in some activity and a free drawing • Drawings rated for presence or absence of factors hypothesized to be markers differentiating sexually abused from nonsexually abused children • 12 "clinically derived" markers rated for presence or absence in drawings	• Drawings obtained by pediatric social workers or art therapists of all sexually abused children and by research associates for comparison group • Standardized format for instructions • Two drawings from each subject (first picture of person; second picture of opposite sex) • Both drawings scored by one rater • Rated for Koppitz Emotional Indicators (EI) • Subjects' scores grouped according to EI categories	• All children asked to draw three pictures, which included a person, a person of opposite sex from first drawing, and complete an outline of a person • Drawings were rated by a pediatrician, pediatric nurse, pediatric social worker, and an elementary school teacher • Drawings were rated for the presence or absence of five body parts	• Authors developed a protocol for scoring for the House-Tree-Person and Kinetic Family Drawings • Total of 86 items were included in comparative analysis of hypothesized indices projecting sexual abuse: - 24 items of betrayal - 32 items of traumatic sexualization - 19 items of stigmatizations - 11 items of powerlessness • Children drew H-T-P and KFDs	• Subjects were instructed to draw a human figure • The samples were randomly selected from a group of human figure drawings collected over a period of several years • Rated on 15 characteristics of potentially disturbed functioning (developed own rating scale from clinical literature) • Ratings by two clinical psychologists

Findings	• Groups differed significantly on EIs • Sexually Abused Group earned higher Louisville subscale scores and drew more EI in their HFD • Groups differed significantly on Flag items (i.e., tiny head, hands cut off, no feet) • Louisville Factor scores alone discriminated the two groups with a 75.49% classification rate • Louisville scores and Koppitz Flag items combined discriminated the two groups with a 77.45% classification rate	• H-T-P and Family drawing contained a slightly higher number of markers for sexually abused versus nonsexually abused children - Markers - Sexual abuse group - 1.28, nonsexually abused group - 0.87 • While differences were statistically significant, the overall frequency of markers was too low to have clinical utility • Art therapists had no better reliability in ratings than nonart-trained	• No statistically significant differences between groups were observed on Emotional Indicators (EIs) • 18 sexually abused children scored one or more indicators in the EI category of Anxiety versus only 8 in the comparison group • One drawing (usually first) was found to be sufficient to emotional indicators	• 10% (5/52) of alleged sexually abused children drew genitalia compared with 2% (1/52) of comparison - Five of 6 drew genitalia on the completion drawing - only one drew genitalia on the free drawing • Substantiated cases considered separately • 9% (3/33) of substantiated victims drew genitalia compared with 10% (2/19) unsubstantiated alleged sexually abused children	• Abused boys and girls were identifiable using the KFD • Abused girls could be identified using the Person drawing, while boys could be identified using Tree drawings • Chi square analyses performed on the four hypothesized indices of sexual abuse: *Betrayal Items* Significant group differences on Person drawing. Sexually abused group > number of betrayal items in Person drawings from HTP *Traumatic Sexualization* Sexually abused group > items in Person drawings from HTP *Stigmatization* Sexually abused group > items in the KFD *Powerlessness* Sexually abused group > items in Person drawing from HTP	• Few mean differences between groups • Significant differences found on the dimensions of "control of impulses" and "quality of repression" • Groups differed on dimensions of hypersexualization, maturity, and quality of sublimation
Weaknesses	• Significant differences, possibly due to variables other than sexual abuse (not matched on age, SES, etc.) • No interrater reliability established for individual indicators • Variability of individual's scores within each group on both the checklist and drawing measures • Some children in sexual abuse group earned lower scores than some comparison group children	• Significant differences, possibly due to variables other than sexual abuse (not matched on age, SES, etc.) • Mislabeling the markers "incest markers" • No validity to "clinically derived" markers • Large age range - developmental differences not considered • Sample unbalanced for gender (more girls in victims group, more boys in nonvictims group)	• Only one rater • Insufficient power in sample size to detect differences • Absence of acceptable psychometric properties, including reliability for the Koppitz Emotional Indicators • Possible inclusion of false positives and false negatives in groups - no criteria listed for identification	• Small sample size producing weak statistics • Drawings from sexually abused children collected by child protection workers • Drawings of nonsexually abused children collected by principle investigator • Sample size too small for statistical analysis • Need a comparison group of traumatized children to determine whether it is sexual abuse or trauma in general causing differences	• Lack of information regarding demographics of the study groups - children apparently not matched for age, sex, race, and SES • Administration procedure unknown • Differences in chronological age of subjects (sexually abused girls almost 2 years older than community girls) may confound research findings	• Small sample size • Need comparison group of nonreferred children • Generalizability limited to lower middle and upper middle class • "Manner in which drawings were obtained varied as a function of clinical judgment" • The sexual abuse group may be selective, homogeneous group due to the fact that these children were more impulsive

TABLE 9.5 (Continued)
Comparison of Sexually Abused and Nonsexually Abused Children's Drawings

FACTORS	Chantler, Pelco, and Mertin (1993)	Cohen and Phelps (1985)	Hibbard and Hartman (1990)	Hibbard, Roghmann, and Hoekelman (1987)	Kaufman and Wohl (1992)	Yates, Beutler, and Crago (1985)
Weaknesses (Continued)	• Absence of acceptable psychometric properties, including reliability for the Koppitz Emotional Indicators	• Nonsexually abused subjects were mental health clients in treatment for emotional problems and a control group for comparison was not utilized	• No analyses by characteristics of abuse, including relationship and number of perpetrators, sexual acts and duration of abuse, violence, or response of nonoffending parent • No analysis separating children in therapy from children not in therapy	• No information given regarding gender breakdown of original sample	• Absence of acceptable psychometric properties for the identified indices established by previous research	• Nonstandardized administration of projective device by individuals who are aware of reason for referral
Strengths	• Consensus regarding presence or absence of each indicator was determined between three raters • Good statistical analysis and cautions regarding conclusions drawn from these results	• Blind raters • Specific objective rating criteria • Good statistical analysis	• Groups did not differ in relation to age, sex, race, and SES • Good test-retest reliability	• Groups did not differ in relation to age, sex, race, and SES • Blind raters • Good interrater agreement	• Interesting concept	• Blind raters • Groups matched for age and socioeconomic status

ence in the drawings of sexually abused and nonsexually abused adolescents on the distribution of oversexualized, normally sexualized, and undifferentiated human figures.

Problems with the use of genitalia in children's art as a marker of sexual abuse are illustrated by the following case example:

> Theodore, age 5, was brought by his father and mother to a psychologist following several weeks of Theodore's perseveration on drawing Batman urinating blood. A history from the parents indicated the parents' marriage was stable, Theodore's only babysitter and daycare provider had been his maternal grandmother, and Theodore never showed any aberrant sexual behaviors prior to 2 weeks before the parents contacted the psychologist. Theodore appeared to be a bright, well-adjusted child both in his home and in his public school kindergarten classroom. However, Theodore also was described by his parents as a very sensitive child who, at times, over responded to environmental stimuli. For example, during toilet training, Theodore was fearful of the sound of the toilet flushing and continued, to date, to be fearful of thunder. The parents further reported that Theodore would worry for weeks about homeless people he saw begging on the streets.
>
> Psychological testing revealed Theodore to have a WPPSI-R Verbal IQ score of 159 and a reading score at a fourth grade level. When the parents were further questioned about events that may have coincided with the beginning of Theodore's perseverative drawing of Batman, the mother reported that they were going on a weekend trip and, at that time, she had allowed Theodore to buy five comic books for the trip. She reported that because she was in a hurry, she did not review the comic books; one of the selected materials, reportedly, was very violent. When in the car on their trip, Theodore, reportedly, while reading these comic books, asked his mother what "passing blood" meant. She, reportedly, informed Theodore that it meant "urinating blood." The psychologist asked the parents to bring her these comic books. The psychologist reviewed the comic books and discovered the comic book on Batman was extremely violent and depicted Batman as being beaten, injured, and passing blood due to his injuries. When Theodore was then questioned by the psychologist about where he got the idea of Batman urinating blood, he described the story he had read in the comic book. It appears this story had traumatized Theodore.
>
> The following drawings were created by Theodore, which precipitated his parents bringing him to a psychologist for an evaluation.

Comment: By using these drawings as only one source of data within a larger comprehensive evaluation, appropriate recommendations were able to be made involving Gifted classes at school, parenting Gifted children, and short-term individual therapy for Theodore. The therapy focused on the trauma caused to Theodore by his exposure to violent reading material. Based on the data collected during Theodore's evaluation, there was no indication that Theodore was the victim of child sexual abuse.

SEXUAL SYMBOLISM
IN CHILDREN'S ART

SEXUAL SYMBOLISM
AS EMOTIONAL INDICATORS
OF PSYCHOPATHOLOGY

In an attempt to validate symbolic indicators of emotional disturbance in children's Human Figure Drawings (HFD), Koppitz (1966) identified 30 symbolic items as valid emotional indicators. The 30 items fall into three separate categories:

1. *Quality of Drawing (9 Items)* - poor integration of parts, shading of face, shading of body and/or limbs, shading of hands and/or neck, gross asymmetry of limbs, figure slanting by 15 degrees or more, tiny figure 2 inches in size or less, big figure 9 inches in height or more, and transparencies.
2. *Items Not Usually Found in Children's HFDs (13 Items)* - tiny head 1/10th or less total figure, crossed eyes, teeth, short arms, long arms, arms clinging to side of body, hands as big as head, hands cut off, legs pressed together, genitals, monster or grotesque figure, three or more figures spontaneously drawn, and clouds/rain.
3. *Omission of Items (8 Items)* - no eyes, no nose, no mouth, no body, no arms, no legs, no feet, and no neck. (p. 313)

A review of the Koppitz model of the HFD reported in Keyser and Sweetland's *Test Critiques* (1984) reads

. . . the presentation of HFD analysis by Koppitz begins with the proposition that HFDs can be used to assess both the developmental and emotional status of a child, and that a different set of signs will appear for each purpose . . . the lack of a substantial empirical base for the test must lead one to be very cautious in employing the procedure at all. Clinical specialists having considerable experience with children and with unstructured assessment tools may wish to utilize the procedure on a trial basis to see if their clinical sensitivity can glean clues to the child's behavior from HFDs, but in any case corroborative data will be necessary before judgements can be made with some confidence. (Chase, 1984, p. 193)

SEXUAL SYMBOLISM
AS A MARKER
OF SEXUAL ABUSE

Sexual symbolism represented in children's drawings also has been proposed as a marker of sexual abuse and has been examined by a number of researchers. Cohen and Phelps (1985) listed several features of House-Tree-Person drawings they reported to be indicative of sexual abuse including phallic chimney (defined as disproportionate in size and shape to the house), one window only, one window differing from others, and a red-colored house. Riordan and Verdel (1991) outline indicators of sexual abuse in human figure drawings pooled from several studies and contend that eyes which are without pupils, abnormally small, hidden by glasses, or totally omitted indicate sexual arousal, guilt, and shame. A nose overemphasized by size or linear contrast signifies phallic preoccupation, and an overemphasized or elongated neck is said to suggest difficulty with maintaining control of sexuality. (See Cummings, 1986 for a more comprehensive review of sexual symbolism in children's drawings.) To date, research has not established that any of these symbols are valid or reliable markers of sexual abuse.

Research examining symbolism in children's drawings as markers of sexual abuse has not shown symbolic features to be sensitive or specific to the identification of sexually abused children. Hammer and Kaplan (1966) investigated the normative features of children's human figure drawings for various ages and sex and the consistency of childen's drawings. A total of 1,305 presumably nonsexually abused male and female children attending fourth through sixth grade were evaluated in this study. The children were asked to draw a picture of a person. They were then asked to draw a person of the opposite sex to the one they had just drawn. One week later, the task was repeated under the same conditions.

Results indicated that no generalizing statement regarding markers of pathology or sexual abuse could be made based on omissions of body parts in children's human figure drawings. When the children's drawings were compared (i.e., first-week drawing to second-week drawing), omissions of fingers were found to be consistent at each grade level for both males and females and for both same and opposite-sex drawings. The inclusion or omission of hands, feet, and nose was inconsistent across administrations at all grade levels for both males and females and for same and opposite-sex drawings.

The children's drawing of heads without bodies, shading of hair, and closed mouths were consistent across the first-week and the second-week drawings. The drawings of heads without bodies by boys significantly exceeded the drawings by girls. The shading of hair was found to increase with age for boys but decrease with age for girls. In general, about 80% of the boys shaded the hair on their drawings, while 55% to 60% of the girls shaded the hair more frequently in opposite-sex drawings in contrast to same-sex drawings. Both boys and girls produced significantly more closed mouths than open mouths at each grade level. Boys and girls also were consistent in drawing either an open or closed mouth during the first- to second-week drawings. At each grade level, boys produced significantly more teeth. However, the inclusion of teeth was inconsistent from the first-week drawing to the second-week drawing.

While Hammer and Kaplan (1966) collected normative data on presumably nonsexually abused children's human figure drawings, Chantler, Pelco, and Mertin (1993) attempted to discriminate sexually abused from nonsexually abused children based on emotional indicators and sexual symbolism in the children's human figure drawings. The researchers cite a correct classification rate of 58.82% using a combination of the Louisville Sexual Problems subscale scores and Koppitz Flag Item scores and a 77.45% correct classification rate using a combination of the Louisville Factor scores and the Koppitz Flag Item scores. Koppitz Flag items include poor integration, big figure, head, arms clinging, hand cut off, and no feet. Problems with this study include an absence of consistent empirical research substantiating the Louisville Behavior Checklists as having discriminate power to identify sexually abused children. Specifically, a number of the 11 items related to sexualized behavior, such as "masturbates/plays with self openly," have been found to also be frequently demonstrated by nonsexually abused children (Friedrich et al., 1992). Further problems with this study include the lack of established psychometric properties, including reliability and validity, in the Koppitz scoring system.

Interestingly, within the Chantler et al. (1993) study, the scores obtained within nonsexually abused and sexually abused groups on both measures were variable. Thus, some sexually abused children actually earned lower scores than the nonsexually abused children, and some nonsexually abused children earned higher scores than the sexually abused children. This variability may be a reflection of the heterogeneity of the sexual abuse group, or it may be related to using a nonstandardized test to measure behavior.

FAMILY DRAWINGS

One study examined Kinetic Family Drawings drawn by sexually abused and nonsexually abused children and their mothers (Hackbarth, Murphy, & McQuary, 1991). Drawings were scored with the Like to Live in the Family scoring system (Burns, 1982). Mothers of sexually abused children received significantly higher scores on their drawings than their children, suggesting that the mothers had more positive perceptions of their family than their sexually abused children. Conversely, nonsexually abused children and their mothers did not differ significantly on the scores they received for their drawings. Furthermore, mothers of nonsexually abused children scored higher than mothers of sexually abused children, suggesting that the mothers with nonsexually abused children had more positive perceptions of their family than the other group of mothers. The problems with this study included the absence of blind raters and lack of a comparison group of other types of traumatized children. While the Kinetic Family Drawings cannot be used for diagnostic purposes, the information derived from scoring child and mother drawings with the Like to Live in the Family scoring system has clinical utility for treatment.

RESEARCH ON
DISCRIMINATIVE POWER
OF CHILDREN'S DRAWINGS

Based on the research conducted to date, the assumption that the drawings of sexually abused children will differ from those of nonsexually abused children, on the presence of specific qualitative features in drawings, is unsubstantiated. The studies researching this issue have been confounded by the diversity of both subject samples and measurement criteria. Methodological factors, including recruitment of subjects, collection of drawing samples, training of the raters, ambiguity in measurement criteria, and lack of empirical validation of measurements (or "markers"), have created many comparison problems.

FOCUSED DRAWINGS
AS A CHILD SEXUAL ABUSE
ASSESSMENT TOOL

The utilization of focused drawings may provide yet another source of data for the evaluator. Following a verbal statement by the child that he or she was involved in sexual activity, focused drawings are used by some evaluators as a demonstration aid. For example, the child is asked to draw a picture of the sexual behavior perpetrated on him or her, including what happened and where the abuse took place. Because the focused drawing may provide the child a stimulus to generate details of the sexually abusive experience(s), this drawing task may lessen the need for more directed questioning by the evaluator.

With toddler and young preschool children, focused drawings may not be useful because of this age group's immature fine motor coordination, limited drawing skills, and difficulty using symbolic representations. Additionally, some older children may not think that they are proficient at drawing and thus a drawing task also may not facilitate these older children's disclosures.

Psychometric properties, including reliability, validity, and normative data are not pertinent because the evaluator does not "interpret" the symbolic meaning of the results; rather, the child describes the drawing. The use of a focused drawing task follows:

Shelly, age 7, had tearfully disclosed to her mother that her father tied her arms, made her put his penis in her mouth, and had put his tongue in her vagina. The sexual abuse, reportedly, took place when the mother was gone for the day. Following

Shelly's disclosure, the mother did not allow the father to stay in the home. Everyday, the father called the house and talked to the victim. After approximately a week, Shelly recanted her abuse, and the father returned home. The topic of sexual abuse was never again discussed by Shelly or her parents. One year later, Shelly (who was then 8) was brought to a psychologist for an evaluation. Her presenting problem was depression. During a comprehensive evaluation, Shelly disclosed the sexual abuse by her father. She stated that she was frightened of her father. The evaluator then directed Shelly, "Draw a picture for me of what happened." Shelly then drew a very detailed picture of herself lying on a bed with each wrist tied to the bedposts with her mother's scarves. Her father was described as kneeling over her with an erect penis. When describing her drawing, she stated that she had been scared because when her father put his penis in her mouth, he pulled her head up off the bed, and she felt as though she could not breathe. She stated that her father has not sexually abused her since that time because her mother never leaves her alone with him, and her mother tells her to lock herself in her room at night.

Comment: *The drawing task provided a stimulus which allowed Shelly to provide further details of her experience and lessened the need for highly directed questions.*

CONCLUSION

The search for ways to accurately identify sexually abused children has included the use of checklists, projective tests, and projective children's drawings. To date, none of these instruments provide "markers" that can stand alone as criteria diagnostic of child sexual abuse. Although standardized child behavior rating scales traditionally have been used to identify the presence of specific behavior problems, these behavior problems are not specific to sexual abuse. As a result, attempts were made to develop specific behavior rating scales that would differentiate sexually abused from nonsexually abused children. These early behavior rating scales were not standardized, and the majority of the behaviors included on the behavior rating scales were found to be symptoms of children under stress rather than unique markers of child sexual victimization.

Although symptoms of regression in adaptive functioning are not unique to sexually abused children, increased levels of sexualized behaviors are more common in sexually abused children than nonsexually abused children. Based on these findings, Friedrich (1993) designed a behavior rating scale to identify the presence of specific sexualized behaviors exhibited by children. Friedrich's Child Sexual Behavior Inventory is an empirically based objective instrument which presents normative data on the sexualized behavior of nonsexually abused and sexually abused children. However, because this instrument is a behavior rating scale, test validity is dependent on the objectivity of the person completing the instrument. Furthermore, it must be remembered that the demonstration of sexual behavior is not a litmus test for sexual abuse. The problem remains that children are a heterogeneous group and, as a result, not all sexually abused children will exhibit sexual behaviors. Conversely, some nonsexually abused children will exhibit sexual behaviors.

It is important to be aware of base rates of symptoms and behavior problems when forming conclusions about whether a child is the victim of sexual abuse. When examining base rates, the evaluator must establish the rate at which symptoms appear in a nonsexually abused group. If a behavior could be identified that consistently occurred in sexually abused children but never occurred in nonsexually abused children, then the presence of these symptoms could be used to reliably and validly identify children who were sexually abused. Although it was previously thought that nightmares and behavioral regressions were markers that could identify children who were victims of sexual abuse, it was then discovered that nonsexually abused children also showed these same symptoms when under stress. While symptoms that result from a trauma are identifiable, the specifics of the trauma cannot be identified from the symptoms alone.

To date, the use of paper-and-pencil tests, projective tests, or children's projective artwork to identify children who are sexually abused is not supported by research. Currently, there are no paper-and-pencil tests or projective tools, including standardized tests or children's drawings, which discriminate nonsexually abused from sexually abused children.

While professionals debate the utility of the techniques and instruments discussed in this chapter, the problem has not been the instruments per se, but rather the misuse of these techniques and instruments by professionals. Children's drawings used as a "diagnostic" instrument of sexual abuse would not be supported by authorities in the areas of psychological tests and measurement. Nor would the use of data collected from projective personality instruments be viewed as acceptable by these authorities for identifying children who are sexually abused. Misinterpretation and overinterpretation of behaviors, test results, or artwork may be among the greatest errors evaluators can make.

```
┌─────────────────────────────────────────────────────────────────────┐
│                            GUIDELINES                                 │
│                   Considerations and Cautions                         │
└─────────────────────────────────────────────────────────────────────┘
```

- Professionals who formulate diagnostic conclusions based on data from assessment tools that are not reliable and valid instruments are at a higher risk to make false-positive errors (identifying a child as sexually abused who is not) and false-negative errors (identifying a child as not sexually abused who is).
- Many assessment instruments have age limits. Very few standardized measures are available to directly assess very young children. Thus, the assessment of very young children will primarily rely on the reports and observations of caregivers (i.e., parents, teachers, etc.) and observations of the evaluator.
- Nomothetic methods focus on statistical probabilities and compare the child's responses to normative data. Idiographic methods focus on the child's common themes and compare the child's responses for consistencies.
- Standardized observation systems, rather than subjective clinical observations, may be useful in collecting objective data involving parent-child interactions.
- Standardized behavior rating scales have utility in providing the evaluator with information from family members and individuals outside of the family which can then be compared.
- Because items on behavior rating scales are face-valid, respondents can deny or exaggerate the presence of behaviors.
- In a review of the recent empirical studies on the impact of sexual abuse on children, over one-fourth of the sexually abused children were found to show no significant behavior problems on broad-based child behavior rating scales.
- Research suggests that family disruption and stress confound the difference between sexually abused and nonsexually abused children on behavioral measures.
- Behavior rating scales assessing dissociation do not show specificity to behaviors or cognitions exhibited by sexually abused children and, therefore, do not have predictive diagnostic validity.
- Projective tests (standardized or nonstandardized) cannot be used to determine whether the child has been sexually abused but can be used to understand the personality functioning of the child.
- Children's artwork used as a projective tool cannot be used to identify sexually abused children based on the presence of sexual symbolism.
- Attempts to standardize children's drawings as a projective instrument, used in the assessment of underlying psychological dynamics, have failed to satisfy the standards required of psychometric tests. Furthermore, neither an empirical or clinical consensus has been reached regarding the identification of features in drawings that are mutually exclusive "markers" for sexually abused children.
- Genitals drawn on human figures by children cannot be used as a sole criterion to diagnose sexual abuse.
- Focused drawings may have utility as a demonstration aid.
- Overinterpretation of children's behaviors, test results, or artwork can lead to faulty conclusions.

CHAPTER 10

The Evaluation Process

This chapter utilizes a case study to present the step-by-step procedures that might be utilized in a forensic evaluation of child sexual abuse.

*   *   *

ORGANIZING THE EVALUATION

This chapter presents specific steps that could be followed when conducting a forensic evaluation of allegations of child sexual abuse. The relationship between the goals and each of the steps is also addressed. A graphic summary of these steps is contained in the flow chart on page 260. A case study is utilized to demonstrate the application of this step-by-step process.

> **GOAL:** Establish external and internal independence and define the role of the evaluator (refer to Chapter 2).

Prior to accepting a case, the mental health professional must ensure external and internal independence (White & Quinn, 1988). External independence involves the evaluator's ability to remain objective and avoid alliances with any of the individuals involved in the case. This objective stance is optimized through court appointment of the evaluator. Internal independence involves the evaluator's ability to avoid personal biases that would influence obtaining or interpreting information presented by any party. Therefore, cases should be reviewed prior to acceptance. The evaluator should not accept cases that involve issues or family values that would conflict with the evaluator's personal biases.

The first steps in the evaluation process also involve defining the professional role and organizing the evaluation process. At that time, payment expectations, a request for a court order identifying the mental health professional's role, the expectations for the parents' and child's involvement, and the expectations for accessibility to collateral information are delineated.

FLOW CHART OF EVALUATION PROCESS IN COURT ORDERED ASSESSMENT OF ALLEGED CHILD SEXUAL ABUSE EMBEDDED IN A CUSTODY/VISITATION DISPUTE

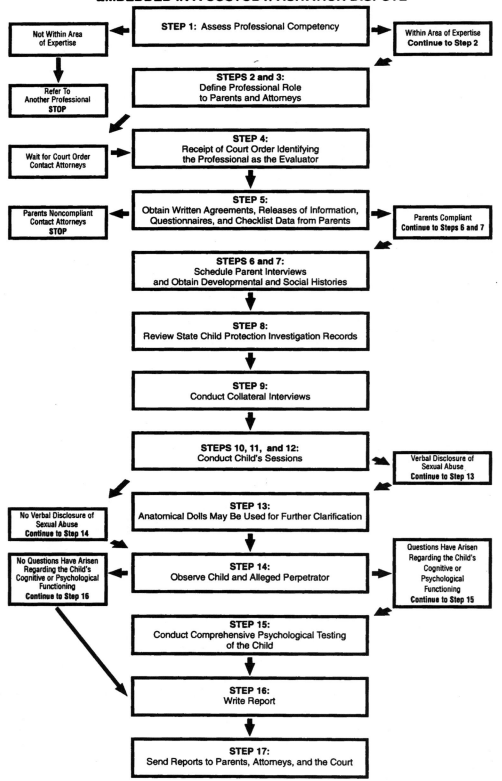

STEP 1: Assess Professional Competency

Not Within Area of Expertise

Within Area of Expertise
Continue to Step 2

Refer To Another Professional
STOP

STEPS 2 and 3:
Define Professional Role to Parents and Attorneys

Wait for Court Order Contact Attorneys

STEP 4:
Receipt of Court Order Identifying the Professional as the Evaluator

Parents Noncompliant Contact Attorneys
STOP

STEP 5:
Obtain Written Agreements, Releases of Information, Questionnaires, and Checklist Data from Parents

Parents Compliant
Continue to Steps 6 and 7

STEPS 6 and 7:
Schedule Parent Interviews and Obtain Developmental and Social Histories

STEP 8:
Review State Child Protection Investigation Records

STEP 9:
Conduct Collateral Interviews

STEPS 10, 11, and 12:
Conduct Child's Sessions

Verbal Disclosure of Sexual Abuse
Continue to Step 13

No Verbal Disclosure of Sexual Abuse
Continue to Step 14

STEP 13:
Anatomical Dolls May Be Used for Further Clarification

No Questions Have Arisen Regarding the Child's Cognitive or Psychological Functioning
Continue to Step 16

STEP 14:
Observe Child and Alleged Perpetrator

Questions Have Arisen Regarding the Child's Cognitive or Psychological Functioning
Continue to Step 15

STEP 15:
Conduct Comprehensive Psychological Testing of the Child

STEP 16:
Write Report

STEP 17:
Send Reports to Parents, Attorneys, and the Court

STEP 1.   Assess the competency to perform tasks and the ability to maintain internal and external independence.

Once an evaluation is requested, the mental health professional determines whether the referral falls within his or her area of expertise and whether there are any conflicts of interest.

STEP 2.   Define the professional's role and delineate the expectations.

During the initial telephone contact, the mental health professional addresses the criteria for contracting his or her services including

- The mental health professional will be court appointed to evaluate the child.
- The court will identify which parties are responsible to pay the evaluation fees.
- Release of information forms must be signed by the mother and father to allow contact with both attorneys.
- The information disclosed during the evaluation will be included in a report to the court and, thus, unlike information disclosed during therapy, is not confidential.
- The parents will agree to stop any further questioning of the child about the alleged sexual abuse.
- The mental health professional will be provided with the following:

  - relevant documents, including previous interviews by professionals
  - written consent to speak with the child's past and present therapists, teachers, daycare providers, and other relevant people
  - the child's developmental history from both parents
  - a minimum of three individual sessions with the child
  - individual sessions observing the child with (a) his or her mother, (b) his or her father, and (c) the alleged perpetrator if a parent figure
  - psychological evaluations on both parents and their respective paramours conducted by the professional evaluating the child or by a separate court-ordered psychologist

The mental health professional sends a letter to both parents identifying the professional's criteria for involvement in the case. (See Form Letter, Appendix W, p. 345.)

STEP 3.   Define the professional's role to the attorneys.

Letters are sent to the attorneys addressing the criteria for the professional's involvement in the case. (See Form Letter, Appendix X, p. 347.)

> **GOAL:**   Collect all data consistently and objectively (refer to Chapter 2).

The mental health professional must be consistent in his or her collection of data from both parents. Similar procedures should be utilized with both parties, with each parent scheduled for the same number of sessions. It also is preferable that each parent bring the child to one of the child's individual sessions. Pertinent documents and reports should be reviewed prior to the parent interviews, if possible.

STEP 4.   Obtain court appointment.

Prior to scheduling appointments, the mental health professional waits to receive the court order appointing him or her as the evaluator. The professional should read the court order to ensure the task is identified correctly.

STEP 5.   Obtain written agreements and collect collateral information.

Both parents are required to sign the following documents:

- Contracts for services delineating their legal rights and responsibilities regarding payment of fees, scheduling and canceling appointments, and so on.
- Release of Information forms for both attorneys.
- Release of Information forms to collect collateral information from additional sources. These sources may include

    - preschool or elementary school teachers (over the past 3 years)
    - Sunday school or synagogue teachers (over past 3 years)
    - babysitters
    - maternal and paternal grandparents
    - state child abuse investigator
    - examining medical doctor
    - pediatrician
    - previous or present therapist(s)

The parents are informed that the written evaluation will be sent directly to each attorney and the court upon completion.

Each parent is informed that his or her child's sessions will be videotaped. The parents are then required to provide verbal or written permission for videotaping the child's interviews with the mental health professional.

Each parent also is required to complete checklists and questionnaires on his or her child in order to provide the mental health professional with further collateral information.

- These checklists may include

  - Child History Checklist
  - Children's Problems Checklist
  - Burks' Behavior Rating Scales
  - Child Sexual Behavior Inventory - Revised

After Release of Information forms are signed by both parents, the child's teachers are sent several checklists.

- These checklists may include

  - Children's Problem Checklist
  - Burks' Behavior Rating Scales
  - Child Sexual Behavior Inventory - Revised

STEP 6.   Schedule the parents' interviews.

Each parent is scheduled for a 2-hour interview that focuses on the child's developmental history. The child's three individual 1-hour sessions are scheduled to follow the parents' sessions. Each parent is advised to bring any documents he or she believes to be relevant. The accusing parent is also requested to write in chronological order his or her first suspicions of sexual abuse, behaviors that precipitated the suspicions, and first verbal disclosures of questionable sexual activity - verbatim (when, where, and to whom the child disclosed).

CASE PRESENTATION

CASE BACKGROUND

This case involves a 6-year-old caucasian male whose parents divorced when he was 2 years old. Both parents have new, live-in partners. The father and his paramour have no children. The mother and her paramour are expecting a baby. This sexual abuse case is embedded in a custody dispute.

Since age 2 Russell has lived 4 days with his mother and then transferred to his father's home for 4 days. This living arrangement began to cause problems between the parents when Russell entered kindergarten. The parents were unable to reach an agreement on where Russell should primarily live during the school week. In the midst of the conflict over residential placement, Russell allegedly reported to his father that his mother's boyfriend showers with him, pinches his penis, locks him in his room, and sticks needles in his penis. Following these allegations, Russell's father was temporarily awarded primary residential custody.

> **GOAL:**   Use a Comprehensive Model in assessing the allegation of child sexual abuse (refer to Chapter 5).

As part of the Comprehensive Model, the collection of collateral information is essential. The historical information provided by the parents is important in understanding the context in which the sexual abuse allegation arises. Other collateral sources, including extended family members and teachers, may provide relevant information. When collecting collateral information, provide people time to be and feel listened to and avoid giving any feedback or answering questions about therapeutic issues (Clark, 1994).

STEP 7.   Obtain Developmental and Social Histories.

DEVELOPMENTAL AND SOCIAL HISTORIES

Russell's parents provided the following developmental information. Russell was born in San Diego, California, to his 19-year-old mother, Patricia Snell, and 20-year-old father, Michael Snell. At that time, Russell's father was in the Marines. The parents reported that there were no complications during the pregnancy with or delivery of Russell. Several weeks after Russell's birth, Russell became very ill and was incorrectly diagnosed with a stomach virus. One month after he was born, Russell had surgery to correct pyloric stenosis - a syndrome in which the muscle in the digestive tract closes. Following Russell's recuperation from surgery, the father and mother moved to Florida and resided with the father's parents. At that same time, the mother was reported to have had postpartum depression. The father began attending Alcoholics Anonymous when Russell was 3 years old. He reported that he has not consumed alcohol for 3 years.

Russell crawled and walked early. He was delayed in his speech. His first words were not spoken until after his first birthday, and he did not talk in sentences until after his second birthday. Russell did not sleep through the night until he was over 1 year old. He was highly sensitive to sounds and tactile sensations, such as being wet. He did not like people to hold him or to interact with him throughout his infancy and toddler years. When he did develop speech, he was electively mute with strangers and would avoid interactions with relatives or family friends whom he saw on a frequent basis.

Russell was enrolled in public daycare from age 4 months until he entered kindergarten. Russell's teachers reported that for the most part, as a toddler and preschooler, Russell was a loner - he infrequently participated with the other children. When he did interact with his peers, he was aggressive. Russell's aggressive behavior has become progressively worse over the past 2 years.

Russell began soiling his pants at age 3. He started with several accidents a week and has become progressively worse over the past 3 years. Currently when angered, he will have a complete bowel movement in his pants. Presently, he spits on children, will not sit still, is defiant with teachers, and has cut his hair and clothing.

Russell's parents divorced when Russell was 2 years old. At that time, the parents agreed upon shared parental custody with neither parent receiving child support. Russell over the past 4 years, has alternated between his mother's and father's homes every 4 days. The parents are both unhappy with this arrangement now that Russell has started kindergarten.

Presently, Russell is attending kindergarten at a public school. He is reported to have social problems with the other children in his class and has had trouble getting his work done. The public school Russell attends is a new school that is piloting a novel academic structure. This pilot program requires Russell to change classrooms and teachers three times during the day. The guidance counselor at school told the mother they were considering placing Russell in a class for emotionally handicapped children. The mother reported that she is upset with the school because many people are angry at Russell for his behavior - "but it's not his fault."

Based on Russell's behavior problems in school, Russell started seeing Dr. Raffa, a psychiatrist, in October. Russell was immediately placed on Ritalin by this psychiatrist. The mother reported that Dr. Raffa focused on the parents and didn't see Russell alone. Russell was reported to be in the room when Dr. Raffa worked with the parents. The mother stated that when in therapy with Dr. Raffa, the father's answer for Russell's problems was to put Russell with him full-time and "give him a chance." The mother said they were in counseling to help Russell "deal with changes," and the mother thought it was wrong that the father wanted to make Russell "suffer" through another change. During the period of time the family was in therapy, Russell, reportedly, told his mother that his father hit him with a belt buckle. This was reported to the state child abuse registry after Russell reported this to Dr. Raffa. The mother stated that the father is too strict, and she is lenient. The father attended three sessions with Dr. Raffa and reportedly then refused to continue. Therapy with Dr. Raffa then also was discontinued by the mother. Although therapy was terminated, Russell maintained medication checks with Dr. Raffa.

The mother recently went to mediation to try to stop the weekday changes in Russell's home placement. She was seeking to have Russell live with her during the weekdays and visit his father on weekends. The father refused to agree to this arrangement.

The father believes that Russell needs both his father and his mother. The father stated that he "is more regimented," and the mother "is more artistic." The father believes he would be the best parent for Russell to live with during school days. The father went to the mother and said he thought the visitation needed to be changed because Russell was unable to cope with kindergarten. The father believes Russell's life needs to be more structured.

Russell's mother and the mother's boyfriend, Donald, began dating 5 months ago, shortly after Russell turned 6 years old. Donald moved into the mother's home last month, after the mother became pregnant with Donald's child. Three weeks ago, the mother's boyfriend was accused of taking a shower with Russell and molesting him. Regarding the allegation, the mother stated that recently, her bathtub became unusable and, the day of the alleged sexual abuse, Russell didn't want to take a shower because he had never taken a shower before. Reportedly, in order to help Russell be less fearful, the mother's boyfriend got into the shower with Russell. The mother said both her mother and she were in the house sitting in the kitchen during Russell's shower with Donald. Following his shower, Russell reportedly came running into the kitchen telling his mother and grandmother that the mother's boyfriend had taught him how to take a shower. He reportedly did not appear upset and did not make any statements indicating sexually inappropriate behavior.

The mother and her boyfriend have separated several times. She feels her "up and down" relationship with Donald has affected Russell's feelings about Donald. Prior to Donald moving into her home, Donald began coming over on days when Russell was at his father's house so that the mother could give separate attention to Donald and Russell.

The father reported that he and his fiancée have been living together for the past 4 months. Russell was 4 years old when he first met his father's fiancée. The father reported that he and his fiancée have a good relationship and that Russell also has a good relationship with his fiancée. The father reported that recently he and his fiancée were talking to Russell about things that Russell does with his mother. Reportedly, Russell said to his father that the mother's boyfriend "takes a shower with me," and "shows me how to wash." Upon further inquiry by the father, Russell then reported to his father that the mother's boyfriend "pinches me down there," and after the shower he "takes me and locks me in my room and shows me how to dress." He then, reportedly, spontaneously stated to his father that the mother's boyfriend "sticks needles in my penis."

The father stated he called the state child abuse registry, and an investigator went out to Russell's school, but Russell did not disclose any information to the investigator. The next week, when Russell was with his father, he reportedly initially denied that he had told his father anything about Donald hurting him. However, Russell later reportedly informed his father that he did not tell the investigator about Donald because it was "a secret."

The father has been given temporary custody of Russell until an evaluation can be conducted. The father said he feels he needs to know whether this happened. The father stated that he and his fiancée showed Russell the video by Henry Winkler on protecting oneself from sexual abuse. The father reported that he and his fiancée have read books on sexual abuse and have learned that "children will be threatened with physical and emotional harm to themselves, as well as other people whom they love." The father reported further concern due to his observation of Russell's masturbating in front of the television and in the bathtub. He has read that this is a sign of sexual abuse.

The father reported that since Russell has been living with him, Russell has improved at school academically but still has trouble with his attention and aggressive behaviors toward peers. The father reported that he is not trying to take Russell away from his mother; however, he feels "she does not make a good structural parent."

STEP 8.   Review child abuse investigative records.

MEDICAL REPORT

A medical evaluation was conducted at the South Community Hospital. Dr. Earlywine, the examining physician, wrote

History of Present Illness

This 6-year-old white male was brought to the Emergency Room at South Community Hospital on this date for examination at the request of his natural father, Michael Snell. The father is divorced from the patient's mother, Patricia Snell, who apparently shares custody of Russell on an alternating basis. The father indicates that Russell, when staying with him, reported that the mother's boyfriend showers with him, pinches his penis, and sticks needles in his penis.

In discussion with the child in the presence of Darlene Preston, RN, with the father not present, the child appeared quite relaxed and readily answered questions in an appropriate manner. He appeared alert and had adequate vocabulary and motor skills, consistent with his age and development. He stated that when he stayed with his mother, he slept in his own room. He absolutely denied that anyone had touched his penis or had inserted anything into his penis or anus.

Genitourinary

The circumcised penis was normal in appearance. Needle marks were absent. The anus was unremarkable with normal sphincter control and no reflex relaxation of the sphincter. There were no tears, bruises, lesions, or scars.

CHILD ABUSE INVESTIGATIVE REPORT

Child abuse investigator, Ron Manaro, interviewed Russell. Mr. Manaro's written report stated Russell denied to the investigator that any individuals had touched his penis or inserted objects in his penis or anus.

STEP 9.   Conduct interviews with teachers and other collateral sources.

INTERVIEW WITH TEACHERS
AND OTHER COLLATERAL SOURCES

Telephone interviews were conducted with Russell's previous preschool teacher, Ms. Knutson, and his present teacher, Ms. Bradley. Russell's maternal and paternal grandparents were also interviewed.

Ms. Knutson was Russell's primary preschool teacher from age 3 to age 5. She stated that during the 2½ years that Russell attended her classroom, he exhibited serious behavior problems toward his peers, including kicking, biting, and pinching. He also was defiant with his teachers. When given time out or reprimands, he would defecate in his pants. Russell lacked cooperative play skills and tended to isolate himself from his peers. He never exhibited any masturbatory behaviors or sexual behaviors with his peers. His behavior did not improve over the 2-year period he attended preschool; rather, it became progressively worse.

Russell's current teacher, Ms. Bradley, reported that Russell is exhibiting serious behavior problems in her classroom. Russell is physically aggressive with his peers when they do not allow him to play with their toys. He also is defiant. Russell wanders around the classroom when the class is seated and working. He ignores her requests to return to his seat. Recently, when sent out of the room, Russell defecated in his pants. Ms. Bradley does not know if Russell can be maintained in a regular classroom. Although Russell was placed on Ritalin, there has been no observable behavior change on this medication. She believes he may be a "slow learner." Russell has never made any statements regarding his involvement in sexual experiences initiated by any of his caretakers. Russell has never been observed to initiate sexual activities with his peers. Ms. Bradley reported that, at times, Russell will fondle his genitals in the classroom, but she does not perceive this behavior to be aberrant for a 6 year old.

Ms. Bradley completed the (Achenbach) Teacher Report form. Six subscales were elevated at the clinically significant level. These included - Anxious/Depressed, Social Problems, Thought Problems, Attention Problems, Delinquent Behavior, and Aggressive Behavior. Ms. Bradley also completed the Child Sexual Behavior Inventory-Revised (CSBI-R). The CSBI-R score of 4 was not significantly elevated for a 6-year-old male, suggesting Russell was not exhibiting aberrant sexual behaviors in the classroom.

The results of the (Achenbach) Teacher Report Form and Child Sexual Behavior Inventory-Revised, with Ms. Bradley as the respondent, were compared with the parents' completed checklist. The (Achenbach) Child Behavior Checklist, with the mother as the respondent, showed seven subscales were elevated at the clinically significant level. These included - Somatic Complaints, Anxious/Depressed, Social Problems, Thought Problems, Attention Problems, Delinquent Behavior, and Aggressive Behavior. The (Achenbach) Child Behavior Checklist, with the father as the respondent, showed clinically significant elevations on the same seven subscales identified by the mother. On the Child Sexual Behavior Inventory-Revised, the mother endorsed 1 sexual behavior, giving Russell a CSBI-R score of 1. The father endorsed 5 sexual behaviors, giving Russell a CSBI-R score of 5. Neither CSBI-R score was significantly elevated for a 6-year-old male.

Russell's paternal and maternal grandparents were interviewed. The maternal grandparents believe Russell's problems stem from the divorce. The paternal grandparents believe Russell's problems stem from a lack of discipline. Neither the maternal or paternal grandparents had questioned Russell about the alleged sexual abuse nor had Russell made any statements to them about the alleged abuse. None of the grandparents have ever witnessed Russell exhibiting any sexualized behaviors.

> **GOAL:** Attempt to utilize verbal interviews with the alleged sexual abuse victim as one component in the evaluation process (refer to Chapter 6).

The child should be seen individually for his or her interviews. Every effort should be made to help the child separate from the parent for these sessions. Sessions should include assessment of developmental abilities, teaching the child skills to enhance resistance to interviewer influence, and movement of interview questions from open-ended to more directive. Time should be taken to build rapport with the child. The child should be provided appropriate play materials to keep him or her seated during questioning. However, play materials that will not distract the child from attending to the interviewer's questions should be utilized. The child should be provided breaks from questioning approximately every 15 to 20 minutes; a single interview session should not extend beyond an hour.

STEP 10. Conduct the child's first session.

FIRST SESSION WITH CHILD

Russell was brought to his first session by his mother. The mother was reminded that Russell's session would be videotaped.

Introduction and Defining the Task

The psychologist introduced herself to Russell by stating, "You must be Russell. My name is Dr. Kuehnle." (pause) "I am a doctor who talks to children. I don't give shots or medicine." (pause) "Your job is to help me learn about you." (pause) "I want you to help me learn about things you like to do." (pause) "I want you to help me learn about things you don't like to do."

Russell was not asked any questions that could be regarded as coercive, such as if he wanted to be the psychologist's friend.

Confidentiality

Russell was told that the psychologist would be videotaping their playing together. He also was told, "Some other people are going to know what you say to me, but this videotape won't be on television shows."

Observations

Russell presented as a 6-year-old, caucasian male who was thin in stature with black hair and dark brown eyes. Manner of dress was appropriate and hygiene was good. Gait and posture were normal. He parted willingly without complaint from his mother in order to accompany the psychologist. Motor behavior was fidgety and restless. He was distracted. Primary facial expression was neutral; eye contact was poor. Speech quantity and quality were normal. However, a speech impairment in the form of mild stuttering was observed. Mood was neutral and affect was blunted. Attention and concentration were moderately impaired. Memory functions were intact.

Russell did not wait for the psychologist to direct the activities; rather, he took control immediately and initially directed his own activities. He, at times, was oppositional and ignored the requests of the psychologist. However, when limits were set, he was compliant.

Developmental Assessment

This first session with Russell involved a developmental assessment; Russell was not asked any abuse-related questions.

Building Rapport

When Russell entered the playroom, he was allowed to select any of the play materials present. These materials included markers, crayons, paints, doll house, sandbox, and puppets. Russell chose to play with the doll house. His doll play did not involve a theme; rather, he held and looked at each of the doll family members and examined the doll house furniture. He did not include the psychologist in his play and made no verbal or behavioral acknowledgement of her presence.

Assessing Language Concepts

When Russell terminated his play in the doll house, the psychologist redirected his play to the Play Doh Fun Factory. The Play Doh Fun Factory allows for physical involvement of the child with the play materials without interrupting his play if conversation is established. Furthermore, this play is not distracting to the conversation. Initially, Russell ignored the psychologist and acted as though she was not speaking to him.

During this play, the following conversation took place:

The Psychologist:	"Russell, how old are you?"
Russell:	"Six."
The Psychologist:	"What grade are you in?"
Russell:	"Kindergarten."
The Psychologist:	"Who are your friends at school?"
Russell:	"Nobody."
The Psychologist:	"I have a friend named Karen. I like to go swimming and ride bikes with my friends."

Assessing Concepts of Who, What, Where, and How

These concepts were not presented in a rapid succession but presented over 5-minute periods of time.

The Psychologist:	(Who)	"Who do you live with?"
Russell:		"My mommy and daddy."
The Psychologist:		"Do your mommy and daddy live together?"
Russell:		"No, my dad lives with Janet."
The Psychologist:	(Where)	"Where do you sleep at your Mommy's house?"
Russell:		"In my room."
The Psychologist:	(Where)	"Where do you sleep at your Daddy and Janet's house?"
Russell:		"In my room there."

[Break in questioning]

The Psychologist:	(When)	"When did you eat breakfast?"
Russell:		"Today."
The Psychologist:		"When today did you eat breakfast?"
Russell:		"When I woke up."
The Psychologist:	(Past Activity)	"What did you eat for dinner last night?"
Russell:		"A hot dog."

[Break in questioning]

The Psychologist:	(Past activity)	"What did Santa Claus bring you at Christmas time?"
Russell:		"A bike."

[Break in questioning]

The Psychologist:	(What)	"What does Mommy do when you are naughty?"
Russell:		"Puts me in my room."
The Psychologist:	(What)	"What does Daddy do when you are naughty?"
Russell:		"Makes me stand in the corner."
The Psychologist:	(How)	"How do you feel when Mommy sends you to your room?"
Russell:		"Sad."
The Psychologist:	(How)	"How do you feel when Daddy stands you in the corner?"
Russell:		"Sad."

Assessing Concepts of Touch

The Psychologist:	(Touch)	"Russell, pinch this bunny (stuffed animal)."
Russell:		(Pinched the bunny.)
The Psychologist:	(Hard Touch)	"Russell, give this bunny a hard pinch."
Russell:		(Pinched the bunny hard.)
The Psychologist:	(Soft Touch)	"Now give this bunny a soft pinch."
Russell:		(Pinched the bunny softly.)

Assessing Concepts of Position

The Psychologist:	(Position)	"Come hop like a bunny with me."
Russell:		(Russell hopped around the room then sat back down.)
The Psychologist:	(Position)	"Were we standing up or lying down when we hopped like a bunny."
Russell:		"Standing up."
The Psychologist:	(Position)	"When you go to sleep, are you lying down or standing up?"
Russell:		"Lying down."

Assessing Concepts of On/Off

The Psychologist:	(On/Off)	(Russell was given a standard doll who was dressed.) "Russell, does this doll have her clothes on or off?"
Russell:		"On."
The Psychologist:	(On/Off)	(Russell was given a standard doll who had her shirt on and pants off.) "Russell, does this doll have her clothes on or off?"
Russell:		"Her shirt is on and her pants are off."

Assessing Concepts of Frequency

The Psychologist:	(Counting)	(Russell was given a page of stickers.) "Russell, put three stickers on me."
Russell:		(Russell put three stickers on the psychologist.)
The Psychologist:	(Counting)	"Russell, put six stickers on you."
Russell:		(Russell put six stickers on himself.)
The Psychologist:	(Frequency Past Events)	"Russell how many times did you brush your teeth yesterday?"
Russell:		"Two times."

Russell's basic concepts were found to be well developed for a 6-year-old child. Therefore, he was assessed to be appropriate for verbal questioning regarding the allegations of sexual abuse.

Ending the First Session

Russell was allowed to select the next play activity. He chose to investigate the sandbox. Russell picked up the lion and tiger animal figures and had the animals fight with one another. His play was aggressive without any theme other than fighting. He chose the strongest and most aggressive animals for his play.

When it was time to end, Russell was told it was time to say goodbye but that he and the psychologist would play and talk again. When Russell and the psychologist walked back to the waiting room to reunite Russell with his mother, Russell's mood and blunted affect did not change. Ms. Snell wanted to know what Russell had told the psychologist. The psychologist responded to Ms. Snell that it was not appropriate to talk in front of Russell.

The psychologist then took Ms. Snell into her office while Russell remained in the waiting room. Ms. Snell was informed that the psychologist knew she was worried, but would not provide any feedback to anyone until her evaluation was complete. Ms. Snell then reported that she had recently learned that Russell's father was sending him to school in diapers, which she considered to be humiliating and emotionally abusive. She requested that the psychologist call the father and tell him how harmful this was and that he stop doing this. The psychologist informed Ms. Snell that as the court-ordered evaluator, she could not become involved in the parenting issues. The psychologist suggested Ms. Snell telephone her attorney to investigate other options.

STEP 11. Conduct the child's second session.

SECOND SESSION WITH CHILD

Two days after Russell's first session (Russell was brought to his second session with the psychologist by his mother), Russell's father was scheduled to bring Russell to this session but canceled the appointment stating that he did not have the money to pay for the evaluation. The mother rescheduled the appointment stating that she would pay for it.

Observation and Building Rapport

Russell presented at his second session appropriately dressed and with good hygiene. Russell's poor eye contact, restlessness, and oppositional behaviors were again noted. When in the office, Russell immediately got out the Play Doh. The psychologist and Russell first talked about what things he had done at school the day before.

Child Questioned About His or Her
Knowledge of Purpose of Evaluation

Russell then was questioned about his understanding of why he was being brought to the psychologist. The following dialogue took place:

The Psychologist:	"Do you know why you are coming to talk to me?"
Russell:	(Shook head no.)
The Psychologist:	"Tell me everything your mommy said to you about visiting me."
Russell:	"She didn't say anything."
The Psychologist:	"Tell me everything your mommy said to tell me."
Russell:	"She didn't tell me to say anything."

[Break in questioning]

The Psychologist:	"Tell me everything your daddy told you about visiting me."
Russell:	"He didn't tell me anything."
The Psychologist:	"Tell me everything your daddy said to tell me."
Russell:	"Nothing."

[Break in questioning]

The Psychologist:	"Tell me everything Donald told you about visiting me."
Russell:	"Nothing. I don't see Donald anymore."

Russell's facial expression did not show anxiety when providing this information; his affect was flat, and mood was neutral.

Enhancing Resistance to Interviewer
Influence and Misleading Questions

During this session, Russell was taught skills that decrease the interviewer's influence and mitigate the negative effect of misleading questions. (With many 6-year-old children these techniques are too complex.)

- The psychologist attempted to not selectively reinforce with her verbalizations or body language any statements made by Russell. A lollipop was offered at the beginning of the session rather than in the middle or at the end of the session.
- Russell was told, "I don't know very much about you. I don't know what you do at school. I don't know what you do at daddy's house. I don't know

what you do at Mommy's house. I need you to tell me about things you do and things that happen to you. I don't know about things that happen to you because I'm not with you at these other places."

- Russell was told, "If I ask you the same question more than once, keep giving the answer that you know is right." Russell and the psychologist role-played this rule. He was told by the psychologist, "I'm going to ask you a question that I want you to answer: Russell, where do you go to school?" Russell responded, "King School." The psychologist questioned again, "Russell, where do you go to school?" Russell responded, "King School." Russell was told, "That's very good. You kept giving me the right answer." He was told, "If I ask you the same question more than once, it's not because you gave me the wrong answer the first time."

- Russell was told, "If you don't want to answer some of the questions I ask, it's okay to say, 'I don't want to answer that'." Russell was asked, "If you don't want to answer a question, what should you tell me?" Russell responded, "I don't want to."

- Russell was told, "I'll be asking you a lot of questions today. If you don't know the answer, say, 'I don't know' or 'I can't remember'." Russell and the psychologist then role-played this rule. Russell was asked, "Russell, how old are you?" Russell replied, "6." Russell was asked, "How old is Donald?" Russell hesitated and then stated, "I forgot." Russell was told, "That was very good. You didn't remember how old Donald was, so you said, 'I forgot.' I'm glad you didn't guess." He then was told, "If you don't know how old Donald is, it is okay to say, 'I don't know'."

- Russell was told, "Some of the questions I ask you may be very hard. Some of the questions may make you feel mixed up. If you feel mixed up, tell me 'I don't know.' Don't guess. I only want you to tell me what you remember." Russell was asked, "If you don't know what I'm saying, what are you supposed to tell me?" Russell responded, "I don't know." Russell and the psychologist then role-played this example. Russell was unable to correctly role-play this rule. Russell was told he had done a good job trying.

- Russell was told, "Sometimes I may say something that you know is wrong. If I say something that you know is wrong, I need you to tell me. Just tell me, 'You made a mistake'." Russell and the psychologist role-played this rule. Russell was told, "Russell, you have a blue shirt on, and you are 3 years old." Russell responded, "I'm not 3; I'm 6 years old!" Russell was told, "That was very good. You told me I made a mistake. I was wrong; I said you were 3, and you are 6."

During these activities of learning the interview rules, Russell's behavior was very restless. He did not stay seated and wandered around the room looking at toys. When limits were set, he initially attempted to ignore these directions. On one occasion, when asked to rejoin the psychologist, he responded, "You're interrupting my play."

Child Is Provided a Break From Questioning

Russell and the psychologist played together to provide him with a break from the evaluation.

Establishing the Narrative Response Set

After approximately 5 minutes of solely focusing on the clay images created by Russell, the psychologist practiced with Russell how to give detailed and complete descriptions of events. The following dialogue took place:

The Psychologist: "Russell, you told me you were 6 years old. Tell me about the birthday when you were 6 years old. Tell me everything about your birthday."

Russell: "My mommy made a chocolate cake."

The Psychologist: "And then what happened? Tell me everything you remember."

Russell: "We sang Happy Birthday, and I got Nintendo, and I tried to blow out the candles, but they wouldn't blow out."

The Psychologist: "Tell me what happened next. Tell me everything. Tell me about what you did on your birthday."

Russell: "We ate cake and ice cream, and I played Nintendo with Mommy and Donald."

The Psychologist: "And then what happened?"

Russell: "I went to sleep."

The Psychologist: "You said you played Nintendo with Mommy and Donald. Tell me everything you remember about playing with your new Nintendo with Mommy and Donald on your birthday."

Russell: "We took turns. Donald didn't know how to do it, and Mommy showed him."

At the end of the dialogue, Russell was thanked for telling the psychologist about his birthday. Russell was told that when he was asked questions about things that have happened to him, the psychologist wanted him to tell everything he could remember.

Child's Knowledge of Telling the Truth

Russell was asked if it was good to tell the truth or if it was good to tell lies. He stated it was good to tell the truth. When asked what happens to children when they tell lies, Russell stated, "They get spanked." Russell was told that when the psychologist asked him questions, it was important for him to say only what he remembered because that would be the truth. He was told not to guess because if he guessed, his guess might not be true. Further dialogue regarding truth and lies was not presented due to Russell's immature developmental level and limited cognitive ability to understand abstract concepts, such as truth and lies. Preschool children's truthfulness will be influenced by external factors, such as interview techniques, to a greater extent than by internal moral factors (refer to Chapter 3).

The Substantive Interview

The substantive interview phase begins by asking open-ended questions. This part of the interview begins with the first level of the Boat and Everson (1986) conceptual framework (refer to Chapter 6). This first level involves questions about critical events or times in the child's life when the sexual abuse may have occurred.

A transitional statement began this phase by alerting Russell that he and the psychologist were going to focus on the problem that had brought him to see her.

Since the allegation of sexual abuse involved showering with his mother's boyfriend, the following dialogue, moving from open-ended to directed, then took place:

The Psychologist:	"I'm going to ask you questions about showers and baths. Tell me everything you remember about taking showers when your bathtub is broken."
Russell:	"I take showers at my mommy's because the bathtub is broken. At first I was scared."
The Psychologist:	"Tell me more."
Russell:	"Now I'm not scared."
The Psychologist:	"Tell me some more things about taking showers."
Russell:	"I don't know."
The Psychologist:	"Tell me about taking baths. Tell me everything."
Russell:	"I take baths at my Daddy's."
The Psychologist:	"Tell me about that."
Russell:	"I can't splash the water on the floor, or I'll get in trouble."
The Psychologist:	"You said at first you were scared to take showers. Tell me about being scared to take showers."
Russell:	"The water got in my eyes."
The Psychologist:	"Tell me what else made you scared."
Russell:	"Nothing else."
The Psychologist:	"Who do you take showers with?"
Russell:	"Nobody."
The Psychologist:	"Who do you take baths with?"
Russell:	"Nobody."
The Psychologist:	"Would it be good or bad to take a bath or a shower with a grownup?"
Russell:	"Good."
The Psychologist:	"Who helps you wash?"
Russell:	"Nobody."

General Assessment of Child's
Feelings About His Family Members

The first level of Boat and Everson's (1986) conceptual framework did not produce any information regarding the allegation of sexual abuse. As a result, escalation to the second level was pursued. At this next level the child is asked in general terms about the alleged perpetrator. At this level, direct reference to the sexual abuse is avoided. The child is also asked about other family members so undue attention is not drawn to the alleged perpetrator.

The Psychologist:	"Tell me everything you can think of about Daddy."
Russell:	"Daddy rides bikes."
The Psychologist:	"Tell me everything Daddy does."
Russell:	"He fixes my bike, but it has a flat tire now."
The Psychologist:	"What else?"
Russell:	"I don't know."
The Psychologist:	"Now we're going to talk about Mommy. Tell me everything you can think of about Mommy."

Russell:	"She plays Nintendo with me, but she can't do it as good as me."
The Psychologist:	"Tell me other things about Mommy."
Russell:	"She cries when she fights with Donald."
The Psychologist:	"Tell me more about Mommy."
Russell:	"She makes Donald leave when they fight."
The Psychologist:	"What else does Mommy do?"
Russell:	"I don't know."
The Psychologist:	"Now we're going to talk about Donald. Tell me everything you can think of about Donald."
Russell:	"He plays Nintendo, but he can't beat me."
The Psychologist:	"Tell me everything Donald does."
Russell:	"He likes Mommy's fried chicken."
The Psychologist:	"Tell me more about Donald."
Russell:	"He yells at Mommy and makes her cry."
The Psychologist:	"What else does Donald do?"
Russell:	"I don't know."
The Psychologist:	"Now we're going to talk about Janet. Tell me everything about Janet."
Russell:	"She cooks good."
The Psychologist:	"Tell me other things about Janet."
Russell:	"She rides bikes with Daddy and me."
The Psychologist:	"Tell me more about Janet."
Russell:	"I don't know."

Russell was then asked to draw a picture of a happy face. When queried about things that make him happy that he does with his mother, Russell stated that he is happy when he plays cards with his mother. When queried about things that make him happy with his father, he stated that he is happy when he is with his father and Janet when they play with the waterhose. When queried about things that make him happy with Donald, he stated he is happy when they play Nintendo. Russell was then asked to draw a sad face. When Russell was queried about things that make him sad when he is with his mother, Russell stated that he is sad when he cannot play with the Nintendo. When Russell was queried about things that make him sad when he is with his father, he stated that he is sad when his father spanks him. Upon inquiry, Russell stated that nothing makes him sad when he is with Janet or Donald. Russell was then asked to draw a scared face. When Russell was queried about things that make him scared when he is with his mother or Donald, he stated that he is not scared of anything. When queried about things that he is scared of when he is with his father or Janet, he stated that he is not scared of anything. Russell did not report any sexual exploitation as reasons that he feels sad or frightened when he is with his mother or Donald.

Russell was administered the Grunes Interview Procedure and an incomplete sentence test in order to assess Russell's relationships and his perceptions of the important people in his life. These are not standardized tests. The following questions and Russell's responses that are of interest from the Grunes Interview Procedure are as follows:

- Who in your family is the strongest? *"Daddy."*
- Who cooks the best? *"Janet."*
- Who is the most fun to play with? *"Mommy."*

- Who laughs the most? *"Mommy."*
- Who is the nicest? *"Mommy."*
- Who does Daddy like the most? *"Janet."*
- Who likes Daddy the most? *"Janet."*
- Who does Mommy like the most? *"Donald."*
- Who likes Mommy the most? *"Donald."*
- Who makes you happy? *"Daddy and Mommy."*
- Who makes you sad? *"Nobody."*
- Who makes you mad? *"Eric."* (a male peer in Russell's kindergarten class)

The following are Russell's answers to the incomplete sentences:

- I am happiest with *"Daddy and Mommy."*
- I wish *"I was superman."*
- When I am with my mother, I feel *"happy."*
- Nothing scares me so much as *"witches."*
- When I feel upset, I'd like to be with *"Grandma and Grandpa."*
- Of all the people in my family, the one I like best is *"Mommy, Daddy, Uncle Joey, and Grandma and Grandpa."*
- When I am with my father, I feel *"great."*
- When I am away from my father, I feel *"sad."*
- When I am sick, the person I want to take care of me is *"my whole family."*
- The difference between my mother and father is *"Mommy has different rules than Daddy - she lets me turn on the car."*
- When I am away from my mother, I feel *"sad."*
- I worry most about my *"Mommy and Daddy."* (Russell was asked when he worries about them, he responded, *"When I'm away from them."*)
- I feel safest with *"Mommy and Daddy."*
- I love a lot of people, but most of all, I love *"Mommy and Daddy."*
- If I do something wrong, the person who should punish me is *"Mommy and Daddy and Grandma and Grandpa."*
- When my parents yell at each other, I feel *"sad - it hurts my ears."*

Following the administration of the incomplete sentences, Russell was asked by the psychologist to draw a picture of his family doing something together. He then drew a picture of him and his mother playing Nintendo. Both figures were of the same size and included head, torso, limbs, and all body parts. The figures were clothed and smiling. Genitalia were not present on either figure.

Russell was asked to draw a picture of himself and Donald doing something together. He then drew a picture of himself and Donald playing Nintendo. The figure of Donald was drawn larger than the figure of Russell. Both bodies included a head, trunk, limbs, and all of the body parts; body parts were drawn fairly proportional. Both figures were clothed and smiling. Genitalia were not present on either figure.

When questioned, Russell stated that he did not know why he presently lived with his father instead of his mother. When queried about where he likes to live, he responded that he likes to live with his mother. Russell was unable to articulate why he likes to live with his mother. The following dialogue then took place:

The Psychologist: "Does your daddy like your mommy?"
Russell: "No."
The Psychologist: "How do you know?"

Russell:	"'Cause every time she calls, they'll hang up on me when I talk to her."
The Psychologist:	"Does your mommy like your daddy?"
Russell:	(Shook head no.)
The Psychologist:	"How do you know she doesn't like your daddy?"
Russell:	" 'Cause she yells at him."

Child Is Provided a Break From Questioning

The interview was interrupted while Russell and the psychologist played a game of Hot Potato. Russell demonstrated immature play skills; he was able to follow the rules of the game but became upset if he did not win. Russell showed deficiencies in his ability to become engaged in a play activity and to have fun. Following 5 minutes of play, the verbal questioning resumed.

The Substantive Interview Continued

Russell was asked to draw a picture of Janet and himself doing something together. Russell drew Janet cooking and drew himself watching television. Both bodies included a head, trunk, limbs, and all of the body parts; body parts were drawn fairly proportional. Both figures were clothed and smiling. Neither figure had genitalia. Russell was then asked to draw a picture of his father and himself doing something together. He drew a picture of himself and his father riding bikes together. The figure of his father was drawn larger than the figure of Russell. Both bodies included a head, trunk, limbs, and all of the body parts; body parts were drawn fairly proportional. Both figures were clothed and smiling. Neither figure had genitalia.

Since during previous questioning Russell did not disclose any inappropriate or sexualized interactions initiated by any adults, questioning moved to Boat and Everson's (1986) third level of escalation. At the third level, the child is asked directly about sexual abuse; the alleged perpetrator's name is not mentioned. At this level, a structured interview format was administered by the psychologist. This structured interview is not a standardized test; however, it provides a structure utilizing anatomical drawings for questioning the child about the various types of touch (both positive and negative) that the child has received. This procedure involves the use of anatomical drawings that are specific to the child's age, gender, and race.

Russell was first shown the drawing of a nude, caucasian preschool male. The following dialogue took place:

| The Psychologist: | "This is a picture of a little boy. He gets hugged. Who hugs you?" |
| Russell: | "Mommy, Daddy, Grandma, Grandpa, Uncle Joey, and Uncle Ted." |

Russell was shown a second drawing, identical to the first drawing, of a nude, caucasian male. The following dialogue took place:

The Psychologist:	"This is a picture of a little boy. He gets hit. Who hits you?"
Russell:	"Eric Smith." (a male peer in Russell's kindergarten class)
The Psychologist:	"Who else hits you?"
Russell:	"My daddy spanks me with a belt."

The Psychologist:	"Tell me everything you can remember about Daddy spanking you with a belt."
Russell:	"He spanks me when I tell a lie."
The Psychologist:	"Tell me more."
Russell:	"He spanks me when I'm bad."
The Psychologist:	"Where on your body does your Daddy spank you with a belt?"
Russell:	"On the butt."
The Psychologist:	(Russell was shown two drawings of a nude, caucasian pre-school male - front view and rear view.) "Russell, point on the boy where your daddy spanks you with a belt."
Russell:	(Russell pointed to the buttock on the drawing of the male child.)

Russell was shown a third drawing, identical to the first drawing, of a nude, caucasian male. Russell was asked to identify the body parts on the drawing (e.g., eyes, nose, mouth, chest, penis, arms, hands, legs, and feet). Russell was also asked to articulate the functions of the various body parts. The following dialogue took place while the psychologist pointed to the specific body part of focus:

The Psychologist:	"Russell, what is this called?" (Pointed to the eyes.)
Russell:	"Eyes."
The Psychologist:	"What do you do with your eyes?"
Russell:	"See."
The Psychologist:	"What is this called?" (Pointed to the nose.)
Russell:	"Nose."
The Psychologist:	"What do you do with your nose?"
Russell:	"Smell."
The Psychologist:	"What is this called?" (Pointed to the mouth.)
Russell:	"Mouth."
The Psychologist:	"What do you do with your mouth?"
Russell:	"Eat and kiss."
The Psychologist:	"What is this called?" (Pointed to the chest.)
Russell:	"Boobies."
The Psychologist:	"What do you do with boobies?"
Russell:	"One side has a heart in it."
The Psychologist:	"What is this called?" (Pointed to penis.)
Russell:	"A penis."
The Psychologist:	"What do you do with your penis?"
Russell:	"Go pee."
The Psychologist:	"Has someone ever done something to your body that you didn't like?"
Russell:	"No."
The Psychologist:	"Have you ever been asked to do something to someone's body that you didn't like?"
Russell:	"No."

Child Is Provided a Break From Questioning

Russell and the psychologist took a 5-minute break from verbal questioning. During this break Russell was taken outside to see the fish pond.

The Substantive Interview Continued

Since the allegation of sexual abuse involved Russell having his penis "pinched," the following dialogue, moving from open-ended to directed, took place:

The Psychologist:	"Now we're going to talk about pinching. Tell me about pinching. Tell me everything you can think of about pinching."
Russell:	"You go like this." (Showed the motion with his thumb and index finger.)
The Psychologist:	"Tell me more about pinching. Tell me everything."
Russell:	"Ralph and Jonathan pinch me."
The Psychologist:	"Who are Ralph and Jonathan?"
Russell:	"They're mean kids at school."
The Psychologist:	"Point on the picture of the boy where they pinch you."
Russell:	"Here and here." (Pointed to arms and hands on the drawing of the boy.)
The Psychologist:	"Where else on your body do you get pinched?"
Russell:	"No where."
The Psychologist:	"Tell me about grownups pinching you."
Russell:	"They don't."

Russell was not asked a directed question about being pinched on his penis because this type of directed question might influence his future responses. Since the allegation of sexual abuse involved Russell having needles stuck in his penis, the following dialogue moved from open-ended to directed regarding his experiences of being stuck with needles:

The Psychologist:	"Now we're going to talk about needles. Tell me everything you can remember about being stuck with a needle."
Russell:	"The doctor pricked my finger when he was getting blood, and I cried."
The Psychologist:	"Tell me more about being stuck with needles."
Russell:	"I don't know."
The Psychologist:	"The doctor stuck you with a needle. Has someone else stuck you with a needle?"
Russell:	"No."

Russell was not questioned about his penis immediately preceding or following questions about needles. Russell was then shown the drawing of a nude, caucasian male child (back view). Russell named the buttock a "butt." The following dialogue then took place:

The Psychologist:	"Now we're going to talk about butts. In your butt, there's a place that poop comes out of. Tell me everything you can think of about touching poop holes."
Russell:	"I wipe my caca off."
The Psychologist:	"Tell me more."
Russell:	"I don't know."
The Psychologist:	"Tell me about grownups touching caca holes?"
Russell:	"My mommy used to wipe my caca."
The Psychologist:	"What other grownup has touched your caca hole?"

Russell:	"Nobody."
The Psychologist:	"Has someone ever put something in your caca hole?"
Russell:	"No!" (Russell appeared somewhat surprised and amused by this question, as he emphasized "No" and smiled at the question.)

The dialogue then escalated to Boat and Everson's (1986) fourth level of questioning. At the fourth level the child is asked directly about the sexual abuse allegation. Questioning at this level is implemented with extreme caution.

The Psychologist:	"Now we're going to talk about penises. Tell me everything you know about putting things in your penis."
Russell:	"You don't."
The Psychologist:	"Has somebody put something in your penis?"
Russell:	"No."
The Psychologist:	"Tell me everything you can remember about a child or grownup hurting your penis."
Russell:	"No one did."
The Psychologist:	"Has your daddy ever hurt your penis?"
Russell:	"No."
The Psychologist:	"Has Donald ever hurt your penis?"
Russell:	"No."
The Psychologist:	"Who would you tell if someone hurt your penis?"
Russell:	"My mom."

This second session was ended, and Russell was returned to the waiting room to reunite with his mother. Consistent with the first session, Russell's mood and affect did not change.

STEP 12. Conduct the child's third session.

THIRD SESSION WITH CHILD

Russell was brought to his third session with the psychologist by his mother. Russell again appeared detached when the psychologist entered the waiting room to get him. He acknowledged the psychologist's presence by getting out of his chair and accompanying her to her office. However, when in her office, he again was noted to be extremely restless, moving from one toy to another.

Initially, the psychologist and Russell talked about activities at home and at school in which he had participated since his last evaluation session. The psychologist then presented a previously asked question by rewording the question asked about taking showers. At this session, Russell was asked questions that would elicit past experiences regarding showers:

The Psychologist:	"Now we're going to talk about showers. Who is the first person you ever took a shower with?"
Russell:	"Donald."
The Psychologist:	"Tell me about taking a shower with Donald."
Russell:	"He showed me how to shower."
The Psychologist:	"Tell me everything about how Donald showed you how to shower."

Russell:	"He put soap on himself."
The Psychologist:	"Tell me more about Donald putting soap on himself."
Russell:	"He put soap on his stomach and arms and legs and penis."
The Psychologist:	"Tell me what he did then. Tell me everything you remember."
Russell:	"He told me to put the soap on."
The Psychologist:	"Then what happened?"
Russell:	"I washed myself."
The Psychologist:	"Then what happened next?"
Russell:	"We got out and dried off."
The Psychologist:	"Who washed Donald?"
Russell:	"He washed himself."
The Psychologist:	"Tell me more about washing you."
Russell:	"I put soap on my stomach and arms and legs and penis and rubbed the dirt off real good."
The Psychologist:	"Did Donald help you rub the soap on your body?"
Russell:	"No."

> **GOAL:** Utilize anatomical dolls with the alleged sexual abuse victim as one technique for assessing the veracity of the child's verbal statements and/or to assess the child's sexual knowledge (refer to Chapter 8).

During this step, anatomical dolls can be utilized to gather further information from the child regarding his or her general knowledge of adult sexual activities. The dolls can also be used for further clarification of the adult sexual activities in which the child alleges to have been involved. When children 4 years and older claim to have been sexually abused but are unable to provide a demonstration of the sexual abuse with the anatomical dolls, the veracity of the allegation might be questioned. However, children under the age of 4 may not be able to demonstrate their sexual abuse with the dolls because they do not comprehend using a symbol (i.e., doll) to represent themselves. The functional use of the dolls (e.g., Icebreaker, Anatomical Model, Demonstration Aid, or Memory Screen) must be determined prior to presenting the dolls to the child. A verbal disclosure of sexual abuse by the child must occur prior to presenting the child with the dolls when using them as a Demonstration Aid. The dolls should be presented to the child fully clothed and only presented one time during the forensic evaluation. The child should not be given the dolls to play with over repeated sessions.

STEP 13. Present the anatomical dolls to the child.

PRESENTATION OF ANATOMICAL DOLLS

The anatomical dolls were not presented to Russell because he did not make a verbal disclosure of sexual abuse during his three evaluation sessions. The dolls would not have added further information without questioning Russell about incidents for which he already had provided answers.

> **GOAL:** Utilize the observation of the child and the alleged perpetrator as one component in the evaluation process (refer to Chapter 5).

Joint sessions with the child and the alleged perpetrator, if a parent or parent surrogate, may be helpful to assess the overall quality of the relationship between these two individuals. It may be beneficial to conduct all of the individual observations and verbal interviews with the child prior to observing the child and alleged perpetrator together. When observing the alleged victim-alleged perpetrator interaction, the evaluator must consider the circumstances surrounding the allegation. The length of time since the child has seen the alleged perpetrator and the negative or positive image of the alleged perpetrator that the child may have been intentionally or unintentionally provided by others must be taken into account. When observing this dyad, if the parent becomes inappropriate in any manner, the evaluator should intervene. For example, if a parent attempts to criticize the other parent to the child or to the evaluator, the evaluator should direct the parent to stop.

STEP 14. Observe the child and alleged perpetrator to assess the quality of the relationship.

OBSERVATION OF CHILD AND ALLEGED PERPETRATOR

Russell was seen at his fourth session with his mother's boyfriend, Donald. At the time of the visit, Russell had not seen Donald in over a month.

Russell responded "okay" in a neutral manner when informed that Donald had come to spend the session with Russell and the psychologist. Russell was taken to a different room than the room in which he and the psychologist had previously played. When Russell entered the room where Donald was waiting, he looked at Donald, said, "Hi," and went to explore the new room. When Russell sat on the floor with a game, Donald joined him on the floor. Russell showed no fear of Donald and intermittently engaged Donald in his play, similar to Russell's behavior when playing with the psychologist. At one point during the session, Russell asked Donald why he was not at the house when Russell came to visit. Donald replied that he hoped he would be able to visit Russell again soon, but he was unable to visit him at this time. Russell accepted this answer and continued to play. Later in the session, Russell found the Play Doh Fun Factory and showed Donald how to use it.

Following this 1-hour session with Donald, Russell was escorted back to his mother. Donald remained in the play room until Russell and his mother had departed.

> **GOAL:** Utilize standardized psychological testing with the alleged sexual abuse victim as one component in the evaluation process (refer to Chapter 9).

Comprehensive psychological testing assists the evaluator by providing information on the child's cognitive, social, and emotional functioning. Not all sexually abused evaluations require comprehensive psychological testing. Psychological testing should be administered when the child is exhibiting academic, social, or emotional problems. Testing may assist the evaluator in making appropriate recommendations. The results of the psychological testing are not used to make diagnostic decisions about sexual abuse.

STEP 15. Conduct comprehensive psychological testing.

PSYCHOLOGICAL EVALUATION

A psychological evaluation using standardized tests was determined to be necessary based on the social, emotional, and behavioral problems exhibited by Russell at school and observed by the psychologist.

Russell was administered the Wechsler Intelligence Scale for Children - Third Edition (WISC-III). Russell earned a Verbal IQ of 131, a Performance IQ of 99, and a Full Scale IQ of 117. While the Full Scale IQ score placed Russell in the High Average range of intelligence, his Verbal IQ score fell within the Very Superior range. The 32-point difference between the higher Verbal IQ score and the lower Performance IQ score was statistically significant beyond the .001 level.

Russell was administered the Woodcock-Johnson Psycho-Educational Battery - Revised (WJ-R). Russell's standard scores on the Woodcock-Johnson Tests of Cognitive Ability subtests ranged from a low of 93 to a high of 132. The cognitive ability scores indicated that Russell has difficulty processing information quickly when the information is presented auditorally. Russell's scores suggest he may absorb information more rapidly if it is presented visually.

Russell's standard scores on the Woodcock-Johnson Tests of Achievement subtests ranged from a low of 113 to a high of 124. These scores were below expected achievement levels based on Russell's Verbal IQ.

Russell was administered the Roberts Apperception Test and the Rorschach Inkblot Technique in order to assess his relationships and personality functions. Throughout the testing, Russell was distractible and oppositional. On numerous occasions, he would get out of his chair and wander around the room during testing. During administration of the Rorschach Inkblot Technique, Russell defecated in his pants.

Personality test results showed Russell to have serious problems in the way he perceives and thinks about the world and other people. Russell's coping mechanisms also were found to be extremely immature, and included an unusually high level of regressive behavior. These coping deficits and his immaturity may affect Russell's judgment and hinder his development of peer relationships. His inability to be playful and spontaneous may add to his problems with peers.

Russell is not a child who anticipates positive relationships with other people. Within his projective stories, Russell's perception of relationships is reflected as conflictual or conditional. For example, one of his stories on the Roberts Apperception Test reads

> *"The mother and the father are fighting. They are telling the rules. The mother is saying she'll take them to work and the father says no he'll take the rules to work to explain them. (How the story ends) The mother and father are mad at each other because they have different rules."*

Another of Russell's stories reads

> *"The mother and father are loving their son. The son thinks they don't love him when he's bad. The son is sad because he thinks they only love him when he's good. (How the story ends) The son is sad because he has to move away. He had to move away because he didn't listen to his mom about playing Nintendo and yelling at her."*

> **GOAL:** Interpret and integrate data collected from all sources into a formal written document (refer to Chapters 3, 4, and 7).

The purpose of the report is to present to the court and to the parents in a clear and scientific manner the findings of the forensic evaluation. The conclusions that are drawn should be supported by the data collected during the evaluation; this information should be clearly identified. Several competing hypotheses should be addressed and evidence should be presented to support and/or negate these hypotheses. The report should address the strengths and weaknesses of the evidence. In the report, the evaluator can directly address whether the child appears credible or appears to be confused or "contaminated" by previous questioning and how the child's credibility affects the conclusions that can be drawn. The ultimate legal issue of whether the child has been sexually abused by the alleged perpetrator should be left to the court to determine.

STEP 16. Review tests, checklists, and all other sources of data. Consider alternative hypotheses.

STEP 17. The written report is created from all data sources.

WRITTEN REPORT

Only a subsection of the Summary and Recommendations of the written report of Russell's evaluation will be presented here.

Summary and Recommendations

In November, Russell was court ordered to be evaluated regarding the allegation of sexual abuse. Russell was seen by the psychologist over a series of five sessions.

During his evaluation, Russell was (a) given structured interviews in order to address the question of sexual abuse, (b) observed with his mother's boyfriend, the alleged perpetrator, and (c) administered comprehensive psychological testing in order to address Russell's cognitive and personality functions.

Intelligence test results indicate that Russell's Full Scale IQ (117) places him within the High Average range of intelligence. However, there was a 32-point discrepancy between his higher Verbal (131) and lower Performance (99) IQ scores. Russell's verbal skills are clearly much more advanced than his perceptual motors skills. Further testing did not indicate perceptual organization impairments or neuropsychological problems. Russell's advanced verbal skills indicate that he would be able to participate in a verbal interview if concepts were not presented beyond his developmental level.

Personality test results suggest that Russell is an emotionally disturbed child whose coping mechanisms are more like those of a 2- to 3-year-old child. Russell's encopresis (i.e., bowel movements in his pants) may be representative of how he attempts to assert himself and express his feelings. Test results suggest that Russell is not a child who will express his anger in dramatic, explosive temper tantrums. Rather, he tends to be excessively guarded related to expression of emotions. His expression of angry feelings at this time appears to be made through anal expulsion, primitive aggressive behaviors used in reaction to his peers' behaviors, or impulsive outbursts. Although some sexually abused children are found to demonstrate encopretic behavior, Russell's encopresis predates his relationship with Donald by several years. Rather than a symptom of sexual abuse, Russell's encopresis appears to be a general regressive coping mechanism.

Test results further indicate that Russell's thinking and perceptions are not always logical and accurate. This disturbance in thinking and distortion of perceptions makes Russell at risk to use poor judgment and to respond inappropriately to situations. These problems may be at the root of Russell's poor peer relationships. For example, when interacting with peers, Russell is prone to misinterpret peers' play as hostile and then respond in an inappropriately aggressive manner. Russell also may be at risk to have difficulties in his relationships with adults. Furthermore, because of Russell's disturbed thinking, he may be at greater risk to be confused if presented erroneous information when questioned about his experiences.

Although Russell's behavior is clearly more distractible and restless than most 6 year olds, and may suggest an Attention-Deficit Disorder, Russell shows many features that are not consistent with a diagnosis of Attention-Deficit/Hyperactivity Disorder (ADHD). Unlike an ADHD child, Russell's behavior does not appear to be impulsive or out of control.

Although distractibility has been found to be exhibited by some sexually abused children, Russell's distractible and restless behavior also predates his relationship with Donald by several years. Russell's preschool teachers have observed these behaviors since Russell was 3 years old. Thus, the distractible and restless behaviors exhibited by Russell appear to be related to a cause other than sexual abuse alleged to have been perpetrated by Donald.

Regarding the allegation of sexual abuse involving Donald (a) showering with Russell, (b) pinching Russell's penis, and (c) sticking needles in Russell's penis, the following data have been considered:

- It has been confirmed that Russell showered with Donald the day of the alleged sexual abuse incident. The mother and Russell independently confirmed this information to the psychologist.

- When asked open-ended questions and nonleading focused questions by the state child abuse investigator, the examining physician, and the psychologist, Russell did not disclose that Donald pinched his penis or touched his penis in an inappropriate manner. Russell reported to focused but nonleading questions presented by the psychologist that Donald showed him how to wash himself. Russell stated that Donald applied soap to his own adult body and instructed Russell to apply soap to his own body.
- When asked open-ended questions and nonleading focused questions by the state child abuse investigator, the examining physician, and the psychologist, Russell did not disclose that Donald locked him in his room and stuck needles in his penis. When questioned if he had ever been stuck with a needle, he reported he had his finger pricked by the doctor once, and he cried. When asked by the psychologist if any other person had ever stuck a needle in any part of his body, he stated no one else had stuck him with a needle.
- When observed during a session with Donald, Russell did not appear fearful or anxious in the presence of Donald.

In summary, the behaviors that Russell initially alleged to his father as initiated by Donald are possible. However, Russell has made no further statements to authorities confirming his initial allegations. Although Russell was consistent in his denial to authorities that Donald had pinched his penis or inserted needles into his penis, some child victims of sexual abuse have been found to deny their sexual abuse when questioned by authorities. Thus, denial cannot solely determine that sexual abuse did not occur.

During the forensic evaluation, Russell openly described the shower he took with Donald and described washing that did not involve sexual abuse. Young sexually abused children who are avoiding disclosure typically do not provide a detailed scenario of a bogus event to cover up an event of sexual abuse. Most young children are not cognitively sophisticated enough for this type of deception. Typically, if young children are reluctant to disclose the sexual abuse, they completely avoid talking about the event.

Russell did not exhibit any overt sexualized behaviors at home or at school, nor did he exhibit fear of Donald, whom he alleged sexually abused him, in a manner that would have involved pain. Furthermore, Russell's father reported that when he discovered Russell was showering with Donald, he questioned his son about possible sexual abuse. Due to Russell's emotional disturbance, he may be at greater risk than the average 6 year old to interviewer influences. However, Russell's increased risk for interview influence is based on a clinical assumption and not on empirical data.

Russell's current severe emotional and behavior problems have a lengthy history and predate Donald's involvement in Russell's life. Additionally, medical evidence was absent, including evidence of needles inserted into Russell's penis. While these factors do not negate any possibility of sexual abuse, neither do they support a finding of sexual abuse.

The following recommendations should be considered:

- Data do not substantiate a finding of the sexual abuse of Russell by Donald. However, it would be in the best interest of both Donald and Russell that Russell not be left alone in the care of Donald.
- Russell shows serious impairments in his ability to think things through in a logical and coherent fashion. He also has serious problems in accurately

perceiving events and interactions that take place in his environment. He further exhibits strange ways of thinking about his experiences as well as strong preoccupations with his bowel functions. While he clearly is a distracted and, at times, overly active child, Russell shows features that are not consistent with ADHD. Given this finding and his lack of a positive response to Ritalin, it may be helpful to review Russell's medication.

- Russell should be placed in individual therapy with a child specialist who possesses advanced training in the treatment of child psychopathology. Russell is a seriously disturbed child who requires intensive treatment. This is not a child with a minor adjustment problem. Russell should not be placed in a sexual abuse treatment form of therapy.
- Further assessment of special education services for Russell should be conducted.
- Further assessment of Russell's family placement should be conducted.

> **Postscript:** While the allegations of sexual abuse in this case were not substantiated, Russell received multiple benefits from his involvement in a court-ordered evaluation. Following Russell's evaluation, the parents were ordered to be psychologically evaluated. His parents also both were ordered to enroll in parenting classes. Following the parents' evaluations, Russell's father was awarded primary residential custody due to his more structured home environment. Russell's mother was awarded every other weekend visitation with additional visitation on Wednesdays for dinner. Russell also was provided consistent individual therapy. His medication was changed from Ritalin to a combination of Dexadrine and Imipramine. At school, Russell has been provided services from both the Emotionally Handicapped Special Education and Gifted Programs. He made straight A's during the first grading period of his new school year. He has shown a significant decrease in his oppositional behaviors; peer and teacher relationships have improved. Russell has a new baby brother and appears to be developing a more stable and consistent relationship with Donald. Both parents are reported to have made improvements in their parenting skills.

The steps previously delineated would be somewhat different if the allegation identified a nonfamily member as the alleged perpetrator. If the alleged abuser is not a parental figure, observation of the child and the alleged perpetrator typically does not occur. However, the evaluator of nonincestuous child sexual abuse allegations also seeks multiple sources of information on which to base an opinion.

CHAPTER 11

Final Comments

Clinicians and researchers continue to struggle with a multitude of yet-to-be-answered questions about child sexual abuse. An accurate count of child sexual abuse victims continues to elude us. Presently, we are unable to determine what percentage of the unsubstantiated sexual abuse cases are false negatives or what percentage of substantiated cases are false positives. The occurrence of false negatives is suggested by research findings (Elliott & Briere, 1994; Keary & Fitzpatrick, 1994; Lawson & Chaffin, 1992; Sauzier, 1989; Sorenson & Snow, 1991) that show some children who are victims of sexual abuse are reluctant to disclose their abuse and may deny sexual abuse when initially interviewed by authorities. Additionally, the occurrence of false positives is suggested by research which shows children's verbal reports may be altered or contaminated by some interviewing techniques, procedures, or styles (Bruck, Ceci, Francoeur, & Barr, 1995; Ceci, Crotteau, et al., 1994; Ceci, Loftus, et al., 1994; Leichtman & Ceci, 1995).

Child sexual abuse is an external physical event; it is not an internal mental condition. Based on children's heterogeneity, the occurrence of sexual abuse does not interact with children's internal psychological processes to elicit a group of predictable symptoms and characteristics. Rather, the event of sexual abuse interacts with a complex matrix of factors, including the child's personality, the child's and family's interpretations of the event, the family and socioeconomic environment, and the specific abuse characteristics (Friedrich, 1990). Therefore, there are no diagnostic behavioral "markers" of child sexual abuse that are exhibited by all victims.

Preliminary research indicates that fear of being left with a particular person, fear of men, developmentally unusual knowledge about sex, and heightened interest in sexual matters and genitals are exhibited more frequently by sexually abused children than nonsexually abused children (Friedrich, 1993; Friedrich et al., 1992; Wells et al., 1995). However, not all sexually abused children interact in a consistent and predictable manner with an alleged perpetrator or show heightened interest in sex. Furthermore, these behaviors are not specific to children who have been sexually abused.

Because children who have been sexually abused are not a homogeneous group, children cannot be identified as having experienced the event of sexual abuse based solely on the presence of behavioral symptoms. Additionally, within the general population, high percentages of preschool and elementary school-age children are found to exhibit problems such as nightmares, sudden changes in mood, poor concentration, fearfulness, disobedience, and temper tantrums (Achenbach, 1991b,

1992), suggesting that children who have not experienced sexual abuse may exhibit these behaviors as a part of their normal development. Thus, when attempting to draw conclusions in cases of alleged child sexual abuse, the rate at which specific symptoms appear in a nonsexually abused group must be considered.

While the presence of behavioral symptoms cannot solely be used to identify the occurrence of sexual abuse, the absence of symptoms cannot be used to conclude that a child has not experienced sexual abuse. Some sexually abused children who deny their abuse attempt to suppress awareness or expression of abuse-related psychological distress (Elliott & Briere, 1994). Additionally, developmental and cross-cultural research (Piaget, 1970; Stoller & Herdt, 1985) suggests that some children do not interpret their sexual experiences with an older person as harmful.

The presence or absence of specific verbal statement components also cannot solely serve to confirm or negate whether a child is a victim of sexual abuse. Developmental limitations, personality factors, family and cultural contexts, characteristics of the abuse, interviewing techniques, and other factors may affect children's narration of their abuse. For example, young children may have difficulty reporting events in exact chronological order and may appear unreliable and illogical when they attempt to use their immature verbal skills to narrate what they observed.

Research further indicates some children, especially those who are very young, are susceptible to pre- and post-event suggestions and interviewer influence. While even young children are accurate reporters when they are asked nonleading questions in calm, supportive, nonthreatening situations (Saywitz, 1995b), the accuracy of their reports decreases when the environment and type of questioning becomes pressured and leading. Because certain children resist acquiescing to leading questions, interviewing techniques may have different effects on children depending on their personalities. However, little is known at this time about the interaction of interviewing techniques and personality variables.

The search for ways to accurately distinguish sexually abused from nonsexually abused children has included examining the diagnostic potential of various checklists, projective tests, and projective children's drawings. While some of these instruments may be sensitive to trauma symptoms, none of the instruments show specificity to sexual abuse. That is, the symptoms that are identified by these instruments are not unique to sexual abuse.

Although standardized child behavior ratings scales (e.g., Achenbach, 1991b, 1992; Conners, 1990) traditionally have been used to identify the presence of specific behavior problems, the behaviors these scales measure also are not unique to child sexual abuse. Due to the lack of predictive diagnostic validity of behavior rating scales in assessing sexual abuse, attempts were made to develop specific behavior rating scales that could differentiate sexually abused from nonsexually abused children. However, the early behavior rating scales were not standardized on nonsexually abused and sexually abused children. Rather than unique markers of child sexual abuse victimization, the majority of the behaviors included on these early rating scales were found to be normative behaviors or symptoms of children under stress (e.g., eating problems, disturbed sleep, nightmares, masturbation, etc.).

Because heightened sexual interest and sexualized behavior are exhibited more frequently by sexually abused children than nonsexually abused children, checklists that identified children's sexual behaviors were developed. The Child Sexual Behavior Inventory-Revised (Friedrich, 1993; Freidrich et al., 1992) is one such standardized instrument that has utility in measuring children's aberrant sexual behaviors. However, it is face valid; therefore, the accuracy of the results is dependent on the response set of the individual who completes the checklist.

While projective tools have frequently been administered as part of a battery of psychological tests in child evaluations, the use of projective materials to identify child sexual abuse is not supported by research. Projective tools, including projective tests, drawings, or anatomical doll play do not discriminate nonsexually abused from sexually abused children. Additionally, while children's drawings of genitalia have shown sensitivity to sexual abuse trauma, these drawings are not specific to trauma caused by sexual abuse.

Cautioning mental health professionals to be careful in their interpretation of behavioral symptoms, children's statements, and projective data should not negate the importance of this information. It is not unimportant when a child exhibits a developmentally unusual preoccupation with genitals or sexual acts nor is it unimportant when a child exhibits fear of a particular person. However, professionals must ask what the meaning of this information is before formulating conclusions. While lying or source misattribution may account for a nonsexually abused child's bizarre or implausible narrative of abuse, a mismatch between the linguistic and cognitive worlds of adults and children may also elicit bizarre and implausible narratives from the sexually abused child. Therefore, the issues of credibility and competency must always be assessed.

Because of the complexity of identifying children who have experienced sexual abuse, professionals must adhere to a high standard of care when accepting the evaluator role in cases of alleged child sexual abuse. As a forensic evaluator, the professional acts as a scientist who organizes, interprets, and integrates data drawn from a number of sources in order to understand behavior. Evaluators should consider all relevant hypotheses and review multiple sources of data. The evaluator must carefully identify the parameters of his or her professional role and not blend the roles of therapist and evaluator.

Professionals evaluating allegations of child sexual abuse are at greater risk to misinterpret their observations and the collateral data when they do not possess formal training in forensic evaluation methods and a thorough knowledge of the base rates of children's behaviors across development. An evaluator's failure to consider alternative hypotheses when conducting an evaluation of alleged sexual abuse poses a serious risk. Failure to consider alternative hypotheses to the evaluator's suspicion can cause the evaluator to ignore inconsistent evidence and shape the interview toward accessing information consistent with the evaluator's preconceived belief (Borum, Otto, & Golding, 1993; Ceci, 1994).

Four primary evaluation models, the Comprehensive Model, the Child Interview Model, the Parent/Child Observation Model, and the Child Observation Model, have emerged to structure and guide the evaluator (Everson, 1993). The Comprehensive Model is consistent with a forensic evaluation model and is structured on the premise that allegations of child sexual abuse are complex and require examination of multiple sources of information.

The strength of the Comprehensive Model is that its format allows the information derived from the child interview to be compared to relevant background material and empirically derived data (Everson, 1993). For example, background variables would include a complete developmental history, as well as observational data provided by neutral parties regarding the alleged victim's prior relationship with the alleged perpetrator. Additionally, attempts are made whenever possible to include both the nonaccused and accused parent in the evaluation process. Research findings are then examined and considered when drawing conclusions about the historical and interview data. The American Professional Society on the Abuse of Children utilizes a Comprehensive Model as its prototype for child sexual abuse evaluations.

The development of protocols and guidelines aimed at increasing the quality of evaluations of young alleged victims of sexual abuse continues. To date, a definitive standard of practice does not exist at either a state or national level. Thus, assessing allegations of child sexual abuse is a complex task, only to be conducted by well-trained professionals. We presently have some understanding of the potentially devastating psychological effects of child sexual abuse; however, we know little about the psychological damage that may be caused to a child who grows up falsely believing he or she has been sexually abused by a loved parent.

Appendices

Appendix A

AMERICAN HUMANE ASSOCIATION -
ESTIMATE OF CHILD PHYSICAL/SEXUAL
ABUSE AND NEGLECT 1976 TO 1987

In 1976, the first collection of national data on reported cases of child abuse and neglect was conducted by the American Humane Association. From 1976 until 1987, the American Humane Association collected statistics from state agencies on child abuse and neglect reporting (see Table A1, below). Because not all states collected statistical data on child abuse cases, the national figures published by the American Humane Association were estimates based on extrapolated data. In addition to data from those of the 52 states collecting data, these numbers include data from the District of Columbia, Puerto Rico, Guam, the Virgin Islands, and Marianas. Overall, the reported cases of child abuse and neglect increased 225% between 1976 and 1987. While there was consistent growth in reported cases annually, there was a predominantly downward trend from 1983 to 1987. The figures in Table A1 (below) include substantiated and unsubstantiated reports.

TABLE A1 National Estimate of the Numbers of Children Reported as Physical/Sexual Maltreated and Neglected from 1976 to 1987*				
REPORTED YEAR	ESTIMATE OF TOTAL CHILD ABUSE AND NEGLECT REPORTS	ESTIMATE OF CHILD ABUSE AND NEGLECT REPORTS PER 1,000 CHILDREN	NUMBER OF STATES PROVIDING CASE DATA	AVERAGE PERCENTAGE CHANGE
1976	669,000	10.1	30	—
1977	838,000	12.8	32	25.26%
1978	836,000	12.9	32	-0.24%
1979	988,000	15.4	33	18.18%
1980	1,154,000	18.1	39	16.80%
1981	1,225,000	19.4	37	6.15%
1982	1,262,000	20.1	36	3.02%
1983	1,477,000	23.6	36	17.04%
1984	1,727,000	27.3	30	16.93%
1985	1,928,000	30.6	28	11.64%
1986	2,086,000	32.8	28	8.2%
1987	2,178,000	34.0	40	4.4%

*From *Highlights of Official Child Neglect and Abuse Reporting - 1986,* by American Association for Protecting Children, 1988, and from *Highlights of Official Child Neglect and Abuse Reporting - 1987,* by American Association for Protecting Children, 1989, both Denver, CO: American Humane Association.

Appendix B

AMERICAN HUMANE ASSOCIATION -
ESTIMATE OF CHILD
SEXUAL ABUSE 1976 TO 1986

The national estimates of the numbers of child sexual abuse cases, derived from the American Humane Association data, during the 10 year time span from 1976 to 1986, are presented in Table B1 (below).

TABLE B1 National Estimate of the Number of Children Reported as Sexually Abused*		
REPORTED YEAR	ESTIMATE OF CHILD SEXUAL ABUSE	NUMBER OF STATES PROVIDING DATA
1976	6,000	30
1977	11,000	32
1978	12,000	32
1979	27,000	33
1980	37,000	39
1981	35,000	37
1982	57,000	36
1983	74,000	36
1984	100,000	30
1985	127,000	28
1986	132,000	28

*From *Highlights of Official Child Neglect and Abuse Reporting - 1986,* by American Association for Protecting Children, 1986, Denver, CO: American Humane Association.

Analysis of the 1986 child sexual abuse national statistics indicates that the average age of children reported as sexually abused was 9 years old. (It must be noted that the age of the child when the report was placed is not necessarily synonymous with the age of occurrence or the age of onset.) Seventy-seven percent of the sexual abuse cases reported were female, while 23% were male. In 42% of the cases, the alleged perpetrators was a parent, 23% was another relative, and 35% of the alleged perpetrators were not related to the victim. The average age of the perpetrators was 32 years old; 82% were males, and 18% were females.

Appendix C

NATIONAL INCIDENCE STUDIES - ESTIMATE OF CHILD SEXUAL ABUSE 1980 TO 1986

The National Center on Child Abuse and Neglect (NCCAN) funded national studies of reported child abuse and neglect cases in 1980 in the National Incidence Study-1 (NIS-1; NCCAN, 1981), and in 1986 in the National Incidence Study-2 (NIS-2) (Sedlak, 1991). In order to collect a broader measure of reported figures than those collected by the American Humane Association, the NIS-1 and NIS-2 conducted by Westat, Inc. for NCCAN collected data from a random sample of 29 counties that represented different regions of the country and different degrees of urbanization. While the American Humane Association Study only collected information from state Child Protection Services, the NIS-1 and NIS-2 attempted to count all abuse and neglect cases that came to the attention of other professionals (e.g., schools, hospitals, police departments, juvenile probation authorities, etc.) from within the 29 counties. However, these studies were not exhaustive in their collection of data from other professionals. For example, no attempt was made to count cases that came to professionals, such as private doctors, mental health professionals in private practice, private schools, and so on. The national estimate of numbers of child sexual abuse cases, derived from the studies conducted by Westat, Inc. are presented in Table C1 (below).

The NIS-1 and NIS-2 estimates of child sexual abuse, using the definition of abuse from the 1980 study, showed an increase of 178% over a 6-year period. In 1986, both the original and a revised set of definitions of abuse and neglect were assessed. While the original definition of abuse and neglect only allowed inclusion of children who had experienced demonstrable harm, the revised definition allowed inclusion of endangered children regardless of whether they exhibited observable injuries or impairments which is more consistent with contemporary child protection standards. Utilizing the broader definition, the incidence numbers were more consistent with the American Humane

TABLE C1 National Estimate of Numbers of Children Reported as Sexually Abused*				
YEAR	ESTIMATE OF CHILDREN SEXUALLY ABUSED (ORIGINAL DEFINITION)	ESTIMATE OF CHILDREN SEXUALLY ABUSED (RATE PER 1,000)	PERCENTAGE OF CHANGE OVER 6 YEARS	ESTIMATE OF CHILDREN SEXUALLY ABUSED (REVISED DEFINITION)
NIS-1 1980	42,900	0.7	—	—
NIS-2 1986	119,200	1.9	+178%	133,600

*From *National Incidence and Prevalence of Child Abuse and Neglect: 1988 - Revised Report*, by A. J. Sedlak, 1991, Rockville, MD: Westat, Inc.

Association's 1986 estimate of child sexual abuse (Finkelhor, 1991). (Refer to Table C1, p. 303.)

Using the original definition, children who had suffered demonstrable harm were approximately equally divided between those who had been abused and those who had been neglected. However, under the revised definition, when endangered children were considered, neglected children outnumbered abused children by a ratio of approximately 3:2. In addition, the revised definition accounted for an increase of 12% of the children identified as victims of sexual abuse.

Appendix D

ESTIMATE OF CHILD PHYSICAL/SEXUAL ABUSE AND NEGLECT 1986 TO 1992

From 1986 to the present, the National Center on Child Abuse Prevention Research, a subdivision of the National Committee on Child Abuse, has collected national incident data from 50 states (McCurdy & Daro, 1993). Table D1 (below) presents the National Center on Child Abuse Prevention Research data of reported child abuse and neglect cases from 1986 to 1992. Because not all states provided statistics on child abuse and neglect cases, these figures also are extrapolated estimates. As these data indicate, between 1986 and 1992, child abuse and neglect reports have steadily grown at an average rate of about 6% a year.

TABLE D1		
National Estimate of the Numbers of Children Reported as Physical/Sexual Maltreatment and Neglect from 1986 to 1992*		
REPORTED YEAR	**ESTIMATED NUMBER OF REPORTED CHILD VICTIMS**	**AVERAGE PERCENTAGE CHANGE**
1986	2,086,000	—
1987	2,157,000	1986-1987 + 3.0%
1988	2,265,000	1987-1988 + 5.0%
1989	2,435,000	1988-1989 + 7.5%
1990	2,557,000	1989-1990 + 5.0%
1991	2,723,000	1990-1991 + 6.5%
1992	2,936,000	1991-1992 + 7.8%

*From *Current Trends in Child Abuse Reporting and Fatalities: The Results of the 1992 Annual Fifty State Survey,* by K. McCurdy and O. Daro, 1993, Chicago, IL: The National Committee for Prevention of Child Abuse.

Only 31 states in 1992 classified child abuse cases according to percentages of specific types of maltreatment. Sexual abuse accounted for 17% of all the child maltreatment reports from the 31 states reporting statistics. This figure rose to 19% when only substantiated child maltreatment reports were considered. Table D2 (p. 306) presents the percentage for all cases of child abuse and neglect by type of maltreatment.

The national statistics indicate that more children are in life-threatening situations through neglect and physical abuse than through sexual abuse. National child fatality data indicate that many more children die from neglect than physical abuse. Data have not provided answers to whether the lower rates are accurate representations of sexual abuse occurring at a lower frequency than physical abuse and neglect or if sexual abuse is just more difficult to identify.

TABLE D2 1992 Maltreatment Reports: Type of Maltreatment*									
	PHYSICAL ABUSE		SEXUAL ABUSE		NEGLECT		EMOTIONAL MALTREATMENT		OTHER	
	Mean	SD	Mean	SD	Mean	SD	Mean	SD	Mean	SD
Average Percentage For All Cases (N = 31 states)	27%	7.7	17%	10.7	45%	13.2	7%	7.6	8%	8.5
Breakdown for Substantiated Cases Only (N = 19 states)	24%	6.1	19%	12.7	43%	14.9	10%	8.7	11%	10.2

*From *Current Trends in Child Abuse Reporting and Fatalities: The Results of the 1992 Annual Fifty State Survey*, by K. McCurdy and O. Daro, 1993, Chicago, IL: The National Committee for Prevention of Child Abuse.

Appendix E

FACTORS ASSOCIATED WITH INCREASES AND DECREASES IN ABUSE/NEGLECT REPORTS

In order to identify the factors associated with increases or decreases in reports of child abuse and neglect cases, The National Center on Child Abuse Prevention Research (McCurdy & Daro, 1993), in its 1993 survey, had states identify the most significant factors which accounted for the reporting trends in their state. While the answers were not based on quantitative data, they offer descriptive appraisals from each state.

The majority of states with increased reports, identified the escalation in child abuse and neglect reports to reflect actual maltreatment of children as a consequence of economic stress and substance abuse (McCurdy & Daro, 1993). Economic stress due to poverty, unemployment, and related work concerns were identified by 38% of the state respondents, while 32% of the states identified substance abuse as a major contributor. The impact of public awareness and reporting changes were also identified as increasing the number of reports. The state of Montana reported that the recent practice of lawyers advising clients to allege abuse during custody battles contributed to an increase in total child abuse reports for that state (McCurdy & Daro, 1993). Currently, research does not exist which substantiates these causative speculations made by state authorities.

There are no reliable baselines from past statistics against which to make comparisons with present statistics. Besharov (1993) does not believe it is possible to determine if deteriorating economic and social conditions have contributed to a rise in the level of abuse and neglect because so many maltreated children previously went unreported.

Analysis of the increase in reported cases led researchers to conclude that the increase was most likely due to the ongoing development of better reporting procedures and data collection. Some researchers believe that any true increase in child abuse is typically accompanied by a statistically significant increase in the most serious cases (Finkelhor, 1989). Because there was no significant increase between 1980 and 1986 in the number of fatal and serious child abuse cases (e.g., broken bones, etc.), a finding of a true increase was not suggested.

The majority of states with decreased abuse and neglect reports identified inundation from increased screening of cases as a reason for the decline in reports rather than successful prevention efforts. At least six states reported that their reporting systems had reached the saturation point, resulting in fewer reports investigated or counted as a report. McCurdy and Daro (1993) observed, "In some states, the overwhelming number of reports have caused workers to investigate only the most serious allegations of abuse and neglect" (p. 6).

Appendix F

PROBLEMS IN COMPARING
INCIDENCE FIGURES
ACROSS STATES

The collection of national data for estimating the incidence of child sexual abuse has been complicated by the significant variation in states' reporting procedures. In a survey of 50 states, the National Committee for Prevention of Child Abuse found the only common ground of states' data collection process was that the majority of states utilized a centralized reporting registry (Daro & McCurdy, 1992).

One area of variation in states' reporting procedures involves the definition of sexual abuse and what constitutes a report. Further discrepancies have existed in the identified familial/nonfamilial relationship between the child and perpetrator for inclusion in the states' social service statistics. For example, the National Center on Child Abuse Prevention Research (Daro & McCurdy, 1992) found 19 states do not include alleged sexual abuse by a neighbor or acquaintance in their reporting statistics. Sixteen states do not count sexual abuse perpetrated by school personnel as a reported case. Twelve states do not accept reports against an out-of-home girlfriend or boyfriend of the parent, and nine states do not count sexual abuse by an out-of-home relative as a reportable case.*

Because of the legal definition of child sexual abuse, in all of the previously mentioned cases, the majority of the child protection agencies only investigated cases in which the identified perpetrator was in a caretaking position with the alleged child victim at the time of the incident. Furthermore, only 21 states included alleged sexual abuse by a person who was a stranger to the child in their total count of reports.

States also are inconsistent in how they count cases of child sexual abuse. The majority of states use multiple methods of counting (i.e., child, family, incident, or other measures). While a number of states count two or more reports concerning the same episode of sexual abuse as one report, 30 states count two or more reports of the same episode of sexual abuse as separate counts (Daro & McCurdy, 1992).

While the American Humane Association, the National Center on Child Abuse and Neglect, and the National Center on Child Abuse Prevention Research data offer general estimates of the number of cases that public agencies handle, the debate over how to estimate the prevalence and incidence of child sexual abuse continues. The national data have been widely recognized as inadequate in terms of accurately estimating the actual numbers of sexually abused children.

---

*While these cases are not reported to state child protection agencies, the cases involve criminal acts and are reported to law enforcement agencies.

SUBSTANTIATION OF REPORTED
ABUSE/NEGLECT CASES

The difficulty in estimating accurate national child abuse figures is reflected in the disparity of the findings from national studies that have investigated substantiation rates. For example, in 1986, both the American Humane Association Study (American Association for Protecting Children, 1988) and Westat Incidence Study (Sedlak, 1991) were conducted to estimate the national incidence of child abuse and neglect. Of those child abuse and neglect reports, the American Humane Association study estimated a 40% to 42% substantiation rate, while the 1986 Westat Incidence Study estimated a substantiation rate of 53%.

Complicating the interpretation of substantiation rates is the lack of a standardized method for recording this statistic (McCurdy & Daro, 1993). States vary in the manner in which they calculate this statistic. Some states provide the number of substantiated incidents, while others provide the number of substantiated families. For some states, the substantiation rate is based on investigated reports, while for other states, it is based on all reports.

The 1992 National Center on Child Abuse Prevention Research Annual Fifty State Survey (McCurdy & Daro, 1993) found 37 states provided substantiation rate figures which ranged from 13% to 72% for the 1992 calendar year. Nine states did not have 1992 rates but presented 1991 rates ranging from 33% to 49% for the 1991 calendar year. Using these percentages for years 1991 and 1992, the 46 states reporting these statistics had an average substantiation rate of 40%. These overall substantiation rate figures of the inclusive category of "abuse and neglect" have all too often been improperly assigned to the subcategory of sexual abuse, thereby creating an inaccurate substantiation estimate for this subcategory of abuse.

Appendix G

THE PARENT-CHILD
INTERACTION PLAY ASSESSMENT

The Parent-Child Interaction Play Assessment is one type of standardized observation system (D. T. Smith, 1991). When using this system, observations are coded across two 15-minute periods of time. As discussed by D. T. Smith, the first 15 minutes, the parent is directed to engage in free play with the child "as you might at home." After 15 minutes of observation in an unstructured situation, the parent is then instructed to direct the child to carry out three tasks. After the child has completed the third task or the 15 minutes has expired, the structured situation is complete (D. T. Smith, 1991).

Behavior is coded for the unstructured period across 13 dimensions:

1. Parent's Affect
2. Parent's Intrusiveness
3. Parent's Praise
4. Parental Attention
5. Parent's Developmental Sensitivity
6. Parent's Responsiveness
7. Parent-Child Involvement

8. Child's Social Responsivity
9. Child's Attention to Activities
10. Child's Activity Level
11. Child's Aggressiveness
12. Child's Responsiveness to Parent's Interaction
13. Child's Responsiveness to Questions

Behavior is coded for the structured period across 8 dimensions:

1. Frequency of Parental Commands
2. Clarity of Commands
3. Parent's Follow Through With Commands
4. Parental Praise

5. Punishment Level
6. Child's Compliance
7. Child's Willfulness
8. Child's Aggressiveness

D. T. Smith (1991) suggests that the observer utilize the following methods to increase validity: (a) be as nonobtrusive as possible, (b) allow clients to become adapted to the situation, and (c) use the procedure after good rapport has been established. The author cautions that this observational procedure lends itself to be manipulated by a parent who wishes to look "good" or "bad."

Appendix H

Standardized Behavior Rating Scales Used to Screen for Psychological Adjustment

CHECKLIST	FORMS	DESCRIPTION	RELIABILITY
Burks' Behavior Rating Scales (BBRS)	**Preschool and Kindergarten Edition** • Combined parent and teacher form - 3 to 6 years **Grades One - Nine Edition** • Combined parent and teacher form Scoring completed on profile form on which scores fall within "Not Significant," "Significant," and "Very Significant" categories	Specifically designed to identify particular behavior problems and patterns of problems shown by children **Scales - 3 to 6 years** Excessive Self-Blame, Excessive Anxiety, Excessive Withdrawal, Excessive Dependency, Poor Ego Strength, Poor Physical Strength, Poor Coordination, Poor Intellectuality, Poor Attention, Poor Impulse Control, Poor Reality Contact, Poor Sense of Identity, Excessive Suffering, Poor Anger Control, Excessive Sense of Persecution, Excessive Aggressiveness, Excessive Resistance, Poor Social Conformity **Scales - Grades 1-9** Scales identical to Preschool and Kindergarten Edition, with the addition of one category - Poor Academics	**Test-Retest:** **Preschool and Kindergarten Edition** Correlation coefficients at 10 days = .74 to .96 (however, children rated very low at first rating, so correlations should be expected to be high) **Grades One Through Nine Edition** Correlation coefficients at 10 days = .60 to .80 for children (grades one to six) rated as high on many items at first administration
Child Behavior Checklist (CBCL)	• Parent forms - 2 to 3 years and 4 to 18 years • Teacher form - 6 to 18 years T-scores that are equal to or exceed T-70 are considered elevated and clinically significant	Designed to record in a standardized format children's competencies and problems as reported by their parents and teachers **Problem Scales** Withdrawn, Somatic Complaints, Anxious/Depressed, Social Problems, Thought Problems, Attention Problems, Delinquent Behavior, Aggressive Behavior, Sex Problems	**Test-Retest (Scale Scores):** • Correlation coefficient mean for competence scales at 7 days = .87, mean for problem scales = .89 • Over 1- and 2-year periods, changes in means were not considered significant. Means over 1 year = .62 for competence scales, .75 for problem scales. Means over 2 years = .56 for competence scales, .71 for problem scales **Interparent Agreement:** • Agreement correlations ranged from .74 to .76 on competence scales • Agreement correlations ranged from .65 to .75 on problem scales

Appendix H (Continued)

Standardized Behavior Rating Scales Used to Screen for Psychological Adjustment

CHECKLIST	FORMS	DESCRIPTION	RELIABILITY

Conners' Rating Scales	• Parent form - 3 to 17 years
	  - CPRS-93 long
	  - CPRS-48 short
	• Teacher form - 3 to 17 years
	  - CTRS-39 long
	  - CTRS-28 short
	
	T-scores that are equal to or exceed T-65 are considered elevated and clinically significant
		Designed to categorize patterns of children's behavior
		
		Parent CPRS-93
		
		Conduct Disorder, Anxious-Shy, Restless-Disorganized, Learning Problem, Psychosomatic, Obsessive Compulsive, Antisocial, Hyperactive-Immature, 10-Item Hyperactivity Index
		
		Teacher CTRS-39
		
		Hyperactivity, Conduct Problem, Emotional Overindulgent, Anxious-Passive, Asocial, Daydream-Attention Problem, 10-Item Hyperactivity Index
			Test-Retest:
			
			CPRS-93 at 1 year = .40 to .70
			CPRS-48 - no studies have been published to date
			CTRS-28 - no studies have been completed to date
			CTRS-39 at 1 month = .72 to .90
			CTRS-39 at 1 year = .53 (Conduct), .55 (Hyperactive), .37 (Antisocial), and .33 (Depressed Mood)
			
			Interparent Agreement:
			
			CPRS-48 = .46 to .57 between mother's and father's ratings

Louisville Behavior Checklist (LBC)	• Combined parent and teacher form
	  - E1 - 4 to 6 years
	  - E2 - 7 to 12 years
	  - E3 - 13 to 17 years
	
	T-scores that exceed T-65 are considered elevated and clinically significant
		Designed to discriminate between children with emotional and behavioral disorders from children in the general population
		
		E1 and E2 Scales in Common
		
		Forms E1 and E2 have the following scales in common: Infantile Aggression, Hyperactivity, Antisocial Behavior, Aggression, Social Withdrawal, Sensitivity, Fear, Inhibition, Immaturity, Normal Irritability, Severity Level, Prosocial Deficit, Rare Deviance, Neurotic Behavior, Psychotic Behavior, Somatic Behavior, and Sexual Behavior
		
		Additional Scales
		
		In addition, Form E1 has the scales Intellectual Deficit, Cognitive Disability, and School Disturbance Predictor; and Form E2 has the scales Academic Disability and Learning Disability
			Test-Retest:
			• Reliability coefficients for broad-band factor scales ranged from .80 to .92
			• Reliability coefficients for narrow-band scales ranged from .70 to .88
			• Reliability coefficients or special scales ranged from .85 to .97 (except for sexual behavior, which was .60)
			• Over 3- period, the central tendency of scales remained constant (Caution: all means were low to begin; therefore, elevated scales may not remain as constant)

| Personality Inventory for Children (PIC) | • Parent form - 3 to 16 years

Validity and Clinical Scales have specific individual cutoffs for clinical interpretation

T-scores that are equal to or exceed T-70 are considered elevated and clinically significant | Designed to screen for intellectual and general psychological adjustment

Four Factor Scales:

I: Undisciplined/Poor Self-Concept
II: Social Incompetence
III: Internalization/Somatic Symptoms
IV: Cognitive Development

Validity and Screening Scales:

Lie, Frequency, Defensiveness, Adjustment

Clinical Scales:

Achievement, Intellectual Screening, Development, Somatic Concern, Depression, Family Relations, Delinquency, Withdrawal, Anxiety, Psychosis, Hyperactivity, Social Skills | **Four Factor Scales:**

I: .92
II: .89
III: .82
IV: .81

Test-Retest:

• Children reassessed 4 to 103 days later
• 10 of 12 correlations fell between .82 and .97

Factor I: .91
II: .91
III: .90
IV: .82 |

Appendix I

BURKS' BEHAVIOR
RATING SCALES (BBRS)

The Burks' Behavior Rating Scales (BBRS) are intended to measure areas of behavioral problems in children (Burks, 1977). The BBRS are designed to gauge the severity of negative symptoms that children present as perceived by parents and teachers. The BBRS have two separate age level forms: The Preschool and Kindergarten Edition for ages 3 to 6 years, and the Grades One - Nine Edition for ages 6 to 14 years. The parent and the child's teacher are respondents; the same form is utilized with both parent and teacher. Before rating a child, the teacher should have sufficient time to observe the child. The authors suggest an observation period of at least 6 to 8 weeks. The required reading level of the respondent is not listed in the manual. The authors advise that some training in child development is needed in order to make proper use and interpretation of the test data. The BBRS' usefulness with normal groups of children is limited. A review of the BBRS found in Keyser and Sweetland's Test Critiques (1985) reads:

> Although it should not be used alone for diagnosis, it can be a valuable tool in the differential diagnosis of children with behavior problems when used in conjunction with other sources of information about the child. It can gauge the severity of the negative symptoms presented by the child, and the profile can point to areas of disturbance that should be the focus of intervention. (Lerner, 1985, p. 112)

Appendix J

CHILD BEHAVIOR
CHECKLISTS (CBCL)

The Child Behavior Checklists (CBCL), developed by Achenbach (1991a, 1991b, 1992), is designed to assess in a standardized format the social competencies and behavior problems of children ages 2 through 18. The checklists require the respondent to have a fifth grade reading level. The CBCL has two separate age level forms - for children 2 to 3 years and 4 to 18 years with the parent as the respondent. However, there is only one age level form - for children 6 to 18 years - with the teacher as the respondent. As a result, if the evaluator wants teacher data on a child below the age of 6, the Burks' Behavior Rating Scales, Preschool and Kindergarten Edition, the Conners' Rating Scales, or the Louisville Behavior Checklist might be utilized. A review of the CBCL found in Keyser and Sweetland's Test Critiques (1985) reads:

> While many checklists have been developed, none has been done so in as careful and well-constructed a manner and is as potentially useful across a wide variety of settings as the Child Behavior Checklist. It is easy to administer, well normed, has outstanding psychometric properties and is appropriate for a large clinic-referred population . . . It is quite useful in distinguishing clinical from non-clinical populations and in providing a broad overview of a child's behavior problems from the parent's perspective . . . Its usefulness with normal groups of children appears to be quite limited. (Mooney, 1984, pp. 181-182)

Appendix K

CONNERS' RATING SCALES

The Conners' Rating Scales were designed to identify hyperactive children; these scales now are used to identify a broader range of behavioral problems in children (Conners, 1990). The Conners' Parent Rating Scales (CPRS) come in two forms, one containing 48 items and the other containing 93 items. The shorter version is not a subset of the longer version; the two have different scales and psychometric properties; the CPRS-48 item version is normed on children ages 3 to 17, and the CPRS-93 is normed on children ages 6 to 14. The Conners' Teacher Rating Scales (CTRS) come in two forms, one containing 28 items and the other containing 39 items. The shorter form is not a subset of the longer form; the two contain different scales and have different psychometric properties. The CTRS-28 is normed on children ages 3 to 17. The CTRS-39 is normed on children ages 4 to 12. The required reading level of the respondent is not listed in the manual.

Appendix L

LOUISVILLE
BEHAVIOR CHECKLIST (LBC)

The Louisville Behavior Checklist (LBC) is designed to differentiate between children with psychopathology and children in the general population (Miller, 1984). There are three separate age level forms: E1 for children 4 to 6 years, E2 for children 7 to 12 years, and E3 for children 13 to 17 years. The parent and teacher complete the same forms. The respondent must have a sixth grade reading level. The Normal Irritability Scale is identified as an index of internal validity. Parents who tend to understate pathology are more likely to score low on this scale, while parents who tend to overstate or scapegoat are more likely to score high. The LBC, as a screening instrument, is reported to offer the evaluator comprehensive, descriptive data about a child's behavior and to provide insights into family dynamics (Miller, 1984).

Appendix M

PERSONALITY INVENTORY
FOR CHILDREN (PIC)

The Personality Inventory for Children is a 420-item inventory designed to provide comprehensive and clinically relevant descriptions of child behavior, affect, and cognitive status, as well as family characteristics for children ages 3 to 16 (Wirt et al., 1990). The parent is the respondent; a form for the teacher as the respondent does not exist. The respondent must have a sixth or seventh grade reading level. The respondent should also have had close contact with the child for at least 6 months preceding completion of the inventory. The inventory provides summary scores on validity, cognitive, clinical, and factor scales. The authors of the PIC caution against interpretation of the inventory by nonprofessionals or by professionals who are limited in their understanding of the inventory's psychometric properties. Criticisms of the inventory have included its excessive length (Achenbach, 1981; Breen & Barkley, 1983).

Appendix N

CHILD DISSOCIATIVE
CHECKLIST (CDC)

Putnam (1990) has developed a 20-item Child Dissociative Checklist (CDC). The CDC is a behavior rating scale on which the respondent is asked to rate whether the 20 symptoms describe the child at present or within the past 12 months. The rating scale is a three-point scale (Not True = 0, Somewhat or Sometimes True = 1, and Very True = 2). The CDC is completed by parents, foster parents, teachers, or other individuals who are very familiar with the child's behavior. It is primarily designed to be used with children ages 6 to 12 years old. Putnam, Helmers, and Trickett (1993) delineate the purpose of the CDC as follows:

> The CDC is designed as both a clinical and research tool. Clinically, it is intended to be a screening measure for the detection of significant levels of dissociative behavior in children. The CDC is not a diagnostic instrument and does not systematically inquire about the DSM-IIIR/DSM-IV criteria for dissociative disorders. When considered in the context of a full clinical evaluation, the CDC can provide important diagnostic information. In a research setting, the CDC is designed to quantify dissociative behavior. It can be used to investigate dissociative contributions to the psychopathology of different diagnostic groups, to identify dissociative subgroups within a given diagnostic category, to explore clinical, psychological, and biological correlates of dissociative behavior in children, and to study developmental trajectories of dissociation in normal and clinical samples. (p. 737)

Putnam et al. (1993) report that the Child Dissociative Checklist has progressed through three major versions (1.2, 2.2, and 3.0) over its development. The most current version, the CDC V3.0-2/90 (Putnam, 1990), has a 1 year test-retest reliability of .69 for a sample of normal and sexually abused girls. The version number, month, and year are listed underneath the title in the authentic versions. Reportedly, several unauthorized versions bearing Putnam's name are known to be in circulation and include other questions and use different answer formats (Putnam et al., 1993). These unauthorized versions are not standardized and would not be considered reliable or valid instruments.

The Child Dissociative Checklist questions were derived from clinical experience with children exhibiting dissociative disorders. Conceptually, the CDC items tap several domains of dissociative behaviors that have been identified as central to pathological dissociation behaviors in adults and children (see Putnam et al., 1993 for references). These domains include (Putnam et al., 1993, p. 734)

- dissociative amnesias
- rapid shifts in demeanor, access to information, knowledge, abilities, and age appropriateness of behavior
- spontaneous trance states
- hallucinations
- identity alterations
- aggressive and sexual behaviors

A score of 12 or higher on the Child Dissociative Checklist is generally considered indicative of significant dissociative behavior, particularly in older children. The reliability and validity of the CDC in children younger than age 6 has not been established. Putnam et al. (1993) warn that scores in younger children should be interpreted cautiously since these behaviors are normatively more common at younger ages. The authors further caution that the predictive diagnostic validity of the CDC has not been established.

Appendix O

CHILDREN'S IMPACT OF TRAUMATIC EVENTS SCALE - REVISED (CITES-R)

The Children's Impact of Traumatic Events Scale - Revised (CITES-R), developed by V. V. Wolfe et al. (1987), is a 54-item, child self-report instrument. It provides a structured format for interviewing children about their perceptions and attributions concerning their sexual abuse. The instrument consists of nine subscales, six related to impact (betrayal, guilt, helplessness, intrusive thoughts, sexualization, and stigmatization) and three related to attributions about abuse (internal-external, global-specific, and stable-unstable).

Development of the CITES-R was based on the Finkelhor and Browne (1985) model, in which the impact of sexual abuse is considered to relate to four traumatogenic factors (betrayal, guilt, sexualization, and stigmatization) and the PTSD model (intrusive thoughts and numbing responses) (V. V. Wolfe, Gentile, & D. A. Wolfe, 1989). Alpha coefficients ranged from .54 (Betrayal) to .86 (Intrusive Thoughts) with the exception of the Helplessness subscale, which was .22. The average of the subscale alpha coefficients was .71 (Gentile, 1988).

Using the CITES-R, V. V. Wolfe et al. (1989) found that the majority of the 5- to 16-year-old sexually abused children in their study did not report many feelings of stigmatization, betrayal, guilt, or negative sexualization. In contrast, however, the majority of the children reported a substantial degree of intrusive thoughts. Younger children were found to be more distressed by sex-related situations. Data further indicated that the severity of sexual abuse factors were significant in predicting negative feelings about sexualization (CITES-R Negative Sexualization Scale).

Results on the CITES-R - Global Negative Scale, which measures intrusive thoughts, stigmatization, and anxiety, indicated that beliefs that the world was a dangerous place and that many people exploit children appeared to have a comforting effect on children. V. V. Wolfe et al. (1989) suggest that the children's beliefs that similar things happen to other children may be comforting to these victims. Predictive diagnostic validity has not been established for the CITES-R.

Appendix P

TRAUMA SYMPTOM
CHECKLIST - CHILDREN (TSC-C)

The Trauma Symptom Checklist - Children (TSC-C), developed by Briere (1989), is a 54-item child self-report measure that assesses a variety of symptoms related to traumatic events and was developed to be sensitive to sexual abuse in particular. The instrument consists of six subscales: Anxiety, Depression, Posttraumatic Stress, Sexual Concerns, Dissociation, and Anger. The Dissociation Subscale primarily measures depersonalization but also includes one item pertaining to amnesia. The Sexual Concerns Subscale includes items ranging from sexual interest and preoccupation to discomfort about sexual activity. The TSC-C is to be primarily used with children 8 to 18 years old. Lanktree, Briere, and deJonge (1993) report acceptable alpha coefficients with a mean alpha coefficient for the TSC-C subscales of .84. The highest subscale reliability was for the Dissociation Scale (.89), and the lowest was for the Sexual Concerns Scale (.76).

Elliott and Briere (n.d.) reported that sexual abuse was related to higher TSC-C scores for all subscales and suggest that the TSC-C may have utility as an assessment instrument for sexual abuse. In this study, sexual abuse characteristics most related to the TSC-C scores were the presence of anal, vaginal, or oral penetration, and abuse that resulted in charges being pressed against the alleged perpetrator.

Appendix Q

PTSD REACTION INDEX

The PTSD Reaction Index, developed by Pynoos and his colleagues, is a child self-report measure based on the criteria for Post-Traumatic Stress Disorder as described in the DSM-III-R (Pynoos et al., 1987). With this assessment device, the child is asked questions that assess the degree to which the child is affected by flashbacks and revivification. The child is also questioned about the degree to which he or she avoids situations similar to that in which the trauma occurred. A parent form, on which the parents report their observations of the child's PTSD-like behaviors, also is available. The purpose of this instrument is to assess the impact of the trauma after the trauma has been identified. This assessment device is not specific to child sexual abuse. The author of this book was unable to obtain any additional information regarding this measure.

Appendix R

THE CHILDREN'S ATTRIBUTIONS
AND PERCEPTIONS SCALE (CAPS)

The Children's Attributions and Perceptions Scale (CAPS) is a child self-report measure that is designed to measure children's attributions and perceptions of self (Mannarino et al., 1994). It consists of 18 items and 4 subscales: Feeling Different from Peers, Personal Attributions for Negative Events, Perceived Credibility, and Reduced Interpersonal Trust. The instrument was developed so that these factors could be addressed without any direct reference to sexual abuse. This was done in order to make the CAPS also appropriate for use with nonsexually abused populations. The authors report that two of the CAPS' subscales - Feeling Different from Peers and Reduced Interpersonal Trust - correspond to two factors (i.e., Stigmatization and Betrayal) of Finkelhor's (1987) child sexual abuse four-factor traumatogenic model. The CAPS is to be primarily used with children 7 to 18 years old.

Research by Mannarino et al. (1994) found internal consistency to be .68 for Feeling Different from Peers subscale, .65 for Personal Attributions for Negative Events subscale, .73 for Perceived Credibility subscale, and .64 for Reduced Interpersonal Trust subscale. Test-retest reliabilities after 2 weeks were found to be .82 for Feeling Different from Peers, .70 for Perceived Credibility, .62 for Reduced Interpersonal Trust, .60 for Personal Attributions for Negative Events, and .75 for the total scale (Mannarino et al., 1994).

Preliminary comparative research on the CAPS, conducted by Mannarino et al. (1994), found that sexually abused children reported a greater sense of feeling different from peers, heightened self-blame for negative events, lower perceived credibility, and reduced interpersonal trust compared to nonsexually abused children. However, a confounding variable with this study was that the sexually abused group was significantly lower in SES than the nonsexually abused group. Predictive diagnostic validity has not been established for the CAPS.

Appendix S

THEMATIC
APPERCEPTION TEST (TAT)

The TAT consists of 31 cards containing vague black and white pictures of children and/or adults and one blank card. Card 13 of the TAT, a man standing over a woman lying on a bed, is thought to pull for sexual content. The TAT must be individually administered by a psychologist specifically trained in use of projective instruments. The evaluator presents the pictures one at a time in a set order, asking the child to tell a story about the picture.

There have been a number of scoring systems developed for the TAT. The most commonly used scoring system was developed by Bellak (1993). Bellak's TAT scoring system focuses on content and dynamics of interpersonal relationships and contains 10 scoring categories: main theme, main hero, main needs and drives of the hero, conception of the environment, what the figures are seen as, significant conflicts, nature of anxieties, main defenses against conflicts and fears, nature of punishment for offenses, and ego integration. Bellak suggests that the 10 scoring variables should be used primarily as a frame of reference and that not all variables will be relevant to every story (see Bellak, 1993 for a more complete description of other scoring systems).

CHILDREN'S
APPERCEPTION TEST (CAT)

While the TAT is said to be applicable to children as young as 4, the CAT was specifically designed for children ages 3 to 10 (Bellak, 1993). The CAT -Animal (CAT-A) form consists of 10 pictures depicting animals portrayed in human situations. The use of animals rather than human figures was based on the assumption that children of these ages would identify more readily with appealing drawings of animals than with drawings of humans. Bellak intended the stimulus cards to assist in understanding the child's drives and relationships to important figures. He also intended the stimulus cards to elicit problems, including sibling rivalry, aggression, and the child's personality structure, including defenses. The administration of the CAT parallels Bellak's recommendations for the TAT.

Two other Children's Apperception Test sets that are much less used are the Children's Apperception Test - Human Figures (CAT-H) and the Children's Apperception Test - Supplement (CAT-S). On the CAT-H, the human figures are substituted for the animals in almost identical scenes from the CAT-A. The Human Figures set was developed in reaction to criticism of the assumption that children identify more easily with animal figures than with human figures.

Psychometric properties, including validity and reliability of the TAT and CAT, are weak. Test-retest reliability can only be considered relevant if the variable being measured is also consistent over time. According to Obrzut and Boliek (1986), because most of the traits and characteristics that are measured with projective devices are motivational and emotional in nature, there is no reason to assume these characteristics are temporally stable. Although a number of studies with adult populations have found acceptable reliability for specific variables on the TAT, there are few studies that have demonstrated this same substantial reliability with child populations.

Appendix T

PROJECTIVE
STORY TELLING TEST

The Projective Story Telling Test is one of the most recently developed projective storytelling tests. This test consists of 47 pictures depicting the interaction of adults and children and was specifically designed to assess physically and sexually abused children. The test author (Caruso, 1988) writes

> Each card was basically designed to cover a specific theme, which should not be limited in the minds of the user to only that theme. Each card has a set of sample questions and instructions that the user can utilize to encourage verbal input by a child, primarily through storytelling. Because there is no rigid administration and scoring methods, each user can develop his or her own style of presentation to the subject, and do so, not only in a manner that is comfortable to the user, but in a manner that best appears suited to the parameters and needs of the user-subject relationship. (p. 7)

The author of the Projective Story Telling Test does not present normative data and comparative data on sexually abused and nonsexually abused children with this instrument. Therefore, empirical data does not exist showing how the projective storytelling stories of children who are sexually abused differ from stories of children who are not sexually abused.

Appendix U

ROBERTS' APPERCEPTION
TEST FOR CHILDREN (RATC)

The Roberts' Apperception Test for Children (RATC) is one of the most recently developed thematic approaches (McArthur & Roberts, 1990). It consists of 27 stimulus cards, of which 16 are administered. Sets of 11 cards have male ("B"- boy) and female ("G"- girl) versions. Pictorially, the cards include scenes depicting parental disagreement, parental affection, aggression, peer relationships, and observed nudity. Card 15, of a young boy looking through a partially open bathroom door at the side view of a woman bathing, is thought to pull for sexual content.

The administration is similar to the TAT and CAT in that the RATC task requires the child to create stories to the stimulus cards. After the 16-stimulus cards have been presented and the child's stories recorded verbatim, the responses are scored on a number of quantitative rating categories.

The scoring system includes 13 profile scales made up of 8 adaptive scales and 5 clinical scales. The 8 adaptive scales include (a) reliance on others, (b) support to others, (c) support of the child (self-sufficiency and maturity), (d) limit setting (by parents and authority figures), (e) problem identification (the child's ability to formulate concepts beyond the scope of the stimulus card), and (f to h) three resolution scales indicating how the child resolves particular problems included in a story. The 5 clinical scales measure feelings about self and/or the environment. The clinical scales include Anxiety, Aggression, Depression, Rejection, and Unresolved.

The RATC was standardized on a sample of 200 "well-adjusted" male and female children, with efforts to include a range of socioeconomic representation. Psychometrically, interrater and split-half reliabilities have been reported to be in the acceptable range (McArthur & Roberts, 1990). The scales with the highest reliability estimates are Limit Setting, Unresolved, Resolution 2, Resolution 3, Problem Identification, and Support. Both convergent and discriminate validity have been obtained for the RATC using subgroups of 200 well-adjusted and 200 clinic children. Results also indicate the independence of the Aggression, Depression, and Rejection Scales.

Appendix V

RORSCHACH

The Rorschach task requires the individual to provide responses to 10 ambiguous inkblots. In the past, the several different techniques of administering and scoring the Rorschach made the collection of reliable and comparable data difficult. The development of the Rorschach Comprehensive System by Exner (1986) has overcome these psychometric problems. The Comprehensive System designed by Exner presents detailed normative information on children and adolescent performance on the Rorschach. Developmental norms are based on the protocols of 1,870 nonreferred 5- to 16-year-old children tested by 147 examiners in different parts of the country (Weiner, 1986). Normative data also includes the Rorschach performance of children and adolescents with various types of adjustment difficulties. There is substantial interscorer agreement (correlations of .85 or more) among trained examiners on all of the scoring codes in the Comprehensive System (Exner, 1986).

Exner defines the Rorschach as a problem-solving task with the nature of the test situation forcing the subject to convert the blot into something that it is not. The stimulus is thought to provoke a complex of psychological operations into activity that ultimately culminate in decision making (Exner, 1986). The manner in which the child articulates his or her impressions of the inkblots provides a representative sample of how the child structures other kinds of perceptual-cognitive experiences. Weiner (1986) writes

> . . . to the extent that the Rorschach is a problem-solving situation, people will attempt to solve it in the same manner as they attempt to solve problems in their lives, and they will utilize the same kinds of coping mechanisms or styles that they employ whenever they are faced with making decisions or taking action. Consistent with trait-state distinction, moreover, some features of the Rorschach behavior will reflect characteristic ways in which subjects cope with experience, whereas other features will reflect more transient, situationally determined tendencies to deal with the Rorschach in a particular manner. (p. 144)

Appendix W

FORM LETTER TO
PARENT SEEKING EVALUATION

Dear __(Parent's Name)__ :

This letter follows our telephone conversation on __(Date)__ . As I stated during our initial telephone contact, I require the following procedures for my involvement as an evaluator when there is an allegation of child sexual abuse:

1. The court appoint me as an evaluator of your child.
2. The court order address who is responsible to pay my fees.
3. My access to all relevant documents, including previous interviews of your child, conducted by other professionals.
4. I be given written permission by the custodial parent to contact previous and present therapists, teachers, daycare providers, and other relevant individuals.
5. Individual sessions with each parent in order to obtain a developmental history on the child.
6. A minimum of three individual sessions with your child and myself. These sessions will be videotaped.
7. Observation of your child with you.
8. Possible observation of your child with the child's other parent.
9. Psychological evaluations on both parents by a court-appointed psychologist.
10. __(Child's Name)__ not be further questioned about the alleged sexual abuse by any family member or other professionals.

As I stated over the telephone, the information that is gathered from interviews, observations, and other documents will be included in a report to the court and, therefore, confidential information you provide to me will be shared with the court.

Prior to scheduling our first appointment, I will need to be in receipt of the court document appointing me the evaluator.

I look forward to working with __(Child's Name)__ and to meeting you.

Sincerely,

__(Evaluator's Name)__

Appendix X

FORM LETTER
TO ATTORNEY

Dear __(Attorney's Name)__ :

I have been requested by your client, __(Parent's Name)__ , to conduct an evaluation of his or her child, __(Child's Name)__ , regarding possible sexual abuse. I require the following procedures if I am to be involved as the evaluator:

1. The court appoint me as an evaluator of the child.
2. The court order address who is responsible to pay my fees.
3. My access to all relevant documents, including previous interviews of the child, conducted by other professionals.
4. I be given written permission by the custodial parent to contact previous and present therapists, teachers, daycare providers, and other relevant individuals.
5. Individual sessions with each parent in order to obtain a developmental history on the child.
6. A minimum of three individual sessions with the child and myself. These sessions will be videotaped.
7. Observation of the child with the client/parent.
8. Possible observation of the child with the child's other parent.

Prior to scheduling any appointments, I will need to be in receipt of the court order. Thank you for your consideration.

Sincerely,

__(Evaluator's Name)__

Appendix Y

Child Sexual Abuse Resources*

ORGANIZATION/AGENCY	ADDRESS/PHONE NUMBER	INFORMATION
• American Association for Protecting Children • American Humane Association	63 Inverness Drive, East Englewood, CO 80112-5117 (303) 792-9900 (800) 227-5242	• Publications regarding child abuse and neglect
American Professional Society on the Abuse of Children (APSAC)	332 S. Michigan Avenue Chicago, IL 60604 (312) 554-0166	• Provides information on child abuse and neglect
National Center on Child Abuse and Neglect (NCCAN)	PO Box 1182 Washington, DC 20013 (703) 385-7565 (800) FYI-3366	• Responsible for the Federal Government's involvement in child abuse and neglect cases • Responsible for overseeing grants to public and private organizations
NCCAN (Sponsored) • Clearinghouse on Child Abuse and Neglect	PO Box 1182 Washington, DC 20013 (703) 385-7565 (800) FYI-3366	• Provides publications and information services on child abuse and neglect • Under the U.S. Department of Health and Human Services
• National Resource Center on Child Abuse and Neglect (operated by American Humane Association)	63 Inverness Drive East Englewood, CO 80112-5117 (303) 792-9900 (800) 227-5242	• Provides publications • Inquires regarding child protective service • Inquires regarding child abuse and neglect
• National Resource Center on Child Sexual Abuse	107 Lincoln Street Huntsville, AL 35801 (205) 534-6868 (800) KIDS-006	• Disseminates research and general information on child sexual abuse
National Council on Child Abuse and Family Violence	1155 Connecticut Avenue, NW Washington, DC 20036 (202) 429-6695	• Provides education services, professional development and organization development in family violence prevention, and treatment programs

*For a more comprehensive listing see National Center on Child Abuse and Neglect, 1992.

References

Achenbach, T. M. (1981). A junior MMPI? *Journal of Personality Assessment, 45,* 332.

Achenbach, T. M. (1991a). *Manual for the teacher's report form and 1991 profile.* Burlington, VT: University of Vermont, Department of Psychiatry.

Achenbach, T. M. (1991b). *Manual for the child behavior checklist/4-18 and 1991 profile.* Burlington, VT: University of Vermont, Department of Psychiatry.

Achenbach, T. M. (1992). *Manual for the child behavior checklist/2-3 and 1992 profile.* Burlington, VT: University of Vermont, Department of Psychiatry.

Ainsworth, M. D. (1973). The development of infant-mother attachment. In B. M. Caldwell & H. N. Ricciuti (Eds.), *Review of child development research* (pp. 1-94). Chicago: University of Chicago Press.

Ainsworth, M. D., & Bell, S. M. (1970). Attachment, exploration and separation: Illustrated by the behavior of one-year-olds in a strange situation. *Child Development, 41,* 49-67.

Alexander, P. C. (1992). Application of attachment theory to the study of sexual abuse. *Journal of Consulting and Clinical Psychology, 60*(2), 185-195.

Alexander, P. C., & Anderson, C. L., (1994, May). *An attachment approach to psychotherapy with the incest survivor.* Unpublished paper presented at the Second National Colloquium of the American Professional Society on the Abuse of Children, Cambridge, MA.

Alexander, P. C., & Lupfer, S. L. (1987). Family characteristics and long-term consequences associated with sexual abuse. *Archives of Sexual Behavior, 16,* 235-245.

American Academy of Child and Adolescent Psychiatry. (1988). Guidelines for the clinical evaluation of child and adolescent sexual abuse. *Journal of the American Academy of Child and Adolescent Psychiatry, 27,* 655-657.

American Academy of Child and Adolescent Psychiatry. (1990). *Guidelines for the clinical evaluation of child sexual abuse.* Washington, DC: Author.

American Association for Protecting Children (AAPC). (1988). *Highlights of official child neglect and abuse reporting - 1986.* Denver, CO: American Humane Association.

American Association for Protecting Children (AAPC). (1989). *Highlights of official child neglect and abuse reporting - 1987.* Denver, CO: American Humane Association.

American Professional Society on the Abuse of Children. (1990). *Guidelines for psychosocial evaluation of suspected sexual abuse in young children.* Chicago: Author.

American Professional Society on the Abuse of Children. (1995). *Practice guidelines - Use of anatomical dolls in child sexual abuse assessment.* Chicago: Author.

American Psychological Association. (1992). Ethical principles of psychologists and code of conduct. *American Psychologist, 47*(12), 1597-1611.

American Psychological Association. (1994). Guidelines for child custody evaluations in divorce proceedings. *American Psychologist, 49*(7), 677-680.

American Psychological Association, Council of Representatives. (1991, February). *Statement on the use of anatomically detailed dolls in forensic evaluations.* Washington, DC: American Psychological Association.

Anastasi, A. (1988). *Psychological testing* (6th ed.). New York: MacMillan.

Anthony, E. J. (1970). The behavior disorders of childhood. In P. Mussen (Ed.), *Carmichael's manual of child psychology* (Vol. II, 3rd ed., pp. 667-764). New York: John Wiley & Sons.

August, R. L., & Forman, B. D. (1989). A comparison of sexually abused and nonsexually abused children's behavioral responses to anatomically correct dolls. *Child Psychiatry and Human Development, 20,* 39-47.

Baker-Ward, L. E., Hess, T. M., & Flanagan, D. A. (1990). The effects of involvement on children's memory for events. *Cognitive Development, 5,* 55-70.

Bauer, P. J., & Mandler, J. M. (1990). Remembering what happened next: Very young children's recall of event sequences. In R. Fivush & J. Hudson (Eds.), *Knowing and remembering in young children* (pp. 9-29). New York: Cambridge University Press.

Bays, J. (1990). Are the genitalia of anatomical dolls distorted? *Child Abuse & Neglect, 14,* 171-175.

Bellak, L. (1993). *The T.A.T., C.A.T. and S.A.T. in clinical use* (5th ed.). Needham Heights, MA: Allyn and Bacon.

Bender, L. (1952). *Child psychiatric techniques.* Springfield, IL: Charles C. Thomas.

Benedek, E. P., & Schetky, D. H. (1987). Problems in validating allegations of sexual abuse. Part I: Factors affecting perception and recall of events. *Journal of the American Academy of Child and Adolescent Psychiatry, 26*(6), 912-915.

Berliner, L. (1988). Deciding whether a child has been sexually abused. In E. B. Nicholson & J. Bulkley (Eds.), *Sexual abuse allegations in custody and visitation cases: A resource book for judges and court personnel* (pp. 48-69). Washington, DC: American Bar Association.

Berliner, L. (1992). Should investigative interviews of children be videotaped? *Journal of Interpersonal Violence, 7*(2), 277-288.

Berliner, L., & Conte, J. R. (1993). Sexual abuse evaluations: Conceptual and empirical obstacles. *Child Abuse & Neglect, 17,* 111-125.

Bernstein, E., & Putnam, F. (1986). Development, reliability and validity of a dissociation scale. *Journal of Nervous and Mental Disease, 174,* 727-735.

Berson, N. (1994). *Personal communication on anatomical dolls.* Chapel Hill, NC: University of North Carolina at Chapel Hill.

Besharov, D. J. (1993). Overreporting and underreporting are twin problems. In R. J. Gelles & D. R. Loseke (Eds.), *Current controversies on family violence* (pp. 257-272). Newbury Park, CA: Sage.

Blau, T. H., & Blau, R. M. (1988). The competency and credibility of children as witnesses. In J. T. Reese & J. M. Horn, *Police psychology - operational assistance*. Unpublished manuscript.

Boat, B. W., & Everson, M. D. (1986). *Using anatomical dolls: Guidelines for interviewing young children in sexual abuse investigations*. Chapel Hill, NC: University of North Carolina at Chapel Hill, Department of Psychiatry.

Boat, B. W., & Everson, M. D. (1988). Use of anatomical dolls among professionals in sexual abuse evaluations. *Child Abuse & Neglect, 12*, 171-179.

Boat, B. W., & Everson, M. D. (1993). The use of anatomical dolls in sexual abuse evaluations: Current research and practice. In G. S. Goodman & B. L. Bottoms (Eds.), *Child victims, child witnesses* (pp. 47-69). New York: Guilford.

Boat, B. W., & Everson, M. D. (1994). Exploration of anatomical dolls by nonreferred preschool-aged children: Comparisons by age, gender, race and socioeconomic status. *Child Abuse & Neglect, 18*(2), 139-153.

Boat, B. W., Everson, M. D., & Holland, J. (1990). Maternal perceptions of non-abused young children's behavior after the children's exposure to anatomical dolls. *Child Welfare, 64*, 389-399.

Borum, R., Otto, R., & Golding, S. (1993). Improving clinical judgment and decision making in forensic evaluation. *Journal of Psychiatry and Law, 21*, 35-76.

Bottoms, B., Goodman, G., Schwartz-Kenney, B., Sachsenmaier, T., & Thomas, S. (1990, March). *Keeping secrets: Implications for children's testimony*. Paper presented at the American Psychology and Law Society Biennial Meeting, Williamsburg, VA.

Bowlby, J. (1969). *Attachment and loss: Vol. 1. Attachment*. London: Hogarth Press.

Brainerd, C. J., Kingma, J., & Howe, M. L. (1985). On the development of forgetting. *Child Development, 56*, 1103-1119.

Brainerd, C. J., Reyna, V. F., Howe, M. L., & Kingma, J. (1990). The development of forgetting and reminiscence. *Monographs of the Society for Research in Child Development, 55* (3-4, Serial No. 222).

Breen, M. J., & Barkley, R. A. (1983). The personality inventory for children (PIC): Its clinical utility with hyperactive children. *Journal of Pediatric Psychology, 18*, 359-366.

Briere, J. (1989). *Trauma Symptom Checklist - Children (TSC-C)*. Los Angeles: University of California, Los Angeles.

Briere, J., & Conte, J. (1993). Self-reported amnesia for abuse in adults molested as children. *Journal of Traumatic Stress, 6*(1), 21-31.

Briere, J., & Runtz, M. (1990). Differential adult symptomatology associated with three types of child abuse histories. *Child Abuse & Neglect, 14*, 357-364.

Browne, A., & Finkelhor, D. (1986). Impact of child sexual abuse: A review of the research. *Psychological Bulletin, 99*, 66-77.

Bruck, M., Ceci, S. J., Francoeur, E., & Barr, R. (1995). "I hardly cried when I got my shot": Influencing children's reports about a visit to their pediatrician. *Child Development, 66*(1), 193-208.

Bruck, M., Ceci, S. J., Francoeur, E., & Renick, A. (1995). Anatomical detailed dolls do not facilitate preschoolers' reports of a pediatric examination involving genital touching. *Journal of Experimental Psychology: Applied, 1*, 95-99.

Buck, J. N. (1970). *The house-tree-person technique, revised manual.* Los Angeles: Western Psychological Services.

Burgess, A. W., & Hartman, C. R. (1993). Children's drawings. *Child Abuse & Neglect, 17,* 161-168.

Burks, H. F. (1977). *Burks' behavior rating scales preschool and kindergarten.* Los Angeles, CA: Western Psychological Services.

Burns, R. C. (1982). *Self growth in families.* New York: Brunner/Mazel.

Burns, R. C., & Kaufman, S. H. (1972). *Actions, styles and symbols in kinetic family drawings (KFD): An interpretive manual.* New York: Brunner/Mazel.

Bussey, K. (1990, March). *Adult influence on children's eyewitness reporting.* Paper presented at the biennial meeting of the American Psychology and Law Society, Williamsburg, VA.

Bussey, K. (1992). Children's lying and truthfulness: Implications for children's testimony. In S. J. Ceci, M. D. Leichtman, & M. E. Putnick (Eds.), *Cognitive and social factors in early deception* (pp. 89-109). Hillsdale, NJ: Lawrence Erlbaum.

Campbell, D., & Stanley, J. (1963). *Experimental and quasi-experimental designs for research.* Chicago: Rand McNally.

Caruso, K. R. (1988). *Basic manual (Version 1).* Redding, CA: Northwest Psychological Publishers.

Ceci, S. J. (1991). Some overarching issues in the children's suggestibility debate. In J. Doris (Ed.), *The suggestibility of children's recollections* (pp. 1-9). Washington, DC: American Psychological Association.

Ceci, S. J. (1993, August). *Cognitive and social factors in children's testimony.* Paper presented at the annual meeting of the American Psychological Association, Toronto, Canada.

Ceci, S. J. (1994). Cognitive and social factors in children's testimony. In B. Sales & G. VandenBos (Eds.), *The psychology in litigation and legislation* (pp. 11-54). Washington, DC: American Psychological Association.

Ceci, S. J., & Bruck, M. (1993). Suggestibility of the child witness: A historical review and synthesis. *Psychological Bulletin, 113*(3), 403-439.

Ceci, S. J., Crotteau, M. L., Smith, E., & Loftus, E. F. (1994). Repeatedly thinking about non-events: Source misattributions among preschoolers. *Consciousness and Cognition, 3,* 388-407.

Ceci, S. J., & Leichtman, M. D. (1992). "I know that you know that I know that you broke the toy": A brief report of recursive awareness among 3-year-olds. In S. J. Ceci, M. D. Leichtman, & M. E. Putnick (Eds.), *Cognitive and social factors in early deception* (pp. 1-9). Hillsdale, NJ: Lawrence Erlbaum.

Ceci, S. J., Leichtman, M. D., Putnick, M. E., & Nightingale, N. N. (1993). The suggestibility of children's recollections. In D. Cicchetti & S. Toth (Eds.), *Child abuse, child development, and social policy* (pp. 117-138). Norwood, NJ: Ablex Publishing.

Ceci, S. J., Leichtman, M. D., & White, T. (in press). Interviewing preschoolers: Remembrance of things planted. In D. P. Peters (Ed.), *The child witness: Cognitive, social and legal issues.* Netherlands: Kluwer.

Ceci, S. J., Loftus, E. F., Leichtman, M. D., & Bruck, M. (1994). The possible role of source misattributions in the creation of false beliefs among preschoolers. *The International Journal of Clinical and Experimental Hypnosis, XLII*(4), 304-320.

Ceci, S. J., Ross, D. F., & Toglia, M. P. (1987a). Age differences in suggestibility: Narrowing the uncertainties. In S. Ceci, M. Toglia, & D. Ross (Eds.), *Children's eyewitness memory* (pp. 79-91). New York: Springer-Verlag.

Ceci, S. J., Ross, D. F., & Toglia, M. P. (1987b). Age differences in suggestibility: Psycholegal implications. *Journal of Experimental Psychology, 117,* 38-49.

Ceci, S. J., Toglia, M. P., & Ross, D. F. (1988). On remembering . . . more or less. *Journal of Experimental Psychology: General, 118,* 250-262.

Cernoch, J. M., & Porter, R. H. (1985). Recognition of maternal axillary odors by infants. *Child Development, 56,* 1593-1598.

Chantler, L., Pelco, L., & Mertin, P. (1993). The psychological evaluation of child sexual abuse using the Louisville behavior checklist and human figure drawing. *Child Abuse & Neglect, 17,* 271-279.

Chase, C. I. (1984). Psychological evaluation of children's human figure drawings. In D. J. Keyser & R. C. Sweetland (Eds.), *Test critiques* (Vol. I, pp. 189-194). Kansas City, MO: Test Corporation of America.

Chi, M. T. H., & Ceci, S. J. (1987). Current knowledge: Its role, representation, and restructuring in memory development. In H. W. Reece (Ed.), *Advances in child development and behavior* (Vol. 20, pp. 91-142). New York: Academic.

Clark, B. (1994, August). *Child custody: A clinician's survival guide.* Advanced training workshop presented at the annual meeting of the American Psychological Association, Los Angeles.

Clarke-Stewart, A., Thompson, L., & Lepore, S. (1989, April). Manipulating children's testimony through interrogation. In G. Goodman (Chair), *Can children provide accurate eyewitness testimony?* Symposium presented at the biennial meeting of the Society for Research in Child Development, Kansas City, MO.

Cohen, F. W., & Phelps, R. E. (1985). Incest markers in children's artwork. *The Arts in Psychotherapy, 12,* 265-283.

Cohn, D. S. (1991). Anatomical doll play of preschoolers referred for sexual abuse and those not referred. *Child Abuse & Neglect, 15,* 455-466.

Committee on Ethical Guidelines for Forensic Psychologists. (1991). Specialty guidelines for forensic psychologists. *Law and Human Behavior, 15*(6), 655-665.

Conners, C. K. (1990). *Conners' rating scales manual.* New York: Multi-Health Systems.

Conte, J. R., & Schuerman, J. R. (1987). Factors associated with an increased impact of child sexual abuse. *Child Abuse & Neglect, 11,* 201-211.

Conte, J. R., Sorenson, E., Fogarty, L., & Pella Rosa, J. (1991). Evaluating children's reports of sexual abuse: Results from a survey of professionals. *American Journal of Orthopsychiatry, 61*(3), 428-437.

Corwin, D. (1988). Early diagnosis of child sexual abuse: Diminishing the lasting effects. In G. Wyatt & G. Powell (Eds.), *The lasting effects of child sexual abuse* (pp. 251-269). Newbury Park, CA: Sage.

Corwin, D. (1990). Child interviews: Current research and practice. *The Advisor, 3*(2), 1.

Cummings, J. H. (1986). Projective drawings. In H. M. Knoff (Ed.), *The assessment of child and adolescent personality* (pp. 199-244). New York: Guilford.

Dale, D. S., Loftus, E. F., & Rathbun, L. (1978). The influence of the form of the question on the eyewitness testimony of preschool children. *Journal of Psycholinguistic Research, 7,* 269-277.

Dana, R. H. (1986). The Thematic Apperception Test used with adolescents. In A. I. Rabin (Ed.), *Projective techniques for adolescents and children* (pp. 14-36). New York: Springer.

Daro, D., & McCurdy, K. (1992). *Current trends in child abuse reporting and fatalities: The results of the 1991 annual fifty-state survey.* Chicago: National Committee for Prevention of Child Abuse.

Davies, G. M. (1993). Children's memory for other people: An integrative review. In C. A. Nelson (Ed.), *Memory and affect in development* (pp. 123-157). Hillsdale, NJ: Lawrence Erlbaum.

Dawes, R. M., Faust, D., & Meehl, P. E. (1989). Clinical versus actuarial judgment. *Science, 243,* 1668-1674.

DeLoache, J. S. (1987). Rapid change in the symbolic functioning of very young children. *Science, 238,* 1556-1557.

DeLoache, J. S. (1993). *The use of dolls in interviewing young children.* Paper presented at the 1993 Kent Psychology Forum, Kent, OH.

DeLoache, J. S., & Marzolf, D. P. (1993). *Young children's testimony may not be improved by using dolls to question them.* Paper presented at the biennial meeting of the Society for Research in Child Development, New Orleans, LA.

DeWitt, C. B. (1992, May). *New approach to interviewing children: A test of its effectiveness.* Washington, DC: U.S. Department of Justice, National Institute of Justice, Research in Brief.

de Young, M. (1987). Disclosing sexual abuse: The impact of developmental variables. *Child Welfare, 66*(3), 217-223.

DiLeo, J. H. (1970). *Young children and their drawings.* New York: Brunner/Mazel.

DiLeo, J. H. (1983). *Interpreting children's drawings.* New York: Brunner/Mazel.

Edelbrock, C. (1983). Problems and issues in using rating scales to assess child personality and psychopathology. *School Psychology Review, 12,* 293-299.

Egeland, B., & Farber, E. A. (1984). Infant-mother attachment: Factors related to its development and changes over time. *Child Development, 55*(3), 753-771.

Egeland, B., & Sroufe, L. A. (1981). Developmental sequelae of maltreatment in infancy. In R. Rizley & D. Cicchetti (Eds.), *New directions for child development, developmental perspectives on child maltreatment, No. 11* (pp. 77-92). San Francisco: Jossey-Bass.

Egeland, B., Sroufe, L. A., & Erickson, M. F. (1983). Developmental consequence of different patterns of maltreatment. *International Journal of Child Abuse, 7,* 459-469.

Elliot, D. M., & Briere, J. (n.d.). *The trauma symptom checklist for children: Validation data from a child abuse evaluation center.* Unpublished manuscript, Harbor - UCLA Medical Center, Torrance, CA.

Elliot, D. M., & Briere, J. (1994). Forensic sexual abuse evaluations of older children: Disclosures and symptomatology. *Behavioral Science and the Law, 12*(3), 261-277.

Erickson, M. F., & Egeland, B. A. (1987). Developmental view of the psychological consequences of maltreatment. *School Psychology Review, 16*(2), 156-168.

Erickson, M. F., Sroufe, L. A., & Egeland, B. (1985). The relationship between quality of attachment and behavior problems in preschool in a high-risk sample. In I. Bretherton & E. Waters (Eds.), *Monographs of the Society for Research in Child Development, 50*(1-2), 147-166.

Everson, M. D. (1993, January). *Evaluating young children for suspected sexual abuse.* Paper presented at the San Diego Conference on Responding to Child Maltreatment, San Diego, CA.

Everson, M. D. (1994) *Personal communication on anatomical dolls.* Chapel Hill, NC: University of North Carolina at Chapel Hill.

Everson, M. D. (1995, February). *Understanding unusual, improbable, and fantasy-like statements in children's accounts of abuse.* Paper presented at the Multidisciplinary Team Meeting, Chapel Hill, NC.

Everson, M. D., & Boat, B. W. (1990). Sexualized doll play among young children: Implications for the use of anatomical dolls in sexual abuse evaluations. *Journal of the American Academy of Child and Adolescent Psychiatry, 29,* 736-742.

Everson, M. D., & Boat, B. W. (1994). Putting the anatomical doll controversy in perspective: An explanation of the major uses and criticisms of the dolls in child sexual abuse evaluations. *Child Abuse & Neglect, 18*(2), 113-129.

Everson, M. D., Boat, B. W., & Sanfilippo, M. (1993, January). *Functional uses of anatomical dolls in sexual abuse evaluations.* Paper presented at the San Diego Conference on Responding to Child Maltreatment, San Diego, CA.

Everson, M. D., & Faller, K. (1994, May). *The art and science of forensic interviewing of children.* Paper presented at the Second National Colloquium of the American Professional Society on the Abuse of Children, Cambridge, MA.

Everson, M. D., Hunter, W. M., Runyon, D. K., Edelsohn, G. A., & Coulter, M. L. (1989). Maternal support following disclosure of incest. *American Journal of Orthopsychiatry, 59*(2), 197-207.

Everstine, D. S., & Everstine, L. (1989). *Sexual trauma in children and adolescents: Dynamics and treatment.* New York: Brunner/Mazel.

Exner, J. E. (1986). *The Rorschach: A comprehensive system. Vol. 1: Basic foundations* (2nd ed.). New York: John Wiley & Sons.

Fagot, B., & Kavanagh, K. (1991). Play as a diagnostic tool with physically abusive parents and their children. In C. Schaefer, K. Gitlin, & A. Sandgrund (Eds.), *Play diagnosis and assessment* (pp. 203-218). New York: John Wiley & Sons.

Faller, K. C. (n.d.). *Abuse focused child interviewing.* Unpublished manuscript, University of Michigan, Ann Arbor, MI.

Faller, K. C. (1984). Is the child victim of sexual abuse telling the truth? *Child Abuse & Neglect, 8,* 473-481.

Faller, K. C. (1988). Criterion for judging the credibility of children's statements about their sexual abuse. *Child Welfare, 67*(5), 389-401.

Faller, K. C. (1993, January). *Evaluating young children for possible sexual abuse.* Paper presented at the San Diego Conference on Responding to Child Maltreatment, San Diego, CA.

Faller, K. C., Froning, M. L., & Lipovsky, J. (1991). The parent-child interview: Use in evaluating child allegations of sexual abuse by the parent. *American Journal of Orthopsychiatry, 61*(4), 552-557.

Finkel, M. A. (1988). The medical evaluation of child sexual abuse. In D. H. Schetky & A. H. Green (Eds.), *Child sexual abuse: A handbook for healthcare and legal professionals* (pp. 82-103). New York: Brunner/Mazel.

Finkel, M. A. (1989). Anogenical trauma in sexually abused children. *Pediatrics, 84,* 317-322.

Finkelhor, D. (1979). *Sexually victimized children.* New York: Free Press.

Finkelhor, D. (1986). *A sourcebook on child sexual abuse.* Beverly Hills, CA: Sage.

Finkelhor, D. (1987). The trauma of child sexual abuse: Two models. *Journal of Interpersonal Violence, 2,* 348-366.

Finkelhor, D. (1989). New national child abuse study findings released. *The Advisor, 2*(1), 7.

Finkelhor, D. (1991). Mistakes found in national child abuse study statistics: Westat releases revised estimates for 1986. *The Advisor, 4*(1), 9.

Finkelhor, D., & Browne, A. (1985). The traumatic impact of child sexual abuse: A conceptualization. *American Journal of Orthopsychiatry, 55*(4), 530-541.

Finkelhor, D., Hotaling, G., Lewis, I. A., & Smith, C. (1990). Sexual abuse in a national survey of adult men and women: Prevalence, characteristics, and risk factors. *Child Abuse & Neglect, 14,* 19-28.

Fisher, R. P., & McCauley, M. R. (1995). Improving eyewitness testimony with the cognitive interview. In M. Zaragoza, J. Graham, G. Hall, R. Hirschman, & Y. Ben-Porath (Eds.), *Memory and testimony in the child witness* (pp. 141-159). Thousand Oaks, CA: Sage.

Fivush, R. (1993). Developmental perspectives on autobiographical recall. In G. S. Goodman & B. L. Bottoms (Eds.), *Child victims, child witnesses* (pp. 1-24). New York: Guilford.

Fivush, R., & Hamond, N. R. (1990). Autobiographical memory across the preschool years: Toward reconceptualizing childhood amnesia. In R. Fivush & J. A. Hudson (Eds.), *Knowing and remembering in young children* (pp. 223-248). New York: Cambridge University Press.

Fivush, R., Hamond, N. R., Harsch, N., Singer, N., & Wolf, A. (1991). Content and consistency in early autobiographical recall. *Discourse Processes, 14,* 373-388.

Fivush, R., Hudson, J., & Nelson, K. (1984). Children's long term memory for a novel event: An exploratory study. *Merrill-Palmer Quarterly, 30,* 303-316.

Flin, R., Boon, J., Knox, A., & Bull, R. (1992). The effect of a five month delay on children's and adults' eyewitness memory. *British Journal of Psychology, 83,* 323-336.

Foley, M. A., & Johnson, M. K. (1985). Confusions between memories for performed and imagined actions: A developmental comparison. *Child Development, 56,* 1145-1155.

Foreward, S., & Buck, C. (1978). *Betrayal of innocence.* Middlesex, England: Penguin.

Friedemann, V., & Morgan, M. (1985). *Interviewing sexual abuse victims using anatomical dolls: The professionals guidebook.* Eugene, OR: Shamrock Press.

Friedrich, W. N. (n.d.). *Child sexual behavior inventory.* Unpublished manuscript, Mayo Clinic & Mayo Foundation, Rochester, MN.

Friedrich, W. N. (1988). Behavior problems in sexually abused children: An adaptational perspective. In G. E. Wyatt & G. J. Powell (Eds.), *Lasting effects of child sexual abuse* (pp. 171-191). Beverly Hills, CA: Sage.

Friedrich, W. N. (1990). *Psychotherapy of sexually abused children and their families.* New York: W. W. Norton.

Friedrich, W. N. (1993). Sexual behavior in sexually abused children. *Violence Update, 3*(5), 1, 4, 8-11.

Friedrich, W. N., Grambsch, P., Damon, L., Hewitt, S. K., Koverola, C., Lang, R. A., Wolfe, V., & Broughton, D. (1992). Child sexual behavior inventory: Normative and clinical contrasts. *Psychological Assessment, 4,* 303-311.

Friedrich, W. N., Jaworski, T. M., Huxsahl, J. E., & Bengtson, B. S. (in press). Assessment of dissociative and sexual behaviors in children and adolescents with sexual abuse. *Journal of Interpersonal Violence.*

Friedrich, W. N., Urquiza, A. J., & Beilke, R. L. (1986). Behavior problems in sexually abused young children. *Journal of Pediatric Psychology, 11*(1), 47-57.

Gabriel, R. M. (1985). Anatomically correct dolls in the diagnosis of sexual abuse of children. *Journal of the Melanie Klein Society, 3,* 40-51.

Gardner, R. A. (1987). *The parental alienation syndrome and the differentiation between fabricated and genuine child sex abuse.* Cresskill, NJ: Creative Therapeutics.

Gardner, R. A. (1992). *True and false accusations of child sex abuse.* Cresskill, NJ: Creative Therapeutics.

Gary, E. (1993). *Unequal justice.* New York: Free Press.

Geiselman, R. E., Fisher, R. P., Firstenberg, I., Hutton, L. A., Sullivan, S., Avetissian, I., & Proski, A. (1984). Enhancement of eyewitness memory: An empirical evaluation of the cognitive interview. *Journal of Police Science and Administration, 12,* 74-80.

Geiselman, R. E., & Padilla, J. (1988). Interviewing child witnesses with the cognitive interview. *Journal of Police Science and Administration, 16,* 236-242.

Geiselman, R. E., Saywitz, K. J., & Bornstein, G. K. (1991). *Effects of cognitive interviewing, practice and interviewing style on children's recall performance* (NI-IJ-CX-0033). Washington, DC: National Institute of Justice.

Gentile, C. (1988). *Factors mediating the impact of child sexual abuse: Learned helplessness and severity of abuse.* Unpublished master's thesis, University of Western Ontario, London, Ontario.

Giardino, A. P., Finkel, M. A., Giardino, E. R., Seidl, T., & Ludwig, S. (1992). *A practical guide to the evaluation of sexual abuse in the prepubertal child.* Newbury Park, CA: Sage.

Ginsberg, H., & Opper, S. (1969). *Piaget's theory of intellectual development.* Englewood Cliffs, NJ: Prentice-Hall.

Glaser, R., & Chi, M. T. H. (1988). Overview. In M. T. H. Chi, R. Glaser, & M. J. Farr (Eds.), *The nature of expertise* (pp. xv-xxviii). Hillsdale, NJ: Lawrence Erlbaum.

Glaser, D., & Collins, C. (1989). The response of young, non-sexually abused children to anatomically correct dolls. *Journal of Child Psychology and Psychiatry, 30,* 547-560.

Goldman, R., & Goldman, J. (1982). *Children's sexual thinking.* Boston: Routledge & Kegan Paul.

Goldman-Rakic, P. (1987). Circuitry of the prefrontal cortex: Short term memory and the regulation of behavior by representational knowledge. In F. Blum (Ed.), *Handbook of physiology: Higher functions of the nervous system* (Vol. 5, pp. 373-417). Bethesda, MD: American Physiological Society.

Goodenough, F. L. (1926). *Measurements of intelligence by drawings.* New York: Harcourt, Brace & World.

Goodman, G. S. (1993, August). *Child victims, child witnesses.* Paper presented at the meeting of the American Psychological Association, Toronto, Canada.

Goodman, G. S., & Aman, C. (1990). Children's use of anatomically detailed dolls to recount an event. *Child Development, 61,* 1859-1871.

Goodman, G. S., Aman, C., & Hirschman, J. (1987). Child sexual abuse and physical abuse: Children's testimony. In S. J. Ceci, M. P. Toglia, & D. F. Ross (Eds.), *Children's eyewitness memory* (pp. 1-23). New York: Springer-Verlag.

Goodman, G. S., Bottoms, B. L., Schwartz-Kenny, B., & Rudy, L. (1991). Children's memory for a stressful event: Improving children's reports. *Journal of Narrative and Life History, 1,* 69-99.

Goodman, G. S., & Clarke-Stewart, A. (1991). Suggestibility in children's testimony: Implications for sexual abuse investigations. In J. Doris (Ed.), *The suggestibility of children's recollections* (pp. 92-105). Washington, DC: American Psychological Association.

Goodman, G. S., & Hegelson, V. S. (1985). Child sexual assault: Children's memory and the law. *University of Miami Law Review, 40,* 181-208.

Goodman, G. S., Hirschman, J. E., Hepps, D., & Rudy, L. (1991). Children's memory for stressful events. *Merrill Palmer Quarterly, 37,* 109-158.

Goodman, G. S., Rudy, L., Bottoms, B., & Aman, C. (1990). Children's concerns and memory: Issues of ecological validity in the study of children's eyewitness testimony. In R. Fivush & J. Hudson (Eds.), *Knowing and remembering in young children* (pp. 249-284). New York: Cambridge University Press.

Gordon, B. N., Ornstein, P. A., Nida, R. E., Follmer, A., Crenshaw, M. C., & Albert, G. (1993). Does the use of dolls facilitate children's memory of visits to the doctor? *Applied Cognitive Psychology, 7,* 459-474.

Gordon, B. N., Schroeder, C. S., & Abrams, J. M. (1990). Age and social-class differences in children's knowledge of sexuality. *Journal of Clinical Child Psychology, 19,* 33-43.

Gray, E. (1993). *Unequal justice: The prosecution of child abuse.* New York: MacMillan.

Graziano, A. M., DeGiovanni, I. S., & Garcia, K. A. (1979). Behavioral treatment of children's fears: A review. *Psychological Bulletin, 86,* 804-830.

Gruber, K. J., & Jones, J. R. (1983). Identifying determinants of risk of sexual victimization of youth: A multivariate approach. *Child Abuse & Neglect, 7,* 17-24.

Gunderson, B. H., Melas, P. S., & Skar, J. E. (1981). Sexual behaviors of preschool children: Teachers' observations. In L. L. Constantine & F. L. Martinson (Eds.), *Children and sex: New findings, new perspectives* (pp. 45-62). Boston: Little Brown.

Hackbarth, S. G., Murphy, H. D., & McQuary, J. P. (1991). Identifying sexually abused children by using kinetic family drawings. *Elementary School Guidance and Counseling, 25*, 255-260.

Halverson, H. (1940). Genital and sphincter behavior of the male infant. *Journal of Genetic Psychology, 56*, 95-136.

Hammer, M., & Kaplan, A. M. (1966). The reliability of children's human figure drawings. *Journal of Clinical Psychology, 22*(3), 316-319.

Hamond, N. R., & Fivush, R. (1990). Memories of Mickey Mouse: Young children recount their trip to Disneyworld. *Cognitive Development, 6*, 433-448.

Harris, D. B. (1963). *Children's drawings as measurements of maturity.* New York: Harcourt, Brace & World.

Harris, D. B. (1972). The draw a person. In O. K. Buros (Ed.), *Seventh mental measurements yearbook* (Vol. 1, pp. 401-404). Highland Park, NJ: Gryphon Press.

Haynes-Seman, C., & Baumgarten, D. (1994). *Children speak for themselves.* New York: Brunner/Mazel.

Heiman, M. L. (1992). Annotation: Putting the puzzle together: Validating allegations of child sexual abuse. *Journal of Child Psychology and Psychiatry, 33*(2), 311-329.

Herman, J., & Schatzow, E. (1987). Recovery and verification of memories of childhood sexual trauma. *Psychoanalytic Psychology, 4*, 1-4.

Hertsgaard, L., & Matthews, A. (1993). The ontogeny of memory revisited: Commentary on Nelson and Fivush. In C. A. Nelson (Ed.), *Memory and affect in development* (pp. 79-86). Hillsdale, NJ: Lawrence Erlbaum.

Hibbard, R. A., & Hartman, G. L. (1990). Emotional indicators in human figure drawings of sexually victimized and nonabused children. *Journal of Clinical Psychology, 46*(2), 211-218.

Hibbard, R. A., Roghmann, K., & Hoekelman, R. A. (1987). Genitals in children's drawings: An association with sexual abuse. *Pediatrics, 79*, 129-137.

Hoffman, M. L. (1988). Moral development. In M. H. Bornstein & M. E. Lamb (Eds.), *Developmental psychology: An advanced textbook* (2nd ed., pp. 497-548). Hillsdale, NJ: Lawrence Erlbaum.

Horner, T. M., Guyer, M. J., & Kalter, N. M. (1993). The biases of child sexual abuse experts: Believing is seeing. *Bulletin of the American Academy of Psychiatry and Law, 21*(3), 281-292.

Hornstein, N. L., & Putnam, F. W. (1992). Clinical phenomenology of child and adolescent dissociative disorders. *Journal of the American Academy of Child and Adolescent Psychiatry, 31*, 1077-1085.

Howe, M. L. (1991). Misleading children's story recall: Forgetting and reminiscence of the facts. *Developmental Psychology, 27*, 746-762.

Hudson, J. A. (1988). Children's memory for atypical actions in script-based stories: Evidence for a disruptive effect. *Journal of Experimental Child Psychology, 5*, 1-15.

Hudson, J. A. (1990a). The emergence of autobiographical memory in mother-child conversation. In R. Fivush & J. A. Hudson (Eds.), *Knowing and remembering in young children* (pp. 166-196). New York: Cambridge University Press.

Hudson, J. A. (1990b). Constructive processes in children's autobiographic memory. *Developmental Psychology, 26,* 180-187.

Hudson, J. A., & Fivush, R. (1987). *As time goes by: Sixth grade children recall a kindergarten experience* (Emory Cognition Project #13). Atlanta: Emory University.

Hudson, J. A., & Nelson, K. (1986). Repeated encounters of a similar kind: Effects of familiarity of children's autobiographic memory. *Cognitive Development, 1,* 253-271.

Humphrey, H. H., III, (1985). *Report on Scott County investigations.* St. Paul, MN: Attorney General's Office.

Husain, S. A., & Cantwell, D. P. (1991). *Fundamentals of child and adolescent psychopathology.* Washington, DC: American Psychiatric Press.

Jampole, L., & Weber, M. (1987). An assessment of the behavior of sexually abused and nonsexually abused children with anatomically correct dolls. *Child Abuse & Neglect, 11,* 187-192.

Jolles, I. (1971). *A catalog for the quantitative interpretation of the house-tree-person.* Los Angeles: Western Psychological Services.

Katz, S., Schonfeld, D. J., Carter, A. S., Leventhal, J. M., & Cicchetti, D. V. (1995). The accuracy of children's reports with anatomically correct dolls. *Developmental and Behavioral Pediatrics, 16,* 71-76.

Kauffman, I., Peck, A., & Tagiuri, C. K. (1954). The family constellation and overt incestuous relations between father and daughter. *American Journal of Orthopsychiatry, 24,* 266-277.

Kaufman, B., & Wohl, A. (1992). *Casualties of childhood: A developmental perspective on sexual abuse using projective drawings.* New York: Brunner/Mazel.

Kavanagh, K. A., Youngblade, L., Reid, J. B., & Fagot, B. I. (1988). Interactions between children and abusive versus control parents. *Journal of Clinical Child Psychology, 17*(2), 137-142.

Keary, K., & Fitzpatrick, C. (1994). Children's disclosure of sexual abuse during formal investigation. *Child Abuse & Neglect, 18*(7), 543-548.

Kelley, K., & Byrne, D. (1992). *Exploring human sexuality.* Englewood Cliffs, NJ: Prentice-Hall.

Kempe, C. H., & Helfer, R. E. (1968). *The battered child.* Chicago: University of Chicago Press.

Kendell-Tackett, K. A. (1991). Believing children versus being neutral: What you think can influence your judgments about suspected victims of sexual abuse. *The Advisor, 4*(3), 4.

Kendall-Tackett, K. A. (1992). Professionals' standards of "normal" behavior with anatomical dolls and factors that influence these standards. *Child Abuse & Neglect, 16,* 727-733.

Kendall-Tackett, K. A., & Watson, M. W. (1992). Use of anatomical dolls by Boston-area professionals. *Child Abuse & Neglect, 61,* 423-428.

Kendall-Tackett, K. A., Williams, L. M., & Finkelhor, D. (1993). Impact of sexual abuse on children: A review and synthesis of recent empirical studies. *Psychological Bulletin, 113,* 164-180.

Kennedy, M. L., Faust, D., Willis, W. G., & Piotrowski, C. (1994). Social-emotional assessment practices in school psychology. *Journal of Psychoeducational Assessment, 12,* 228-240.

Kenyon-Jump, R., Burnette, M. M., & Robertson, M. (1991). Comparison of behaviors of suspected sexually abused and nonsexually abused preschool children using anatomical dolls. *Journal of Psychopathology and Behavioral Assessment, 13*(3), 225-239.

Keyser, D. J., & Sweetland, R. C. (Eds.). (1984). *Test critiques - Vol. I.* Kansas City, MO: Test Corporation of America.

Keyser, D. J., & Sweetland, R. C. (Eds.). (1985). *Test critiques - Vol. II.* Kansas City, MO: Test Corporation of America.

Kilpatrick, A. C. (1987). Childhood experiences: Problems and issues in studying long-range effects. *Journal of Sex Research, 23*(2), 173-196.

Kilpatrick, A. C. (1992). *Long range effects of child and adolescent sexual experiences, myths, mores, and menaces.* Hillsdale, NJ: Lawrence Erlbaum.

King, M. A., & Yuille, J. C. (1987). Suggestibility and the child witness. In S. J. Ceci, M. P. Toglia, & D. F. Ross (Eds.), *Children's eyewitness memory* (pp. 24-35). New York: Springer-Verlag.

Kinsey, A. C., Pomeroy, W. B., & Martin, C. E. (1948). *Sexual behavior in the human male.* Philadelphia: W. B. Saunders.

Kinsey, A. C., Pomeroy, W. B., Martin, C. E., & Gebhard, P. H. (1953). *Sexual behavior in the human female.* Philadelphia: W. B. Saunders.

Klajner-Diamond, H., Wehrspann, W., & Steinhauer, P. (1987). Assessing the credibility of young children's allegations of sexual abuse: Clinical issues. *Canadian Journal of Psychiatry, 32,* 610-614.

Klopfer, B., Ainsworth, M. D., Klopfer, G. W., & Holt, R. R. (1954). *Developments in the Rorschach technique: Vol. I. Technique and theory.* New York: World Book Company.

Knoff, H. M. (1986). Identifying and classifying children and adolescents referred for personality assessment: Theories, systems, and issues. In H. M. Knoff (Ed.), *The assessment of child and adolescent personality* (pp. 3-33). New York: Guilford.

Kohlberg, L. (1976). Moral stage and moralization: The cognitive developmental approach. In T. Lickona (Ed.), *Moral development and behavior: Theory, research and social issues* (pp. 31-53). New York: Holt, Rinehart & Winston.

Koppitz, E. (1966). Emotional indicators on human figure drawings of children: A validation study. *Journal of Clinical Psychology, 22*(3), 313-315.

Koppitz, E. (1968). *Psychological evaluation of children's human figure drawings.* New York: Grune & Stratton.

Kuhn, D. (1988). Cognitive development. In M. H. Bornstein & M. E. Lamb (Eds.), *Developmental psychology: An advanced textbook* (2nd ed., pp. 205-260). Hillsdale, NJ: Lawrence Erlbaum.

Lamb, M. E., Sternberg, K. J., & Esplin, P. W. (1994). Factors influencing the reliability and validity of statements made by young victims of sexual maltreatment. *Journal of Applied Developmental Psychology, 15,* 255-280.

Lanktree, C. B., Briere, J., & deJonge, J. (1993, August). *Effectiveness of therapy for sexually abused children: Changes in Trauma Symptom Checklist for Children*

TSC-C scores. Paper presented at the meeting of the American Psychological Association, Toronto, Canada.

Lawson, L., & Chaffin, M. (1992). False negatives in sexual abuse disclosure interviews. *Journal of Interpersonal Violence, 7*(4), 532-542.

Leichtman, M. D., & Ceci, S. J. (1995). The effects of stereotypes and suggestions on preschoolers reports. *Developmental Psychology, 31*(4), 568-578.

Leifer, M., Shapiro, J., Martone, M., & Kassem, L. (1991). Rorschach assessment of psychological functioning in sexually abused girls. *Journal of Personality Assessment, 56*(1), 14-28.

Leitenberg, H., Greenwald, E., & Tarran, M. J. (1989). The relationship between sexual activity among children during preadolescence and/or early adolescence and sexual behavior and sexual adjustment in young adulthood. *Archives of Sexual Behavior, 18,* 299-313.

Lerner, J. V. (1985). Burks' behavior rating scales. In D. J. Keyser & R. C. Sweetland (Eds.), *Test critiques* (Vol. II, pp. 108-112). Kansas City, MO: Test Corporation of America.

Lewis, M., & Michalson, L. (1983). *Children's emotions and moods.* New York: Plenum.

Loftus, E. F. (1993). The reality of repressed memories. *American Psychologist, 48*(5), 518-537.

Loftus, E. F., & Ketcham, K. (1991). *Witness for the defense.* New York: St. Martin's Press.

Loftus, E. F., Polonsky, S., & Fullilove, M. T. (1994). Memories of childhood sexual abuse. *Psychology of Women Quarterly, 18,* 67-84.

Lubin, B., Larsen, R. M., & Matarazzo, J. D. (1984). Patterns of psychological test usage in the United States: 1935-1982. *American Psychologist, 39,* 451-454.

Lubin, B., Wallis, R. R., & Paine, C. (1971). Patterns of psychological test usage in the United States: 1935-1969. *Professional Psychology, 2,* 70-74.

Maccoby, E. (1983). Social-emotional development and response to stressors. In N. Garmezy & M. Rutter (Eds.), *Stress, coping and development in children* (pp. 217-234). New York: McGraw-Hill.

MacFarlane, J. W., Allen, L., & Honzik, M. P. (1954). *A developmental study of the behavior problems of normal children between twenty-one months and fourteen years, University of California Publications in Child Development: Vol. 2.* Los Angeles: University of California Press.

Machover, K. (1949). *Personality projection in the drawing of the human figure.* Springfield, IL: Charles C. Thomas.

Mannarino, A. P., & Cohen, J. (1987). *Psychological symptoms of sexually abused children.* Paper presented at the Third National Family Violence Research Conference, Durham, NH.

Mannarino, A. P., Cohen, J. A., & Berman, S. R. (1994). The children's attributions and perceptions scale: A new measure of sexual abuse-related factors. *Journal of Clinical Child Psychology, 23*(2), 204-211.

Martin, R. P., Hooper, S., & Snow, J. (1986). Behavior rating scale approaches to personality assessment in children and adolescents. In H. M. Knoff (Ed.), *The assessment of child and adolescent personality* (pp. 309-351). New York: Guilford.

McArthur, D. S., & Roberts, G. E. (1990). *Roberts apperception test for children.* Los Angeles: Western Psychological Services.

McCarthy, D. (1954). Language development in children. In L. Carmichael (Ed.), *Manual of child psychology* (pp. 492-630). New York: John Wiley & Sons.

McCartney, K., & Nelson, K. (1981). Children's use of scripts in story recall. *Discourse Processes, 4,* 59-70.

McCauley, M., & Fisher, R. (1992, March). *Improving children's recall of action with the cognitive interview.* Paper presented at the meeting of the American Psychology and Law Society, San Diego, CA.

McCloskey, M., & Zaragoza, M. (1985a). Misleading postevent information and memory for events: Arguments and evidence against memory impairment hypotheses. *Journal of Experimental Psychology: General, 114,* 1-16.

McCloskey, M., & Zaragoza, M. (1985b). Postevent information and memory: Reply to Loftus, Schooler, and Wagenaar. *Journal of Experimental Psychology: General, 114,* 381-387.

McCurdy, K., & Daro, O. (1993). *Current trends in child abuse reporting and fatalities: The results of the 1992 annual fifty state survey.* Chicago: The National Committee for Prevention of Child Abuse.

McGough, L. (1994). *Child witness: Fragile voices in the American legal system.* New Haven, CT: Yale University Press.

McIver, W., Wakefield, H., & Underwager, R. (1989). Behavior of abused and nonabused children in interviews with anatomically correct dolls. *Issues in Child Abuse Accusations, 1*(1), 39-48.

Meiselman, K. C. (1978). *Incest.* San Francisco: Jossey-Bass.

Melton, G. B., & Limber, S. (1989). Psychologists' involvement in cases of child maltreatment: Limits of role and expertise. *American Psychologist, 44,* 1225-1233.

Melton, G. B., & Thompson, R. A. (1987). Getting out of a rut: Detours to less traveled paths in child-witness research. In S. J. Ceci, M. P. Toglia, & D. F. Ross (Eds.), *Children's eyewitness testimony* (pp. 209-229). New York: John Wiley & Sons.

Miller, L. C. (1984). *Louisville behavior checklist manual - revised.* Los Angeles: Western Psychological Services.

Minnesota Psychological Association. (1986, Winter). Minnesota Psychological Association guidelines for the practice of psychology in child sexual abuse cases. *Minnesota Psychologist,* pp. 1, 17-19.

Moan-Hardie, S. M. (1991). *Reducing suggestibility in children's eyewitness testimony: A training program to improve children's competence to resist misleading questions and aid retrieval.* Unpublished doctoral dissertation, University of California, Los Angeles.

Mooney, K. C. (1984). Child Behavior Checklist. In D. J. Keyser & R. C. Sweetland (Eds.), *Test critiques* (Vol. I, pp. 168-184). Kansas City, MO: Test Corporation of America.

Morison, S., & Greene, E. (1992). Juror and expert knowledge of child sexual abuse. *Child Abuse & Neglect, 16,* 595-613.

Morrow, K. B. (1991). Attributions of female adolescent incest victims regarding their molestation. *Child Abuse & Neglect, 15,* 477-483.

Moston, S. (1987). The suggestibility of children in interview studies. *First Language, 7,* 67-78.

Myers, J. E. B. (1992). *Legal issues in child abuse and neglect.* Newbury Park, CA: Sage.

Myers, J. E. B. (in press). Expert testimony. In L. Berliner, J. Briere, & J. Buckley (Eds.), *APSAC handbook on child maltreatment.* Newbury Park, CA: Sage.

Myers, J. E. B., Berliner, L., Conte, J., & Sauders, B. E. (1994, May). *The scientific basis for expert psychological testimony regarding child sexual abuse.* Paper presented at the Second National Colloquium of the American Professional Society on the Abuse of Children, Cambridge, MA.

Myers, J. E. B., & White, S. (1989). Dolls in court? *The Advisor, 2*(3), 5-6.

Nader, K., & Pynoos, R. S. (1991). Play and drawing techniques as tools for interviewing traumatized children. In C. E. Schaefer, K. Gitlin, & A. Sandgrund (Eds.), *Play diagnosis and assessment* (pp. 375-389). New York: John Wiley & Sons.

National Center for Child Abuse and Neglect. (1981). *Study findings: National study of the incidence and severity of child abuse and neglect* (DHHS Publication No. OHDS 81-30325). Washington, DC: Clearinghouse on Child Abuse and Neglect.

National Center for the Prosecution of Child Abuse. (1993). *Investigation and prosecution of child abuse* (2nd ed.). Alexandria, VA: Author.

National Center on Child Abuse and Neglect. (1992). *Child abuse and neglect: A shared community concern.* Washington, DC: U. S. Department of Health and Human Services.

Nelson, K. (1986). *Event knowledge: Structure and function in development.* Hillsdale, NJ: Lawrence Erlbaum.

Nelson, K. (1990). Remembering, forgetting and childhood amnesia. In R. Fivush & J. A. Hudson, *Knowing and remembering in young children* (pp. 301-316). New York: Cambridge University Press.

Nelson, K. (1993). Events, narratives, memory: What develops? In C. A. Nelson (Ed.), *Memory and affect in development* (pp. 1-24). Hillsdale, NJ: Lawrence Erlbaum.

Nurcombe, B. (1986). The child as witness: Competency and credibility. *Journal of the American Academy of Child Psychiatry, 25,* 473-480.

Oates, K., & Shrimpton, S. (1991). Children's memories for stressful and non-stressful events. *Medicine, Science and the Law, 31,* 4-10.

Obrzut, J. E., & Boliek, C. A. (1986). Thematic approaches to personality assessment with children and adolescents. In H. M. Knoff (Ed.), *Assessment of child and adolescent personality* (pp. 173-198). New York: Guilford.

Ornstein, P. A. (1993, April). *Abuse and victimization in life span perspective - trauma and memory - clinical and legal dimensions.* Paper presented at the Harvard Medical School Conference, Boston, MA.

Ornstein, P. A., Gordon, B. N., & Larus, D. M. (1992). Children's memory for a personally experienced event: Implications for testimony. *Applied Cognitive Psychology, 6,* 49-60.

Ornstein, P. A., Larus, D. M., & Clubb, P. A. (1991). Understanding children's testimony: Implications of research on the development of memory. *Annals of Child Development, 8,* 145-176.

Ornstein, P. A., & Naus, M. N. (1985). Effects of the knowledge base as children's memory strategies. In H. W. Reece (Ed.), *Advances in child development and behavior* (pp. 113-148). Orlando, FL: Academic Press.

Paveza, G. J. (1987, July). *Risk factors in father-daughter child sexual abuse: Findings from a case-control study.* Paper presented at the Third National Family Violence Research Conference, Durham, NH.

Perry, N. W. (1992). How children remember and why they forget. *The Advisor, 5*(3), 1-2, 13-15.

Perry, N. W., & Wrightsman, L. S. (1991). *The child witness.* Newbury Park, CA: Sage.

Peters, D. P. (1987). The impact of naturally occurring stress on children's memory. In S. J. Ceci, M. P. Toglia, & D. F. Ross (Eds.), *Children's eyewitness memory* (pp. 122-141). New York: Springer-Verlag.

Peters, S. D. (1988). Child sexual abuse and later psychological problems. In G. E. Wyatt & G. J. Powell (Eds.), *Lasting effects of child sexual abuse* (pp. 101-117). Beverly Hills, CA: Sage.

Peters, S. D. (1991). The influence of stress and arousal on the child witness. In J. L. Doris (Ed.), *The suggestibility of children's recollections* (pp. 60-76). Washington, DC: American Psychological Association.

Peters, S. D., Wyatt, G., & Finkelhor, D. (1986). Prevalence. In D. Finkelhor & Associates (Eds.), *Sourcebook on child sexual abuse* (pp. 15-59). Beverly Hills, CA: Sage.

Petty, J. (1990). *Checklist for child abuse evaluation - professional manual.* Odessa, FL: Psychological Assessment Resources.

Piaget, J. (1932/1965). *The moral judgment of the child.* Harmondsworth, England: Penguin.

Piaget, J. (1970). Piaget's theory. In P. Mussen (Ed.), *Carmichael's manual of child psychology* (Vol. I, 3rd ed., pp. 703-730). New York: John Wiley & Sons.

Piotrowski, C., & Keller, J. W. (1992). Psychological testing in applied settings: A literature review from 1982-1992. *Journal of Training & Practice in Professional Psychology, 6*(2), 74-82.

Pipe, M. F., Gee, S., & Wilson, C. (1993). Cues, props, and context: Do they facilitate children's event reports? In G. S. Goodman & B. L. Bottoms (Eds.), *Child victims, child witnesses* (pp. 25-45). New York: Guilford.

Poole, D. A., & Lindsay, D. S. (1995). Interviewing preschoolers: Effects of nonsuggestive techniques, parental coaching, and leading questions on reports of nonexperienced events. *Journal of Experimental Child Psyschology, 60*(1), 129-154.

Poole, D. A., & Warren, A. R. (1995). *Recent challenges to three commonly held assumptions about children's eyewitness testimony.* Paper presented at the biennial meeting of the Society for Research in Child Development, Indianapolis, IN.

Poole, D. A., & White, L. T. (1991). Effects of question repetition on the eyewitness testimony of children and adults. *Developmental Psychology, 27,* 975-986.

Poole, D. A., & White, L. T. (1993). Two years later: Effects of question repetition and retention interval on the eyewitness testimony of children and adults. *Developmental Psychology, 29*(5), 844-853.

Prout, H. T. (1983). School psychologists and social-emotional assessment techniques: Patterns in training and use. *School Psychology Review, 12,* 35-38.

Putnam, F. W. (1990). *Child Dissociative Checklist* (Version 3.0 - 2/90). Laboratory of Developmental Psychology, National Institute of Mental Health, Bethesda, MD.

Putnam, F. W. (1991). Dissociative phenomena. In A. Tasman (Ed.), *Annual review of psychiatry* (pp. 159-174). Washington, DC: American Psychiatric Press.

Putnam, F. W., Helmers, K., & Trickett, P. K. (1993). Development, reliability, and validity of a child dissociation scale. *Child Abuse & Neglect, 17,* 731-741.

Pynoos, R. S., & Eth, S. (1984). The child as witness to homicide. *Journal of Social Issues, 40*(2), 87-108.

Pynoos, R. S., Frederick, C., Nader, K., Arroyo, W., Steinberg, S., Eth, S., Nunez, F., & Fairbanks, L. (1987). Life threat and posttraumatic stress in school-age children. *Archives of General Psychiatry, 44,* 1057-1063.

Pynoos, R. S., & Nader, K. (1988). Children's memory and proximity to violence. *Journal of the American Academy of Child and Adolescent Psychiatry, 28,* 236-241.

Quinton, D., & Rutter, M. (1984). Parents with children in care, II: Intergenerational continuities. *Journal of Child Psychology and Psychiatry, 25,* 231-250.

Rabinowitz, M. J. (1985). The child as an eyewitness: An overview. *Social Action and the Law, 11*(1), 5-10.

Raskin, D. C., & Esplin, P. W. (1991). Assessment of children's statements of sexual abuse. In J. Doris (Ed.), *The suggestibility of children's recollections* (pp. 153-164). Washington, DC: American Psychological Association.

Raskin, D. C., & Yuille, J. C. (1989). Problems in evaluating interviews of children in sexual abuse cases. In S. J. Ceci, D. F. Ross, & M. P. Toglia (Eds.), *Perspectives on children's testimony* (pp. 184-207). New York: Springer-Verlag.

Realmuto, G., Jensen, J., & Wescoe, S. (1990). Specificity and sensitivity of sexually anatomically correct dolls in substantiating abuse: A pilot study. *Journal of the American Academy of Child and Adolescent Psychiatry, 29,* 743-746.

Reed, D. L. (1993). Enhancing children's resistance to misleading questions during forensic interviews. *The Advisor, 6*(2), 3-8.

Renninger, K. A., & Wozniak, R. H. (1985). Effect of interest on attentional shift, recognition and recall in young children. *Developmental Psychology, 21,* 624-632.

Riordan, R. J., & Verdel, A. C. (1991). Evidence of sexual abuse in children's art projects. *The School Counselor, 39,* 116-121.

Rovee-Collier, C., & Hayne, H. (1987). Reactivation of the infant memory. In H. W. Reese (Ed.), *Advances in child development and behavior* (pp. 185-238). New York: Academic Press.

Rudy, L., & Goodman, G. S. (1991). Effects of participation on children's reports: Implications for children's testimony. *Developmental Psychology, 27,* 527-538.

Salzinger, S., Kaplan, S., Pelcovitz, D., Samit, C., & Krieger, R. (1984). Parent and teacher assessment of children's behavior in child maltreating families. *Journal of the American Academy of Child Psychiatry, 23,* 458-464.

Sarafino, E. P. (1986). *The fears of childhood.* New York: Human Sciences Press.

Sauzier, M. (1989). Disclosure of child sexual abuse - for better or worse. *Psychiatric Clinics of North America, 12*(2), 455-469.

Saywitz, K. J. (1987). Children's testimony: Age-related patterns of memory errors. In S. J. Ceci, M. Toglia, & D. Ross (Eds.), *Children's eyewitness memory* (pp. 36-52). New York: Springer-Verlag.

Saywitz, K. J. (1989). Children's conceptions of the legal system: Court is a place to play basketball. In S. Ceci, D. Ross, & M. Toglia (Eds.), *Perspectives on children's testimony* (pp. 131-157). New York: Springer-Verlag.

Saywitz, K. J. (1992). Enhancing children's memory with the cognitive interview. *The Advisor, 5*(3), 9-10.

Saywitz, K. J. (1994). Effects of a multidisciplinary interview center on the investigation of alleged child sexual abuse. *Violence Update, 5*(4), 3, 6.

Saywitz, K. J. (1995a). *Personal communication on interviewing alleged child victims of sexual abuse.* Los Angeles: University of California.

Saywitz, K. J. (1995b). Improving children's testimony: The question, the answer, and the environment. In M. Zaragoza, J. Graham, G. Hall, R. Hirschman, & Y. Ben-Porath (Eds.), *Memory and testimony in the child witness* (pp. 113-140). Thousand Oaks, CA: Sage.

Saywitz, K. J., Geiselman, R. E., & Bornstein, G. K. (1992). Effects of cognitive interviewing and practice on children's recall performance. *Journal of Applied Psychology, 77*(5), 744-756.

Saywitz, K. J., & Goodman, G. S. (in press). Interviewing children in and out of court: Current research and practical implications. In L. Berliner, J. Briere, & J. Bulkley (Eds.), *APSAC handbook on child maltreatment.* Newbury Park, CA: Sage.

Saywitz, K. J., Goodman, G. S., Nicholas, G., & Moan, S. (1991). Children's memories of physical examinations that involve genital touch: Implications for reports of child sexual abuse. *Journal of Consulting and Clinical Psychology, 59*(5), 682-691.

Saywitz, K. J., & Moan-Hardie, S. (1994). Reducing the potential for distortion of childhood memories. *Consciousness and Cognition, 3,* 408-425.

Saywitz, K., Moan-Hardie, S., & Lamphear, V. (in press). The effect of preparation on children's resistance to misleading questions. In K. Pezdek & W. P. Banks (Eds.), *Consciousness and cognition,* special issue on the recovery of lost childhood memories for traumatic events.

Saywitz, K. J., & Snyder, L. (1993). Improving children's testimony with preparation. In G. S. Goodman & B. L. Bottoms (Eds.), *Child victims, child witnesses: Understanding and improving testimony* (pp. 117-146). New York: Guilford.

Saywitz, K. J., Snyder, L., & Lamphear, V. (1990, August). *Preparing child witnesses: The efficacy of memory strategy training.* Paper presented at the meeting of the American Psychological Association, Boston, MA.

Schaffer, H. R. (1971). *The growth of sociability.* Harmondsworth, England: Penguin.

Schaffer, H. R. (1974). Cognitive components of the infant's response to strangeness. In M. Lewis & L. A. Roseblum (Eds.), *The origins of fear* (pp. 11-24). New York: John Wiley & Sons.

Schaffer, H. R., & Emerson, P. E. (1964). The development of social attachments in infancy. *Monographs of the Society for Research in Child Development* (Vol. 29 [3], Serial No. 94). Lafayette, IN: Child Development Publications of the Society for Research and Child Development, Inc.

Sedlak, A. J. (1991). *National incidence and prevalence of child abuse and neglect: 1988 - Revised report.* Rockville, MD: Westat.

Sgroi, S. (1982). *Handbook of clinical intervention in child sexual abuse.* Lexington, MA: Lexington Books.

Sgroi, S. (1988). *Vulnerable populations.* Lexington, MA: Lexington Books.

Shapiro, J. P., Leifer, M., Martone, M. W., & Kassem, L. (1990). Multimethod assessment of depression in sexually abused girls. *Journal of Personality Assessment, 55*(1-2), 234-248.

Sidun, N. M., & Rosenthal, R. H. (1987). Graphic indicators of sexual abuse in draw-a-person tests of psychiatrically hospitalized adolescents. *The Arts in Psychotherapy, 14,* 25-33.

Sivan, A. B., Schor, D. P., Koeppl, G. K., & Noble, L. D. (1988). Interaction of normal children with anatomical dolls. *Child Abuse & Neglect, 12,* 295-304.

Smith, D. T. (1991). Parent-child interaction play assessment. In C. E. Schaefer, K. Gitlin, & A. Sandgrund (Eds.), *Play diagnosis and assessment* (pp. 463-492). New York: John Wiley & Sons.

Snyder, L. S., Nathanson, R., & Saywitz, K. J. (1993). Children in court: The role of discourse processing and production. *Topics in Language Disorders, 13*(4), 39-58.

Sorenson, T., & Snow, B. (1991). How children tell: The process of disclosure in child sexual abuse. *Child Welfare, 70,* 3-15.

Spiegel, D., & Cardena, E. (1991). Disintegrated experience: The dissociative disorders revisited. *Journal of Abnormal Psychology, 100,* 366-378.

Sroufe, L. A. (1983). Infant-caregiver attachment and patterns of adaptation in preschool: The roots of maladaptation and competence. In M. Perlmutter-Hillsdale (Ed.), *Development and policy concerning children with special needs* (pp. 41-83). Hillsdale, NJ: Lawrence Erlbaum.

State v. Wright, 775 P. 2d 1224 (1989, aff'd 497 U.S. 805 1990).

Stein, N., & Glenn, C. (1978). *The role of temporal organization in story comprehension* (Technical Report No. 71). Urbana, IL: University of Illinois, Center for Study of Reading.

Steward, M. S. (1992). Preliminary findings from the University of California, Davis, Child Memory Study: Development and testing of interview protocols for young children. *The Advisor, 5*(3), 11-13.

Steward, M. S. (1993). Understanding children's memories of medical procedures: "He didn't touch me and it didn't hurt!" In C. A. Nelson (Ed.), *Memory and affect in development* (pp. 171-225). Hillsdale, NJ: Lawrence Erlbaum.

Steward, M. S., Bussey, K., Goodman, G. S., & Saywitz, K. J. (1993). Implications of developmental research for interviewing children. *Child Abuse & Neglect, 17,* 25-37.

Steward, M. S., & Stewart, D. (in press). *Interviewing young children about body touch and handling.* Monograph series for the Society for Research in Child Development.

Stoller, R. J., & Herdt, G. (1985). Theories of origins of male homosexuality. *Archives of General Psychiatry, 42,* 399-404.

Terr, L. (1988). What happens to early memories of trauma? A study of twenty children under age five at the time of documented traumatic events. *Journal of the American Academy of Child and Adolescent Psychiatry, 27,* 96-104.

Terr, L. (1990). *Too scared to cry.* New York: Harper & Row.

Tessler, M. (1986). *Mother-child talk in a museum: The socialization of memory.* Unpublished manuscript, University of New York.

Todd, C., & Perlmutter, M. (1980). Reality recalled by preschool children. In M. Perlmutter (Ed.), *New directions for child development, No. 10: Children's memory* (pp. 69-86). San Francisco: Jossey-Bass.

Tucker, A., Mertin, P., & Luszcz, M. (1990). The effect of a repeated interview on young children's eyewitness memory. *Australian and New Zealand Journal of Criminology, 23,* 117-124.

Usher, J., & Neisser, U. (1993). Childhood amnesia and the beginnings of memory for four early life events. *Journal of Experimental Psychology: General, 122,* 155-165.

Wade, T. C., & Baker, T. B. (1977). Opinions and use of psychological tests. *American Psychologist, 32,* 874-882.

Wakefield, H., & Underwager, R. (1988). Psychological assessment of suspected victims. In H. Wakefield & R. Underwager (Eds.), *Accusations of child sexual abuse.* Springfield, IL: Charles C. Thomas.

Walker, A. G. (1993). Questioning young children in court: A linguistic case study. *Law and Human Behavior, 17,* 59-81.

Warren, A., Hulse-Trotter, K., & Tubbs, E. (1991). Inducing resistance to suggestibility in children. *Law and Human Behavior, 15*(3), 273-285.

Warren, A., & Lane, P. (1995). Effects of timing and type of questioning on eyewitness accuracy and suggestibility. In M. S. Zaragoza, J. R. Graham, G. C. Hall, R. Hirschman, & Y. S. Ben-Porath (Eds.), *Memory and testimony in the child witness* (pp. 44-60). Thousand Oak, CA: Sage.

Wehrspann, W., Steinhauer, P., & Klajner-Diamond, H. (1987). Criterion for assessing credibility of sexual abuse allegations. *Canadian Journal of Psychiatry, 32,* 615-623.

Weiner, I. B. (1986). Assessing children and adolescents with the Rorschach. In H. M. Knoff (Ed.), *The assessment of child and adolescent personality* (pp. 141-171). New York: Guilford.

Wells, D., McCann, J., Adams, J., Voris, J., & Ensign, J. (1995). Emotional, behavioral, and physical symptoms reported by parents of sexually abused, nonabused, and allegedly abused prepubescent females. *Child Abuse & Neglect, 19,* 155-163.

White, S. H. (1994, August). *Assessing child sexual abuse allegations in custody disputes.* Advanced training workshop presented at the meeting of the American Psychological Association, Los Angeles, CA.

White, S. H., & Pillemer, D. B. (1979). Childhood amnesia and the development of a socially accessible memory system. In J. F. Kihlstrom & F. J. Evans (Eds.), *Functional disorders of memory* (pp. 29-73). Hillsdale, NJ: Lawrence Erlbaum.

White, S. H., & Quinn, K. (1988). Investigatory independence in child sexual abuse evaluations: Conceptual considerations. *Bulletin of the American Academy of Psychiatry and the Law, 16*(3), 269-278.

White, S. H., Strom, G., Santilli, G., & Halpin, B. M. (1986). Interviewing young sexual abuse victims with anatomically correct dolls. *Child Abuse & Neglect, 10,* 519-530.

White, S. H., Strom, G., Santilli, G., & Quinn, K. (1987). *Clinical guidelines for interviewing young children with sexually anatomically detailed dolls.* Unpublished manuscript, Case Western Reserve University School of Medicine at Cleveland, OH.

Williams, L. (1994). Recall of childhood trauma: A prospective study of women's memories of child sexual abuse. *Journal of Consulting and Clinical Psychology, 62*(6), 1167-1176.

Winnicot, D. W. (1971). *Therapeutic consultations in child psychiatry.* New York: Basic Books.

Wirt, R. D., Lachar, D., Klinedinst, J. K., & Seat, P. D. (1990). *Multidimensional description of child personality: A manual for the Personality Inventory for Children revised 1984.* Los Angeles: Western Psychological Services.

Wolfe, D. A., & Mosk, M. D. (1983). Behavioral comparisons of children from abusive and distressed families. *Journal of Consulting and Clinical Psychology, 51,* 702-708.

Wolfe, V. V., Gentile, C., & Wolfe, D. A. (1989). The impact of sexual abuse on children: A PTSD formulation. *Behavior Therapy, 20*(2), 215-228.

Wolfe, V. V., Wolfe, D. A., Gentile, C., & LaRose, L. (1987). *Children's Impact of Traumatic Events Scale-Revised.* Unpublished manuscript, University of Western Ontario at London, Ontario.

Wolfner, G., Faust, D., & Dawes, R. (1993). The use of anatomically detailed dolls in sexual abuse evaluations: The state of the science. *Applied and Preventive Psychology, 2,* 1-11.

Wyatt, G., & Mickey, M. R. (1988). The support by parents and others as it mediates the effects of child sexual abuse: An exploratory study. In G. E. Wyatt & G. J. Powell (Eds.), *Lasting effects of child sexual abuse* (pp. 211-226). Beverly Hills, CA: Sage.

Yates, A., Beutler, L. E., & Crago, M. (1985). Drawings by child victims of incest. *Child Abuse & Neglect, 9,* 183-189.

Yates, A., & Terr, L. (1988a). Anatomically correct dolls: Should they be used as a basis for expert testimony? - Yates response. *Journal of the American Academy of Child and Adolescent Psychiatry, 27*(2), 254-257.

Yates, A., & Terr, L. (1988b). Anatomically correct dolls: Should they be used as a basis for expert testimony? - Terr's response. *Journal of the American Academy of Child and Adolescent Psychiatry, 27*(3), 387-388.

Yuille, J. C., Hunter, R., Joffe, R., & Zaparniuk, J. (1993). Interviewing children in sexual abuse cases. In G. S. Goodman & B. L. Bottoms (Eds.), *Child victims, child witnesses: Understanding and improving testimony* (pp. 95-115). New York: Guilford.

Yuille, J. C., & Wells, G. L. (1991). Concerns about the application of research findings: The issue of ecological validity. In J. Doris (Ed.), *The suggestibility of children's recollections* (pp. 118-128). Washington, DC: American Psychological Association.

Zivney, O. A., Nash, M. R., & Hulsey, T. L. (1988). Sexual abuse in early versus late childhood: Differing patterns of pathology as revealed on the Rorschach. *Psychotherapy, 25*(1), 99-106.

Subject Index

If You Found This Book Useful . . .

You might want to know more about our other titles.

If you would like to receive our latest catalog, please return this form:

Name: _____
(Please Print)

Address: _____

Address: _____

City/State/Zip: _____
This is ▢ home ▢ office

Telephone: (_____)_____

I am a:

_____ Psychologist   _____ Mental Health Counselor
_____ Psychiatrist   _____ Attorney
_____ Clinical Social Worker   _____ Other:_____

◆   ◆   ◆

Professional Resource Press
P.O. Box 15560
Sarasota, FL 34277-1560

Telephone #800-443-3364
FAX #941-343-9201
Email at mail@prpress.com

Add A Colleague To Our Mailing List . . .

If you would like us to send our latest catalog to one of your colleagues, please return this form.

Name: _____
(Please Print)

Address: _____

Address: _____

City/State/Zip: _____
This is ☐ home ☐ office

Telephone: (_____)_____

This person is a:

_____ Psychologist   _____ Mental Health Counselor
_____ Psychiatrist   _____ Attorney
_____ Clinical Social Worker _____ Other: _____

Name of person completing this form: _____

◆   ◆   ◆

Professional Resource Press
P.O. Box 15560
Sarasota, FL 34277-1560

Telephone #800-443-3364
FAX #941-343-9201
Email at mail@prpress.com